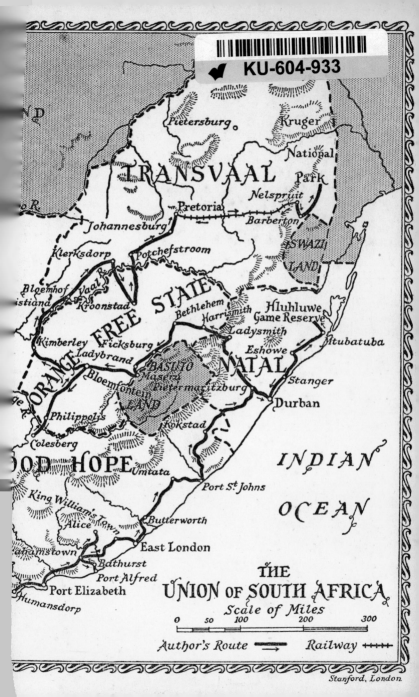

THE
UNION OF SOUTH AFRICA
Scale of Miles

0   50   100   200   300

Author's Route ———→   Railway ++++

Stanford, London.

KU-604-933

IN SEARCH OF
SOUTH AFRICA

TABLE MOUNTAIN FROM THE GARDENS, CAPE TOWN

IN SEARCH OF
SOUTH AFRICA

by

H. V. MORTON

METHUEN & CO. LTD., LONDON
36 Essex Street, Strand, W.C.2

First published in 1948

CATALOGUE NO. 3452/U

THIS BOOK IS PRODUCED IN
COMPLETE CONFORMITY WITH THE
AUTHORISED ECONOMY STANDARDS

PRINTED IN GREAT BRITAIN

FOR
TIMOTHY

INTRODUCTION

WHILE I was in the Union of South Africa I was constantly reminded of the classical world, in which illusion I was assisted by the clarity of the air and the architecture of Sir Herbert Baker. It seemed strange to me, as indeed it still does, that a part of the earth which the Greeks and the people of the Hellenistic world would have adored, and the Romans have found so profitable, should have remained concealed from them.

Such thoughts came early in my travels. Flying to South Africa, which sophisticated friends told me would be boring, turned out to be a sheer delight from beginning to end. During its thirty-six hours I looked down upon practically the whole length of the tremendous Continent of Africa. I saw North Africa and the site of Carthage; I saw the Nile Valley lying like a green snake on two deserts; and by the time darkness came we had left all trace of life behind and were flying above a desolation that stretched from sky to sky. In the morning the sun lit a wilderness of arid bush, a landscape dominated by drought, the tsetse fly and the mosquito, whose hot monotony persisted beneath us nearly all that day. That impenetrable country, from whose jungles our advancing shadow occasionally flushed a herd of wild elephant, was the most interesting and instructive sight of all.

One glance proved why no people of the ancient world were able to discover and colonise South Africa, why Nero's attempt to find the source of the Nile petered out in the Sudan, and why Africa to the Greeks and the Romans meant simply the northern coast belt from Tangier to the Delta of the Nile. Had there been any possible way across the deserts and through the bush the Ancient Egyptians, the Hellenistic Greeks and the Romans would have followed it, and in South Africa they would have created the civilisation which existed

in the North. Those interested in the " ifs " of history may
not think it unprofitable to speculate upon the effect on the
trade routes of the world had South Africa been discovered in
the time of Alexander the Great, or the effect upon the
economic life of the Roman Empire if South African diamonds
and gold had been mined in the time of the Caesars.

However, none of this happened. The Transvaal and the
Free State were never to see a temple to Amen Rē, the mountains of the Cape were not to know cities like Pergamos, no
Hellenistic temples were ever to be mirrored in the waters of
the Indian Ocean. South Africa, like its counterpart in the
north, was virtually an island protected by deserts and bush,
and by seas on the west; and this isolation was to continue
until modern times. South Africa, the southern extremity of
a Continent that boasts the Pyramids, was to remain hidden
as if she were a portion of the New World and to be revealed
in the age of Vasco da Gama and Columbus.

As I flew over North Africa I reflected that the only two
peoples who have attempted to bring Europe into Africa were
the present South Africans and the Greeks and Romans who
for so many centuries maintained a brilliant civilisation in
the north. It is doubtful whether a South African ever gives
them a thought, though they were his brothers in endeavour,
and it might be imagined that their triumphs, and particularly
their failures, would have an absorbing interest for him.

It is a sad reflection that of that great civilisation in North
Africa nothing now remains but ruins. Some are enormous
like Timgad, while cities such as Roman Carthage, greater
and more brilliant than a dozen Johannesburgs, have vanished,
leaving hardly a trace behind. Temples, colonnades, libraries,
theatres, baths, triumphal archways and aqueducts have been
shattered and overthrown by the barbarian and only the
names of the great Africans, like Tertullian and St Augustine,
remind us that Europe once blossomed upon the North
African shore.

This may seem a melancholy reflection as one approaches
South Africa, though it might be argued that many of the
circumstances which brought about the fall of Roman Africa
are not likely to face her successor. But it cannot be denied

that the fundamental problem at the heart of these cultures was, and is, the same: how to safeguard civilisation—that always besieged citadel—from the threat of the barbarian who, whether he be white or black, is no more ready, or able, to-day to assimilate civilisation than he was in the Fourth Century.

With thoughts such as these I alighted in a country of haunting beauty and found myself among a people whose kindness and warmth of heart are not anywhere exceeded. As I travelled about the country, I learnt a page of history new to me, and one, I might add, which is not too well known in Europe or America. This book is an attempt to put into words something of the pleasure I experienced during my travels: it is not, nor was it ever intended to be, an exposition of South African problems. The newcomer to South Africa, having shed his omniscience, quickly discovers the complexity of those problems, and the longer he stays in the country the less likely is he to be ready with solutions. Indeed, he may leave the Union, as I did, with an admiration for the people he met there mingled with indignation that the good name of South Africa should sometimes be questioned in international assemblies by those who possess no first-hand knowledge of South African affairs.

It may seem to some, who know how swiftly the illusion of security can vanish in a world of revolutionary change, that the Union is a land basking in almost incredible good fortune. It is a land unravaged by war and uncomplicated by economic doubts and depressions, and a land that has enjoyed immunity from real, searing sorrow for something like half a century. The stranger from less sunny regions may ask himself at times whether all South Africans are fully conscious of their blessings. Their faith in the future and their belief in the continuing prosperity of their homeland is a stimulating optimism in these days of doubt and hesitancy, and the visitor can only go on his way with crossed fingers and a prayer that good fortune may continue to be the lot of the happy Dominion. The family feud between Boer and Briton, though it may strike the stranger as not the most serious, may seem the most regrettable, of all the problems of the Union. Seen against the dark background of the world—which is so easily forgotten in the sunlight of South Africa—it appears like a dispute between two brothers conducted on a railway line in the path of an advancing express.

Were I to mention all those South Africans in the four provinces who lavished kindness upon me and gave me hospitality and advice, I should now embark upon a great catalogue of names. I have thanked them personally on stoeps all over South Africa; and I do so again. Hospitality is the oldest tradition in the Union, and the traveller everywhere encounters kindness and generosity which it is a pleasure to experience and a delight to remember.

My debt to those who have written about South Africa is an obvious one, and I have acknowledged it in my bibliography. I hope my narrative will encourage some who read it to dip deeper into this subject and obtain the books I have indicated. My thanks are due to Mr Winston Churchill for permission to print for the first time the text of the letter he left on his bed the night he escaped from prison in Pretoria in December, 1899. This interesting document has been cherished ever since as a family heirloom, and I am grateful to Mrs O. E. de Souza of Barberton for showing it to me. In a letter authorising its publication, Mr Churchill says, " You are at liberty to contradict the story of my having swum the Aapies River." Thus one of South Africa's most pleasing, but less solemn, legends is hereby laid to rest.

CONTENTS

ILLUSTRATIONS

Other photographs reproduced by courtesy of South African Railways.

MAPS

IN SEARCH OF
SOUTH AFRICA

CHAPTER ONE

I fly to South Africa in thirty-six hours, take a train to Cape Town, ascend Table Mountain, remember the great spice trade and the arrival from Holland of Jan Anthony van Riebeeck.

§ 1

THIRTY-SIX hours after leaving London upon a cold October morning, the aeroplane landed on an air-field near Johannesburg and I stepped out into a warm African night. I was aware of a pleasant feeling of disembodiment, of not really being there at all, and it seemed to me strange that the Customs officials found me visible and audible.

A summer storm of great violence was rumbling over the Transvaal. Thunder sounded far off and the sky was noiselessly opened by flashes of violet light. As I was driven to the city through the hot night, wearing my warm winter overcoat, the lightning, like a conjurer, produced from the darkness startling white pyramids, which were gold-mine dumps, and the sky-line of a city. I sat looking out at the strange scene, hugging to myself the astonishing knowledge that the clothes I was wearing had been put on in London yesterday morning.

I was thankful to reach the sanctuary of an hotel bedroom, where I sat anxiously waiting for my luggage so that I might change my unsuitable garments and conceal the fantastic liberty I had taken with time and space. The flight itself had been nothing but sitting in a comfortable arm-chair high up in the air, but the arrival was most disconcerting. I felt declimatised and unreal.

There was a knock on the door. A gleaming Zulu, dressed like a small boy in a white tunic and white shorts, entered with my luggage. He had a smooth, shining body, which looked as though it had been oiled. The lobes of his ears were deformed by two wooden objects like coloured reels

B   I

of cotton. There was a thin brass ring tightly round his left calf, and his feet were bare.

He could not speak English, but he made it clear that he wanted to know whether I would like the luggage in the bedroom or in the hall outside. When I gave him sixpence, he bent his body slightly and, cupping both his hands together, took the coin as if I had given him the Holy Grail.

There was another knock at the door. A grey-haired woman came in, wearing a black gown.

" Good evening," she said. " And do you wish early morning tea? "

" Glasgow! " I said. This was becoming incredible!

" Och no, I haven't been to Scotland at all," she said with a laugh. " I was born in Cape Town and I came up here in an ox-wagon many a long year ago. But my mother came from Sco'land . . ."

" Glasgow," I insisted.

" No, it wasn't Glasgow," she said stubbornly. " It was Paisley."

I went out and rang for the lift. The doors were flung wide by a little Indian boy. Down in the restaurant an orchestra was playing, and an Italian *maître d'hôtel* waved me to a table heaped with summer flowers.

§ 2

I knew, of course, that South Africa had grown up in the course of the last fifty years, but the full extent of this growth, whose most spectacular proof is perhaps Johannesburg, was striking and unexpected. Johannesburg, like the word Klondyke, builds up in the mind a picture of gold rush, bars, and tin shacks, a picture that was perfectly true fifty years ago. But I stepped out the next morning into a city which seemed to me to bear some resemblance to a small New York, while at the same time retaining something which reminded me of Kingston, Jamaica.

It was a vast collection of shining white concrete and marble buildings, varied by Edwardian Renaissance and the wrought-iron verandas one used to see in Wild West films, where the heroine waves to the hero while the sheriff sucks a cheroot. A noisy surge of traffic filled the roads; the pavements swarmed with white and black humanity. Hard sunlight transformed the ordinary into the heroic and saved the commonplace from squalidity.

I went to the General Post Office to send a cable. I was fascinated by the queue of natives in which I found myself. They were careless, jolly people with broad grins on their faces and fine teeth. Some were in suits of khaki drill and some wore shabby European garments; others, like the luggage porter in the hotel, were six feet statues in white shorts and vests. When I reached the counter the clerk, lifting a pained eyebrow, told me that I was in the wrong queue. I had entered by the " nie blankes nie ", the non-white door. I committed a similar solecism later on when bus after bus, half empty, refused to stop for me. I could not understand why until a native crossed the road and told me that I was standing at a " natives only " bus stop. I discovered that a little way up the road other buses readily pulled up for the " baas ".

So I was gently introduced by a black man to my automatic place in the aristocracy. In such little ways a stranger is made aware of the leading fact in South African life : that every white person is by virtue of his whiteness an aristocrat and consequently burdened with the anxieties and responsibilities that should go with that status. Ready to do his bidding are those queues of black men with whom it is so easy to become mixed up. They are countless and everywhere. They swarm. They are even eager to become cooks and domestic servants! I reflected, as I was swept on among the crowds, that the number of white South Africans who habitually clean their own shoes, wash up dishes, and lend a hand in the kitchen, must be very few, or perhaps no such exist. The taxi-driver who drove me round for half-an-hour told me that his wife had a manservant. So the Englishman of middle-age, who belongs to the class once ministered to by servants, recognises, the moment he sniffs the temperature of South Africa, the pleasing social climate of his childhood and youth. If he rings a bell, someone will answer it. The word " sir ", now almost discarded in England except by public school boys, is still in full swing in South Africa as the word " baas ", or boss. If you are white, you are a " baas ", and if you have been accustomed to servants in your youth, you feel again the desire, so firmly implanted in the nursery, to be worthy of baas-dom.

I thought also, as I mixed with those vivid and vital crowds in the sunlight of a Johannesburg morning, that of all the inhabitants of the Commonwealth the white South African is the most difficult to describe. Canadians, Australians, and New Zealanders may be distinguished at a glance, certainly as soon as they speak, but there seems to be no such thing as the typical South African : neither is there such a thing as a South African accent. When for the first time you find your-self in a crowd of South Africans, your first impression is that these people look, speak, and dress more as we do in Great Britain than any other folk. And this is true also of those South Africans of Dutch, French, and German descent who have no wish to be like us in any way, for they belong to the same racial stock and cannot help it. Even their language— Afrikaans—has the same roots as English, and gives one the impression that any student of Chaucer should be able to learn to speak it, or at any rate to read it, in a few weeks.

Those were my first impressions of Johannesburg. It was my belief, which experience has not contradicted, that the only proper place from which to begin a tour of South Africa is Cape Town, and I went there in the Blue Train. It is a long journey of a day and a night, so that I had plenty of time to study four books which I commend to the stranger : the Union Castle's masterpiece of fact, the *South and East African Year Book and Guide*; *South Africans* by Gertrude Millin; *South Africa* by A. W. Wells; and *Here are South Africans* by Julian Mockford.

To me the most surprising thing about South Africa is the thought that it is not impossible to travel from Cape Town to Istanbul without once taking ship, and that South Africa belongs to the Old World. Hidden from all the ancient empires and the Middle Ages, Southern Africa appears suddenly and unexpectedly during the great period of maritime discovery that revealed America. When the Portuguese saw the coast of South Africa in the Fifteenth Century, on their way to India, it was just as though a new island had been discovered and not the tip of an old continent.

And a desert island, feared and remote, Southern Africa remained for a century and a half. No one wanted to live there, and the country which belonged geographically to the Old World, but in every other way to the New World, was going begging. Not until 1652 did the Dutch East India Company decide to send out about two hundred of its employees to open up a half-way house to India, where Dutch East Indiamen could take in vegetables and meat. The first commander of this station, and the founder of South Africa, was a capable Dutchman, Jan Anthony van Riebeeck.

There were about twenty thousand Dutch and Dutch-Huguenot inhabitants of the Cape when a hundred and fifty years later Britain decided to seize the Cape in order to prevent Napoleon from doing so. After Waterloo the colony was ceded to Britain by the Dutch. Only British officials went there until 1820, when a few thousand British emigrants arrived. British and Dutch continued to inhabit the seaboard. The high interior plains, cut off by mountains, were unknown except to hunters and missionaries.

Then came the Voortrekkers—the forerunners. It is impossible to explain to any South African that few Europeans have ever heard of these heroic people. They were a few thousand farmers of Dutch, French, and German descent— the Boers—who preferred to leave their homes rather than live under British rule. Placing all their moveable possessions in covered wagons, they crossed the mountains into the empty north and founded the republics of the Orange Free State and the Transvaal. In these northern regions diamonds and then gold were discovered, and from a poor agricultural country South Africa became one of the richest lands in the world.

It is surprising to realise that the teeming black men, called the " natives ", were unknown to the first South Africans. The people seen by the first settlers were bushmen, still to be found in the Kalahari Desert, and Hottentots, a people who no longer exist in racial purity. The Bantu-speaking African

" native ", now seen everywhere, was, like the European, an invader. While the white men were advancing from the west, the Bantu tribes were advancing from the east, and the two races were fated not to meet for a century.

With the British occupation, missionaries flocked to the Cape, sent there by the many societies which had sprung up in Nineteenth Century England on the wave of middle-class Evangelicanism. From these men England gained her first ideas of the country and its people. Some of the missionaries were narrow-minded and some were half-educated, and, as in the Pacific, they strove for mastery of the native population. The Boers considered themselves slandered by the missionaries, and this was one of the most powerful reasons for their withdrawal from the Colony.

What of modern South Africa? The self-governing Dominion known as the Union is composed of four regions which were once separate provinces or states: The Cape Province, Natal, the Orange Free State, and the Transvaal. These came together in legislative unity only in 1910. The white South Africans in the Union number about two and a half millions; the black and coloured population number nearly eleven millions. A large proportion of this native population works in the towns and factories, on the farms and in the houses, but a proportion is still in a tribal stage of development and lives in the large native reserves.

Five minutes in any South African city will inform the stranger that the country is divided into black and white, and that the white are further divided into two racial groups. There are the Afrikaners, who are chiefly those of Dutch, French, and German ancestry, and those of British ancestry. Just over half of white South Africa is non-British in origin, and this racial distinction has resulted in dualism. There are two official languages, English and Afrikaans. Every official publication must be duplicated. There are two flags, the Union Jack and the Union Flag, which are flown side by side on police stations and official buildings. There are two national anthems, " God Save the King " and " Die Stem van Suid Afrika ", " The Voice of South Africa ". There are two capitals, Cape Town, where Parliament meets, and Pretoria, where the Government offices are situated. These two capitals are a thousand miles apart.

In South Africa the European seasons are reversed. The hottest months of the year are December, January, and February, autumn occurs in March, April, and May, and winter in June, July, and August.

While I was deep in such matters an attendant came along playing a xylophone, filling the train with a mellifluous sound and summoning us to luncheon. I kept the menu, which was, of course, bi-lingual.

Tomato Soup
Tamatiesop

Consommé   Brunoise
Groentesop

Fried fillet of Sole, sauce Tartare.
Gebakte tongvis met tartaresous

Ribs of lamb, demiglace
Lamsribbetjies met bruinsous

Roast Turkey and salad
Gebraaide kalkoen met slaai

Yellow rice and Raisins
Geelrys met rosyntjies

Assorted vegetables
Groentesoorte

Apple flan meringues
Appelskuimpies

Peach Melba
Perske-melba

Cheese   Biscuits   Coffee
Kaas   Beskuitjies   Koffie

Fruit
Vrugte

Few people in the world to-day, I think, would have questioned the bill, which was 4s. 6d.

§ 3

It was a train of great splendour and finer than any train at present running in Europe, and as fine as the best the United States can boast. It was a train of blue sleeping-coaches and restaurant cars, each coach, even each compartment, air-conditioned, as I discovered when I found it possible to raise or lower the temperature by moving a little chromium switch above the bed.

South African railways, airways, harbours, and most forms of public transport are owned by the State. The guards, restaurant-car attendants, and the coloured men who make up the beds at night, are a good advertisement for the Union, for they are the most polite public servants you will find in a day's march. The railways are unusual, because their rolling-stock of normal size does not run upon the European gauge of four feet, eight and a half inches, but on a narrower gauge of three feet, six inches. This gauge has been dictated by the enormous distances to be covered and by the mountainous character of the Cape and Natal, and the example has been followed by most of the railways in Africa.

I went along to the observation car after lunch. We were now running through a country of clear-cut distances, broken by low ridges and detached koppies, or hills. Cattle grazed and horses cropped the thin grass that grew on the parched soil. The red roads ran for miles beside the track and then struck off across country to the sky.

Certain little things, not necessarily the most important things or the most characteristic, fix themselves in the mind of a traveller in his first moments of exploration and remain there for ever. I knew I should always remember the Free State when I saw the queer, undulating flight of the widow bird. Out of the mealie-fields, or maize as we call it, these small finches rose into the sunlight, carrying the absurd black streamer of a tail which the male birds grow in the mating season; hampered by this impediment, they would undulate and flutter until they seemed hardly air-borne, and would sink, it would seem gratefully, to earth a few yards away. An agile boy, I thought, would surely be able to catch these gay, preposterous little birds in his hands while they were on the wing.

Then I saw a sight which, of all the things to be encountered upon a road, is essentially South African: I saw red oxen yoked two by two, drawing a wagon, and in front walked a small half-naked black boy, while a native in a blanket who might have been his father walked beside the wagon and seemed to be singing or shouting to the oxen as he walked. The train sped on. There was a horseman on the road. Far away a farmer's car was speeding like a comet, drawing a tail of red dust across the landscape.

We came to a line of blue gum trees and a station. In the shade of the trees were American cars, Cape carts, and wagons. Upon the platform was a crowd of white South Africans and black South Africans. They were on the same platform, but on different parts of it. The natives had collected at the far end, near the locomotive, where they knew the " natives only " coaches would be; the Europeans were together elsewhere. There were station benches and lavatories labelled for black or white, and thus I learnt again the first lesson of South Africa: that there is a white South Africa and a black South Africa.

Another interesting feature of this railway station, and of all stations in the Union, was its interest in altitude, for beside the name of the station was printed its height above the distant ocean. I saw that we were four thousand feet above sea level.

Away we went into the sunlight and the wide spaces of the veld, and I looked at this country and knew that its attraction is twofold: its colour, which is the red of the roads, the green and gold of the grass, and the blue of the distance, and its resemblance to the sea; for the eye is constantly roving to the horizon as it does at sea, searching and probing into the distance and finding there refreshment, peace, and freedom. So we ran south on our long way to Cape Town, into the heart of a burning afternoon.

§ 4

In the first light of morning I glanced out of the window and saw that we were traversing a lone, wild region which I thought must be the Karoo. It was a parched, hilly land like the glimpses I have seen in films of Arizona. The rocky earth was tufted with small shrubs which, as the light became stronger, I could see were beautifully shaped, like dwarfed

Japanese trees. And when the train stopped to take in water, I noticed that each square yard of this land was like a small garden of succulents. As the light grew, the ragged hills were etched against a pale greenish glow, then the sky was flushed with pink and the sun rose upon barren hills which reminded me of Samaria.

The morning advanced, and we dropped down from the plateau towards the sea. There came a time when, traversing the Hex River Pass, the train became a snake which twisted back upon itself, so that the locomotive was seen puffing valiantly now at the left-hand window and now at the right. All round were mighty mountains, each cleft and corrie filled with pale blue shadow, the shadows we know on the west coast of Ireland as " Atlantic blue " ; and so we came down into a happy land of peach-blossom and grape-vines, where a stream of ice-clear water ran beside the train for a long time.

And I, newly from an island where no one is far from the sea, perceived something thrilling to me beyond words; for I could feel a promise in the air, and see some clear intensity of the light, which told me that we drew near at last to that wonderful place at the tip of Africa where the warm currents of the Indian Ocean meet the cool waves of the Atlantic.

§ 5

I came to Cape Town upon a blue morning : the sea was blue, Table Mountain was blue, the sky was blue; and there was a girl with blue eyes in Adderley Street, who pinned a little flag to my coat. And over Cape Town was a golden hush of summer that had come, they told me, in the wake of a south-easterly wind. The sun-blinds were down and people walked in the shade of colonnades.

As I looked at Cape Town, the thought came to me that, of all the cities I had ever seen, this one alone brought Athens to my mind. Why should this be so, I wondered, for the physical resemblance is not great. Athens lies four miles from the sea, and is built on a plain in a circle round a golden hill which rises like a castle. Cape Town is almost on the water's edge and lifts itself, gently at first and then more steeply, towards the slopes of Table Mountain, whose flanks and gorges defy the architect, and make Cape Town, not a circle like Athens, but a half-moon round the mountain's base.

I walked in the streets and entered a garden in the heart of the city where doves were cooing in tall trees, and the memory of a day in Greece came back so vividly that I might have been crossing the Athenian plain again. It was a day of sun as this was, the cicadas in the olive trees were beating in the hot air like the pulse of summer, and the mountains that enclose the plain, Pentelicus, the long range of Hymettus, and the lower hills of Ægaleos, which lead to Daphni, were standing in a faint mist, as Table Mountain stood that morning. And as the eye is drawn inevitably to the golden hill of Athens upon whose summit stands that lovely thing which is all the longing of the world and all the aspirations of Man made visible in stone, just as inevitably the eye is drawn always to the great Acropolis of South Africa.

More notable than mountain or sea was the light, the fine clarity of air, that bathed this city as it does Greece, a light both warm and intensely clear, with something about it that Plutarch compared to spun-silk. Such was my first impression of Cape Town: a city of dignity and beauty seated at the foot of a blue mountain where two oceans meet, and washed by a magic light that should make of men poets, artists, and philosophers.

§ 6

Some days before I arrived in Cape Town a dead body had been found upon the slopes of Table Mountain, and the news of the discovery, which occupied considerable space in the newspapers, was as eagerly discussed in the city as a Ben Nevis climbing disaster in Fort William or an Alpine tragedy in any Swiss village. It was strange that this large city with its wide interests could talk about practically nothing for days but the body on the mountain. And as I listened to the conversations I must say that I began to think of Table Mountain not as a benevolent giant, but as something primitive and wild that now and again demanded a sacrifice. There are several tracks to the top of Table Mountain, but my desire to get there as quickly as possible led me to the cable-way.

Steel cables the size of your arm connect the earth with the top of Table Mountain, three thousand, five hundred feet above. Two little cages, starting one from the top and the other from the bottom and meeting half-way, go slowly into the air and carry you almost vertically until you feel that you are hovering in a gyroscope. The enormous precipices of the mountain grow nearer and nearer and the view of Cape Town becomes ever more a bird's-eye view as you are smoothly lifted through the air.

My companions were two middle-aged ladies and a small girl who was not tall enough to look over the edge of the cage. One of the ladies was robust and tough-looking and the other was thin and frail. It was the tough-looking one who, as we passed the descending cage, sat down and covered her eyes with her hand and remained in that position until we had reached the top, while the frail one gazed with unflinching interest into the void.

" Are we nearly at the top, Margaret? " asked the robust lady, peeping cautiously through her fingers.

" Nowhere near the top," replied her friend heartlessly. " You're missing a wonderful sight. It looks as though you could throw a tennis ball into Adderley Street."

" I'd rather not hear any more," said her companion.

The cable-way ends in a little shop where there is a letter-box so that you can post letters to friends from the top of Table Mountain, and where you can buy films and post-cards. Stepping out upon a rock-ledge, I looked down upon one of the grandest views in the world. Cape Town lay below, every street visible, van Riebeeck's garden, the harbour, the docks, Robben Island lying out in Table Bay; and the land curved round to the north, where, seen faintly in a mist thirty miles off, were the white farms and stubble-fields round Malmesbury.

The top of Table Mountain is unlike any other mountain I have ever seen. It is not a small eminence upon which you stand and regain strength for a descent: it is a wide world of its own where you can walk for miles, and at one point see the Indian Ocean on one side and the Atlantic on the other. You could build a city upon Table Mountain, and the Hellenistic Greeks would have done this. No matter what it might have cost them in treasure, energy, and inconvenience, they would somehow have built a city like Pergamos, even though its inhabitants would have spent half the year in mist and storm and wind.

Not far from the cable station is a solid little café constructed of stone that was surely shot up there from a village in Sussex. It is administered by a waitress driven almost dumb, I conjectured, by the silly questions she is asked during the day's work. With the greatest reluctance she told me that six people live on Table Mountain all the year round, that it is sometimes cold, often windy, and, of course, lonely.

All mountain tops have a spell, sometimes agreeable, sometimes horrible, sometimes terrifying, but there is nothing either gruesome or horrible about Table Mountain. It is not frigid and bare of vegetation, neither is it sterile and free of animal life. Lizards flash everywhere among the rocks, and if you watch carefully, you can see large, prosperous-looking striped mice at the back of the cable station. There are, I believe, less pleasant snakes. There are many kinds of wild flowers. The slopes on the way up, as Dr. Hutchinson tells in his *Botanist in Southern Africa*, are a garden in themselves.

It is remarkable to be told, when you are on the top of Table Mountain, that you are two thousand, three hundred feet lower than Johannesburg. It is, I think, one of the many surprising things about South Africa that nearly half of the country is higher than Table Mountain. The great mountain ranges of the Cape, which look so high from sea level, are, so to speak, a rampart on the top of which lie the Free State and the Transvaal.

Sitting upon a rock and glancing down at Table Bay, I thought of the enormous influence of pepper in human affairs. It was pepper and spices, silk and pearls, and all the riches of the Spice Trade—but especially pepper—which led to the discovery of the Cape route to India and the European settlement of the Cape. The Spice Trade would seem to be the oldest commerce in the world. The business of carrying bits of animal and vegetable matter from the East to the West would appear to have begun before recorded history. When Moses upon Sinai was instructed in the making of holy oil, God commanded him to use three noted Indian spices— cinnamon, cadamus, and cassia. The Arabs who sold Joseph into bondage were on their way to Egypt with spices for the perfumers and embalmers.

As far as we can see into the remoteness of history, men were loading pepper upon the backs of buffaloes at Malabar and Travancore, they were gathering spikenard from the trees overhanging the Ganges and the Jumna, they were digging alluvial gold from Dardistan in India, mining emeralds and rubies, fishing for pearls, drying ginger, cloves, and nutmegs, and loading all these things upon the backs of camels and asses for the great empires of the Euphrates and the Nile.

It was in Ancient Rome that pepper caught the taste of western man and achieved a fame it has never really lost. Nearly every dish in the books of Apicius contains pepper, and Roman doctors prescribed it even for malaria. With the fall of Rome the Spice Trade went to Constantinople, where it piled up riches for the Byzantine Empire. After the Turkish capture of Constantinople, it went to Venice and the Lion of St Mark's rose with his feet in spices. The Crusaders went home to their bleak castles taking back with them little boxes of spice, and Europe began to long for pepper to season the horrible salt meat and fish of the mediæval winter. The baron and his lady in their moated keeps hankered for musk and cinnamon, for pearls and silk, for ivory and ebony, and to satisfy them the Venetian galleys sailed at regular times to bring the East to the West.

If the world were really a sphere, argued Henry of Portugal, " the Navigator ", it should be possible to find a way round Africa to India and so cut out Venice and bring the treasures of the East to Lisbon. Gradually the Portuguese seamen found their way down the west coast of Africa, each voyage venturing a little farther to the south. Then in 1486 Bartholomew Diaz was blown round the Cape in a storm, reaching the point where Port Elizabeth is now, and he knew what no other European had known, that Africa had a southern end which a ship could sail round. On his way home he saw the Cape Peninsula and called it the Cape of Storms, a name which either Diaz himself or John II of Portugal changed to the Cape of Good Hope—the Cape which offered a Good Hope of reaching India by sea.

Eleven years later this hope was fulfilled when Vasco da Gama sailed round the Cape and up the east coast, which he called Natal because it was the time of the Nativity, dropping anchor at last off Calicut. From that moment Venice was ruined. The Mediterranean world was incredulous, for all the old trade routes were now out-of-date. In her alarm, Venice even proposed to cut a Suez Canal. And year after year the treasures of the East came round the Cape in Portuguese ships to Lisbon. There the Dutch picked them up and carried them north. So Holland began to learn her first lessons in the Spice Trade. No apter pupil ever out-classed her master. For a full century and a half Holland held " the gorgeous East in fee ", and Table Mountain was the half-way milestone on her route.

It is strange for a man who has flown to South Africa in thirty-six hours to sit on Table Mountain and reflect that it once took the seamen of Portugal and Holland six months to reach the Cape, by which time some were dead of the Land Disease, or Scurvy, while others were emaciated and fevered, their gums rotted. Lime juice, fresh vegetables, and the land itself were the only cures for this distressing complaint. Some measure of the utter remoteness of the Cape is the neglect of all the fierce competitors in the India trade to make a foothold there. To the men of that time the Cape, swept by tempests where two angry oceans met, must have seemed infinitely more dangerous and desolate than the calm West Indies or the most distant portions of the American coast.

To the Portuguese it was a place where venomous little savages flung poisoned barbs; to the Dutch and English it was a place where herbs and fresh water were to be found, a place where letters might be left under a flat stone with the knowledge that someone gathering sorrel would come across them and take them forward. But no one wished to live there. Once, when the spirit of comedy was in the ascendant, it was suggested that the Dutch and English East India Companies might pool their resources and open a joint station there for the refreshment of their men and ships. But nothing was done. Two English sea captains, probably in want of exercise, climbed the Lion's Rump in 1627 and planted a Union Jack there in the name of James I. But again nothing was done. And it was not until 1652, when Jan van Riebeeck landed with his company and set up house there, that white men came to live, that chimney smoke came to curl, that white babies came to cry, upon the southern end of Africa.

§ 7

It is a warm summer morning at Sea Point—one of Cape Town's delightful suburbs—and I go out upon my balcony soon after sunrise. I watch the rollers come crashing in from the Atlantic, line after line of them, curling over, poised for a second, then breaking upon the beach. The October sun is warm and seems to grow warmer every morning. There are several energetic men in bathing-slips on the same patch of grass at the same time each morning, with a medicine ball and a keenly interested dog. There are other men who swim in a rock pool whose waters are freshened by the sea. In the garden beneath the balcony a coloured nursemaid wheels a perambulator, and a coloured garden boy waters a bank of red and yellow cannas. Sometimes a ship passes eastwards on its way to Port Elizabeth, East London, or Durban.

If I move to the side of the balcony, I can see the Lion's Head lifted into the morning sunlight, and round about are neat white villas and clear-cut blocks of flats, stark and modern, gazing at the Atlantic over gardens gay with bougain-villea, hibiscus, and the familiar, energetic Dorothy Perkins. There is an extraordinary sense of well-being in this climate. I think I should never get tired of it. Many a time I have heard men who live in Africa say how the sunlight has wearied them and thinned their blood, and how often they have longed for a grey, wet day in England, but I find it difficult to believe this.

Electric trolley buses run with a rubbery smoothness into Cape Town. They are called, quaintly, "trackless trams", or "trembusse" in Afrikaans; and this, strange as it may seem, is a meticulously accurate description. Another word used in South Africa, but long discontinued in England, is robot for traffic lights.

It is delightful to have nothing to do but to go out about ten o'clock on a sunny morning and look at Cape Town. The trackless tram drops me in St George's Street, where at this time in the morning women are just coming out to shop. Here, it seems, no one has yet flung a spanner into the machinery of civilisation. Women look happy, cheerful, and well, which is a tribute to the balance of life in any country.

There are two peoples in the streets, white people and people of every colour from yellow to black. It is disconcerting and puzzling to see so many queer, alien faces against a purely European background. Some of these Cape Coloured have European skulls and Bantu noses and hair, some have Asiatic eyes and pale hair, some, especially young girls, who walk with a lithe, slender grace, might be Spaniards or Jewesses; then there are some who are nearly black and others who might be mistaken for Englishmen suffering from that heart disease which turns the complexion blue. Some of these people look quick, intelligent, and appealing; others look fit for treasons and stratagems and are people to be avoided on a dark night. Then there are Moslems, the descendants of Malay slaves brought here in the days of the Dutch East India Company. There are Indians. A more varied non-European population, so different from the more uniform Bantu population of Johannesburg, could not be imagined.

There are so many of these people, fetching and carrying and pushing carts, working lifts and opening doors, and doing all the menial and manual work, that it is hardly surprising to realise that there are two hundred thousand coloured folk in the city. They must mean something different to almost everyone: to the anthropologist, a fascinating study, to the social reformer, a paradise of effort, to the sentimentalist, a heartrending invitation, to the agitator, a perfect field for power, and to the ordinary person and the puzzled stranger, a

C

pathetic and frightening display of centuries of dock-side inter-breeding.

The white people are no different from those seen in any European city before the last war. I use the past tense because the people of Europe are not at the moment looking as cheerful or as well-dressed as the people of Cape Town. They speak English with no accent or twang, unless it be a tendency here and there to pronounce A as O. I hear a girl say to a friend : " I'm just going to pork the cor," which means " I'm just going to park the car," but, said by a pretty girl in Adderley Street on a summer morning, this sounds charming.

The first thing I do when I arrive in Cape Town is to glance at Table Mountain to see if the table-cloth is laid or not. Sometimes a white cloud lies on the mountain, with the blue sky above and all round it. There are no other clouds in the sky, only that queer white covering like something that went up there to sleep in the dark and has been caught by the daylight. Often it peels away in an hour; sometimes it lies there with deliberation and appears to summon other clouds to come and join it, which they do with unfailing regularity. People who live here know what kind of weather to expect by glancing at Table Mountain. It is the world's largest barometer.

When I step off the trembus and make sure that the "robot" is green, I walk across to Adderley Street, where I idle away my time in two good bookshops, one of which carries high on its façade the only statue of Shakespeare in South Africa. Then I look at the shops and wonder how Cape Town can consume so many brand-new Swiss watches, and I wander on thinking how fortunate are the women of South Africa who inhabit this agreeable land of servants, shops, and leisure.

My impression of Cape Town is that it carries itself with an air of quality. This springs from its history. It has not grown up in a tearing hurry, but has been composed over a fairly long period, long not as we in Europe reckon time, but for South Africa it is the ultimate antiquity. Adderley Street runs straight up from the docks to the public gardens, which are on the site of the famous garden of the Dutch East India Company. This street, and this garden, around whose trees and flower-beds are grouped with Greek fitness and rightness the most important public buildings, are the making of Cape Town.

I cannot remember another city which has grouped all its chief intellectual institutions together in such an unforgettably beautiful setting. At one end of the gardens is the South African Museum, at the other the fine Public Library; on one side is the exquisite little white Art Gallery, with a formal garden and water in front of it, and almost opposite are South Africa's State Archives. You must imagine this with cannas in bloom and roses in full flower, shrubs, and tall trees, many of them a century old, rising in a warm hush of summer, children's voices as they play in the gardens, the cooing of doves, and, behind it all, immensely high and pale blue and withdrawn in the haze, the riven, ageless flanks of Table Mountain.

Here, I think, is something unusually fine and memorable, something which I am right to compare with Athens, for here is natural beauty, cultivated and wild, and here is good architecture suitable to the sunlight in which it stands, and here also are those things of the mind, art and literature, interest in the past and love of tradition, without which a city, no matter how fine, is just a body of buildings without a spirit.

From the spine of Adderley Street spring the ribs of the city, and in these side streets you will find several fine old houses and buildings. I think one of the finest ancient buildings in South Africa is the Old Town House, straight from the Holland of the mid-Eighteenth Century, a building in the classical tradition that is fit to be the pride of any city. Next I should place the Slave Lodge at the top of Adderley Street, which, although much later, has dignity and style and would be a sad loss to Cape Town should it ever disappear.

The House of Representatives, peeping coyly from the foliage of an oak avenue, wears a perpetual maidenly blush, due to the attractive pink tone of its brick; and when the sun shines full on the stone columns of its porticoes and the warm brick flushes in the light, the building wears an air of greater cheerfulness and gaiety than most buildings dedicated to argument. I am sorry to say that the one architectural blemish on Cape Town is, in my opinion, the new Cathedral of St George. Why this Gothic battleship should have been put in dry dock there, where it has hardly room to move an inch, is difficult to imagine, and why the Gothic style should have been imported to the sharp sunlight of South Africa from less fortunate climes, which it suits admirably, is even more difficult to understand.

But when all is said and done the glory of Cape Town is van Riebeeck's garden. It was planned in Amsterdam nearly three hundred years ago. It was the reason why white men went to South Africa. It served its purpose well, and now in retirement the trees are full of turtle doves and the gardener's hose tends banks of flaming cannas and roses in the place where cabbages and onions were grown for the East India fleets. The old summer house which grew into a guest house has grown still further into Government House; not far from it is a cage full of little birds like jewels, and the most beautiful perhaps are the Red Bishop birds, which are like bullfinches at a fancy dress ball.

White South Africa would apparently stop if it did not drink tea in the morning. Nowhere is it easier to contract the habit of elevenses than in the tea garden beneath the trees, with the doves cooing, the water prickling on the green leaves, and the great wall of Table Mountain rising into the heat. Even the greatest misanthrope would recognise this as the place where Cape Town lovers meet. Children play there in the shade of trees while coloured nursemaids knit and tell each other endless stories. It is the Kensington Gardens of Africa.

§ 8

South Africa's founder stands at the foot of Adderley Street and gazes towards Table Mountain. What van Riebeeck was really like we know from his sombre, competent face in the Rijks Museum, Amsterdam. He was just the right man to send out to a savage part of the world. He was quick, enterprising, and resolute, and his devotion to the grasping concern which employed him was uncritical. He was very much the child of a ruthless commercialism.

His ten years of hard work at the Cape are well known and heavily documented, but his origins and the place he came from in Holland may not be so familiar. His birthplace was the mediæval town of Culemborg, which is fifteen minutes by electric train from Utrecht, on the line to Arnhem. It lies in a serene landscape typical of Guelderland. Black and white cattle graze in the meadows, windbreaks of shivering poplars shelter neat regiments of pear and apple trees, and here and there precise clumps of woodland dot the distance. As so frequently happens in Holland, the clouds play the part of mountains and rise over the level land in golden ranges and pinnacles, and the sky, reflected in water channels which intersect the fields in all directions, brings down to the green earth a touch of blue and gold. Such is the tranquil country in which van Riebeeck spent his boyhood, a land strangely different from the wild and sometimes stormy undulations of the Cape.

Culemborg has grown old with grace and without losing its shape or putting on too much suburban tissue. If van Riebeeck could see it, he would instantly recognise it as the town where he was born, and he could identify many a building which has not altered from his day to ours. To-day van Riebeeck's nine thousand industrious fellow townsmen make cigars, cigar-boxes, and furniture.

You enter Culemborg beneath a massive gate-house which in van Riebeeck's time was one of several town gates, but is now the only survivor. Framed in the curve of its arch, you see a wide main street ahead, a street made for mediæval fairs and junketings, and now lined on each side by little shops and cafés whose steep pitched roofs are almost the colour of geraniums. In the background, and so nearly in the centre of the road as to seem to turn the street into a market square, rises a superb building of red brick which was already a century old when van Riebeeck was a boy. It is a slender, tall building with step gables culminating in an almost ecclesiastical tower and cupola, and is now the Stadhuis. I have been told that it was built in 1534 for a knight who had married a daughter of the House of Culemborg.

A branch of the Lower Rhine, called the Lek, flows a few

hundred yards from Culemborg, and its waters once filled the town moat, and also the moat of the fairy-tale castle with its pointed pinnacles, of which not a trace remains to-day, where the Counts of Culemborg lived like mediæval barons far into the Eighteenth Century. Under the Counts the town remained a mediæval State where the Netherlands law had no authority, with the natural result that it became a sanctuary for those who wished to escape the Dutch courts. Once within the walls of Culemborg, nothing could touch a fugitive, and this extraordinary state of affairs lasted until 1795, when the French invaders demolished Culemborg's independence and obliged it to fall into line with the rest of Revolutionary Holland.

The townsfolk still talk with reverence of the aristocratic Counts of Culemborg who, among other peculiarities, had the macabre fancy to have their portraits painted after death. In the local orphanage, in a dark room crossed by massive beams, you can see portraits of numbers of these pale gentlemen with their pointed beards, lying dead, clothed in black velvet and with lace collars at their throats. They, too, have vanished, but their name lingers in the title of Countess of Culemborg, which is one of the titles held by the Queen of Holland.

Culemborg was also the birthplace of Anthony van Diemen, who gave his name to Van Diemen's Land, now Tasmania, and it may be that van Riebeeck was named Anthony— although he never used this name and preferred Jan—after his distinguished townsman, his senior by many years and Governor General of the Dutch East Indies. The people of Culemborg are proud of their two famous sons. They show with pride the brass chandelier with the van Riebeeck arms upon it, which the founder of Cape Town gave to the church of St Barbara before he left for South Africa. They also point out three artisans' dwellings in Katten Street, which occupy the site of the house in which van Riebeeck is said to have been born in 1618. It was apparently a large house, but nothing of it now remains except a carved lion's head which is let into the façade of the present building.

At the beginning of the Seventeenth Century Culemborg

was still moated and walled and in every way a self-contained mediæval city. From their romantic stronghold the Counts dominated the Lek and its traffic, and many a time young van Riebeeck must have seen those knightly gentlemen ride out across the drawbridge, falcons on wrist, and have heard their hunting-horns ranging the autumn stubble. They brought into the tidy, mercantile Holland of the Seventeenth Century a touch of the wilder, more prodigal, and more passionate mediæval world.

Van Riebeeck came of good country stock. His mother was Elizabeth van Gasbeek, who died at Shiedam in 1629 and is buried there. Her father was a burgomaster of Culemborg. The van Diemens were also on the town council, and it is as certain as any undocumented fact can be that the van Riebeecks, the van Gasbeeks, and the van Diemens were well acquainted.

It is believed that van Riebeeck's father was a sea captain who was away from home when his son was born, and indeed he never comes into the picture at all, and is said to have died in Brazil in 1639, and to lie buried in the Church of St Paul at Olinda, Pernambuco. So van Riebeeck lost his mother when he was eleven and his father when he was twenty-one. Dr E. C. Godée-Molesbergen, the Dutch writer and historian who has investigated van Riebeeck's early life, thinks it possible that the young man, after going to school at Culemborg and studying to be a barber-surgeon there, was helped into the Dutch East India Company by Anthony van Diemen, who became Governor General of the East Indies in 1636. Three years later van Riebeeck, then twenty-one, became a sub-surgeon on the Company's books at a monthly wage of twenty-two gulden.

I do not know whether he ever visited Culemborg after his departure in 1651. His gift of a chandelier to the church before he left for South Africa is proof enough that he had strong local attachments. There are now no van Riebeecks in the district, neither does the name appear in the Amsterdam telephone directory, so that it may have died out in Holland.

It is fascinating to walk about Cape Town to-day and to think of Culemborg, as no doubt van Riebeeck often did.

When he looked up at Table Mountain, or saw the dragon's teeth of the Hottentot's Holland Mountains above False Bay, he must have remembered, for the contrast is so acute, the flat meadows with the broad Lek flowing through them in which he ran and played as a boy.

Culemborg has weathered many a storm. During the Middle Ages English and Scottish soldiers of fortune were to be found in its garrison, and their names, altered almost beyond recognition, are still to be found there. For instance, there is a family called Kinnegin which can be traced back to a Scot named Cunynghame, who was Lieutenant of the garrison in 1580. During the last war Culemborg saw a lot of the German army, for the bridge over the Lek is one of the main strategic points in that part of Holland. The townsfolk still speak of the terrific noise from the direction of Arnhem the night the parachutists dropped.

The first Allied soldier to be seen in Culemborg was a Canadian who was met on the road outside the town. The inhabitants, who covered him with kisses, were so overjoyed to see him that they refused to allow him to go in on foot. They tell me that he entered Culemborg sitting on a cow!

§ 9

It is not a bad idea to begin a tour of South Africa in Amsterdam. Beside the canals of that beautiful and ancient city you will probably gain a fairly accurate idea of the first South Africans, who were the same mixed seafaring breed that you find on the quaysides to-day.

Holland planted two important seeds of life in the Seventeenth Century, one in America, which has grown into New York, and the other in South Africa, which has grown into Cape Town. Both cities had the same origin, and so similar was their history for a long time that one might almost be reading about the same place. It is interesting that the buildings in which New York and Cape Town were born are still standing in the heart of old Amsterdam.

West India House is to be found upon the Prins Hendrik Kade, once the Y-Gracht, and is now split up into tenements and storehouses.   It is a massive five-storeyed building pierced everywhere with windows.   Its gables still bear the date 1641, and projecting from the top storey you notice the pulleys which three centuries ago drew up into the warehouses the beaver and otter pelts and the other products which the Iroquois had traded with the first Manhattan islanders.

Ten minutes walk into the maze of canals and narrow streets will bring you to East India House, at the corner of Oude Hoog Straat and the Kloveniers-Burgwal.   The great Spicery which formerly rose from the banks of the canal was destroyed by fire many years ago, but it was here that barges from the East India Docks came through a network of canals to discharge cargoes of musk, ambergris, cinnamon, cloves, nutmegs, and mace.   Round the corner in Oude Hoog Straat you come to an ancient archway which leads to a paved quadrangle around which rises the old headquarters of the Netherlands East India Company.   To-day it is a tax office.   The courtyard is filled with innumerable bicycles, but in the evening, when all the clerks have cycled home, you see East India House much as van Riebeeck saw it when he received his instructions to open a station at the Cape of Good Hope.

As a ship's surgeon, van Riebeeck may have been familiar with the head office, for here all the drugs and medical supplies were stored.   The medicine chests used by the doctors of the merchant fleet, and in all the stations, posts, and factories throughout the East, were made up on the premises, in rooms near the gate-house, by a staff of resident chemists.

Van Riebeeck was born in 1618, at the end of what we should call the Elizabethan Age.   Shakespeare had been dead only two years; Walter Raleigh was executed that same year. The era of voyages and exploration was over and the age of commercial exploitation had begun.   All the time, while van Riebeeck was growing up in Culemborg, the great Spice War rumbled over the hot Java seas.   First, the Dutch merchant fleets bombarded the Portuguese forts; then at sea the Dutch and British flags were seen through cannon smoke, and in the courts of rajah and sultan British and Dutch intrigued against each other with skill and cunning.

By the time van Riebeeck had grown up and gone to sea,

the Netherlands East India Company had emerged from the first phase of the Spice War as the richest commercial organisation in the world. The British East India Company had to be content with its leavings. All the other East India companies were nowhere. The Governor General in Batavia was a potent viceroy, and the centre of the world-wide network was the building in the Oude Hoog Straat in Amsterdam, where the Council of Seventeen, as the Directors were dramatically named, held their court.

In 1651, when the Cape station was finally decided upon, Holland was at the peak of her Golden Age. There was no other country so rich, so uncomplicated by political or religious disputes, so happy, so confident, and so purse-proud. She had flung a series of chain stores across the Orient and was paying forty per cent. Bankruptcy was still far off in the unbelievable future. England at this time had recently executed a king. It was the year young Charles II was crowned at Scone, beaten at Worcester by Cromwell, and driven into exile. France was involved in civil war. Spain and Portugal were in decline. Germany had been devastated by the Thirty Years War. Turkey was planning a conquest of distracted Europe. Holland alone was happy and cheerful, a country of spices and pictures.

Her mood has been caught on a thousand glowing canvases. It was the mellow Holland of Pieter de Hooch, where house-wives scoured copper pans in red-brick backyards; the Holland of Cuyp, where fat cattle drowsed beneath enormous golden skies; the Holland of Breughel, where old and young skated in winter with mufflers over their mouths, while church spires, roofs, and windmills rose in an ice-blue hush; it was the Holland of Teniers, where drunken clowns and their wenches kissed outside wayside inns; above all it was the Holland of those grave, unsmiling merchant princes and their placid wives, whose shrewd faces gaze at us from a snowfield of lace collars.

When van Riebeeck was busying himself about the docks and enlisting his first South Africans, Rembrandt had just gone to live in the house with the shutters in the Breedstraat; Franz Hals, an old Falstaff of seventy, had been forced to sell all he had to pay the baker; Vermeer was twenty; de Hooch was thirty-four; and Wouwerman was painting his white horses. That was the well-known, immortal Holland out of which South Africa was born.

Van Riebeeck was a man of great experience when he stood before the Seventeen and agreed to open a ship's station at the Cape. He had seen the Company's activities from Greenland to Japan. On his way home from Batavia he had even visited the Cape and landed there, and had for three weeks surveyed the scene of his future endeavours. There was at that time a wreck lying in Table Bay, the *Haarlem*. A salvage party from her crew had been camping on what is now Green Point Common, growing little patches of vegetables and trying to save the spices as they fermented in the sea-water and the hot sun. The founder of the Cape station cast an experienced eye round Table Bay and upon his arrival in Amsterdam was able to lay before the Seventeen some " considerations and criticisms " of their scheme to establish a fortress and a garden there.

It is not difficult to imagine the scene in the council chamber of East India House as the Seventeen in their wide-brimmed hats, ribbons at knee, starched collars and wrist bands, and keen faces with Van Dyck beards—it is all in Rembrandt's *De Stallmeesters*—questioned their devoted servant; for van Riebeeck was one of those men whose loyalty to the company was a personal piety.

Possibly Manhattan Island cropped up in the course of their discussion about the Cape. Although much the junior concern, the West India Company had twenty-five years before planted upon the shore of America a little Company post which might have been a blue-print for the Cape. A man like van Riebeeck, Peter Minuit, had built an earth fort on Manhattan Island and had called it the Good Hope, a reference to the hope of good trading to come. This fort stood on land now occupied by the New Customs House and Battery Park. And the name of Minuit's settlement was New Amsterdam. The land on which it stood had been bought from the Redskins for six pounds worth of beads and finery, the kind of bargain that both Companies adored. If similar bargains were to be had from the Hottentots, you may be sure van Riebeeck was not going to be outdone by Peter Minuit!

The difference between New Amsterdam and the Cape was that while both were ship's stations, New Amsterdam was a trading post and the Cape was to be nothing but a vegetable garden and meat market. Nevertheless the experience gained in America may have been useful to the Seventeen. They underlined certain difficulties inherent in both propositions. First of all, the Manhattan Dutch had been wayward and turbulent people. Their story had been roughly that of drifting away from slavish obedience to the Company into regions of private profit and nothing could be more hateful to the Companies. Upon one occasion these Manhattan Dutch had even charged one of their governors with having lined his own pockets and had carried the charge to Holland. Then the company employees showed a regrettable tendency to become boers, or farmers, and to stray off into the country. Their farms, or " boueries ", had already spread into the district which to this day perpetuates their memory in the Anglicised form of the Bowery. And it is not improbable that at the moment when van Riebeeck may have been warned about all these matters (every one of which was to be repeated at the Cape), there was already in Amsterdam a petition from the Boers of New Amsterdam demanding burgher rights, a privilege which was conferred the following year at much the time when van Riebeeck was landing in Africa.

Such things may well have been discussed, because that was exactly what the Seventeen did not wish to happen at the Cape. It must not become a town and then a colony, with all the expense and responsibility implied in such a state of affairs. It must be nothing but a ship's station where East Indiamen could take on green food and meat. No development, no nonsense about private farming, nothing but slavish obedience to the Company, and everything to be run as cheaply as possible. Those were the hard, the impossible, conditions to which van Riebeeck had to agree. As a man of the world who knew the many ways of evading the cast-iron Company regulations, he may have had his own ideas, but these he was no doubt wise enough to keep to himself.

It was in December of the year 1651 when van Riebeeck and his company of rather more than a hundred men and women sailed from Holland in the usual convoy bound for Batavia. He was accompanied by his wife, a lady of Huguenot ancestry, Maria de la Quellerie, and their baby, a girl but twelve months old. There were also two nieces of van Riebeeck's, Elizabeth and Sebastiana van Opdorp. Two other women were among the passengers, Annetje Boom, the gardener's wife, and the wife of the sick comforter, or catechist, who, poor lady, must have viewed her ordeal with some dismay, for two months after her arrival she became the mother of a son, the first European to be born in South Africa.

It is of the women rather than the men that one thinks in contemplating ventures of this kind: women torn from the ancient and settled domesticity of Europe to begin house-keeping and child-rearing in an unknown land and among fabulous beasts and primitive savages. In the Seventeenth Century the world was still not fully explored and the minds of travellers were a medley of strange and terrifying stories of perils and mysteries, many of them as old as the Middle Ages. It required courage and devotion of a high order to face the appalling discomfort and danger of a long sea voyage, then to set the standard of home life in a barbarous land. Colonial existence, with its hunting and fishing and its untidy extemporisation, comes naturally to the male; to the woman it is a more difficult problem, for her task is to normal-ise the abnormal, to teach the children their prayers while a lion is prowling round the house, and to bring gentleness and comfort where none have previously existed.

Standing upon the water-front of Amsterdam you may see the picture of van Riebeeck's departure as if it were hanging in the Rijks Museum: the fleet of East Indiamen advancing like slow swans through the narrow winding channel to the Zuider Zee, and among them three smaller ships loaded for the Cape. Behind them the long blue line of Amsterdam lies against the winter sky, the windmills turning on the bastions, the dense thicket of bare masts in the harbour, the smoke of chimneys, the abrupt, slim towers full of sweet bells; the hammering shipyards and the barges entering the still canals.

Upon the docksides stand the bales and boxes from the Spice Islands, the beaver skins and hickory from western lands where the moose stretch up to the frozen pine trees and the redskins come silently on icy rivers in shells of silver birch bark. The voyagers turn to look for the last time towards the Schreyer-storen, the Weeping Tower, where a crowd is always waving goodbye, always watching ships go out to sea, always waiting for them to return.

No one knows, as the *Dromedaris*, the *Reiger*, and the *Goede Hoop*—van Riebeeck's ships—move from sight beyond the low meadows, that they carry the germ of a nation. As they pass from Holland the eye of Time may already see the wagons of the Voortrekkers poised above Natal, the assegais whistling towards Boer and Briton; the bullets thumping from the wheels of laagered wagons; Piet Retief riding up to Umgun-gundhlovu; Dick King riding to Grahamstown; Dr Jameson riding to folly; Cecil Rhodes dreaming of a hinterland; Oom Paul dispensing justice on a stoep. . . . Botha. . . . Hertzog. . . . Smuts.

It is all written in the future as those ships pass out to sea.

§ 10

To a stranger few portions of the earth can be more confusing topographically than Cape Town. The slender, mountainous peninsula that stretches from Cape Town some thirty miles to the south is washed on one side by the Atlantic and on the other by the Indian Ocean, and the stranger usually spends his first few days confusing the one with the other. I think this confusion is caused because most people see only maps of Africa upon which the Cape Peninsula is so small an object as to be almost invisible, and also when we read of ships " rounding the Cape " we imagine perhaps that the portion rounded was Table Bay, forgetting that Table Bay faces the north-east and that thirty miles of peninsula separate it from the Cape of Good Hope. Diaz, for instance, probably never saw Table Bay when he was first blown round the end of the peninsula, and not until he was on his way home and, circling the Cape of Good Hope, sailed thirty miles north-ward would he have come to the site of the future Cape Town.

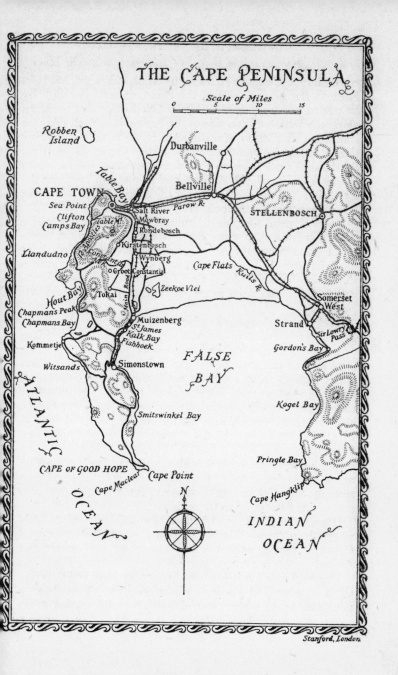

A splendid road called the Marine Drive, which greatly resembles the Corniche Road in the South of France, has been built on the Atlantic side of the Peninsula, and it is an easy matter to run down to the Cape of Good Hope and to return along the Indian Ocean side of the Peninsula. Both sides are studded with a chain of seaside places, those on the Atlantic side more bracing and those on the Indian Ocean side warmer, for the difference between the sea temperatures is from ten to twelve degrees. South Africans paddle and sun bathe on the Atlantic side, but they swim on the Indian side, where the famous sands of Muizenberg are " spun before the gale ".

Upon a warm October morning I could think of nothing more delightful than a run down to the Cape of Good Hope, and I set off along the Atlantic side, where the Marine Drive hugs the base of the mountains, with the ocean a few yards to the right. Every now and then I glanced over a precipice to delicious little bays where an emerald sea creamed upon the sands.

Rocks and mountains appear to encourage the South African architect. No ascent is too steep, no rock too sharp or perpendicular, to defy a bungalow or a chalet. There are houses along this coast poised like mountain goats, and others whose garages are at roof level, while the house itself descends from the road on rock ledges towards the sea. All this gives the same air of sparkle and gaiety that you notice on the French and Italian Rivieras, which are the only parts of the earth to which I can compare the Cape Peninsula, never having seen California.

Sun-bathers were lying far below upon the sand, or walking at the edge of the waves ; dogs in an ecstasy of approval were rushing about with children ; and in the distance blue mountains fell steeply to the sea.

It was most difficult to believe that this was Africa. It might have been Biarritz or San Tropez, with a bit of Cornwall during a heat wave thrown in, but—surely not Africa !

The road now left behind the little rocky bays and their gay villas and pressed on into wilder country. There was a mountain range whose clear, defined, seaward-leaning peaks

MARINE DRIVE, CAPE PENINSULA

are called the Twelve Apostles, and in whose valleys and clefts the morning light was pressed like grape-juice, now blue, now purple. Hawks hung in the quiet sky. The waves came whitening from the sea, sometimes halting at a rock ledge and rushing onward in palest blue to spill into an emerald pool. Upon this lovely Cape Peninsula, where mountain and sea combine to compose themselves into a hundred unpaintable pictures, lay the burning hand of the sun.

I looked down at one point into a cove which might have been Mullion, where in pale, shallow water a company of coloured children were splashing, their bodies golden-brown and lemon-yellow. Just before the road turned inland I came to a place called, most improbably, Llandudno, a quiet little rock bay with a single road running down to it and elsewhere completely cut off by rocks and mountains.

The valley which led inland to Hout Bay was streaked with hills of drift-sand as white as snow. Upon the right there was a shimmer of silver trees: soft, velvety leaves which, when I was a child, returning Anglo-Indian uncles gave to little boys as bookmarkers; and thousands of them must still lie pressed like limp grey velvet in old Bibles.

The mountains piled up to the left, the road became a gorge, the sea grew every moment more distant, and the overhanging peaks and the bends in the road cut off the sun, so that I passed through patches of light and shade. The road turned inland and went for some way into a valley, and then, turning westward, came to the beautiful bay of Kommetje, to more mountains and a road which took me to a vast beach of silver sand that needed only a three-masted schooner in the bay, and a group of pirates on shore burying an iron chest, to make it the bay of one's boyhood. A little farther on is a small game reserve where I caught my first glimpse of wild animals. Beneath a tree in the sun-dappled woodland two eland were standing as still as stone.

The Cape of Good Hope occupies a rocky promontory which is battered by wave and wind even on a warm summer's day, and rises to the considerable height of nearly nine hundred feet. A disused lighthouse stands upon a rocky ledge above a wide concrete platform, and far below, at the end of a steep

D

track, but invisible from the old lighthouse, is the Cape Point Light.

The view is grand. I looked down into smugglers' coves where the sea dashed itself against rocks while the birds mewed and darted, and I looked away across the rocky spine of the Peninsula stretching north to Table Mountain. Like all such promontories, the Cape of Good Hope impresses by its air of dramatic finality and also by the knowledge, which every visitor takes with him, that this, of all the capes in the world, is the most famous and the most notorious.

And it is, surely, of the cruel and terrifying aspects of the Cape that one thinks, even on a fine day: of the sudden hurricanes from a blue sky, like a quarrel between the eastern and the western oceans, causing ships in Table Bay to drag their anchors and drift before the gale; of the five hundred British soldiers who stood on parade in a night of mad storm while their wives and children took to the boats and the *Birkenhead* went down.

" Do you know," said the lighthouse keeper, " I've sometimes surprised visitors by rolling a barrel over the cliff and then waiting for the wind down there to pick it up and throw it back! You ought to come here some night when a real gale is blowing and the updraught comes over the cliff at a hundred miles an hour! "

I asked if he had ever seen the *Flying Dutchman* and to my disappointment he said no. This is the greatest legend of the sea. And in the story of a seaman condemned for his misdeeds to sail for ever round the Cape, never reaching harbour, I think we can discern the fear and horror which this place inspired in the minds of the early navigators. Van der Decken is the name of the unfortunate seaman in the Dutch story, although van Straaten is another candidate, and in the German version the name is von Falkenberg. All three Captains are said to have cast dice with the devil for their souls.

Walter Scott examined this legend and traced it to a ship laden with bullion, on which a murder had been committed or in which plague had broken out. The ship sailed on and on, only to find that each port, learning of its history, was closed to it.

The most surprising thing I know about the *Flying Dutchman* is that he was seen in the year 1881, well off his usual beat, and vouched for by the late King George V. The spectre is well described in *The Cruise of Her Majesty's Ship Bacchante*, written by George V and his brother, Prince Albert Victor (afterwards the Duke of Clarence), who were midshipmen at the time.

The young Princes, after visiting South Africa and commenting on its problems in a grown-up and solemn way, steamed with the squadron to Australia. Their ship, *Bacchante*, reversed the usual procedure by meeting disaster before, not after, seeing the *Flying Dutchman*, for she lost her rudder at Melbourne, and the Princes were transferred to *Inconstant*, another ship of the squadron.

Two nights before they sailed the Princes note that they were given two platypus skins, commenting with schoolboy avidity that " each skin is worth a couple of guineas " !   Then the night before they sailed, while attending a ball at Government House, they say that " just before dancing began part of the cornice of the western side of the room came down with a bang: it hurt nobody, but part of it, unfortunately, fell on the head of an officer of the Public Works Department, under whose care the room was. . . . It was a beautiful ball."

The princely concern, combined with the ill-concealed pleasure of the word " bang ", together with the magnificent accuracy of " the western side of the room " make this extract typical of the whole diary.   But no doubt the accuracy of the Princes, which extended to measuring everything that could be measured, to assessing the velocity of winds and to noting the height of mountains, and so on, all, no doubt, under the eagle eyes of Admiral and tutor, must surely increase our respect for the account of the spectral ship which follows.

The squadron sailed soon after midnight on July 9, 1881, and on July 11th the following entry appears in the royal diary:

" At 4 a.m. the *Flying Dutchman* crossed our bows. A strange red light as of a phantom ship all aglow, in the midst of which light the masts, spars and sails of a brig 200 yards distant stood out in strong relief as she came up on the port bow. The look out man on the forecastle reported her as close on the port bow, where also the officer of the watch from the bridge clearly saw her, as did also the quarterdeck midshipman, who was sent forward at once to the forecastle; but, on arriving there, no vestige nor any sign whatever of any material ship was to be seen either near or right away to the horizon, the night being clear and the sea calm. Thirteen persons altogether saw her, but whether it was *Van Diemen* or the *Flying Dutchman*, or who else, must remain unknown. The *Tommaline* and *Cleopatra*, who were sailing on our starboard bow, flashed to ask whether we had seen the strange red light."

Then follows the remarkable piece of news:

" At 10.45 a.m. the ordinary seaman who had this morning reported the *Flying Dutchman* fell from the foretopmast cross-trees and was smashed to atoms. At 10.45 p.m. after quarters we hove to with the headyards aback, and he was buried in the sea. He was a smart royal yardman, and one of the most promising young lads in the ship, and everyone feels quite sad at his loss. (At the next port we came to the Admiral was also smitten down.) "

Then the third disaster is chronicled:

" The midshipmen's half yearly examination began to-day with the Algebra paper."

And the ship sailed on to Sydney.

I continued my northward journey back to Cape Town along the Indian Ocean side of the Peninsula. About five miles from Cape Point I came to a little place called Smits-winkel Bay. In Dutch and Afrikaans " winkel " is a shop. Rip van Winkle was Rip-from-the-shop, or Rip, the shop-keeper.

Beyond this point the road runs along the edge of the cliff while mountains, rising through dense woodlands, tower on the left. It was here that I surprised a company of baboons as they crossed the road ahead of me. I think they were as astonished as I was. They gazed at me for a fleeting moment with the expression reserved by all pedestrians for dangerous drivers, and then, levering themselves on their knuckles, they hurled their hairy bodies straight into the trees on the opposite side. Although I got out and looked down into the wood, they had vanished; only the faintest movement of branches far off in the green depths spoke of their swift descent.

I passed through many small seaside places and bays, and at last I arrived at Simonstown, the naval base, with its elegant Admiralty House, its dockyard, and its rocky coves where the children of naval officers and men bathe and get sunburnt.

From Simonstown the scenery became even more Mediterranean, and the beauty of False Bay was immensely enhanced by the gorgeous outline of the Hottentot's Holland Mountains on the far side, which lifted their fretted pinnacles into a sky hardly less blue than themselves. Rocky bays succeeded one another, each one with its villas climbing hills at the back, and some with little harbours where yachts and fishing boats were mirrored in the emerald water on which they rode at anchor. Small boys surrounded the fishermen, so that these harbours presented a view of many thin little posteriors in khaki shorts whose owners, leaning perilously over walls and breakwaters, waited breathlessly to see what queer fish might come from that enchanted sea.

A lovely spot, which brings back memories of Capri, is St James. Here, with a view across the water to the heroic blue mountains on the sky, that distinguished writer, Francis Brett Young, has settled; and South Africa must be proud to have him there. His novels, *They Seek a Country* and *The City of Gold* —the third novel to complete the trilogy is yet to be written— have done much to explain South Africa to the world. Admirers of those novels will like to know how they came to be written.

" In 1915 or 1916 it was my fate to serve under Smuts in the German East Africa campaign," Mr Brett Young told me. " I had already fallen in love with the Cape and was distressed by a great deal of talk about racial differences in what I believed to be a country with a vast future. On the transport sailing northwards from Durban, I sat at the table between two men. One was a dear friend of mine, a surgeon who has since died, and the other was a Brigade Major named Andries Brink, who later became Chief of Staff to the Union Defence Force, and died only the other day.

" As we sat and talked it emerged that these men had fought, on opposite sides, in the South African War. It appeared likely that the shot which wounded my surgeon friend at one of the battles in Natal had been fired by my other neighbour. It was an inspiring thing to hear these two men discussing, without any rancour, the events of that campaign. We were all three the best of friends and I could not help feeling that this encounter was not only intensely dramatic but also significant of the community of feeling which, sooner or later, must unite the two racial strains in a new and, as I believed, a great South African nation. The proper title for my book was, of course, *The Birth of a Nation*, but in this I had been forestalled. But this was the theme of the book which I planned that day, though it had to wait more than twenty years before I set pen to paper. And I still believe that my theme was something more than a romantic dream which the liberal wisdom of the Act of Union made possible."

Both races in South Africa agree that these two books have made a great contribution towards that issue. I remember reading them long before I came to South Africa and they were the first books that gave me an idea of the spiritual background of the Boer.

Next to St James is the celebrated Muizenberg, where white waves in successive arcs were advancing upon miles of sand. Upon the main road is the humble little cottage in which Cecil Rhodes died. It is now a national monument, but, although I knocked upon the door on this and two subsequent occasions, the place was empty and I was never able to see inside.

CHAPTER TWO

In which I see the original diary of van Riebeeck, steam over to Robben Island, visit Cape Town Castle with its memories of Lady Anne Barnard, visit Groot Constantia and go to Groote Schuur, the house which belonged to Cecil Rhodes.

§ 1

THE pen of the South African historian must drop from a nerveless hand when he lets his thoughts stray towards the State Archives in Cape Town. You may find there the whole history of South Africa from the first week of its existence until the day before yesterday, all neatly filed away ready to refute the historian; and never, I should think, has any country possessed a more completely documented account of itself. Such phrases as " it is assumed that " or " there is little doubt that ", which bridge the merciful gaps in ordinary historical sources, are not possible to the writer on South Africa, who, every time he puts pen to paper, is inviting some-one to catch him out with an original document.

It was in this bewildering vault of history that I had the great pleasure of holding in my hands the diary of van Rie-beeck; and I can assure you that in modern Cape Town, with the throb of an urgent city all around, it was indeed touching and impressive to turn the yellowed pages which recorded man's first endeavours on those shores. It is a portly little volume, its leaves as pale as straw, but the ink still good and black, written in the difficult handwriting of the Seventeenth Century. It is, of course, written in Dutch and in the hand of a secretary, but the Commander himself vouches for the truth of each day's entry.

It was one of the many regulations of the Netherlands East India Company that the Commander at every one of their posts had to keep in triplicate a day to day record of his stewardship. One copy went to Amsterdam, another to Batavia, and the third copy he retained. As the Batavian copy of van Riebeeck's *Journal* has been lost, there are only two now in existence, in Cape Town and at the Hague. Unfortunately the Cape Town copy appears to have been bound by the public executioner, who has shaved it so closely that a line is missing from nearly every page, but the Hague copy is perfect. Working with a photostat of this copy, the Van Riebeeck Society is preparing a translation of this, the first South African document, to celebrate the tri-centenary of the landing.

The *Journal* is without doubt the most interesting piece of " Africana " in existence, and to hold it is to pass in imagination into those days when it was penned in the white sunlight of the Cape, or by the gleam of rushlights, while the first Europeans were making their experiments in the scattered dwellings round the fort. They had landed, many of them sick, after a voyage of seventeen weeks. The construction of the fort was van Riebeeck's first care and his next was the laying out of the twenty-six acres of vegetable garden, and the planting, in order to catch the rains of May and June, of the seeds he had brought in tubs of sand from Holland.

In the first days life at the Cape was naturally one long round of work. It was necessary, as van Riebeeck said, " to bring forth everything out of nothing ", and to cajole or drive some of his followers, who were not all of heroic mould. Some he considered " as raw as the whole world had ever seen ", but that, of course, was not a fault and might be cured by experience; others were intractable and disobedient and took the earliest chance to stow away and disappear on the first ship. Van Riebeeck himself, although he strove so valiantly and accomplished so much, did not love the Cape. After only a year he begged to be sent to the Indies away from the " dull, stupid, lazy, stinking " Hottentots, who might not be punished by order of the Company, even though they came and stole crops by night and drove off the cattle.

This Swiss Family Robinson era in South Africa is fascinating, and it is interesting to see how soon the pattern of South African life asserted itself among a tiny population. In addition to the residents, there was a fluctuating number of invalids suffering from scurvy, probably every fleet landed some of these, and those visitors who were not ill made life no easier by haunting the taverns, filling themselves with arak or anything else they could get, trampling down the cabbages and roaring that " they would rather be hanged than live in this damned country ". Even if van Riebeeck had been surrounded by saintly characters, all anxious to put their shoulders to the wheel, his achievements in ten years would have been remarkable, but when he had to contend with more than his due share of grousing, desertion, and insubordination, we can only marvel that he built so much and so well. For had he failed, might not the Cape have become French, or would the English have come over from St Helena? Certainly the Dutch element in South Africa would have gone for ever with van Riebeeck.

His labour problem appeared to him to be such that he had to import slaves. It is strange to think of slaves in that Mediterranean climate so fitted for the manual labour of white men. Nevertheless they came. By Dutch law aboriginal populations were exempted from slavery, so that the Hottentots were free, and slaves were imported from Angola and Guinea, and afterwards from Madagascar and Malaya. Thus the Seventeenth Century habits of hot countries were transferred to the mild wine-growing Riviera of the Cape.

Within a few seasons passing Dutch merchantmen were taking on cargoes of fresh vegetables and fresh meat. Wheat was being cultivated with difficulty, and a wonderful new crop imported from Guinea, maize or mealies, was being grown with success. Beer, which was considered good for scurvy, was first brewed in 1658; wine and Cape brandy were made in the following year. Walnut, oak, chestnut, and ash trees had been planted; the first Guelder rose was plucked in 1659 —what a moment!—the first ripe oranges in 1661 and the first apples in 1662. As early as 1658 the blacksmith was making ploughshares, spades, and knives from steel sent from Holland.

It was van Riebeeck who wrote home to his masters asking for " lusty farm wenches " as wives for his settlers; accordingly those gracious institutions in Amsterdam which still house orphans, and until recently clothed them in attractive mediæval dress, one side black, the other red, were canvassed for the right type of girl. Whether the story of Manhattan Island had influenced him, who can say, but it is plain that van Riebeeck saw from the start that men would break out of the shackles of the hated Company into a free life of private profit, and, with the reluctant knowledge of the Seventeen, he actually settled the first freemen on their own farms within five years of the landing.

When van Riebeeck left after ten years of hard, solid work, the white population numbered a few hundred, and the settlement was well upon the way to becoming Cape Town. Already that division of the population into free burghers and Company servants, which it took New York longer to achieve, was in operation, and people round Table Bay already had friends or relatives farming land outside the settlement, who sometimes trekked into the Cape with their produce.

The old fort was still the Governor's residence. At its entrance were the Company stores and offices, also a hospital where, upon palliasses filled with straw, the scurvy-stricken sailors of Holland nursed their sore gums and tried to get rid of the fleas. A wooden jetty ran into the bay with a little shipbuilding yard nearby; a handful of low, one-storey, thatched dwellings was scattered on either side of the fresh-water stream, and, higher up, where the land begins to lift slightly towards the mountain, the Company garden, well hedged and traversed by irrigation canals, produced enormous crops of cabbages, radishes, potatoes, melons, and maize.

In van Riebeeck's private garden at Boschheuvel, the solace of whatever spare time he had—and it is always the busiest man who has spare time—the grapes grew blue in the sun; oranges, lemons, and the homely apple thrived; the quince, the cherry, the pear, the walnut, and the chestnut, perhaps drew back his mind to Europe, for, of course, van Riebeeck was not really a true South African!

Now and again a leopard would come out in the dusk and raid a hen-roost, more often a Hottentot would snatch washing from the line, cut brass buttons from a child's jacket, or snatch a hat from a passing stranger and be off and away like a deer. Drums were always beating, warning sailors to return aboard;

guns were always booming from Signal Hill to announce a sail coming up over the horizon; pungent smells of smoked fried porcupine or salted dassie rose in the morning air; and in the gathering African dusk, as the beacon on Robben Island blazed like a bush fire at sea, the Night Watch, fusees on shoulder, would shamble reluctantly on duty with many a backward glance towards the shouts and songs from the taverns of the Cape.

It was not a polite society, neither was it a cultured one. Like all ports of call, the Cape was subject to sudden violent eruptions of raging, roaring sailors who for months, as with torn fingers and split nails they grappled with sails in wind and sleet, had been savagely dreaming of bottomless casks of arak.

There was, however, one place at the Cape where from the first days the Sabbath had been kept when possible; in the hall of van Riebeeck's fort the Word of God had been heard for the first time in South Africa, and that Book read which the Voortrekkers were to carry with them over the mountains into the new lands of the north.

When van Riebeeck sailed away with his family his ten years of office had established more than a garden: he left the Cape with a native problem, a budding aristocracy, and an abiding hatred of government.

§ 2

As I walk about Cape Town, I think how much I should like to spend a day there with van Riebeeck. He would, of course, recognise the place at once because of Table Mountain and the Bay, but there is hardly anything else he would remember, except the position of his garden.

With luck he might, by prowling round the post-office and the City Hall, spot the place where the old fort had stood, but he would be puzzled by the disappearance of the river, which in a reminiscent moment he had called the Amstel, and astonished by the way the sea has retreated. Strand Street, which was once upon the foreshore of the bay, is now some good distance inland.

He could not fail to be interested in postal matters, because the Cape was a post-office long before he turned it into a market garden. He would be the first to agree that the present system is an improvement upon the more casual early method of leaving ships' papers under a stone.

We would go up to the Museum at the top of the Gardens, where van Riebeeck would be quite at home. He would recognise with a grim smile all the Hottentot exhibits and he would show interest in the astonishingly life-like casts of bushmen and their remarkable and steatopygous females. No doubt he would recognise some of the old ships' stones, all of which were lying about Table Bay in his time.

I should like to ask him how it happened that three hundred years ago, when ships' companies were chiefly composed of tough and illiterate characters, there were men among them capable of cutting inscriptions upon granite as exquisite as a title-page by Caxton. The English stones are particularly good. Take the stone inscribed *London*, 1622, a ship captained by Richard Blyth, and another, dated 1631, with the name Richard Arnott upon it, and the Dutch stone, dated 1632, bearing the name of Dirk van der Lee, and, even supposing them to have been the work of stone-masons, they are still masterpieces in the art of Roman lettering.

Van Riebeeck would be fascinated and thrilled to see the zoological section: the life-like lions and lionesses and the hippopotami, which he knew as " sea cows ", and he would be glad but surprised to know that these animals no longer haunt the shores of Table Bay. The rhino he would know well, for these creatures roamed the Cape in his time; many of the buck would be familiar to him; the leopard would be only too familiar; so would the civet cat—an animal that on one occasion invaded his bedroom! But the giraffe would be entirely new to him.

Perhaps the greatest thrill one could give van Riebeeck would be to take him to the top of the Old Mutual Building, probably the finest modern building in South Africa. If we must have skyscrapers, let them be like this. It is a Babylonian Temple, a Chaldæan ziggurat, if you like, but it is a triumphant solution to the problem of erecting a skyscraper in the vicinity of Table Mountain. It is nearly three hundred feet high, and four lifts shoot noiselessly to the summit. You step out upon a roof which affords what can only be described as a breath-taking view of Cape Town, Table Mountain, and Table Bay.

I made this ascent three times, and on each occasion I thought the experience more memorable. I expected to find every visitor to Cape Town on top of the building, but instead I had it all to myself.

§ 3

Before I set foot in South Africa I had never heard the word " tickey ". It is the South African name for a threepenny-bit. It is almost impossible to live through a day anywhere in the Union without hearing this strange word mentioned. The coin, which is the old-fashioned silver threepenny-bit, has a prestige in South Africa equalled only by the high place it occupies in the affections of Scotland.

Why is it called a tickey? The general impression is that it may be a native imitation of an English or an Afrikaans word. Some people think that it represents the native attempt to enunciate the Afrikaans " stukkie "—a little piece or bit— while others think it comes from the English word " ticket ", because at one time natives employed on public works were paid, not in coin, but with tickets, each valued at threepence, which could be redeemed at the local store.

I discovered a long and inconclusive note about the word in Charles Pettman's *Africanderisms*. The author does not think very highly of the explanations usually given, but offers the suggestion that the word may be much older than people think—that, in fact, it may go back to the days before the white settlement at the Cape. He thinks it possible that it may come from a Hottentot corruption of the Portuguese word " pataca ", a small coin.

Another word the stranger will quickly encounter is " morgen ", the Dutch land measurement, which is just over two English acres. The word " erf ", used in Dutch for " ground " or " inheritance ", means a building plot.

No one in South Africa ever talks about the cinema: it is the "bioscope", a delightfully old-fashioned word which carries the mind of any mature individual back to the far-off days of spotty tours of Venetian canals in the village hall. This does not mean that the South African cinema has lagged behind the rest of the world, for, on the contrary, all the latest films are to be seen in palatial bioscopes, many of which are air-conditioned.

When you are invited out to dinner in a South African home, you will encounter hospitality upon the scale associated with America. The dinner will be admirable and the conversation will be full of vitality. But towards the end of dinner you will become aware of some slight uneasiness in the air. You may intercept meaning glances between your host and hostess, and you will wonder what has gone wrong. Then, as people are eating an ice cream or trying to drink scalding hot coffee, your hostess will address the company.

" I don't want to hurry you," she will say, " but we shall be late for the bioscope! "

No one ever asks if you wish to go to the bioscope, or if you have already seen the film, which sometimes happens! And you crowd into American limousines and desert the reality of an excellent meal for the land of shadows.

§ 4

The " Cape Doctor " is the name of Cape Town's private and personal monsoon, the South-Easter. It blows during the dry season of summer, and is called the " Cape Doctor " because it always blows seaward and is said to carry away all the germs with it. It has been described and feared since Diaz rounded the Cape.

No sooner had I put my head out of doors one morning than I knew the South-Easter was in full blast. Looking up at Table Mountain, I saw that the summit was concealed by a cloud whose grey edges steamed over the flanks like a slow-motion waterfall. Having descended some way, the mist peeled off and frayed away into thin air, but this ceaseless evaporation did not diminish or thin the waterfall. And all the time the wind screamed seaward, the sun shone, the sky was blue, and white horses had been whipped up on the Atlantic.

In Cape Town the wind was tremendous and unforgettable, but quite freakish. It seemed that each tall street was a funnel directing it and aiming it with such force at the cross-roads that men and women travelling against it had to fight their way heads down to the opposite pavement. Yet oddly enough there were unlikely little pockets of calm where the wind was hardly blowing at all.

The South-Easter has the air of being a private wind, something belonging to Cape Town that is let loose from its cave upon Table Mountain, as the Greeks fancied the winds were unleashed from a mountain in Thrace. It can vary in character from day to day. Upon this particular day it was not in a savage or a dangerous mood: it was a big, blustering wind that came gambolling through Cape Town like a puppy, snapping at the hats of men and at the knees of women, and making fantastic whirls and spirals of old newspapers, dust, orange peel, dead flowers, and presumably blowing all the germs out to sea.

This was the windy morning I had selected to go out in a little boat to have a look at Robben Island. From the first moment I arrived in Cape Town the sight of that island lying in Table Bay, apparently as bare as a billiard ball, had roused my curiosity. Its queer history—it was in ancient times a leper and a penal settlement—made me anxious to visit it, but I found this not easy because it now belongs to the Union Defence Force and has been closed to visitors for many years. However, I was kindly given a pass, and upon this gusty morning I was blown down to the docks, where all the ships and the boats were lifting on the swell.

Tied to the dock was an experienced-looking little tug called the *Isie*, whose mission in life is to link Robben Island with the mainland. Military stores, including a plentiful supply of beer for the N.C.O.'s mess, were being loaded and well roped down on deck. The passengers were all in khaki. They were either returning from leave or going out to take a course, for the island is now an artillery school. Slowly the *Isie* moved across the harbour to a line of white which was Table Bay, and as I looked back at Table Mountain and saw the sullen cloud steaming over the edge, and felt the powerful wind blowing us towards the harbour mouth, I recognised a hundred early pictures and engravings of Cape Town: the mountain, the mist, the seaward wind, the tossing ships.

The skipper in his wheel-house said that it was going to be all right going out, but not so good coming back. As we crossed the harbour bar, the long swell met us and now and again the tail of a wave whipped across our low decks, sending us with upturned collars to shelter. There I met a young South African officer who was returning from leave. He told me that life on Robben Island is grand for those who like solitude, but not so much fun for those who long for the bright lights which can be seen across the sea, glittering and winking round the foot of Table Mountain every night. He, a lover of solitude, liked Robben Island and was content to stay there, do his job, read books, and save his pay.

Soon we came into calmer water and Robben Island was now quite near upon our starboard bow, a low, Robinson Crusoe island, bare and featureless, the waves breaking in sunlight upon deserted beaches. There was a little harbour and a new stone pier, named ambitiously Port Murray, and to this pier the *Isie* tied up. A smart young officer was waiting for me with a car.

While we drove to headquarters he told me the recent history of Robben Island: how about 1936 the Government decided to fortify it and put a military force upon it; how this force had taken possession of what had for years been an abandoned and overgrown island where the old buildings and houses of former occupants—the convict and leper settlements—were standing roofless and deserted in a jungle of manitaka trees. Now, the war over, the Army has established a military school on the island with a regular staff and a changing population of soldiers on courses. In addition to the military, several hundred coloured and native labourers have been imported, who, dimly aware of the island's tragic history, believe the place is haunted, as indeed it ought to be.

We came to a Nineteenth Century house, once the residence

THE UNIVERSITY, CAPE TOWN

of the governor of Robben Island and now the headquarters and mess. There were a few shanties near by and a trace of older buildings, for this was evidently the centre of the island's administration.

Not far away is a surprising sight—a perfect little English church complete with a machicolated tower which might have come from any Hampshire village. Two old ships' cannon stand, barrel downwards, on each side of the door, and above is a stone which reads: " Erected in the year of our Lord, 1841. Captain Richard Wolfe, Commandant of the Island." We went inside, and it was as I had thought, a tiny English church, designed, no doubt, in homesick or reminiscent mood by a Royal Engineer.

After lunch we motored round the island, a drive of about seven miles. Most of the land is scrub and tough grass, the rest is a jungle of manitoka, which was introduced about 1910 and has spread almost everywhere. In spring whole acres of Robben Island are covered with white narcissi which, I was told, had spread from bulbs planted in the old graveyards.

On the north of the island we saw an ancient slate quarry from which the Dutch settlers took slate for Cape Town Castle and for the floors and stoeps of the first Cape houses. Not far away is a beach of pulverised shell which is driven up and packed by the tides on this side of the island. This shell beach is mentioned by van Riebeeck, who took from it masses of material for the Cape's first lime-kilns. Upon the only slight eminence on the island, known as Vuurberg—fire mountain—van Riebeeck kept a beacon burning at night for ships entering the Bay: the first light on the coasts of South Africa. There is a modern lighthouse there to-day, whose seven second flash is well known to the people of Sea Point and other places on the Atlantic mainland.

In the Eighteenth Century Robben Island achieved a sad and tragic fame as a leper colony.

" It's a curious thing," said one of the officers, " that the ghosts which the coloured workmen claim to see on the island have no hands or feet. I put this down to the fact that when we came here we found in a house a collection of leper

E

photographs which the doctor had once possessed.   These must have got about among the workmen, with the result which you can imagine ! "

We went off to have a look at what remains of the leper settlement, but not much is left.   The suns of many summers, the rains, and, above all, the advancing jungle, have obliterated nearly all trace.   The queerest thing we saw was the ruin of the Leper Maternity Home, lying in a tangle of what had once been a garden.

The little *Isie* took me back to Cape Town.   The Cape Doctor was still blowing.   The *Isie* was smacked about by the sea this way and that, until we had to hold on to anything that was handy.   And once again the view of Cape Town and Table Mountain, with a tossing blue sea in the foreground, was a sight never to be forgotten.

§ 5

Cape Town Castle is one of those happy fortresses which never fired an angry shot.   It now finds itself, owing to land reclamation, no longer on the edge of Table Bay but some way inland, where it could not do much damage, except possibly to the Blue Train or the nine-fifteen to Wynberg, which run into its line of fire as they leave or enter Cape Town.

It is the most massive, as it is also the oldest, European monument in South Africa.   Though we should not call it ancient—it was begun in 1666, the year of the Great Fire of London—it is to South Africans the most venerable European object in their country, and it is interesting as the type of stronghold which the Netherlands East India Company built in the days of its power to defend itself from the growing rivalry of England.   Van Riebeeck's old fort was a shelter from Hottentots and wild animals; its successor is a more ambitious and powerful structure, in shape the usual pentagonal fortification of the Seventeenth Century.   Its five batteries enclose a great barrack square around which rise the old administrative headquarters of the colony and the delightful Residency of the Governor; for by the time the castle was built the Commander at the Cape had been promoted.

A sentry in tropical drill stands on guard at the main gate, and every hour visitors assemble in the shade and wait for the guide to come and show them round. The gatehouse is perhaps the most attractive portion of the Castle. It is built of those beautiful small mulberry-coloured bricks that the Dutch made so well, and it rises into a domed belfry which still holds the old alarm bell. Anyone interested in the Netherlands East India Company will notice, carved on the lintel of the main gateway, the arms of the six towns in Holland whose Chambers elected the all powerful Seventeen.

I joined a little crowd, which included a covey of schoolgirls, an elderly English couple who told me they had come to live at the Cape, an American, and a friendly Afrikaans speaking lady with a small boy, who was kind enough to let me practise upon her some of the less inappropriate portions of my Afrikaans phrase book. But is there anything more pointless and disconcerting than the sentences one finds in such books? How can you discover anything to address to a woman you have never seen before from such headings as " Apartments ", " The Customs House ", " Money-changing ", " Post and Telegraph ", or " Worship "? The lady enriched my vocabulary by a glorious word, not in the phrase book, which, by means of intonation, may express affirmation, negation, approval, disapproval, credulity, and incredulity at will. It is just " ja-nee ", which means yes-no.

We entered the Council Chamber of the Dutch East India Company, where governor after governor held his court from the Seventeenth Century down to the moment when Cape Town reluctantly surrendered to the British in 1795. The rooms are high and cool. There are a few old Dutch dressers in them and some grandfather clocks, and a sinister picture which visits disaster upon anyone who moves it from its position over the fireplace.

In these rooms Lady Anne Barnard gave her parties.

We passed through an archway, where the guide showed us a brackish well and the simple wooden cross from Delville Wood erected by the 1st South African Infantry Brigade. We then mounted steps to one of the bastions. We gazed over the network of railway lines and back towards Cape

Town and Table Mountain. We entered cells and dungeons. I noticed that they bear a record of continuous occupations from the Eighteenth Century down to the present time. One prisoner, in the style of a more graceful age, had carved upon his cell door:

> *Unwelcome stranger to this woeful place*
> *Adieu to friendship and to mental peace.*
> *Content is fled. O, tedious time*
> *When sad reflection ponders o'er no crime.*
> *No chearing comfort glads the wearied eye*
> *As the incessant hours in dull rotation fly.*

In abrupt contrast to this, the productions of an age of compulsory education are surprisingly poor. " The Army can go to Hell for my part " is almost the best that the year 1943 can produce. " I got here through my wife and I got here through my girl," is a puzzling but provoking cry of disillusion. What happened, one wonders? Did the wife and the girl get together and, by some sinister collaboration, condemn the prisoner to that dreary cell?

We wandered round the ramparts for a while, then, passing across the hot courtyard to the gate, we said good-bye, with a *tot siens* or two and one " s'long folks "; and so, drawn together for a moment by Cape Town Castle, we resumed our separate lives.

What a pleasant existence the Dutch created for themselves so far from the storm and stress of Europe, a life with an easy charm, even grace, provincial maybe and perhaps not very intellectual, but comfortable and lived in an unmatchable setting. Those voyagers who arrived from the violence of revolutionary Europe must have felt like staying there. And history is apparently repeating itself. There is something idyllic about the régime of such Governors as old Simon van der Stel, whose memory still pervades the Castle, a man who might be called South Africa's first statesman, perhaps her first gentleman. The Castle has not changed much since his day and one may fancy his coach and six drawing up before the Residency to take him off on some benevolent occasion.

The only other name that leaps readily to the mind is that of a woman, Lady Anne Barnard, the authoress of *Auld Robin Gray*, who arrived at the Cape as the wife of the Secretary to the first British administration.

By that time the Cape had long since outgrown its humble status as a smallholding: it was now the chief strategic point on the road to India. When the French Revolutionary armies marched into Holland in 1793, the Dutch joined them under the exotic name of the Batavian Republic, and the Prince of Orange fled to England. France had also declared war on Britain and so began the long struggle that, with intervals, ended only at Waterloo.

From the outset it was obvious that either Britain or France would have to hold the Cape.

" What was a feather in the hands of Holland, will become a sword in the hands of France," wrote a naval Captain at the time. It was very true.

A British fleet was sent at once to the Cape with a letter which the Prince of Orange had written from Kew, asking the Governor to accept the British as friends and to allow them to stiffen the defence of the Peninsula. This letter did not have the expected result. The Dutch, who thus heard surprisingly and abruptly of the plight of their homeland, did not know what to do. Their loyalties were divided between their exiled Prince and their country. After long discussion they decided to oppose the British landing; but the opposition was of the token variety, and the British troops had no difficulty in reaching Cape Town and running up the Union Jack on the Castle. Thus the Cape came under British rule for eight years, 1795–1803, after which it was returned to the Batavian Republic at the Peace of Amiens.

The brief period of eight years, to which Lady Anne Barnard belongs, is known as the first British occupation. The Cape had been Dutch again for only three years when the Napoleonic Wars began, and this time Britain—now no longer the ally of Holland—had to take the Cape by force. One action was fought, and British forces again took possession of Cape Town. After the fall of Napoleon, the Congress of Vienna confirmed Britain's possession of the Cape and certain other former Dutch possessions upon the payment of six million pounds. That was how Britain came to South Africa.

§ 6

The first English landing caused the tragic death of one who played an interesting and I think not generally appreciated part in Cape history. He was Colonel Robert Jacob Gordon, the officer in command of the Dutch garrison. He is the first Scot in South African history, but although he was of Scots ancestry he considered himself a good Dutchman and was devoted to the House of Orange. Poor Gordon was so distressed by the British landing and, some say, so upset by charges of treachery that he committed suicide.

He belonged to a Scottish family who had evidently followed the Stuarts into exile. He was brought up in Holland and entered the Dutch army. He was well known to everybody who visited the Cape at the end of the Eighteenth Century, and his amiable personality flits pleasantly in and out of travel books and memoirs, kindly and cheerful, full of local knowledge, cultured and hospitable. And he played a notable part in South African exploration.

Though he was not the first white man to see the Orange River, having been preceded by a Dutch elephant-hunter, he was the second to do so, and it was Gordon who named the river in honour of the reigning House of Orange. His own name, by the way, is preserved in Gordon's Bay, near Somerset West. Gordon was an extraordinarily kind, sociable fellow, a classical scholar and a reader, and no doubt at times he felt rather lonely at the Cape and was only too happy to welcome the odd assortment of writers and botanists who were always calling there.

A delightful description of Gordon is to be found in the *Memoirs* of William Hickey. In 1777, when Hickey was a young lawyer of twenty-eight on his way to India, he stopped at the Cape with a party of young men from the ship. Gordon arranged a trip to the top of Table Mountain for them. He sent Hottentot servants ahead with baskets of food and wine, flutes and French horns. When the weary travellers had climbed half-way, they had a breakfast of cold ham and chicken to the sound of flutes, and on the summit they were rewarded by large quantities of food and drink to the sound of French horns. Gordon was of great assistance to Le Vaillant when he was writing his two lively books, and in his company William Paterson made the journeys which he subsequently described.

Australia may not be aware that it owes the start of its wool industry to the Cape, and to sheep owned at one time by Gordon. Towards the end of the Eighteenth Century the "father" of New South Wales, John Macarthur, who was contemplating the possibility of breeding fine-woolled sheep, asked two sea captains to look out for likely animals for him. These men arrived at the Cape after Gordon's suicide and at a time when his widow was selling some of his possessions, including a flock of merino sheep with an unusual history. They had belonged to the celebrated Escurial flock and had been presented to the Dutch Government by the King of Spain.

With the idea that the Cape might go in for wool, the Dutch Government sent out these merinos, but as soon as they arrived they encountered the prejudice of the farmers. Mutton, not wool, was the tradition at the Cape in those days, and as on one was interested in them, they passed into the possession of Gordon. Many years were to pass before South Africa could think of a sheep in terms not of mutton but of wool.

Gordon's sheep were welcomed in Australia, where Macarthur took the greatest care of them. As soon as possible he went to London, taking with him a sample of their wool. He interested manufacturers in the quality of Australian wool, and from that moment the great industry never looked back.

Gordon was a magnificent cartographer and water-colourist, and among his possessions were four hundred beautiful water-colour drawings of South African scenery, and particularly the coastline of the Cape. This collection is now in the Rijks Museum in Amsterdam, and is bound in six enormous volumes. All the plans and views are mounted on linen and are signed and dated by Gordon. Perhaps the most interesting are the first pictures ever made of the Orange River.

There is also a delightful view of Swellendam, showing the Drostdy with the Dutch flag planted in a field opposite and six little white farms dotted about the landscape. Some of the panoramas, notably those of the Orange River and the Cape coast, are over thirty feet long and are best examined on the floor.

§ 7

South Africa was still an unknown country when Lady Anne Barnard stepped ashore at the Cape in 1797 with the first British administration. Considering its place on the world trade routes, remarkably little had been written about it. Father Tachard, who went to Siam in 1685 with a party of Jesuits, gave an incidental description of Cape Town of very great interest, proving how many secret Roman Catholics lived under the Dutch East India Company; a German called Peter Kolben wrote an unreliable book in 1719, and a Scot, William Paterson, wrote a dull one in 1789. But the flood of books on South Africa did not begin until the Nineteenth Century. It was therefore into a novel and fascinating land that Lady Anne Barnard stepped in 1797, equipped with a keen eye, a witty pen, and a charitable heart.

This Scotswoman was the first person who attempted to show the Cape Dutch that all British people were not haughty or ill-mannered, and she had considerable success in bringing British and Dutch together in Cape Town Castle in a happy atmosphere of wine, cold chicken, candlelight and fiddles. Her descriptions of Cape life were penned in the form of letters to friends in England.

There is, perhaps, something eternally youthful about the name of Anne, so that it is rather a surprise to realise that the originator of all this gaiety was a mature woman of forty-seven when she first set eyes on Table Mountain. There was nothing girlish about her: she was an accomplished woman of the world, a Scottish noblewoman whose life had been spent amongst the " quality " in Edinburgh and London, a woman whose fate it was to go through life in love with one man, but contentedly, even happily, married to another twelve years her junior. She was sane and practical, and, in my opinion, few things show more clearly this side of her character than the fact that she took with her to the Cape " a map of a sheep and an ox ", thinking it likely that Dutch butchers might cut meat awkwardly.

In her youth, as Lady Anne Lindsay, daughter of the old Earl of Balcarres, she moved with wit and, as a miniature by Cosway proves, with beauty, through the elegant social world of the late Eighteenth Century. When she was twenty-one she composed the ballad *Auld Robin Gray*, whose fame was a life-long embarrassment to her. It describes the problem of a married woman faced by the return of her old true love from foreign parts, and it was inspired by her sister's life. In order not to implicate her sister, she stubbornly denied her authorship until she was an old lady of seventy-three, when she confessed the authorship to Sir Walter Scott, but never admitted the source of her inspiration.

Although her husband was only Secretary, Lady Anne found herself the official hostess at the Castle, because Lady Macartney, the Governor's wife, had not accompanied her husband to the Cape. Lord Macartney, sixty and suffering from gout, decided to live in the Garden House, now Government House, and to hand over to the Barnards the more sumptuous apartments in the Castle which were rightfully his. So poor Lady Anne set about furnishing those large and enormously high rooms with the aid of military carpenters and tailors, and everything must have been upon a simple, even frugal, scale.

The first lady of South Africa discovered a society that to her eyes was provincial, and also politically opposed to the occupation, believing that when the war was over the Cape would either become French or would be handed back to the Dutch, as indeed it was by treaty. Therefore many of those far-seeing people were not at all anxious to label themselves pro-British and so earn the hostility of the next rulers. She noted that some of the most important men who attended official functions, " appeared for a short time and then vanished, as if they were almost afraid of being seen there by each other ".

It was that frigid, suspicious atmosphere which she decided to break down by kindness and hospitality, and all those qualities of sympathy and sincerity which were a part of her nature. She observed the members of her own sex with a pitiless feminine eye. Lady Anne's first impression of them, on a gala occasion when they were sitting around in their best dresses, was that they reminded her very much of the women one might find at an assize ball in a country town. " What they want most is shoulders and manners."

Angling first for these ladies and their daughters, and gradually casting her net wider, with the blue coats from Simonstown and the red coats of the garrison as bait, Lady Anne soon drew to the Castle a lively company which drank her wine, ate her chicken, flirted and danced to the music of black fiddlers beneath the glow of the old Dutch chandeliers. Such warmth and good nature as there were in Cape Town during those extremely difficult years proceeded from her. She was no snob, neither was she burdened in any way with the prejudices of her class and time; the social peculiarities she noticed at the Cape came, as she well knew, from no ill nature, but were the natural result of a self-contained, semi-rural society which had been cut off for centuries from Europe and was poised remotely upon the toe of Africa.

The Cape Town she saw had grown into quite a large place. There were over six thousand white inhabitants, served by a larger number of slaves. The town, although so much smaller and lower in its roof-lines than to-day, impressed the visitor with the same air of brightness and liveliness. It was an exciting place to discover after weary months at sea.

The sun shone upon rectangular streets lined with reed-thatched houses, many of them the stately, classical houses of the Seventeenth Century, their many-paned windows set with regularity on either side of a tall, dignified door, pilasters lifting themselves from street to roof level, and each house with a stone stoep upon which the Kapenaars sat in the cool of summer evenings. Those buildings must have related themselves in Lady Anne's eyes to the old Jacobean houses of England, and the tall windows and the great doors, high enough for a horseman to enter in the saddle, may have reminded her of the Dutch architecture of the London of William and Mary. Many streets were unpaved, the town was ill-lit at night, parts of it smelt most vilely, and the dozens of single storey, thatched taverns, called by such names as De Witte Swan, De Roode Os, De Konig van Pruizen, De Goode Anker, never lacked their own thirsty international clientele.

There were no visible shops, but you could buy anything by arrangement, for a monstrous contraband tradition had grown up, the result of the Dutch East India Company's ban on shopkeeping. Nearly every ship that anchored in the Bay had mysterious dealings with Cape Town's invisible stores. The central feature of the town, the Herrengracht, called after the most fashionable canal of Seventeenth Century Amsterdam, was a wide street lined with trees which led gracefully to the Company Garden, then, as now, the joy and pride of Cape Town.

It was a vivid and ever-fascinating scene to a woman of Lady Anne's quick perception, who was also a capable water-colourist: the lead-complexioned Malay slaves trotting along with fish, fruit, or firewood on shoulder-poles; the broad, blue-coated Boers in vast hats and velskoen; the out-spanned oxen in the town square, clucked at by naked Hottentots; the gorgeous flowers in the fruit market; the muscular slaves advancing with some well-nourished beauty enshrined within a sedan-chair; the female slaves crouched in the sun, sewing, their raven hair transfixed by a silver pin.

At nine o'clock in the evening a Castle gun was fired. The sedan-chairmen awakened and flexed their muscles and, grasping the poles of their little glass boxes, went to collect their mistresses. Lanterns bobbed above the holes and craters in the streets as the mooi meisies and their mammas went home, fanning themselves beneath the Southern Cross, humming to the stars the tune of a catchy cotillon, or maybe remembering what lieveling Ensign Robinson had whispered about to-morrow night. Then, just to remind the ladies that they were not in Paris, or London or the Hague, all the watch-dogs would bark and the hyænas would back out of the starlight with their offal.

Lady Anne would go up to bed, believing she had done

a good deed, and in the Garden House old Lord Macartney, with the crickets trilling and the moths charging the candles, would open his despatches and read with satisfaction that England had not been beaten yet.

After Lady Anne Barnard and her husband returned to England in 1802, the Cape was handed back to the Dutch. The Barnards lived the usual London life for four years. Then the Napoleonic struggle began. England seized the Cape. Andrew Barnard was asked to go out again with young Lord Caledon, the Governor. He agreed to go for six months, leaving his wife at home.

" Where will this find you, my best beloved? " she wrote swiftly after him. " Oh, Barnard, if this matter were to be acted over again, I would not consent to a separation. Do not let your absence be longer than it must. Fair winds attend you and blow you soon back again. . . ."

He was ill on the voyage out, but wrote in May, 1807, giving her all the Cape Town news. In October he died on a journey up country and was buried in the Dutch Reformed Cemetery on the way to Green Point. Lady Anne lived to be seventy-four, carrying into her old age that vivid interest in the world around her which she employed so well at the Cape of Good Hope.

§ 8

I shall never forget the magic of those days spent in the country about Cape Town, among orchards and vineyards where the white walls of the old Dutch farms stand glittering in the sunlight as if carved in snow. The old farmers loved to give their houses names which expressed a reposeful sentiment, like Welgemeend—well-meant—or Vergelegen—far-away, or such poetic names as Morgenster—Morning-star, just as the Dutch do to this day.

The Cape farmhouse is the oldest type of domestic architecture in South Africa, and the style runs like a theme song in the work of many modern architects. In its purest form, as seen in the Cape, it is a style exquisitely adapted to the country and the climate. It is to South Africa what Spanish Colonial is to South America, and English Colonial to Carolina and Virginia.

The usual farm in Holland is a building of one storey, and the standard house of the wealthy Amsterdam merchant in the Seventeenth Century was a building of six or seven storeys, ending in a decorative gable in which there was always a little attic room. When the Dutch found themselves in South Africa they married the one storey farm to the Amsterdam gable with the greatest success. It might be thought that to give such prominence to the gable, and to bring it down so near the eye level, would have been unfortunate, but it is the reverse. The gable becomes the most interesting feature. It redeems the building from the commonplace and gives it style and quality.

The Cape farm is a long, roomy, thatched building, in size and proportion not unlike a large Hampshire barn. The ends of the building have gables which follow the line of the thatch, and the third and most important gable is in the centre over the front door and contains an attic, used in the old days as a storeroom or a schoolroom. The farms are always whitewashed and they dazzle the eyes, but this gives them a delightfully cool appearance in the warm climate. Trees—oak trees generally—are planted so near to them that the leaf-shadows at some moment of the day are silhouetted upon the walls. Some few yards from the farmhouse stands a slender white arch with a bell—the slave bell—hanging in it, and grouped about at convenient distances are the barns, stables, storehouses, and wine-presses, all built in the same style and all whitewashed.

Those old Dutch farms impressed me by their solidity and their dignity. Life must have passed very pleasantly there; no one went hungry or thirsty, and agriculture and viticulture were pursued not at a run, but at a gentle walk.

One of the most beautiful of the Cape homesteads is Groot Constantia, about twelve miles from Cape Town. This is the estate which produced the Constantia wine so famous in

Europe during the Eighteenth Century. Though the house itself is now a museum, its ancient vineyards still thrive. You approach Groot Constantia by way of a long avenue lined by trees, and when you come to it standing in white serenity among the shadows, it seems almost a pity to disturb its afternoon sleep.

A caretaker admitted me to a high, cool hall, the voorhuis, on either side of which were tall rooms. Behind was a long saloon—the dining-hall—and at the back were the kitchens and the spare rooms. The house breathed the spacious dignity of the Seventeenth Century. It was the right background for a grandee of the time. The man who built it had lived in a fine house in Holland, and he did the best he could to surround himself with the air of space and quality to which he was accustomed, as Englishmen did who went to Virginia and Carolina and built themselves the same kind of houses they had lived in at home.

The presses and storerooms in which the celebrated Constantia was made and matured may be seen near the house. This wine was a dessert wine of such quality and distinction that the experienced drinkers of the Eighteenth Century proclaimed it to be among the great wines of its type. Its excellence was due to the peculiarity, well known in wine-growing countries, that certain vineyards produce superb wine-grapes, while the next, separated only by a hedge or a ditch, may be commonplace. And it has also been suggested that the custom of twisting the stems of the bunches to arrest the flow of sap, and so turn the grapes almost into raisins before they went to the wine-press, helped the characteristic heavy sweet flavour. The grapes which grew so admirably at Constantia were the Muscadel and the Muscadel de Frontignac. The care with which this wine was made and shipped also maintained its reputation in Europe.

It is natural that Sheridan should have liked the wine, but more interesting, I think, that it should have been the last thing Napoleon asked for as he lay dying at St Helena. He was supplied with this wine by his devoted Las Cases. Among the guests who dined at Constantia in the year 1769 was the French navigator, Antoine de Bougainville. It is pleasant to think of him in a country where his name is now written so exquisitely upon a thousand sunlit walls.

§ 9

There are many memorials to Cecil Rhodes, but none, I fancy, more interesting or unusual than Groote Schuur, the fine house which Rhodes built outside Cape Town. He was so busy dreaming of an Anglo-Saxon world in which war would be no more, and of the United States of South Africa, that objects like rooms and bedsteads and tables never mattered very much to him. Rhodes was happy in a tin shed with a camp bed and perhaps a gladstone bag as a bolster. Of course, he was a bachelor.

But eventually, at the height of his power, he bought an ancient building called the Big Barn—Groote Schuur—in which the Dutch East India Company had once stored grain. He decided to convert this barn into a fine house for himself. It was the only time he gave any indication that he was aware of the domestic elegancies.

Meeting a shy young architect at dinner one night, he casually gave him the task of transforming Groote Schuur into a mansion, and that was the beginning of one of the happiest of South African associations: the collaboration between Cecil Rhodes and Herbert Baker. When a new wing had been built and a fine bedroom was ready for him, Rhodes continued to live in a hut in the garden which had been part of the old slave quarters, and it was not without great difficulty that Baker managed to get him out of this dwelling and into his own quarters in Groote Schuur. Even when the house was completed and furnished, Rhodes, proud as he was of it, showed a tendency to slip out by the back door at times and run off to one of his shacks or cottages. One wonders whether Rhodes really built Groote Schuur for himself, or whether it may be that the " brooding spirit ", or the feminine intuition which served him as a wife, told him, as he surveyed a South Africa of corrugated iron, that the time had come to set an æsthetic standard for the future.

Until Rhodes built Groote Schuur and filled it with old

Dutch furniture, no one except a few enthusiasts like Madame Koopmans de Wet thought highly of Cape architecture or Seventeenth Century Dutch furniture and craftsmanship. Then suddenly it became the fashion. This fortunate event not only established a South African style in domestic architecture, but it also created the modern manufacture of the sometimes excellent reproductions of Seventeenth Century furniture. When Rhodes died, he left Groote Schuur to the nation and nominated the house as the future residence of the Prime Minister of the Union of South Africa—several years before the Union took place.

I was invited by Field-Marshal Smuts to breakfast at Groote Schuur, and I motored along the De Waal Drive at the glorious hour of half-past seven in the morning. As the road sweeps up out of Cape Town there is a grand view of the Bay, then it runs inland, and soon I was passing the superbly situated University, one of Rhodes' dearest dreams. This splendid group of white buildings is seen against the massive slopes of the Devil's Peak which towers up, dark blue, into a pale blue sky. Next to it is an enclosure where zebra and buck were grazing behind a deer fence, and almost opposite a drive ran down to Groote Schuur.

The house is large, white, and gabled, with a pillared stoep looking out to the mountains. The gardeners were hosing the flower-beds and the sun was getting warm. There is a good bronze plaque over the central gable showing the landing of van Riebeeck.

After breakfast the General—for that is the handier title used in South Africa—took me all over the house, and I was surprised to see how many rooms are just as Cecil Rhodes left them. It is almost as though you might open a door and come face to face with Rhodes in a pair of white drill trousers going out for a ride. How odd it is that a man who cared so little for rooms and interior decoration should have so firmly impressed himself upon walls and chairs and tables.

His bedroom is the most interesting room in the house, interesting in the sense that it reflects his personality. It is a large, barely furnished room, not the room of a millionaire, but rather that of a soldier who has lived most of his life in a

CAPE TOWN AND TABLE MOUNTAIN FROM THE AIR

tent. The windows give a grand view of the mountains, and that, one imagines, was the attraction to Rhodes. The bed is rather hard and uncomfortable, there is the minimum of furniture, and upon the walls hang two photographs of Egyptian pharaohs, a print showing Napoleon crowning himself, and a photograph of a woman.

And who is this woman in the bedroom of Cecil Rhodes? She is a wrinkled old Zulu woman whose mummy-like hands lie on her knees and whose old eyes gaze out of an intricate nest of lines. She was one of the last surviving wives of the Matabele chief, Mzilikazi, and with her aid Rhodes made his daring visit, unarmed, into the Matopos in 1896, and brought the Matabele revolt to an end. The General told me the story briefly, and there is a full and fascinating account of it in Dr Hans Sauer's admirable book of reminiscences, *Ex Africa*. Sauer was one of the three men who went with Rhodes on this daring expedition, believing up to the last minute that they might be massacred.

The old woman was encountered by chance when Rhodes and a few Cape boys were hunting for food during the revolt. As they were catching some chickens, the old woman rushed out of a hut and abused Rhodes as a hen-stealer. It was then discovered that she was Nyambezana, Mzilikazi's only living wife, and the mother of one of the most important rebel chiefs. Rhodes, who had been told that ten thousand troops would be necessary to put down the revolt, decided to try to bring it to an end by going himself into the enemy country and meeting the chiefs. The old woman eventually acted as go-between.

The story of the journey into the hills and the Indaba that followed, which brought peace to Rhodesia, is one of nerve and courage that stands side by side with the journey of Piet Retief to the Zulu king, Dingaan. Retief's journey, however, ended in massacre. So the old woman whose portrait hangs in the bedroom at Groote Schuur was, I suppose, the most important woman in the life of Cecil Rhodes.

Downstairs there is another room just as Rhodes knew it. This is the library. It is a small library, but notable for the presence of several hundred books all bound in uniform red morocco and all in typescript. Here is another remark-

F

able story. Gibbon's *Decline and Fall* was one of the books which Rhodes admired so much that he wished to read the Greek and Latin authorities mentioned in the footnotes. One day, while he was walking along Piccadilly, he turned into a bookshop with the remarkable request that they should engage scholars at Oxford and Cambridge to translate all Gibbon's authorities! This was done. A stream of mainly Greek authorities, all neatly typed and in English, began to appear at Groote Schuur, and the supply did not cease until someone discovered that the bill had mounted to £8,000.

I was interested to see this library, which has often been disparaged as the whim of a rich man who paid heavily for translations of Ovid and Caesar. But how surprised I was to find that by far the greatest number are rare Byzantine texts which had never before been translated, a collection so impressive that they must be the finest library of Byzantine authorities ever put into English. I am sure that Byzantine students will be interested to know that in a few moments, during a brief glance at the shelves, I saw the following: the *History* of Agathias of Myrina; the *Chronographia* of John Cantacuzene; the *History of John Comnenus* by Nicetas; the *History* of Michael Attaliates; the *History* of John Curopalates; the *History* of Theophanes; the *Annals* of Zanaras; and the *Ceremonies* of Constantine Porphyrogenitus. Perhaps someday it might be possible to publish the Groote Schuur Byzantine texts, or some of them, for nothing like them exists anywhere else.

The Spartan masculinity of Groote Schuur impressed Mrs Gertrude Millin, who says in her biography, *Rhodes*: " It is a man's house. And, in fact, Rhodes kept no women servants, and the maids of visitors had orders to remain as inconspicuous as possible. There are fifteen bedrooms and two bathrooms: one of which, in marble, with a terrific granite bath, was Rhodes' great pride. Few of the bedrooms have adequate mirrors. Rhodes' own room possesses no adequate mirror, no bookshelf, no bright pictures, nothing soft."

Rhodes encouraged the public to wander so freely in every part of his estate that strangers were sometimes discovered in the house itself. " Numerous visitors used calmly to walk up and stroll along the back, looking into the windows, even when Rhodes, whom they probably did not recognise, was sitting in his chair at the far end of the stoep ", writes Gordon le Sueur, one of his secretaries. " I have known the bell to be rung by couples, and tea asked for, which was always supplied, and I have come across people strolling about the house quite unattended, having probably walked in through some door left open. One afternoon I went into the library, and saw a rough-looking man sitting in an easy-chair reading a newspaper. I enquired if there was anything I could do for him. ' No,' he replied. ' Then what are you doing here? ' I asked. Oh, just havin' a look round,' he said. ' This is Cecil Rhodes' 'ouse, ain't it? ' "

Like many people who have never done any writing, Rhodes had the delightful idea that you have only to place a poet or a writer in beautiful scenery in order to inspire the production of masterpieces, whereas the truth is that a lot of fine literature has been produced in revolt against ugly surroundings. A poet at the Cape is more likely to sit and do nothing, feeling that the poem has already been written by a greater than he.

However, with this idea Rhodes engaged Sir Herbert Baker to convert a smaller building, known as the Woolsack, and connected to Groote Schuur by a blue river of hydrangeas, into a retreat where artists and writers might live in beautiful surroundings and—in his hopeful words—" be better inspired to interpret through their art the beauty and grandeur of the country ". This charming little house built round an atrium had as its first literary tenant Rudyard Kipling, who used to go out to the Cape and live there every year with his family.

Though Kipling has left a pleasant account of holiday life at the Woolsack in *Something of Myself*, he must have been a disappointment to Rhodes. Apart from the lines:

Under hot Constantia broad the vineyards lie,
Throned and thorned the aching berg props the speckless sky,

and:

White as sand of Muysenberg
Spun before the gale—

Kipling never appeared to have been inspired by the beauty of the Cape. The beauty, of which he was naturally fully aware, acted on him as an anodyne. Rhodes must have looked at Kipling many a time as he used to look at the Big Hole at Kimberley, wondering when the diamonds, which he knew to be there, would come to light. But they never did. And I can understand Kipling perfectly. There are days at the Cape when you just do not work. You are content to look and to enjoy, and anybody can have your pen.

§ 10

I climbed the mountain path behind Groote Schuur to the Rhodes Memorial. In a temple of unfluted columns I saw the bust of a sad-faced man gazing out over the hazy flats to the north. I read these lines by Kipling on the pedestal:

> *His immense and brooding spirit still*
> *Shall quicken and control.*
> *Living he was the land, and dead*
> *His soul shall be her soul.*

The temple, says Sir Herbert Baker, was built upon a clearing where Rhodes had placed a seat because it was " his favourite view ". But surely not. Surely the " immense and brooding " face in the temple is gazing towards his favourite view, where, far to the north, in a country which bears his name, he lies like a pharaoh in a pyramid of living granite.

Many books have been written about Cecil Rhodes and many more will no doubt be written. Perhaps one day his one catastrophic fall from grace, the Jameson Raid, will not entirely overshadow his great virtues. He came from the vicarage of Bishop's Stortford, one of a large family, and went to South Africa as a delicate youth threatened with consumption. He became a millionaire and tied all his vast wealth to a dream: the vision of a Pax Brittanica.

The books draw the picture of a powerful and interesting personality: realist and dreamer; tough bargainer and open-handed giver; shrewd politician and youthful enthusiast;

poetic visionary and hardened cynic (" every man has his price ") ; and all this delightfully mixed with those personal peculiarities and whimsicalities which, since the time of Napoleon, have been expected of self-made Caesars.   He also, one gathers, had Napoleon's unfailing eye for a marshal and could recognise genius at a glance.   He had only to say to some unknown young man " do this " and it was done brilliantly, and the young man became famous.   But I should like to know more about Rhodes' failures, of the people who let him down and double-crossed him and of the swans who turned out to be not even geese.

No man in a life of forty-nine years did more for the Imperial idea which was his religion, and certainly few men have led a more dedicated, selfless life.   And it is fitting that one who created so many undergraduates should have remained so much an undergraduate himself.

§ 11

There were Professor A and Professor B, the Doctor, and someone whose name I never knew, and we were having lunch in a club and talking about Cape Town.

" What a number of words the Cape has prefixed," I said. " How many do you think there are ? "

" Well, there's the Cape Doctor," said Professor B.

" And Cape Cart," said the Doctor.

" And the Cape Gooseberry," I said.

" And Cape Dutch," said the Unknown.

" Yes, and Cape Pigeon—the petrel," said Professor A.

" And *gardenia florida*—Cape Jasmine," said Professor B.

" Oh, and Cape Hen—the albatross," said the Doctor.

" What about Cape Coloured ? " I suggested.

There was an interval.

" Cape Merchant," cried the Unknown triumphantly.

" Cape clouds," said the Doctor firmly.

" Yes," said Professor B, " the Magellan Clouds."

About an hour afterwards, as we were saying good-bye, Professor A, who had gone thoughtfully away, turned back with a gleam of triumph in his eye.

" Cape fly-away ! " he said and strode briskly off.

" He's right," said the Doctor.   " It's a mirage at sea."

A Cape Town night that lingers in my memory was spent in the coloured slum, District Six, with an armed police sergeant.   Things were quiet because on the previous night a gang of thugs, who had been smoking hemp, broke loose armed with razor blades and bicycle chains, and the subsequent arrests had spread an uneasy hush over the place.   I saw all the familiar sights of an exotic slum—the apparently inextricable confusion of good and bad, of infected and clean—but I saw nothing new in the way of vice or squalor.   It was strange to emerge from the mess to find myself in the centre of fashionable Cape Town on a moonlit night.

I returned the next day to attend a Malay wedding which was one of the prettiest things imaginable.   I sat for hours in a little house at a table loaded with crystallised fruits while the vivid little bride and her husband, surrounded by a glowing bouquet of bridesmaids, sat enthroned and received the good wishes of their Moslem kinsfolk.

CHAPTER THREE

*I go to the town of Stellenbosch and the fruit country of the Draken-
stein Valley and Paarl. I stay at Ceres and, passing through Tulbagh,
explore the Piquetberg Mountains, where I find a family that has been
living there for eighty years.*

§ 1

AS soon as the Cape wind ceased to blow, the hot November days continued. Table Bay became a lake, and the
far-off mountains lay upon the sky's edge in a flat wash
of blue and violet.

The spring flowers had died back into the hillside, but in
the gardens, where beds of hollyhocks and dahlias bloomed
side by side with bougainvillea and hibiscus, Europe and
Africa joined hands. Most lovely were the arum lilies of
white and yellow which sprang from any pool of still water
beside the road.

It was strange to see Christmas stealing into South African
shop windows in little dabs of cotton-wool snow; for the
tradition that the Nativity occurred in the climate of Northern
Europe is indestructible. With the temperature steadily
rising, Father Christmas was shown muffled in his heavy
scarlet gown, and he drove his reindeer sledge behind the
plate-glass of Adderley Street, heavily spangled with tinsel
frost upon which the summer sunlight of the Cape shone
strangely.

§ 2

One morning, motoring across the Cape Flats, I came to
green rounded hills which might have been the South Downs.
There was a moment, indeed, when the landscape bore such
a remarkable resemblance to Sussex that I expected to find
the Long Man of Wilmington round the next corner. Then

the resemblance faded, and I saw a screen of jagged mountains ahead which might have been dipped in Prussian Blue and hung against the sky. They were the mountains above the Drakenstein Valley.

I came to the delightful town of Stellenbosch, which was full of early morning bicycles and bells as young men and women with books beneath their arms hurried on their way to lectures and, I trust, to fame and fortune. What a pretty town it is. The University is spread in and around Stellenbosch in a number of fine buildings, but there was no need to construct cloisters, for that was done centuries ago when Governor Simon van der Stel planted his oak avenues. Everywhere in Stellenbosch you see broad streets lined with oak trees, white houses gleaming in tree shadows, tall tunnels of green shade; and in the gutters the water of the Eerste River runs musically tinkling on a hot morning and tempting you to believe that this must be a memory of the Dutch canals.

Next to Cape Town, Stellenbosch is South Africa's most ancient town. For twenty-six long years the first settlers contented themselves with a few expeditions into the " interior ", but they continued to live almost within shouting distance, certainly within gunshot, of the fort. The Cape in those days cannot have encouraged dispersion. There were lions and " tygers ", as they called leopards, there were roving hordes of Hottentots, and farther back in the hills there were bushmen. However, when the greatest of the Cape Dutchmen, Simon van der Stel, took stock of his little kingdom in 1679, he wisely came to the decision that the time had arrived for white men to take their first daring step away from Table Bay.

That first step led them to Stellenbosch. A few brave freemen were given farms in a landscape that had not yet taken on its characteristic appearance. There were no oaks, no vineyards, no firs, and no gum trees. It was a primitive bit of Africa awaiting the transforming hand of man. Holland sent acorns out to the Cape in sacks. When the young trees were as thick as a finger they were planted out in a nursery of good black soil on Table Mountain. In ten years time those not uprooted by baboons were thirty-six feet high, with a diameter of seven to eight inches near the ground! This may seem unbelievable, but we have Simon van der Stel's word for it. The Governor lavished a paternal love upon Stellenbosch, and every year on his birthday he would take his coach and six and go there to sit beneath the oak trees and give cakes to the most promising scholars while a jolly fair, a genuine old Dutch *kermis*, one imagines, took place around him; a scene that Teniers should have painted.

Stellenbosch to-day is an Afrikaans-speaking town. I hardly heard a word of English spoken there. The University, like that of Pretoria, teaches in Afrikaans; Cape Town and the Witwatersrand teach in English. The bookshops were an interesting proof of the enormous amount of Afrikaans literature being printed in South Africa to-day.

The two most famous scholars of Stellenbosch were General Hertzog and Field-Marshal Smuts. Hertzog went on from Stellenbosch to Holland, and Smuts to Cambridge. Although they differed on political matters, they were always in complete agreement on one: the excellence and desirability of Stellenbosch girls. Both Hertzog and Smuts fell in love when students, and both made early marriages; and, from a brief survey of the town, I should say that this was not the most difficult part of their tutelage.

I departed from pretty, leafy Stellenbosch with one question unanswered in my mind. It is a mystery. When Lady Anne Barnard went to that town in 1797, the Landdrost, or magistrate, sent his carriage to meet her, and she was surprised to see from the coat of arms on the door that it had once belonged to the fourth Duke of Queensberry. This was the notorious " Old Q ", who in his seventies used to sit on a balcony in Piccadilly quizzing the ladies, while a mounted groom sat below ready to carry his master's messages here and there. Though almost anything may happen to a second-hand article, the appearance at the Cape of " Old Q's " carriage—that relic of Georgian London—with six horses attached to it and a Hottentot driver on the box, belongs surely to the highest regions of the improbable.

§ 3

The Drakenstein Valley, like many things in the Cape, is completely un-African. It might be France, it might even be Germany; I think if you could slide it quietly into any region west of Bordeaux, towards the Cevennes, no one would be surprised to wake up in the morning and find it there. Mountains enclose it on the north, rising in long ridges or in sharp pinnacles; the slopes are thickly planted with firs; and there is not a thing within sight, except the mountains themselves, that is not there as the result of long European occupation. Every yard of the valley is closely cultivated with orchards and vineyards. White châteaux gleam among the trees, neat vineyards climb the hills as they do in the Rhineland, and altogether you see in the Drakenstein Valley as fine an example as you could wish of an imported landscape.

That lions, leopards or baboons—though these last are still present—should ever have haunted so European a scene seems incredible. Even the labourers in the vineyards look rather out of place when they turn and reveal their dark faces.

At one end of the valley, at a place called Fransch Hoek, there is a memorial to the Huguenots, but their true memorial is the valley itself and the great wine industry of the Cape. Among all the religious and political refugees who at one time or another have left their own land, the Huguenots alone appear to have been welcomed everywhere and to have given their skill and their loyalty unquestioningly to the countries of their adoption. Their arrival at the Cape was one of the fortunate moments in South African history. There were only about two hundred of them, but they have influenced South Africa out of all proportion to their numbers. They were settled round Fransch Hoek, and at the other end of the valley round Paarl, that they might teach the inhabitants what was wrong with Cape wine. Although the Dutch had made wine in South Africa within seven years of their arrival— a gallant effort—their wine had not roused any enthusiasm in Holland or Batavia; indeed, some critics rudely compared it to the crab apple. With the Huguenots came men who knew all the ancient secrets of the French vineyards.

They stepped ashore at the Cape, as they did in so many other lands, with nothing save the clothes they wore, their own great skill and their splendid industry. Living at first in rough bothies, in time they looked out upon their own flourishing acres and upon some of the finest châteaux in the Cape. In a few generations they had intermarried with their Dutch neighbours and had given up their French language and their own customs. When a Frenchman went in search of his compatriots at the end of the Eighteenth Century, expecting to find some faint memory of France, he found the Huguenots completely South African, with nothing to distinguish them but their vivacity, their names, the names of their farms, and their way of baking bread.

In the valley of the Berg River, from Fransch Hoek to Wellington, the names of the French farms remain to this day: La Cotte, La Dauphine, La Terre de Luc, La Provence, Champagne, Cabrière, Le Paris, Dieudonné, Biendonné, Le Rhône, L'Arc d'Orléans, and very many more. And the names of those who live in these farms, and in the wine districts of the Cape, are those of the old Huguenot settlers: du Toit, de Villiers, Marais, Joubert, Malherbe, and so on.

The Huguenot names in South Africa have undergone that transformation in spelling which has occurred also in England. Indeed, among the thousands of people of Huguenot stock in England there must be many who have no idea of their descent. Apart from such weird Anglicisms as Boocock for Beaucoup, many of the Huguenots completely disguised themselves by translating their names into English, so that Leblanc became White, Tonnellier became Cooper, Lejeune became Young, Lenoir became Black, and L'Oiseau became Bird. The same thing happened in Holland. Du Bois became van den Bosch, le Roi became de Koning, Leblanc became de Witt. To what extent this also happened in South Africa, I do not know.

A glance at any South African telephone directory will prove what an enormous number of Huguenot names there are, some in their original form, others with a slight Dutch accent. For instance, du Pré in South Africa is now du Preez, Senecal is Senekal, Villion is Viljoen, Cellier is Cillie, de Clercq is de Klerk, Mesnard has become Minnaar; and there are many more. On the other hand, du Plessis, le Roux, Marais, Malan, Retief, Fourié, and Malherbe, to give only a few, have come down in their pure French form.

I explored this lovely valley from end to end. I saw the coloured workmen in the long, neat vineyards, topping the vines, and in the orchards thinning plums and spraying pear trees to destroy that familiar pest, which has apparently made itself perfectly at home in South Africa—the codling moth. I saw the old French châteaux of the Drakenstein bowered in peace and rooted in dignity: La Provence, Boschendal, La Motte, Le Rhône, and Bourgogne, which is sometimes called Burgundy. They stood white in the sunshine with leaf-shadows printed on their gable ends, watching the serried vines and neat groomed orchards.

All these châteaux were built in the last years of the Eighteenth Century or the first years of the Nineteenth, and they have that strong likeness to each other which you sometimes find in a family of pretty sisters. A pleasant woman who lives in one of these old houses was kind enough to show me over it, and I saw the voorkamer, or general living-room (which the early writers describe as always filled with wife, daughters, and slaves), and the rooms leading from it. The arrangement is simple and adequate in an open-air country. I believe the high winds of the Cape, and the difficulty of importing long lengths of timber, are said to be the reason why the farms of South Africa are always of one storey, but on the other hand this is usual in Holland. The Dutch farm to this day is often a bungalow.

A long drive towards the blue Valhalla of the Simonsberg brought me to a beautiful white homestead standing in its gardens. A swimming-pool near at hand was filled with cool mountain water. From the stoep you look over the valley towards the mountains, and away to the east, at the end of the valley, you see a thin white thread winding up into a gorge. The old name of this pass is a reminder—incredible as it seems to me—that the Drakenstein Valley was visited by elephants less than three centuries ago. It is the old Elephant's Path, now called the Fransch Hoek Pass, which leads over the Hottentot's Holland into the fair land of the Eastern Cape.

My host was an Englishman who has devoted a great part of his life to building roads and bridges, making dams, and extending the orchards and vineyards to supply choice fruits to cheer an English winter. Long years in South Africa have not taken from him the rich flavour of the West Riding.

As we sat on the stoep he told me about the pioneers of the fruit industry—Struben, Malleson, Dicey—and of Pickstone, the father of the industry, who first established nurseries and made possible subsequent development. He paid a great tribute to Pickstone, who did so much to organise the industry and whose contribution to the development of fruit-growing in South Africa stimulated the interest of Cecil Rhodes, whose careless generosity is still talked about by the old coloured men who work on the farms. His old driver Gert says Rhodes never looked at the money he withdrew from his pocket when he gave tips, and " that was the time, Baas, when half a pound was the same size as a sixpence, and he made many mistakes ! "

I admired what I think is one of the great charms of the old Cape Farms, that is the disposition of the farm buildings and the old slave quarters in relation to the main building. A farmhouse the world over is part of a pattern which includes stables, barns, outhouses, and cottages, and a fine farmstead can be ruined by shabby and badly placed farm buildings. But the old builders of the Cape never made that mistake. They saw a farm as a composition, and placed the long, white, thatched outbuildings in exactly the right place in relation to the main building, so that the whole unit is a model of dignity and balance.

In the old days the Cape farmers used to summon their slaves to work by ringing the bell which was hung in the inner curve of a tall, slender archway, always whitewashed like the farmhouse and the farm buildings. These snowy bell-towers are a great feature of the Cape farms, and it is probable that they are to be seen nowhere else in the world. The bell-tower on this farm is remarkable, not only for its beauty, but also for a bronze tablet with this inscription:

In Memory of William Wilberforce,
Born Hull, Yorks, through
Whose efforts slavery was abolished in 1833.

My host, himself a Yorkshireman, told me that he had put up the tablet in 1933, the occasion of the Centenary of the Abolition of Slavery, to remind the workpeople, men and women, of the individuality of that Yorkshireman who in 1833 crowned his life's work by the great emancipation which changed the whole current of the lives of a large section of the people of the world. So the bell-tower stands to-day, and the clear, even notes of the bell ring out across the valley of the Huguenots, recalling through the passage of years the miracle which was brought about, and denoting the starting and stopping times for workers in the surrounding orchards and vineyards. The continuous ringing of farm bells by day or by night is the danger signal which calls out all residents to bush or mountain fires, which frequently occur in the summer, destroying vegetation on the mountain slopes and leading to serious soil erosion.

In the blaze of the afternoon sun we travelled through this fruitful valley, where every peach tree seems to have its valet and every vine its nurse. It was here in the Drakenstein valley that Cecil Rhodes, in a historic combination of fruit-farms, laid the foundation of large-scale export of fruit to Europe. Although fruit was one of the chief products of van Riebeeck's garden, it was not until the time of Rhodes that the mighty problem of transporting these delicate products to a market six thousand miles away was envisaged and tackled in a courageous way. With one of his imperial gestures, Rhodes told his farm manager to buy the whole of the Drakenstein valley! Mrs Millin says in her book on Rhodes that this startled man retorted that it would cost a million. " I don't ask your advice," cried Rhodes. " I want you to buy it. Buy it! "

That was how the Rhodes Fruit Farms began fifty years ago. They have proved of incalculable benefit to the fruit industry of South Africa. Rhodes' enterprise put a stiffening into the small beginnings of the scheme, and focussed the attention of the shipping companies upon the potentialities of an export fruit industry. Rhodes' dream has been realised. The farms are still in existence, though they are no longer administered by the Rhodes Trustees.

The varieties of South African fruit are greater than I had imagined, and there is hardly a time of the year when fruit is unobtainable. Here is a calendar:

October: Strawberries, oranges and lemons, figs, guavas, Cape gooseberries.
November: Oranges, early apricots, early peaches, strawberries, Cape gooseberries.
December: Peaches, apricots, figs, pineapples, bananas, papaws, plums, youngberries.
January: Peaches, plums, pears, pineapples, papaws, early grapes.
February: Grapes, pears, plums, nectarines, melons, pineapples, mangoes, bananas, peaches.
March–April: Grapes, apples, pears, peaches, plums, bananas, papaws, avocado pears.
May–June: Pineapples, bananas, oranges, lemons, naartjes, grapefruit.
July–Sept.: Oranges, lemons, naartjes, grapefruit, pineapples, guavas, bananas.

The tropical and semi-tropical fruits such as mangoes, bananas, papaws, and pineapples are not grown in the Western Cape, but in Natal and the Northern Transvaal. It takes only from three to five years for peach, apricot, and orange trees to yield a small crop, and only from four to seven years for the apple, pear, and plum.

§ 4

Paarl, which means pearl, is the great wine town of the Cape. If you have ever tasted South African sherry, hock, burgundy, or brandy, it is more than probable that the grapes grew round Paarl and that the wine was made in Paarl. Many people will tell you that it is the most beautiful town in the Cape.

The mountains rise round Paarl, the sun shines upon it, and it has a hot South of France look about it: warm dust, cicadas, white houses, sudden sprays of colour, deep enveloping shadows, and the sight everywhere of vines, millions of them, lying out in the sun and climbing the craggy mountain slopes as the grapes swell and sweeten on a summer's day.

Nearly every man you meet in this place appears to be named du Plessis, du Toit, or de Villiers. Everyone is either growing grapes or turning grapes into wine. In the old farms and the white houses along the seven mile long street live these du Plessis, du Toits, and de Villiers—to say nothing of the le Rouxs, the Viljoens, and the Marais—and the general routine of their lives is much as it was nearly three hundred years ago, when their ancestors were teaching the Dutchmen how to keep the vinegar out of the wine. But anyone who expects to find these wine men of Paarl living up to their names would have the same experience that fell to the lot of le Vaillant; for they are, to a man, Afrikaners.

Men with French names who speak Afrikaans and blinding white walls. That is your first impression of Paarl. It will occur to you that whitewash in the Cape is like a uniform or a diploma. Every old-established building shines in spotless purity and exhibits the cool symbol of its antiquity. And wherever you look in Paarl, you see whitewash shining through oak leaves, whitewash with a spray of bougainvillea dropping over it, whitewash on hill-sides surrounded by vineyards, whitewash in gardens surrounded by flowers, and whitewash even on the old thatched church, which stands like a ghost in a graveyard where cypresses hold dark tapers towards the mountains.

Even were Paarl not beautiful to look at, even were it not gracious and peaceful, it would still be worth while to go there to see the church and the superb modern town hall, a beautiful little building with a Spanish-looking atrium under an archway.

Nearly five thousand wine farmers belong to an organisation known as the Co-operative Wine Growers Association, which has enormous vats and cellars at Paarl, also a room in which every visitor is hospitably instructed in South African vintages. These wines are coming back to the English market, and a great difference will be noticed, particularly in South African sherry, which has been improved out of all belief during the last few years. This is because the South Africans are at last

COLOURED BOY WITH GRAPES

" plastering " their sherry as they do in Spain, which is the process of adding gypsum to the must before fermentation. But the most interesting thing is that they can produce the mysterious substance known as " flor ", which was once believed to exist nowhere outside Spain. This is a form of yeast which is able to ferment the must to wine and then to cover the wine with an alcoholic film.

I was told that it is possible to make the cheaper types of sherry without " flor ", but impossible without it to make the finer pale sherries, such as Amontillado, Fino, and Manzanilla. This the South Africans can now do, the result of experiments made with " flor " by the Stellenbosch College of Agriculture. But sherry, although perhaps the best known, is only one of the many wines produced at the Cape. There are port, hock, burgundy, and sparkling wines ; an extraordinary selection to be grown in a comparatively small area. Many a stranger must have thought it surprising that South Africa, although she produces so many delicious wines, is not really a wine-drinking country. Why is this ?

Is there something in the Calvinistic nature of the country that shrinks from wine, something northern and Puritanical that suspects wine, not as alcohol (for I have noticed that South Africans are not scared by their own brandy), but as an expression of the subtle, Papistical south ? It is not impossible. Of course, the history of drink in South Africa is of hot, violent spirits like arak and brandy, which were tossed back by thirsty sailors at *De Opregte Anker* in Strand Street in the old days, then it leaps ahead to the gin and whisky of the Kimberley bars. But of the pressed sunlight of Cape vineyards we hear nothing but an occasional compliment from the candlelight of an Eighteenth Century dinner-table in far-off Europe.

§ 5

Creaking and groaning the old wagon slowly ascended the hill. The voorloper walked ahead with the leading oxen, and the driver walked beside shouting to the animals by name as, with heads bent to the yoke, they thrust forward and upward, moving in a thin white dust.

G

It was impossible to pass, for the road was narrow, so I dawdled behind watching the wagon and the line of red oxen as they curved outward on the hill, slow, methodical, and rhythmic, their horns flashing in the sun. When they reached the top of the hill they paused for a breather, and I pulled up too, and went to talk to the driver, who was a grizzled old Cape "boy". He politely lifted his battered felt hat to me, and seemed delighted when I examined the wagon, and vastly amused when I proceeded to measure it in paces.

The ox-wagon is one of the most interesting sights in South Africa. Although there are thousands of motor lorries, there are still thousands of wagons. The art of making them and the art of driving them over the mountains are two of the oldest achievements of the country. Life has changed in South Africa during the last century, but the pace of the ox has not altered, the creak and groan of the wagon are the same, the crack of the driver's whip, as it curves over the horns, is the same, and the words he shouts to his oxen on the long, slow journeys are the words used by the first South Africans. The ox-wagon is the symbol of Man's progress in South Africa. There are now great steel works in the country. Trains thread their way through the wildest mountain gorges. Electricity is fed here, there, and everywhere. But without the old ox-wagon none of these things would be. It is right that this symbol should have been taken from the old Transvaal flag and placed upon the flag of the Union. The ox-wagon, in the most real and intimate sense, is the symbol of South Africa.

Like all old farm wagons, it is a miracle of the wheelwright's craft. This particular wagon was twenty feet long, which is nearly twice the length of the wagons in which the Voortrekkers travelled. It seems that the longer wagon came into use in the eighteen seventies, and before that time the trek wagon was surprisingly small. Its average length was only twelve feet, the length of the English farm wagon which it so much resembles. This is not surprising, because the trek wagon and the English farm wagon are both adaptations of the Dutch wagon, which was introduced into England during the Sixteenth Century and has been used ever since side by side with the older and rougher English two-wheeled wain.

For the onderstel, or under-frame, the Boer wheelwrights in the old days employed a rare and heavy timber, now no longer used, called ironwood. In more recent times it has been replaced by Australian hickory. The naves of the wheels were made from the iron-hard yellowwood of Knysna, and the wood from which the Bantu made the shafts of their assegais was used for the drawing gear, to which was attached the disselboom, the single pole or shaft to which the first pair of oxen were yoked. But there were other African woods used in the trek wagon, such as red and white pearwood. The main difference between the original Dutch wagon and the African trek wagon was that the Dutch wagon was designed for short journeys and the transport of farm produce, while the African trek wagon was really a caravan in which people lived as they travelled.

This meant the addition of several features unknown to the European wheelwright: the katel, or bed, and the voorkis and agterkis, the front and rear chests or kists, in which clothes and possessions could be carried. The katel is the most interesting of these, a word, by the way, that is said to come from Hindustani. This was a wooden frame on which rawhide throngs were interwoven. It was carried under the wagon-tilt by day and brought out at night, when, with mattresses and pillows, it made a comfortable sleeping-place for the women.

Although such splendid craftsmanship was lavished on the trek wagon, no one invented a brake for it until the eighteen sixties. The most dangerous descents were made in days when there was nothing to check the wagon but the old skid, or remskoen, which was slipped under a rear wheel. I have heard that in the old days the Boer farmer paid great attention to the decoration of his wagon and took pride in the flowers, or blommetjies, which decorated it. Though extremely rare nowadays, you can sometimes see bright flowers painted on the front and back-boards of English farm wagons. Even to-day the English wagon is often to be seen in all its old-time beauty, the body painted a bright blue and the wheel spokes a bright red, colours which have been handed on with surprising success to the mechanical tractor and the plough.

With a great shouting and a cracking of the whip, the Cape wagon went on its way. The oxen were as varied as mankind. Some were anxious to do more than their share, and others were delighted for them to do it. But the old driver knew them all by name and by character. Hearing a crack of the whip in the air overhead and a shouted name, a lazy ox would pull himself together; and so the wagon, with a thin dust rising from the hooves, went on into the lazy afternoon.

§ 6

I stood on the summit of Bain's Kloof and looked down on about forty square miles of the Cape. At the foot of the mountain lay the hot, busy town of Wellington, miles away was Paarl—I could see the Paarl Rock shining like a beacon—and there were miles of yellow cornland stretching away in a haze to a line of blue darker than the sky, which was the Atlantic Ocean.

There was a lot of life on the top of the pass: summer bungalows and an hotel. While I was looking at the superb sweep of country, a man came up and asked if he might borrow my field-glasses. He was a little Londoner, about thirty-five, stocky and pink.

" Do you live here? " I asked.

" Jo'burg," he replied. " I've emigrated."

" How do you like it? "

" Let's go and have a drink," he said.

We carried glasses of icy shandy to a seat under a tree.

" I'm a builder," he said. " I was here in the R.A.F., at a place called George. When I got demobbed, I could see that there was nothing for me at home but putting up pre-fabs, so I thought I'd come out here. My missus cried her eyes out, but she came. With one thing and another, and my gratuity, I'd saved quite a bit of money, so we came out—flew out. Quite a change that was! I hadn't been in Jo'burg a week before I fell into a job. . . . How's London lookin'? "

" Is it a good job? "

" Not 'arf! " he laughed, suddenly relapsing into Cockney.

" It's a beautiful country," I said.

" Been up to Jo'burg? " he asked. " A fair old mix-up that is. Kaffirs! Thousands of them. You ought to see it. And talk about money! Blimey. . . ."

" Do you like your job? "

He took a reflective drink.

" Well, I dunno," he said. " It's all so different. I suppose I shall get used to it. You see, out here there are so many things you can't do—a white man can't do—and I've always been used to getting down to a job myself. What I have to do now is to stand around and boss a lot of blacks. Blimey, talk about slow motion! Still, I suppose I shall get used to it."

As I went on, I came into mountain country as wild and desolate as Glencoe. The pass had been dynamited from the side of the mountains, in places shelves of rock overhung it, and I gazed over the edge of the road to the distant valley where the Wit River tumbled among its boulders. Some of the mountains were covered with thin grass, others towered up in shelves of naked rock, but as the road went down into this solitude any further comparison I might have made with Glencoe ended as a baboon suddenly ran out in front of me.

I came to a rich valley where a river ran through cornlands. It was November, and most of the corn had been cut, and the sheaves were stooked to dry in the long summer days. I asked a man who was walking in a cornfield what kind of wild animals were found in the mountains. He told me that only the week before an old man had shot a leopard which had a hundred and twenty dead sheep chalked up against it. There were buck, monkeys, hares, pheasants, and partridges, but with so much traffic over the Kloof you had to go in the side kloofs if you wanted to see animals.

Another pass almost as wild as Bain's Kloof runs up to Ceres between the Hex River Mountains and the Witzenbergen. It also was made by Andrew Geddes Bain, but bears the name of Charles Michell, who was Surveyor-General at the Cape in 1848, when the pass was opened. The motorist who peacefully travels through these two passes does not perhaps always think of the sight they must have presented when they were the main road to Kimberley. The diamond rush which poured over them must have been the strangest-looking trek in South African history. Sailors deserted their ships, soldiers their regiments, merchants their shops, clerks their offices, farmers their land, and the weirdest crowd ever seen in South Africa, good and bad, came over the mountains on horseback, on foot, in Cape carts, ox wagons, stage-coaches —anything that would take them to the biggest lucky dip in history. A man who saw it says that towns were suddenly quiet, dorps deserted, and only the old men and young boys were left behind.

At the summit of the pass I was nearly two thousand feet above Table Bay and nearing the town with the lovely name of Ceres. What a surprising name to find together with Wellington, Worcester, and Wolseley! It is as though one had come across a maiden from Botticelli's Primavera poised upon one toe on a plinth usually occupied by Mr Gladstone.

It is a little town in the bokkeveld famous for pears. And bokkeveld means goats-veld, so that all kinds of pleasant classical images filled my mind as I ran down Michell's Pass. The word veld, as used by South Africans, can be puzzling. Many a stranger has the idea that it refers to some definite locality, as we should say the Downs or Fenland. But you soon learn that there are all kinds of veld. There is sweet-veld and sour-veld, high-veld and low-veld, back-veld and sand-veld, cold-veld and warm-veld and bush-veld, and probably many more. The word is used in two ways: to describe grazing country anywhere, and also to describe what kind of grazing it is. So a South African could sigh for the veld in general, but if he were buying a farm he would want to know what particular kind of veld it was.

§ 7

Ceres was perfect.

Peace dripped over it in the hot afternoon. The mountains enclosed it. The only sound was the voice of cicadas in gardens and orchards. There was a wide main street shaded by high trees, a few shops, bungalows with gardens, water gurgling in gutters at the back, and a river sliding under willow trees to a bridge.

I had the feeling that came over me sometimes in Andalusia that I ought to walk on tiptoe, for I thought everyone was asleep. There was a tattered old coloured man asleep on his back in the shade of an oak tree, and his donkey, unharnessed from a little cart, stood in the same shade, drooping meditatively; dogs lay curled in the shadow of buildings; venetian shutters were closed, and the only person awake in the hotel was the active little proprietor in shirt sleeves who bustled out and gave me a room over the stoep.

The curtains were drawn and the room was comparatively cool. The hot day showed only in a thin line of white-hot light where the curtains did not meet, and I glanced for a weak moment with interest at the bed before I pulled back the curtains and let in the hot blaze of a November afternoon. The mountains were lying against a sky of aquamarine. There was an old white house opposite and trees. A coloured boy walked in the centre of the road, his bare feet kicking up the dust, his fingers idly touching the strings of a mandolin as he sang to himself. Of what do those dark troubadours sing as they trudge the roads of Africa with their instruments? You meet them miles from anywhere still strumming, still singing, still laughing, their dusty sombreroes cocked over an eye, as they pad on bare feet across the mountains and over the veld like so many dusky Blondels.

As the hotel awakened and people came in from walks and excursions, I sat out on the stoep with a man who had come to Ceres from remote Johannesburg. He told me that unlike many parts of the Cape, where enormous fruit-farms are often the rule, the fruit-growers of Ceres cultivate small-holdings of about forty acres, where the best pears in the Union are grown, together with some of the finest apples, peaches, plums, and apricots. The mountains group themselves round Ceres as if the Goddess had cast her robe round the orchards to shelter them from the South-Easters.

People from all parts of the Union go to Ceres for their holidays, he told me, both in winter and in summer. In

winter, the slopes of the Matroosberg above Ceres often pro-
vide snow for skiers, and in summer the great attraction is an
open-air swimming-pool which he called the most beautiful
one of its kind in the Union.

I climbed a hill behind the town as the sun was setting and
came to a little wood on the slope of the mountain.   Beside
the wood was an enormously long swimming-pool with grass
on one side of it, and the mountains all round.   It was not a
natural pool : it was the most modern kind of pool, edged with
paved walks, an unexpected sophistication to find in the
bokkeveld.   An arm of the river had been dammed, and the
water was filtered into the pool at one end and, after passing
through it, flowed downward to the town, so that the pool was
always fresh and moving.   It was the most romantically sited
swimming-pool I had ever seen; a place where you might well
expect to meet not only Ceres, but perhaps Venus.

A few family parties were still brightly dotting the grass, un-
willing to leave until the last dying blaze of November sun
should have gone.

It was quiet and beautiful, and it is good to be able to say
that even had there been five hundred South Africans there
instead of twenty, it would still have been quiet, for vulgarity
is not among the sins of this nation.   The small white population of South Africa does not contain that element which loves
Coney Island and Blackpool.   No South African ever shouts,
screams, sings, or behaves in public with that lack of restraint
and disregard for the feelings of other people which are sometimes considered the marks of a good democrat.   Even if such
an element existed, it is possible that the size of the country
and its austere character would impose a calming influence
upon it.   I would place in the forefront of my impressions of
South Africa the general good manners encountered everywhere.

Electric fans were revolving in the dining-room as we
sat down to dinner.   The room was full of family parties;
there were three young men in khaki shorts who had arrived
from the mountain slopes with knapsacks on their shoulders,
and there were half a dozen young naval ratings from Simonstown, who were touring the Cape in a car.   After dinner I

strolled about in the dark listening to gramophones, crickets, and stray bursts of radio from illuminated stoeps. Then I did something I had not done for perhaps two years: I went to the bioscope!

The film was one written by a friend of mine about an American soldier who found himself during the war in an English family circle, and it was watched with interest by a large and crowded audience in a long bungalow of a bioscope. I had no idea there were so many people in Ceres.

As I walked back to the hotel, the stars were like a white sheet overhead and every cricket in South Africa seemed to be spending the night at Ceres.

§ 8

I recrossed Michell's Pass on a hot morning, and was soon travelling through those valleys which are known as the granary of the Union. Most of the corn had been cut and carted, but now and again the stubble was varied by a few acres of sheaves. The sun, the fine-spun air, the blue mountains streaked with violet shadows, combined to create such a sense of well-being and happiness that I went on as light of heart as the dusky troubadours who walk the roads of Africa with their mandolins.

An old farmer in a stubble-field told me that the harvest had been an unusually good one. I asked him how many bushels he got to the acre, and we then descended together into impenetrable confusion. At last—for he was a determined old man—he told me how many muids he got to the morgen, and, if our conversion table was correct, we worked out that the yield was the low one of only seven and a half bushels an acre, which no English farmer would think worth growing. I told him, but I think he hardly believed me, that in my part of England we get an average of sixty bushels an acre. Then I was surprised to learn how thinly they sow wheat in South Africa—forty pounds an acre against our hundred and fifty to a hundred and eighty pounds in Hampshire.

I asked him if, in his boyhood, he had seen corn threshed by trotting horses. There is an interesting picture of this in

Peter Kolben's book. The wheat was spread out in a circle inside a breast-high circular wall. Horses, roped together in file, trotted over the sheaves while a man, who stood in the centre with a whip like a ring-master in a circus, kept them in motion.

Oh yes, he said, not only had he seen horses threshing out the corn fifty years ago, but as a boy he had helped to keep them at a trot. Before the threshing-machines were used, all the farmers in the grain districts used this method, which, he said, went back right to old times.

I think it went right back to the Old Testament. In Biblical times oxen were used in threshing—a method which the Israelites probably learned in Egypt. The use of horses by the Boers was only a variation of the oldest method of threshing known to Man. It is interesting that the Dutch farmers, who came from Europe, where the flail had always been in general use, should have found the old Biblical method more efficient and have reverted to the historical method of Africa.

Bidding my old friend good-day, I was soon approaching Tulbagh, which is highly praised in the Cape as the " Queen Anne town of South Africa ". Possibly because I had heard so much about it, I expected greater architectural beauty than I had any right to imagine. I saw an old Cape town with many white buildings hiding amid greenery, pretty and dignified like all the relics of the Seventeenth Century. I was amused by the question of an obliging inhabitant who, after showing me the treasures of Tulbagh, the old Drostdy, some miles out of the town, and the old church, now a museum, asked :

" Are there old buildings like this in England and France? "

When I tried to describe Winchester and Oxford to him, he stood there against a pomegranate hedge interjecting "Wonderlik! " at intervals. But it is not easy to explain to some South Africans, especially when they have proudly shown you a museum full of mid-Nineteenth Century objects, that in Europe three centuries is not particularly old.

Tulbagh is famous for its excellent wines and for the profusion of its spring flowers. I was told that anyone who happens to be at the Cape when Tulbagh holds a flower show ought not on any account to miss it.

The road now led northward through level country. On the way I paused to admire a perfect little Cape landscape. In the background was a blue mountain; in the middle distance a white thatched farm, and in the foreground several ostriches, calves, sheep, pigs, turkeys, and hens, roaming in perfect amity over a stony field of dried-up grass. What a handful for the farmer's wife! I have always understood that ostriches are birds of uncertain temperament, but these specimens seemed to be perfectly domesticated. I have read somewhere that an ostrich egg is equal in bulk to twenty-four hen's eggs and is extremely good when scrambled. Another useful fact remains in my memory: they take one hour to boil hard!

The road led into the little town of Piquetberg, which once was the boundary of white life in the western Cape. Simon van der Stel mentions in his *Journal* that it got its name when a picquet was stationed on the mountain during trouble with a Hottentot chief. If it had been hot in the Drakenstein Valley and in Ceres, that heat was nothing compared with the shadeless heat of Piquetberg. It was quite the hottest place I had struck in South Africa.

It is a small town with no trees. There was not a breath of wind. The vertical sun blazed down on hot brick and stone. The heat pulsated on the white road. Everything was hard, clear-cut, and shadowless. I had promised to call on Mr Versfeld, who, I had been told, lived somewhere in this furnace. I went to the little hotel, where several travellers sheltering from the heat were drinking iced beer in a darkened room, to ask where he lived. The hotel factotum took me round to the back of the hotel and pointed to a mountain.

" Up there," he said.

" How far up? " I asked.

" On the top," he replied.

I went in to luncheon. Here in a dark room were about twenty people purposefully moving through a menu which read: Soup, roast chicken, roast mutton, roast pork, trifle. The heroic contests with menus which go on in South Africa with the temperature over a hundred must be seen to be credited. I watched with fascination a man at a table next to me go right through the menu. When he mopped his head after the roast mutton and took a breath, I thought he had been vanquished; but I was wrong! The coloured boy glided in with a huge plate of roast pork, and that unforgettable eater grasped knife and fork and demolished it. I waited just long enough to make certain that he was not denying himself the trifle, and then went out, debating with myself whether or not I should go up the mountain in search of Mr Versfeld.

This vague type of direction is one only too familiar to all those who have travelled in the remoter parts of Scotland and Ireland. "When you get there," you are always told, " *any-one* will tell you where he lives! " You expect, of course, to be shown a house in the High Street, but instead they say he lives " over yon ben " or " away in the hills "; and it often takes a stout heart, especially if it is raining, to follow such journeys to the end. Anyhow, I told myself, to remain in Piquetberg on such an afternoon was asking to be sun-dried and transformed into biltong; so I decided to tackle the Versfeld Pass.

I was soon high above the earth. I had the same view of the cornlands spread out towards the Oliphant River Mountains that I might have had in an aeroplane flying at about two thousand feet. The pass then began to take itself seriously, and turned its back upon the earth, and I went on with the air seeming to grow a little cooler into a world where domed mountain ridges enclosed me on every side.

For about three miles the pass twisted up into the mountains, with no sign of a house anywhere in view. I came to a rounded hill, and stopped to watch the lovely sight of a herd of perhaps a hundred black and tan goats, suddenly surprised, go leaping and skipping over the rocks with their kids, some of them standing against the sky to watch me, others pouring through the defiles down to an opposite slope. The air was heavy with a smell as pungent as thyme but even more aromatic, and I knew this to be buchu, for I had seen this plant, and smelt it, in a botanical garden. There were acres of it. I got out and picked myself a bunch, and I shall always think of it as South Africa on a hot summer's after-noon pressed into one small nosegay.

It is an interesting plant, too. The Hottentots used to make medicine from it, and I believe it is highly thought of to-day. Latrobe says that when he was in the Cape in 1815 buchu leaves, steeped in brandy and vinegar and allowed to thicken in the sun, were used to heal all kinds of bruises, and brandy with buchu leaves in it was taken for internal complaints. The Hottentots, says le Vaillant, used to make a powder of the leaves and sprinkle it over themselves and their cattle.

The road straightened up, and I was at last on top of the mountain. But what a surprising place it was! It was not in any way like a mountain top. It gave the queer impression that an old and well wooded part of the Cape round about Stellenbosch had been lifted by some volcanic eruption high into the air. There were avenues of ancient oak trees. There were cultivated fields, peach orchards, vineyards, and—orange trees!

I came to a large homestead built on a high platform. Pre-senting my letter of introduction, I was soon talking to two Versfelds, father and son. And from Mr Versfeld Senior I heard a remarkable story.

"The Versfelds came here eighty years ago," he said. "My father trekked from Caledon and farmed this mountain until his death. I followed him, and now I have handed over to the third generation," and he nodded towards his son. "I daresay you saw some of our farm people on your way up. They are the sons and many are the grandsons of the servants my father brought up here with him. They are happy, well looked after, and well fed, and they have never wanted to leave us.

"My father's servants were a queer assortment. With two exceptions they suggested a mixture of Hottentot, Koranna, Malabar, and even a dash of Bushman blood. The two excep-tions were a Makatees—a race very nearly extinct which came from the Crocodile River in the Transvaal—and a Mozam-bique, who had been kidnapped and was trying to get back to his country, after having escaped from a ship that had put in at Cape Town. He never found his way back. He stayed on until he died—only a few months ago."

So here upon the Piquetberg Mountain, as if isolated for observation, was an eighty year old microcosm of South African life: a farmer served by old family servants, and the continuity of effort not only in the homestead, but in the native quarters, going on from one generation to the next. This was possibly, I thought, as good an example as I should come across of the patriarchal state in which the Boers once lived.

" Why did your father decide to subdue this mountain? "

" Well, I suppose the cheapness of land here had a lot to do with it. Then he had farmed similar veld for a doctor round Caledon, and thought he could make a good thing of it. I have often heard my father describe his trek in 1866. He started off in a wagon with my mother and their first two children, and accompanied by the servants and all the stock he possessed. He spent the last night of the trek in a farm at the foot of the mountain, where his host, by way of encouragement, said to him ' You're going up the mountain in a wagon, but before long you'll come down on foot! ' Cheerful, wasn't it?

" In those days the mountain was wild and not very well known. Only a rocky track led to the top. Leopards were so numerous that losses of sheep were considerable. I have often heard my mother tell how, on her first night on the mountain, a leopard came down and took a sheep out of the cattle kraal under their very noses.

" New farming methods soon began to tell. My father introduced merino sheep and tobacco, and he even made wine. But no grain was grown. It was bought below the mountain and taken up on pack-horses. Then in 1879 things were doing so well that my father decided to build the first road up the mountain with the help of his own farm hands and himself as engineer. He made it on the south side of the mountain. Then ten years later he made another one on the east side, and this became famous all over South Africa.

" It was famous as the only big mountain pass in the country made by a private individual, and also because my father, who was well used to handling long teams of draught animals, invented a system of loop turns which enabled a wagon and a team of twelve mules to turn in a smaller space than the usual hairpin bend. Perhaps you don't know that a wagon and a team can turn in a much shorter space on the downgrade than on the up, or even on the level, because the wagon comes round on its own impetus and the team can be ' bunched.' Well, my father devised three loop turns on the pass so that a wagon whether going up or down always turned on the downhill grade—a device that had never before been applied in the history of road-making, certainly not in South Africa.

" You will hardly perhaps credit it, but the Versfeld Pass, which was three miles long, was made in three months at a cost of two hundred pounds! And it was used for fifty-five years, until the new pass was made on the direct route three years ago. How was the old pass made so quickly? I'll tell you! My father employed only his own farm labourers, who co-operated to the full and indulged in friendly competition all the time. Each man was given a strip of twelve feet, and each one strove to finish his strip before his neighbours. This competition was entirely their own idea. They were all strong, contented men, and knew they were working for the ' master ', and took pride in their work. That was how the pass was made! "

I asked him if life was not lonely on the mountain when he was a boy.

" Lonely! " he laughed. " It was anything but lonely! My parents had fifteen children, and thirteen of us grew up. Then they took in, and educated, six children of a widowed sister of my father's, and two belonging to one of his brothers, so that there were twenty-one boys and girls on the mountain! School? Oh, we had governesses. I remember one of them came straight out to the mountain from an English village. She was the granddaughter of an English clergyman. A few years before she came, an English ex-sailor had turned up on the mountain and was employed as handyman. When the governess and the ex-sailor came face to face they were amazed, for they both came from the same village, and he had been baptised by her grandfather! Oh no, life was anything but lonely! Our amusements were mountain climbing, horseback riding—for which we kept a stable full of horses—swimming, and dancing. Our dance music was provided by three coloured fiddlers. Not only were we a large and cheerful family, but we always had visitors and there was always a man or two learning farming.

"When I was a boy not only were the mountains full of leopards, but there were zebra as well. That's why the tallest mountain is called Zebra Kop. I remember them still there in 1903, and a lovely sight they were coming down the face of the mountain in the sunlight. I think they were gradually exterminated after 1903 by coloured men from the mission station, who used to bring guns when they came buchu gathering on the mountain. By the way, my father always shot with a muzzle-loader, but by the time I was able to take over, the breech-loader was quite common."

We walked over the mountain top and beneath the oak avenues. When I got back to the car I found that someone had placed there a box of ripe mountain peaches. I went back over the pass thinking that no one, standing on the plain below and looking up at the Piquetberg Mountains, could imagine that little epic of human endeavour which is its history. And in a world sick and discontented and at odds with itself, that little story of a South African family lifted high above the earth upon its mountain top has the authentic ring of the Golden Age.

As the sun was sinking and losing its fire I passed through Riebeek West, where South Africa's philosopher statesman once herded sheep, and just before the road dives down into Malmesbury I saw, framed in the boles of gum trees, the blue shadow of Table Mountain thirty miles away.

AN OLD CAPE HOMESTEAD

CHAPTER FOUR

In which I leave Cape Town for the East, visit Caledon and Swellendam, where I find a Scotsman; I go on through the Garden Route to George and see hop gardens; at Oudtshorn I see ostriches; at Knysna I meet another Scot and hear about elephants.

§ 1

ONE day in November I motored out of Cape Town without a care in the world; or at least they were forgotten, which is almost the same thing.

South Africa lay before me in vast, hot distances and in bewildering variety, and the road upon which I was travelling was, as recently as a century and a half ago, a lone and perilous track leading to what men called " the interior ". Travelling eastward, I ran into that little country town whose name would seem to defy the compass, Somerset West, but it orientates itself in relation to another Somerset farther to the east.

Palm trees grew beside the wide main road. The white shops with their covered stoeps drew two dark lines of shadow down the street. Coloured boys on bicycles were delivering the groceries, coloured nursemaids were wheeling out the children; here and there I saw people who ought to have been in Cheltenham—ex-colonels with spaniels, English matrons, and a pretty English girl on horseback—and the place had, I thought, a pleasant, friendly air. Behind it rose those magnificently shaped mountains, the Hottentot's Holland, which, seen from Muizenberg, look like the entrance to Valhalla. They rose behind Somerset West as blue as harebells in the morning sun.

In a valley with a gentle trout stream rippling from pool to pool was the old homestead of Vergelegen, which got Adriaan van der Stel into so much trouble, lying now amid farmlands where a herd of Jerseys grazed in green pastures.

A few miles away the Strand, and glorious little Gordon's

Bay, might be part of the Italian Riviera. If peace and quiet are as good for a writer as everyone who has not written a book knows them to be, what could be more wonderful than to rent one of the little bungalows at Gordon's Bay, within sight of blue water, white sand, and violet mountains?

The Strand, which is now a modern seaside place, was once a quiet bay where, in the heat of summer, the fruit farmers of the Drakenstein Valley would come with their families, their ox-wagons, and their retainers. They still come, but in American touring cars.

I had lunch in an hotel where a wedding party was in progress. About thirty guests, with the blushing bride and the bridegroom in their midst, occupied the end of the dining-room and provided entertainment for everyone in the hotel. The bride was a big, competent Afrikaner girl, and the bridegroom looked like the heavy-weight champion of the Union. His mother gazed at him with tearful eyes, as if he were still about ten years of age. For all his sixteen stone, she was losing her dear little boy for ever! There were toasts and speeches and much laughter; and we others sat eating bobotie, thinking how wonderful love is at twenty-one.

An elderly farmer rose and made what must have been a witty speech in Afrikaans, for applause and laughter rang through the hotel. I thought that I had seen precisely the same kind of wedding attended by just the same sort of folk in East Anglia. You might have slipped a few Norfolk farmers into the wedding party, and no one would have been able to spot them as alien. And I remembered that in Norfolk the word 'bor—the last syllable of neighbour, or near boor— is the common mode of address. Indeed, as I well know, until a Norfolk man calls you " 'bor " you can consider yourself an outlander in that county. My Afrikaans dictionary gives " burr " as neighbour, so that perhaps there is some faint justification in linking the sunburnt farmers at a Cape wedding with the equally big and bony inhabitants of Norfolk and Suffolk.

The heat of afternoon had settled over the land. The sun, white, and not golden as in Europe, lit the rocky earth with the hard brilliance of magnesium, shining from a sky in which there was not one cloud. I made for the Sir Lowry Pass, which must be one of the oldest roads in South Africa. Long before the white man came, the migrating eland used it; long before van Riebeeck's time the Hottentot hordes descended it towards the sea to trade their cattle for iron hoops, and in the early Eighteenth Century the first pioneers climbed it on their way to the unknown. From the summit of the pass I turned and said good-bye to Cape Town; and as I did so, I saw thirty miles away the outline of Table Mountain and the outward curve of False Bay enclosing a half-circle of turquoise sea.

As I continued my journey the peaks of the Zonder End Mountains rose before me, growing taller as the mountains came out of the distance, vast and blue like a fretted screen set up against the paler sky. The sun was setting and the important stillness of approaching night stood over the landscape. White farms lay far off against the mountains, and I remembered that in this part of the country the Dutch East India Company once had many of its cattle stations. It was strange to think that this stupendous landscape, having missed the age of chivalry, had no story to tell but of wild animals and men almost as wild, of cattle thieves and poisoned arrows. As I watched the stars come out and burn above the towering peaks, I thought that if ever mountains looked as though they should have a King Arthur and a Merlin, those Zonder End Mountains did; yet the traveller could explore them for ever and never come across an old castle or hear an old song of swords or love. Were they in Europe, rising above the Rhine, or in a Scotch mist, or on the west coast of Ireland, they would hold a hundred stories of men and women, of life and death, of love and despair, of triumph and defeat, of knights and ladies, of gnomes and fairies, of family curses and of spectres. But in this young and lovely country there is no weight of human feeling upon them. They are wild and silent as the world was wild a million years ago.

Darkness fell, and the first stars were green sparks in the

sky. A Cape cart rattled past, but there was nothing else, no sign of life but a yellow window far off in the valley and a bonfire burning away upon the hillside. The crickets were trilling when I came to the mile-long street of Swellendam. Tall gum trees cast their shade. White houses gleamed in the starlight, and there was a black mountain rising up at the back.

My hotel was good, small, comfortable, and friendly. Like many a South African hotel in the country, it had certain architectural peculiarities. The bedrooms were in a separate building at the back, grouped round a covered quadrangle with a little garden in the centre. After the admirable dinner which most small country hotels in South Africa give one, I went out into the warm, windless main street. The crickets were now in full chorus. The sky was a sheet of stars.

I saw through open windows into little lamplit rooms beyond where large photographs of stern, spade-bearded old gentlemen and resourceful-looking old ladies gazed grimly upon their grandchildren, the modern counterpart of the unsmiling portraits by van Dyck and Franz Hals.

There is often a dog in a strange town who assumes the air of a publicity agent. He waits outside the hotel and attaches himself to strangers, snobbishly cutting all his old friends as he trots ahead and shows off the beauties of the town. Then, unlike a human publicity agent, he says good-night outside the hotel and departs with a final tail wag.

The dog of Swellendam led me up the main street to a Baroque building—the Dutch Reformed Church—which was dramatically flood-lit against the blackness of a mountain.

We retraced our steps, my guide trotting ahead, coming back to me now and again to make sure I was having a good time, and at the hotel we said good night; and he went off into the darkness.

§ 2

Swellendam is a good place to pause and consider the origin of the Boer. The word is Dutch for a farmer. Early in Cape history this restless urge to trek off into the blue, which

has played so big a part in South African history, began to
show itself.

In addition to the leisurely life of the Western Cape, where
in the Drakenstein Valley, Stellenbosch, Paarl, Tulbagh, and
the corn country, a settled agricultural life was in progress,
modelled upon that of Europe, a numerous population was
engaged in the more restless task of cattle-ranching. These
men were not tied to the land, but were, on the contrary,
anxious to move on to new pastures with their herds.

In little Holland, where so many of their forebears had
lived, farms were smaller than in most countries, and a few
lush acres were sufficient for a herd of cows; but the Hollander
transported to the Cape, where the grass was not always green,
considered that a few thousand acres were not too many
for his needs. So the Boer went on and on, all the time getting
farther away from his base, which was the Dutch fort on Table
Bay.

This was a life different from that of the western homesteads. It was a life that attracted brave and independent
men and, of course, a few indolent ones as well. It was not
life with a pruning-hook: it was life with a gun and a trek
wagon. It was an open-air life of freedom, of camping out
and of escape; particularly escape from the hated government
of the Dutch East India Company. Some of the ranchers
built themselves little white farms like those of their friends
and relatives in the west, others moved on from loan-farm to
loan-farm—large tracts of leased grazing—where they lived
in sheds and shacks, while others, still more mobile, slept in
their wagons, with the stars for a roof. So early in South
African life the love of camping out and eating roasted meat
on wooden skewers was implanted in the heart of the
Boer.

What happened to the Boer in the wilderness is one of the
most important facts of South African history. He was still only
one generation removed from Europe. Even in 1736, when
the first herds began to approach Swellendam, an old man of
eighty-four might, when a boy, have been rebuked for stealing
apples by van Riebeeck himself! Certainly many an elderly
Boer riding his pony on the limits of the frontier would

have heard at his mother's knee first-hand accounts of the canals and windmills of Holland or the vineyards and rivers of France. But now in his old age those bedtime stories, and memories of rough crowds of festive sailors in the taverns of the Cape, were all that Europe meant to him as he rode his pony over the veld.

Turning his back symbolically upon the sea that led to Europe, the sea which brought the ships from his ever more unreal fatherland, the Boer pressed on into the wilderness. In renouncing Europe he accepted Africa; in taking the frontier as his home he came under new influences which moulded and remade him; in adopting a way of life that demanded a new technique of living, he became a South African. Just as the American frontier was moulding British, Dutch, Germans, and Swedes, and transforming them into Americans, so the wild, fierce land of South Africa was making the first men who dared to love her as truly her sons as an Englishman is of England and a Scot of Scotland.

Think of the change in his environment. With ancestral roots in the quiet water-meadows of Holland, along the Lower Rhine, and in France, the Boer now lived in a hot land of great mountains and gorges, of plains aflame in summer with flowering heaths and wild geranium, of dry water-courses that in winter became violent torrents, a hard, cruel land of extremes, whose every bush and cave might conceal a little yellow man in the act of fitting a poisoned arrow to a bow. Away to the east, although he did not know it, were hordes of organised and valiant warriors who would one day contest every yard of his advance—the war-like Bantu.

Europe, trade, the life of ports and cities had all been forgotten by this man who had turned his back upon the sea. They were not for him. Taking with him from the old world only one thing, the Bible, he went out into Africa, and upon the African veld, and beneath the shadow of African mountains, his women bore their children. So the Afrikaner was born.

At much the same time that the Boers broke away to the east from Table Bay, the varied peoples of the same European stock cooped up on the seaboard of America began to trek to the west. The two treks were vastly different. The Americans, more numerous than the Boers, crossed the mountains which enclosed them and moved west, planning towns as they went, and moving on rather like a great army consolidating its positions during an invasion. The Boers, on the other hand, were few, and might perhaps be compared to a cavalry patrol, moving on and leaving very little behind it. If it would be true to say that the unit of the American trek was a little township, the unit of the South African trek was a lonely ranch separated by miles from the next one.

The motive which sent out both sets of pioneers was the same: a desire for space and freedom, a hunger for new land, a discontent with civilisation as it was represented by the life of the seaboard, an inability to fit in with the scheme of things; and bad luck. The qualities demanded by the new life were the same: courage, individualism, and self-reliance.

The Americans, upon the great crest of the Appalachians, went down into a rich land where they encountered buffalo, elk, deer, bears, wolves, panthers, turkeys, squirrels, and partridges; the Boers, in a fiercer and a poorer land, encountered the lion and the leopard, the rhinoceros and the hippopotamus, the baboon and the cobra; but it was also a land teeming with buck, which, as the white men advanced, began to retreat, and so helped to draw him on. The Americans were opposed from the outset by aboriginals as fierce and as war-like as the black invaders whom the Boers did not at first encounter. But the Boer was harassed by the primitive bushman with his deadly poisoned arrow and his habit of stealing and maiming cattle. The Americans shot down the Red Indian without mercy and offered bounties for his scalp; the Boers shot down the bushmen like vermin.

Frontier life in both countries was intensely individualistic. In South Africa it was founded on the family unit. The old patriarch in his ranch, surrounded by his family, his oxen and his asses, his men servants and his maid servants—most of them technically free Hottentots and half-breeds, for the slaves were nearly all in the settled west—might well open his Old Testament and see in the story of Abraham a faithful reflection of himself.

The frontier was also a military training-ground, for a distance was soon reached from civilisation when the frontiersman had to make his own laws and become his own policeman. The Americans learnt to fight like Red Indians, moving from tree to tree; the Boers became mounted sharp-shooters. The bushman's contribution to South African history was that he imposed the Commando system of warfare upon the frontier. It is a system that produced patriot warriors like Pretorius, Potgieter, and de Wet, and soldier statesmen like Botha and Smuts. In America, the backwoods school of fighting produced George Washington and the " embattled farmers " of the War of Independence.

So, early in the story of South Africa, two ways of life are visible: the settled west, where property descended from father to son, where the vines and the corn and the peaches ripened in fertile valleys, and the tougher, coarser life of the ever-moving east, where long whips cracked over the horns of oxen and loaded wagons flanked by herds of grazing cattle moved slowly in search of new grassland. And as the white ranchers moved eastward, black ranchers in tribal hordes were moving west, and it was only a question of time before they clashed. By the time Britain stepped into the Cape in 1795, the outposts were already in touch. Boer and Bantu had met at last.

That was the South Africa to which a handful of British officials came during the opening phase of the struggle that grew into the Napoleonic War. Soon after came the missionaries.

Some writers have seen in the Boer a man who took with him into the wilderness the mentality of the Seventeenth Century, and if this is so it would explain why those who encountered him in the Nineteenth Century had little in common with him. The Seventeenth Century was one in which the social conscience was not yet awake. The men of the Seventeenth Century divided humanity sharply into Christian men and pagans. Primitive races were lower even than pagans, creatures hardly human and probably soulless. The first cry of horror from the Boer when he encountered the mind of Europe again after all those years was: " Is this the way to treat Christian men!" To him it was inconceivable that the sub-human species should be considered his equals either before God or in the eyes of the law. And that is what he was told. He was expected to accept in ten minutes a change of mind which it had taken Europe a century to achieve.

If there is truth in this, the meeting upon the African veld of the Seventeenth with the Nineteenth Century is surely a remarkable encounter. Perhaps naturally, Rip van Winkle springs to the mind, and, in a sense, the Boer had been asleep for a hundred years. He fell asleep shortly after the Reformation, believing, as his Bible told him, that the curse of Ham was upon his bondsman, and he awakened in a world that had experienced the French Revolution and was well into the Industrial Revolution.

He came into modern times, transformed by the frontier, still firmly holding his Bible and speaking a new language.

§ 3

Sitting upon the stoep in the white sunlight of the morning, I watched Swellendam get into its stride. Coloured boys of various shades and ages swept out the shops. They did this in slow time, talking and laughing together with the greatest zest. How wonderful to have so much to say, so much to laugh about, so much to repeat! Children went to school. Cape carts with mules in the shafts passed towards the station or the country. Light wagons drawn by three or four span of donkeys passed, with a dark boy perched on the shafts.

An old woman came along, a strange old woman with a little brown face scored like a medlar, and she stopped in front of the stoep and looked up at me with sad, brown monkey eyes and with the frank, unwinking interest of a child. She was encased in rags and powdered with dust, and the wire bracelets and ornaments she was wearing hung on her thin arms like jewellery on a mummy. She was different from any of the coloured people round about, and I thought that she must have Hottentot blood in her veins. When she had had enough of me, she brushed a fly away with a little brown hand and deliberately walked on.

The proprietor, who came out at this time, told me that I was right about her and that descendants of the Hessekwa tribe of Hottentots are to be found in Swellendam. There are also people with Bushman blood. I detected this in two yellow women with high, Mongolian cheek-bones and delicately small hands and feet.

The Drostdy, or Courthouse, of Swellendam was once the residence of the magistrate and the place where officials and distinguished visitors stayed. It is one of the fine old buildings of the Cape, a long, white homestead, with Eighteenth Century windows and a vine-covered stoep.

It contains a large and fascinating collection of local bygones. In the tall, gaunt rooms where the business of the frontier was once transacted, coffee-pots, tea-cups, knives and spoons, and churns are reverently preserved in glass cases. They are fascinating to us, although they are at the most only two centuries old, while the majority are much later; and they would also be interesting to the old farmers, could they come back and see Ouma's knitting-needles and Oom Jan's ancient pipe preserved for posterity!

The life revealed in those cases is a hard and frugal one, shared equally by men and women. Most of the relics come, no doubt, from the better-class farms of the district, for the less prosperous trek farmer had nothing to leave but his gun, even to a museum in search of bygones. What a grim, hard life it was, a life which few descendants of those tough old characters would willingly endure to-day.

At infrequent periods the Company buyers would come along to purchase cattle, and pay cash down in rix-dollars which were promptly put away in a wagon kist. Then, upon those rare and surely exciting occasions when a farmer's wife sent salt, butter, and soap to the Cape Town market, out would come the dollars to be returned to the town in exchange for tea, coffee, sugar, tobacco, cloth, and ammunition. Those, incidentally, were precisely the same things needed by the American settlers in return for their cattle, grain, and furs.

An object which delighted me was an eight-foot rod with a church collecting-bag at the end, accompanied by a bell to wake up the somnolent worshipper. Variations of this probably occur in other Calvinistic countries, where a congregation accustomed to the open air fell asleep during a two hour sermon. In America the Puritans used the same sort of thing, but they did not combine it with the collecting bag. It was a rod with a hare's foot at one end and a brass ball at the other. During the sermon, the tithing man, who was responsible for Sabbath observance, kept a keen eye on the congregation, and if he saw an adult dropping off to sleep he would advance and tickle him with the hare's foot; but if an unfortunate boy fell asleep, down came the brass ball.

Among the portraits in the Drostdy are several uncompromising Scottish faces. I came across a photograph of " Captain Benjamin Moodie. 10th Laird of Melsetter, Orkneys. Born 1789 and died 1856 at Swellendam. Descendant of Robert I. the Bruce, King of Scotland, 1274–1329, and seven later Kings." What a people these Scots are!

The Moodie family is an interesting one. During the Jacobite rebellions they were on the Hanoverian side, which caused bad feeling with the Jacobites of Orkney. Moodie's great-grandfather was shot by a Jacobite in the streets of Kirkwall, and this produced a family feud which was avenged when his son rounded up the local Jacobites and sent them to the Tower of London. Remarkably perhaps —for they were on the winning side—the Moodie fortunes declined, and Benjamin Moodie decided to emigrate to the Cape in 1817, taking with him two hundred Scottish labourers and artisans. This was the first attempt to settle British people in South Africa.

Moodie bound his settlers to work for him for eighteen months upon arrival, or else to pay him a sum for their passages and seek work on their own. Unfortunately for him, he had recruited not Orkneymen, who might have felt some veneration for his name, but Edinburgh men, most of whom deserted when they discovered that good jobs were waiting them everywhere. The men quickly scattered, some to towns and others to live the adventurous lives of traders and elephant-hunters.

Moodie himself bought for £600 the old Cape homestead of Groot Vader's Bosch, where seven children were born to him. Donald, a brother who joined him in South Africa, became a well-known figure in Natal and at the Cape, and it is from these two that the numerous clan of Moodies in the Union and the Rhodesias are descended.

A third brother, J. W. D. Moodie, also appeared in South Africa and after a stay of ten years wrote a readable and valuable book about his adventures in the country. When at the Cape, he met Thomas Pringle, the Scottish poet, who had come out with the 1820 Settlers, and it was in Pringle's house in London years later that Moodie met the youngest of the numerous flock of Strickland daughters, Susanna, whose sister, Agnes, was already famous as the author of *The Queens of England*. Susanna Strickland and Moodie married and went to Canada, where they had a large family whose descendants have spread the Moodie name through Canada and the United States.

§ 4

The time has come when South Africans have fallen in love with their great-great-grandparents. A halo of romance has descended upon everything that happened a hundred years ago, and the most common objects of daily life are sure of an honoured place in the local museum.

Like most local museums everywhere, they owe their treasures mainly to the enthusiasm of some sleepless local antiquary who will stop at nothing to secure a candlestick or a churn, while even the larger objects of agricultural life, such as ploughs and farm wagons, are, as the Drostdy proves, sure of a dignified retirement.

I met the local enthusiast in Swellendam. Listening to him, you might think that if the rest of the Union sank beneath the waves, and Swellendam alone were left as a tiny island, everything worth preserving would still be intact, and the voyager, approaching the shores of Swellendam, would be able to cry, " Here is South Africa ! "

He has his eye on old coffee-pots, pipes, guns, kappies,

candle-moulds, and such like, all over the district, and his method of obtaining them from reluctant owners struck me as something original in the art of persuasion.

" I meet an old farmer who has something that ought to be in the Drostdy," he said, " and I ask him, ' How old are you? ' When he tells me, I then ask, ' And where are you going to be buried? ' He tells me. I then say, ' Have you got your tombstone? ' He says, ' Yes.' I then look at him for a moment and ask, ' And who do you think is going to read it? Come man,' I say, ' give that old coffee-pot to the museum! Man, *that's* your tombstone, that coffee-pot! I want to put your name and your wife's name on it, and the date of your birth and where you live; and then people will come to the Drostdy and they will look at the coffee-pot and they will remember you and your good woman. . . . Man, think! Is that your tombstone—that coffee-pot—or is it not? ' "

" And is it? " I asked.

" Ja—certainly! They stroke their chins thoughtfully and after a while they say, ' It might be '. And then—I get the coffee-pot! "

§ 5

I continued my journey to Mossel Bay through an exquisite land of mountains and woody glades. White trickles of water feathered down through dark trees, and there were glens full of sunlight and shadow, then the road opened out to moorlands covered with the most splendid heaths I have ever seen.

The wayfarer in Britain may stop and talk to almost anyone on the road and hear something interesting, but this is not so in South Africa. The only people on foot in South Africa are brown or black. I have no doubt that the South African born, brought up with these people, may, with the right approach and a happy phrase, get them talking. But the stranger is baffled by them.

While I had stopped to admire a view and look at a map somewhere near Albertinia, an intelligent-looking Cape boy— he was about forty, but the native never officially grows up—

came by and pounced avidly on the cigarette I had thrown away. He had no bundle or sack, neither was he carrying one of those enormously heavy brass-bound boxes which the native bears across an endless landscape, so I concluded that he worked locally. But this is the kind of conversation I had with him.

" Good morning. Do you work round here? "

" Ja, baas, ja."

" And what do you do? "

" Work, baas."

" Yes, but what do you do? Do you work on a farm? "

" Work, baas, ja ", and he pointed into the distance as if I ought to be able to see in the sky his niche in the agricultural or industrial life of the Union.

" Are you married? Wife? "

" Ja, baas. Nine piccanin."

At last I was getting some place, as the Americans say!

" How much money do you get? "

He looked shifty, and the iron curtain came down again.

" Not much money, baas."

And so it went on for fifteen minutes. It was like trying to open an oyster with a toothpick. Yet I have no doubt that a South African who could speak the Cape dialect or Afrikaans might have produced a flood of anecdote and amusing conversation from him, for the Cape Coloured are, I have been told, great and amusing talkers. When I gave him sixpence he took it, cupping both his hands together.

At a little dorp on the way to Mossel Bay I went to an unpretentious hotel patronised by farmers. The dining-room looked like the Chelsea Flower Show. Except at a funeral, I have never seen so many lovely flowers in a small room. Every table was loaded—there is no other word for it—with dahlias, heaths, carnations, snapdragons, wallflowers, pink gladioli, Madonna lilies; and some of the dahlias, severed close to the head, were so huge that they obscured the soup plates in which they were floating.

A barefoot, coloured girl came to me and whispered, " Baas want dinner? " While silently admitting that the flowers were a feast in themselves, I replied that was my intention, whereupon she brought me a menu. This is what I read—prepared for a room that held only ten people :

Barley soup.

Pickled herrings
Fried fish and lemon
Curried fish

Haricot ribs of mutton
Braised lamb chops
Fried pork chops
Roast chicken

Cold York ham
Cold corned brisket
Cold roast sucking pig

Boiled potatoes, beans, marrow, green peas

Jelly and canned peaches

Cheese

Five other people came in, and we plunged into that riot of eatables. In South Africa the climate is never allowed to interfere with the appetite. You eat roast pork in a dark room with the shutters drawn and a temperature outside of 100 in the shade. It is natural that a country which began as a meat-producing station should be carnivorous, but to realise how fond the ordinary South African is of meat, you have to leave fashionable and expensive hotels and go out into the country.

" Give them great meals of beef, and iron and steel, and they will eat like wolves and fight like devils," said Shakespeare of the English, but, as far as my observations go, in comparison with the South African, the English were, even in the days of the Roast Beef of Old England, hardly more than vegetarian! There is something Homeric about these great repasts in small hotels. Under the watchful eyes of fellow-eaters, the stranger begins to feel effeminate and feeble unless he, too, plunges into pork after mutton. Like so much else in South

Africa, I have an idea that these Gargantuan meals are a legacy from Seventeenth Century Holland.

After lunch I praised the flowers to the wife of the proprietor, and she took me round to a pretty little patch of garden at the side of the hotel, where all those lovely flowers were flourishing because they were irrigated by the bath-water!

With the feeling that bed would have been infinitely more agreeable than the dusty road, I went out into the afternoon, with a fiery streak lying ahead on which I encountered nothing but occasional coloured men and boys, and little carts drawn by three and four span of donkeys. At the bridge over the Gouritz River I stopped to examine as good an object lesson as you will see anywhere of the placidity and potential violence of a South African torrent.

The bridge, which is a long one and made of girders, is flung across a ravine hundreds of feet deep. In the gorge a thin, rusty-coloured snake of water was lying in a bed of baked sand. The bridge was upheld by three Eiffel towers of four-sided steel girders fixed in immensely strong concrete drums, the whole structure designed to offer as little opposition as possible to the water. The contrast between the present state of the Gouritz, hardly moving and lying in hot pools, and the provision made to guard against what it can do in the rainy season, was dramatic. Many of the rivers of South Africa, some of which are terrifying in the winter, are reduced in the summer to these brown streaks, and for some reason or other South Africans find this humorous. I had already been told several times the story of the man who fell into a river and rose up and dusted himself!

I was soon in the hot streets of Mossel Bay, where there were churches, shops, hotels, bicycles, motor cars, and an air of growth and popularity. It was a hot town that afternoon, and the cooling sea breeze which the publicity folders promise was taking a day off. That this breeze does exist, and has an ugly sister called the wind, is proved by the white patches of blown sand on the inland rocks.

The feature of Mossel Bay is the Poort, and I went there at once to sit in the shade. It must be the finest natural sea-bathing pool in the Union. In shape it is long and

KNYSNA LAGOON FROM THE HEADS

narrow, and is formed by a massive rock formation which has built itself up like a wall against the sea. One end is open to the sea, but is protected by reefs from the crashing surf of the Indian Ocean. The waves break on the reef and send through the narrow rock entrance ripples of water which freshen and fill the pool. But the great feature of the Poort is a floor of sloping silver sand, shallow enough at one end for a child of six to stand in, and deep enough at the other to give a swimmer a good dive.

I thought it would have been pleasant to have spent an afternoon at the Poort. The children who monopolised the pool were having a glorious afternoon. There were little shrimp-like girls in bathing-suits, and little brown eel-like boys, splashing and swimming and diving from the rocks into the sun-shot green water. As I watched them, I thought how good looking they were and how proud their creators must be of them, and I derived an incredulous pleasure from the knowledge that this August scene was happening in November.

The road went on and inland, and I was soon in the town of George.

§ 6

High mountains called the Outeniquas lie round George. They were known to the Portuguese by the lovely name of Serra de Estrella—the Star Mountains—and the present name, that of a Hottentot tribe, means " the honey-laden men ", a reference, no doubt, to the honey made in that land of heaths.

George takes its name from one of South Africa's mysteries, a man named George Rex, who arrived there in 1802, and was believed to be the son of the reigning monarch, George III, and the elusive Quakeress, Hannah Lightfoot. He moved from George to Knysna, where he bought a large estate and lived like an English country gentleman. Many people in South Africa are convinced that Mr Rex had been sent out to the Cape to avoid political complications, but if this were so, surely he would have been persuaded to use a less provoking name?

The Outeniqua Mountains are extraordinarily Scottish; I

I

seem always to be comparing South Africa to Europe, but it is inevitable. They are, indeed, Scotland at her best. When I awakened one morning I could readily have believed that I was at Fort William. The mist—or haar, as the Scots so expressively call that white, smoke-like sea mist—was steaming down the sides of the mountains and creeping with cold fingers through the pine-woods, casting over the landscape an air of suspended awesomeness which you get round Glencoe on a misty day. Then, as the sun rose, the mist retreated, revealing mile after mile of tremendous scarred flanks and green slopes, corries, glens, and dark gorges. The mountain road could be seen winding round the outermost edge of the great flanks, disappearing and emerging higher up to vanish at length over the summit into lands beyond.

The names of those who made the roads and the railways of South Africa should be sung and honoured. So many are the windings of the railway to George, that the train from Cape Town can be seen far up the mountain an hour and a half before it sighs into the station.

I was told that George would remind me of an English town, but the roads are too wide, the vegetation is too luxuriant, and above all the many fine houses, standing back English fashion in beautiful gardens, are all much of the same period, giving to the place that air of uniformity which is absent from everything in England but a housing estate.

The charm of any English town the size of George is that Mr Brown, the tobacconist, has a shop that was built in the reign of Elizabeth; next door, Dr Armstrong's surgery is George III; old Colonel Black is Queen Anne; Miss James at the Grange is Walter Scott Gothic; and so on, with all kinds of variations in between, ancient and modern. The eye, always enchanted or repelled, is at least never wearied.

In South Africa the architect has saved the country from what might so easily have become an almost unbelievable monotony, by varying his styles with great skill and taste. And the vegetation, eagerly responding, provides in a few years trees which in Europe would be half a century growing, so that the South African house, if built only twenty years ago, is always decently embowered and surrounded.

Many of the people who live in George are very English, for it has for years been a favourite place for retired people from India and the Cape Province. The barber who cut my hair was undoubtedly English, and he had pinned up in his shop a coloured photograph of Mr Winston Churchill.

In one of the wide roads I came upon the English Cathedral, a building smaller than many a village church at home, but with a diocese the size of Wales. In one of the memorial windows I noticed St George dressed as a modern soldier in khaki. The Dutch Reformed Church, a fine and imposing temple, was as large as the cathedral was small.

Two sights of George will always anchor that place in my memory: the agapanthus and the hop. Just as the bluebell grows in England, casting a sheet of dark blue upon the earth, so the agapanthus grows round George. And that stately flower is no delicate stranger which has to be hurried into the greenhouse with the approach of winter: it stands over three feet high from its native soil, bearing great flowers of blue or white, which you can just about cup in both hands. I have grown agapanthus in England, but, having seen it round George, I shall never trouble to do so again.

Then the hop. I was surprised to come upon acre after acre at George which looked like Paddock Wood in Kent, or Alton in Hampshire. The hops were strung and tied in the same way, and, apart from the fact that the hop-poles in South Africa are made of eucalyptus wood, I doubt if even an expert could have seen any difference.

The hop is one of the few European plants which has not readily adapted itself to South Africa. Early Dutch attempts to grow it were all failures. In 1902 thousands of plants from England, Germany, and America were distributed all over the Union, but the right soil and the right hop never seemed to come together. After sixteen years of bad luck the experts at George found their attention focused upon a single plant which had been flourishing for several years in the garden of a Miss van Niekerk. That furtive survivor of so many unsuccessful experiments was in the habit of climbing a tree every summer, and efforts were made to trace its history. It appeared to be the sole survivor of some old English variety that had gone out of cultivation. The experts lavished more care upon it than has ever probably been expended upon a single hop plant before or since.

Meanwhile, yet another attempt was made with imported hops, this time from Tasmania. All died except three female plants of a variety sent in error! But it is from those three unexpected cuttings, and the lone male of the garden, that all the hops of George have since been grown. It is to such fortunate accidents that science and industry often owe so much.

I was told that well over a million descendants of the four plants now cover three hundred and twenty acres in George. The name given to the variety is Golden Clusters, and the production is getting near the two hundred tons required by South African brewers.

English hop-growers would be interested to see that the industry at George is carried out to a familiar pattern. The hops are planted in a " garden ", which consists of so many " sets " to a " hill ". The drying-sheds are called kilns, as in Hampshire, and not oast-houses, as in Kent. The buildings are not such a notable feature of the landscape as the old-fashioned oast-houses of Kent, for they do not possess the red-tiled, conical ventilating towers. But what would interest the European hop-grower more than anything is that in South Africa a hop garden can start from zero at about Christmas-time and be ready for picking a few weeks later!

§ 7

Nowhere in the world are you more conscious of mountains than in the Cape Province. They are never out of sight. They are your daily companions. To travel in the Cape is to cross mountains. Looking northward from the south coast of Africa, you must imagine how the mountains lie parallel to the sea, rising like a flight of steps to the interior plain. The first steps are those mountains nearest to the sea, then comes a terrace, and another step to a higher level, and so on until, several thousands of feet above sea level, the great tableland of Southern Africa stretches north to the Limpopo.

In some countries mountains have invited and encouraged the explorer. Their valleys have offered him an easy way into the interior, or rivers have made it a simple matter for him to paddle a canoe, or punt a raft, into the very heart of a country. In South Africa the very reverse has happened. Cut off on the north by hundreds of miles of malarial bush and desert, and on the south by a series of mountain ranges, the " interior ", which is now the Free State and the Transvaal, was until only a little over a century ago an unknown land given over to vast herds of game and to beasts of prey.

It had been raining, but the sudden storm had passed. I set off in the morning to cross the Montagu Pass. Yellow peaty-looking water was tumbling down the rocks and lying in black pools. There were oak glades and the greenest of green ferns. The pass, which was blasted out of the mountain's edge a century or so ago, twists and climbs, sometimes over a thousand feet in a few miles. Here again I must say that it was like motoring in Scotland. From the top of the Pass I looked back and saw the road spiralling down to George.

Once over the Pass, the country changed in a sudden and dramatic way. I was out of Scotland and into Africa. The grass had vanished, and in its place were scrubby, succulent plants, each one growing in its own little desert. Now and again an aloe lifted a spear from a bush of green bayonets and a prickly pear was outlined grotesquely like a scarecrow against the sky. This unexpected desert was the Little Karoo, a stark and threatening country, but with great pictorial charm and atmosphere. It seemed almost a miracle that animals could find anything to keep them alive in that desert, but the best mutton in South Africa is raised on the small moisture-holding vygies of the Little Karoo and the Great Karoo.

The bald land peppercorned with its dry, dusty-looking plants ended abruptly, and I saw before me the extraordinary contrast of a green, lush landscape stretching forward to another mountain range, the Zwartzbergen, which led on to higher land and then another range. In the valley through which I was travelling poplar trees outlined the course of streams and irrigation canals. There were acres sown with lucerne, and the country was well fenced. There were farm-houses and an air of prosperity. Carts drawn by four donkeys, a black boy sitting sideways on the shafts, went past in the dust. There were dairy herds, and the land suggested cream and butter and cheese.

Everywhere I looked I saw ostriches. They were grazing contentedly with sheep and cows. They were corralled in large flocks—or possibly herds better describes a bird that behaves like a quadruped. They were everywhere.

I entered the pleasant town of Oudtshorn, still the centre of ostrich farming, but to-day more interested in dairying, tobacco, green crops, and fruit. Someone had given me an introduction to a merchant. I found him in a hot little office, living in a hurry like an American business man on the films. Could I see an ostrich farm? Certainly! Any-thing else he could do? He dashed into the next room and returned with an armful of ostrich feathers. With the sudden, unaccountable generosity of Israel, he pressed these upon me, and I emerged into the sunny streets grasping the ex-traordinary bouquet like a prima donna; but no one seemed to notice.

The ostrich farm was some way out among green fields.

The owner had just rounded up four hundred birds, which were standing apprehensively in a meadow. We went first into a field to look at what appeared to be fifty hedgehogs running nimbly on thin legs. They were ostrich chicks, and remarkably pretty, covered with drab, parti-coloured down and with little velvet necks, and great film-star eyes and lashes.

" How long do they live? "

" They *can* live over a hundred years," replied the farmer, " but they don't! They generally kill themselves in a fence, or swallow a pair of pliers."

He told me that the ostrich is the most stupid of all birds; in fact, he almost doubted if it had a brain. So far as I could gather, it is merely a fuselage covered with feathers, mounted on a pair of tremendous limbs and with an expression of perpetual apprehension beneath its enormous Hollywood lashes. The male at certain times of the year can become dangerous, and his kick is as powerful as that of a horse. His habit of charging when angry can always be deflected, I was told, if you take a twig with a few leaves on the end and wave it in his face. This has never been known to fail. The bird shuts his eyes, and when he opens them again he is a hundred yards away. The sound he makes in the breeding season has often been mistaken for the roar of a lion and is called "brooming". Apart from stupidity and vanity, the only other human attributes which the ostrich possesses is a love of dancing. Sometimes when the birds are let out from the kraal in the morning, they sail off, feeling good, revolving together in a waltz; some, however, becoming giddy, fall down and break their legs and have to be shot.

We approached the field where the four hundred birds were corralled. There were several coloured herd-boys and two men on horseback. The ostriches were grouped in the remote distance, wing to wing, every neck upright at the same angle, giving the impression of a regiment of lancers waiting the order to charge.

As soon as the horsemen moved off, you could sense the panic that spread through the herd. Still in mass formation they set off at a trot that developed into a gallop, until they were racing flat out at about forty miles an hour.

Watching them in movement I could understand how it was that Pliny thought ostriches in flight flung missiles at their pursuers, for on stony ground many an apparently well-directed stone was hurled backward by their muscular feet.

With great skill the horsemen kept the herd together and drove it forward, each neck upright, until the birds looked like hundreds of cobras on horseback. The herd-boys then surrounded the birds, who kept trying to make a break-through but the boys were always too quick for them. The foreman dismounted and, taking a long crook, advanced to the ostriches and, selecting one, drew it out by the neck just as I have seen a Southdown shepherd pick out a sheep by the leg.

The bird then started to stamp and struggle. The dust rose in clouds. The foreman held on to the neck while two of the boys grasped the wings and a third took an old sock from his pocket, which he neatly slipped over the bird's head. This appeared to calm it slightly, and it was led, still protesting, to a tree, where its neck was placed in a cleft that held it fast. Then the ostrich, instead of lifting its neck, which would have instantly freed it, began to draw back and pull, which held it more firmly. While it was doing this, the boys quickly relieved it—the process is painless—of several fine wing-feathers.

While this was going on, the other ostriches stood bunched together, watching in wide-eyed terror. As soon as the plucked bird was released, it shot away into the distance to stand shaking itself with distended wings and dancing about all the time like an indignant balloon; and the next bird was selected and plucked.

"You can pluck a good bird three times in two years," said the farmer, "but once a year is the average. I've heard old men round Oudtshorn tell of the days, about sixty years ago, when fellows went mad on ostrich farms. It was like a gold rush! You paid from two hundred pounds upwards for a fine pair of birds. Everybody thought he was going to make his fortune; and some did! But those days have gone. . . . What with ostrich biltong at a shilling a pound and an ostrich skin worth five shillings in America, why a bird's often worth more dead than alive!"

And so it happens that the hats women wear in Europe affect life in Oudtshorn. Every time a queen or a princess is pictured wearing an ostrich feather, hearts are lifted in Oudtshorn and optimists dream of another feather boom. If it did happen, I am told there are sufficient fine feathers stored away to clothe nearly every woman in the world from head to foot.

§ 8

Some twenty miles to the north of Oudtshorn are the Cango Caves, which are said to be among the finest in the world. The road is made memorable by the great barrier of the Swartzbergen ahead.

To enter the Caves on a hot day is to pass into a delightful refrigerator. The guide, a cheerful man who loves every stalagmite, was dressed in a khaki shirt and shorts, and as I went in he switched on a battery of electric lights; for the Cango Caves are sophisticated. I descended steps into what looked like a desolate and gaunt London tube station.

The passages and caverns stretch on for two miles, ending in the Devil's Workshop, and it is believed that further caves may yet remain to be discovered. They were seen first in 1780, when a farmer named van Zyl sent his Hottentot boy, Klaas, to look for lost cattle. The boy climbed into the hills and came to a hole in the rocks hidden by brushwood. On the following day a schoolmaster, who was staying on the farm, went with Klaas to see the hole, which impressed him so much that he persuaded van Zyl to go and look too.

Accordingly van Zyl went there with eight slaves and a coil of rope, and was let down into the cave which is now called van Zyl's Hall. It must have required courage to have done that, I think. Since then the history of the Caves has been one of discovery and exploration.

We went down some steps and stood in a fantastic hall, where stalactite dripped and met stalagmite, where spiky waterfalls had apparently been arrested in mid air, where little stalactites were just beginning on the roof like horns on the head of a kid; and the drip of water on the floor was forming into tiny bumps that might be several inches in height when everything now existing on the earth has vanished. The guide switched on lights concealed behind the stalactites, and then directed a battery of floodlights upon the stalagmites, turning the weird cavern into what the guide-book would call " a subterranean fairyland ".

We went on into enormous cathedral-like chambers, vast and silent, where the air was as dead as it is in a broadcasting studio. Every now and again the guide would disappear, and I would hear him busy with the switches. Suddenly the vast, incoherent architecture would be flooded with concealed red light, to be followed by an awful sepulchral green like a scene in a pantomime. I cannot remember whether my favourite cavern was called the Bridal Chamber, the Crystal Palace, the Fairy Chamber, or the Cathedral, but it was, I think, the largest of them all, also the most uncanny; and upon its distant roof were many black dots which dropped off and flapped noiselessly about when the light disturbed them.

Years of sightseers have labelled the stalactites and stalagmites of this remarkable place with many obvious names, like the Pulpit, the Organ Pipes, the Angel's Wings, the Canopied Throne, and the Madonna and Child, for it seems to be a common human desire to recognise in the inhuman architecture of Nature some resemblance to the work of man.

The time taken by water to scoop out the caverns can, I suppose, be estimated by a scientist. First, rain water bearing carbonic acid soaked into the rock, eating away the carbonate of lime and making a cavity that continued to enlarge as the process of infiltration continued for hundreds of thousands of years. The awesomeness of the caves is not, in my opinion, lessened by the Drury Lane transformations which leap to view every time the electric lights are switched on; I think these give the spectator a better idea of the riot of shape and colour created with an utter disregard of time or criticism. The very act of descending into a cave, as into a tomb, is in itself frightening, which is probably why visitors are so ready to assert themselves in banter and cheer themselves with fancied resemblances to things of their own world.

§ 9

The falling of rain and the misty hills increased the inevitable resemblance to Scotland. Miserable natives—for what can look more miserable than a black skin on a wet day?—moved sack-covered through the storm; dense woodlands climbed the hillsides; brown water came tumbling through ferns; and the storm clouds grew greyer with the promise of more rain to come.

Gazing disconsolately from heights where I had promised to pause and admire the view, I saw nothing but a ragged mist moving over a hill a hundred yards away.

No wonder English people and particularly Scots have found themselves at home at George and Knysna—to which I was now going—for in all Africa there can surely be nothing more like a wet day in the Highlands than this Cape drizzle. Had the rain descended savagely and flooded a few towns, or had it been accompanied by a hurricane which lifted off a few roofs, it would have been more in keeping with my idea of African weather.

Turning a corner, I nearly ran down the most sinister figure in South Africa. He wears a tight, grey cut-away coat, black knee-breeches, and flesh-coloured hose. He lifts his long thin legs slowly and apparently rheumatically. A crest of feathers on his head reminded people a century or two ago of quill pens, so they called him the secretary bird.

He looks like the spirit of Eighteenth Century sin incarnate: a senile rake, the wicked earl of melodrama, a monk of Medmenham, or maybe a corrupt old lord chamberlain stealing with a diabolic grin down palace corridors. Yet I am told that these shocking looks belie the secretary bird, who, when tamed, can become an engaging pet; though it must be rather like having Mephistopheles about the house!

When fighting the snakes he loves to eat, he dances round them, warding them off with out-spread wings, and I have heard that he will fly into the air with his victim and, releasing it, dash it to death on the rocks below.

When I reached the hotel at the Wilderness, which welcomes honeymoon couples from all parts of the Union and beyond, I saw groups of storm-bound people sitting at their morning tea, gazing into a garden blazing with wet geraniums. In front of them were sandhills and the sea. Like so many South African hotels, this was surrounded by pleasant rondavels. I should have explained long ago that a rondavel is a type of hut peculiar to South Africa, a circular, thatched European version of the Kaffir hut, and fitted with windows. Groups of them, sometimes electrically lit and with wash-basins and running water, are often built in hotel gardens, and the guests sleep in them. They are roomy and comfortable, and in a hot country infinitely more agreeable than a stuffy hotel bedroom.

When the sun came out, the Wilderness fulfilled all that I had heard in Cape Town about its beauty. It is one of those places which seem created by Nature and the hand of man for honeymoon couples. Why the Wilderness should have been called by such an unsuitable name was explained to me by a resident. In 1835 a young woman in Cape Town agreed to marry a man if he would take her away into the wilderness. He promised to do so. He then bought an estate in this delectable district and called it the Wilderness. Legend does not record what the lady said, and it is surely a reprehensible story for a honeymoon resort to perpetuate! It is also, I might add, an admirable example of what the Afrikaner admiringly terms slimmigheid or slimness.

Beyond the Wilderness are several lochs or vleis, one after the other, where hosts of water-fowl were swimming. I thought this part of the Cape unusually rich in bird life, or they may have just come out to enjoy the " good rains ". I noticed many kinds of birds I had not seen before, and wished I knew their names. You can pick a flower or a leaf and look it up in a book and learn its name, but it is difficult to identify anything as elusive as a bird, especially as bird illustrations are so optimistically coloured that they always appear to represent some more brilliant species than the one you are looking for.

As I came over the hill into Knysna and ran beside the loch, I saw the little town I had expected, where, in spite of poinsettia and bougainvillea, I was again reminded of Scotland. It was therefore hardly a surprise to be met at the hotel by a Fraser.

I told him that in the course of the past few days I had seen seven Glencoes and a couple of Killiecrankies.

" Aye ", he smiled, " and there was a man called Duthie who bought land here years ago because it reminded him of Loch Lomond."

§ 10

Knysna is famous for its sea loch and its fishing, for its boating, for the freedom of its open-air life, but, above all, for the mighty forest where the last members of a tribe of wild elephants, said to be the largest elephants in the world, still live.

I had been out round and about this forest all day with a local driver. He showed me dense jungles where immense trees created a gloom shot with spears of sunlight. The undergrowth was impenetrable, and creeping plants covered the tree trunks with tough tendrils, as if trying to pull them down to destruction. Birds called in the cool greenness, but were rarely seen. Only now and again did we come across a woodcutters' path which enabled us to walk some way into the forest; and then the silence and the feeling of being enclosed, as if the trees had moved to trap us when our backs were turned, were unpleasantly eerie. I was looking all the time for snakes. There was not a moss-covered branch or a swinging tendril that escaped my suspicion. I had never before been in a jungle like this, for the Knysna Forest is a hostile piece of the primeval world. The things that grow there, falling and rotting age after age, have made coal. I understood why, when so much of the world was like this, primitive people lived on downs and high places, where they could at least see what was coming.

My companion was full of stories about the elephants. The forest is Government property, and the last of the herd are protected. They have perfect freedom to roam about and frighten the lives out of woodcutters and tourists, who sometimes encounter them on a road in the dusk. But apparently they are not so dangerous as the ostrich! At Oudtshorn I heard several stories of men who had been killed by ostriches, but the Knysna elephants do not apparently kill people, or, if they do, it is kept very dark; instead they appear suddenly and terrify them out of their wits.

There was once a man in the depth of the forest, with an ox-wagon which he was loading with wood. Suddenly there was a terrible roar and a trampling, and small trees snapped like twigs as a gigantic bull elephant pushed his way forward and stood watching, with his ears fanning slowly back and forth. The oxen panicked, and the man had the presence of mind to free them from the wagon before he took to his heels. While ostrich stories generally end up in the hospital or the cemetery, there is no real end to these elephant stories! What happened? Did the elephant charge the wagon and trample it underfoot, or did it merely go on looking? I do not know. It is not recorded. So the elephants of the Knysna Forest just haunt the place like enormous ghosts, and I suppose people are too frightened to wait and see what happens next.

In 1885 there were about six hundred elephants in the forest, but now there are believed to be only two bulls, three cows, and a calf or two. The biggest bull is said to be a colossal apparition, fourteen feet to the shoulder, with tusks that protrude for ten feet on each side of his trunk. The elephants move about chiefly in the dusk and after dark. They migrate from point to point of the forest, sometimes scaring the wits out of a woodman by invading a clearing and stamping down a mealie patch in the middle of the night. They live on grass, leaves, and ferns, and the forest is full of fallen trees which they have pushed over to get at the milky creepers. A cow elephant calves only once in five or seven years, and when a calf is born the parents gather bushes and form a nest, known as an elephant couch, in which the calf is kept for ten days: but for some reason there has been high mortality among the calves, and many a time in recent years their dead bodies have been found lying in pools of water.

We went to high places in the forest where I could look across eighty miles of trees and mountains to the Tzitzikama Mountains, which are an eastward extension of the Outeniquas. Then we went down into the heart of the forest to the great yellow-wood tree, which is a hundred and forty feet high and twenty-six feet in circumference, and is said to be one thousand and seven hundred years old. This is the giant of Knysna, and everyone goes to see it. If its supposed age is correct, it began its life in the year A.D. 246, when Philip the Arabian was Emperor of Rome, when St Fabian, who was martyred under Decius, was Pope, when Britain was still a remote Province of the Roman Empire, and when the toleration of Christianity was still sixty years off—a truly astonishing thought! I wonder if there is any more ancient living thing in the world.

Other massive and ancient inhabitants of the forest are the stinkwood trees. That horrible name greets the visitor the moment he arrives in South Africa. He sees it in furniture shops, in the advertisement columns of newspapers, and his acquaintances show him with pride rare old stinkwood cabinets, chests, and tables; for this wood is the mahogany of South Africa.

I cannot imagine why a pleasanter name than stinkwood has not been found for a wood which people take so eagerly into their homes. If it really stank, one could understand it, but the only smell I have been able to detect is that of furniture polish. I am told, however, that when freshly felled the tree does smell, but, even so, surely it is rather unnecessary to carry a woodsman's woe into every drawing-room in the Union?

Throughout the forest you come across the most incredible shacks and hovels, made of bits of wood and tin and rag. Like an air-raid shelter beneath a mansion, they show to what depths Europeans can descend in unpleasant circumstances. A native hut would be a palace compared with some of these awful shacks, which are the homes of " Poor Whites ".

This term, though not as contemptuous as the American " white trash ", is the South African equivalent, and denotes those people of European origin who have descended in the social and economic scale.   In Europe and America a skilled worker, falling upon evil times, may descend into the ranks of unskilled labour without loss of prestige, and exist there for a while before climbing out again.   But even if a Poor White blacked his face (which is the last thing on earth he would do!) he could not work side by side with Kaffirs, because the wages would not keep him. Therefore, rather like the genteel poor of a more class-conscious age in England, his lot is to starve in spiritual pride.

I was told that the Poor Whites of Knysna include numbers of people with British names who no longer speak English but Afrikaans.   They are assumed to be the descendants of the servants, grooms, housemaids, and so forth of the English squires who settled in this district over a century ago.   Names like Steel, Monk, Roberts, McCarthy, and McAlpine are to be found among them.

I wanted to speak to some of them and to see inside their shacks, but I was told that, like the poor everywhere, they are naturally suspicious of visitors and questions. Nevertheless, in a clearing we came to the kind of house that Walt Disney might have built in a dense forest. You have the same effect when a snow house encounters a sharp thaw, which slants everything at peculiar angles but at the same time gives it extreme rigidity.

Squalid as the house was, the surroundings were lovely. Vegetables and flowers grew in the little garden patch. The forest trees surrounded it like a hedge. Instead of the gnome one might have expected, the door opened and out came a little old Englishman with a face like a crab apple. His name was English, his face was English, his handshake and smile were English, but he could not speak a word of English. My companion addressed him in Afrikaans and asked his family history. All he knew was that a hundred years ago his father had left London and had come to Knysna, where he had been born. He had spent a lifetime in the Forest as a wood-cutter. He was over seventy. He had a son who was a woodsman and another who was "in the railways", and a granddaughter working in a chocolate factory in East London. So it would seem that now and then the Poor White is able to climb out.

While we were talking, his old wife emerged, and I noticed that she had tidied herself up to meet visitors, and I admired her for it. Her father had been English, but her mother was an Afrikaner. Like her husband, she spoke only Afrikaans. She took me round to the hen-house and showed me her chickens, and in a clearing were two cows. She insisted upon giving me a little bunch of flowers from her garden.

I suppose these people were the better class of Poor White. I did not like to ask if I might go into the house, but I managed to steal a glance. Everything was worn out and broken, but there were a few photographs on the walls, a few broken chairs and a table. There was something heroic in their racial purity and in the fact that they still kept up some kind of standard. In a city such a place would have been terrible ;

in the country, where extreme poverty is never completely squalid, it was, at the best, a haphazard camping out.

It was almost dark as we turned to go back to Knysna. My companion reverted to elephants and wild animals. There are wild boars in the Forest, he told me, also baboons and grey monkeys. Lynxes expelled from the Little Karoo have exterminated the blue buck, but there are still some bush buck.

Above the sound of the engine we heard a terrific crash ahead. The driver stopped immediately.

" Elephants ! " I said, jokingly.

" Yes, elephants all right ! " whispered the driver, turning a serious face to me.

It was now pitch dark. We had stopped on a bend, and the headlights shot into the Forest, revealing vast tree-trunks and white, tangled masses of monkey rope. I felt foolishly brave with the courage of ignorance, and suggested that we might leave the car and have a look round.

" No, no, no ! " said the driver. " We must go on, but— listen ! "

Again we heard, about a hundred yards or so away, more splintering crashes and the sound of a body, or bodies, pressing through the undergrowth.

" They're crossing the road," whispered the driver, and, putting the car into reverse, we went back some way and again stopped to listen. I now began to feel less courageous. I began to see elephants everywhere. Suppose they should come lumbering along the road towards us, what should we do ? Plunge into the forest, which was probably at that hour crawling with snakes, or stay to be trampled to death ?

" They're gone ! " whispered the driver ; and it was like hearing the " All clear ". He stealthily advanced.

" Look ! " he cried when we had travelled a few hundred yards, " the spoor ! "

And there, sure enough, was evidence that we had not been dreaming.

K

§ 11

Early one morning I ran out to the Heads, which is the name of the narrow rock channel through which the sea enters the Knysna lagoon.

A couple were camping in a tent within a few yards of the water. A girl in a sweater and a pair of shorts was frying breakfast on a paraffin stove, and a young man, who had propped a piece of mirror on a rock, was having a painful shave in cold water. It was one of those uncomfortable moments which are remembered with a glow of happiness twenty years after.

Knysna, with the grey lagoon in front of it and the Outeniquas at the back, looked so like—but I will not continue to make this comparison. This was South Africa ! And as if in answer to my thoughts, out of a gate came a herd of cows driven by a little boy like a black bat. He was naked except for a triangular sack from which his thin black arms protruded ; with his black legs running and the sack flapping, he might have flittered from the roof of the Bridal Chamber in the Cango Caves.

I went into the little church of St George, which lies opposite the hotel, and wandered round the graveyard, noting that John Benn, born at Deptford in 1812—probably a shipbuilder—had died at Knysna in 1877, and another Englishman born in the same year at Bristol, and perhaps also to do with the sea, had died there in 1885.

At the edge of the forest I found the grave of the most mysterious immigrant South Africa has ever received. It was a neglected grave. An agapanthus grew upon it. Oak trees and two pines stood guard over it. On the tombstone was the inscription : " In memory of George Rex esquire, proprietor and founder of Knysna. Died 3rd April 1839."

This mysterious person arrived in Cape Town about the year 1796, and was said to bear an unmistakable resemblance to the reigning king, George III. He was given the position of Marshal of the Vice Admiralty Court and a salary of £1,000 a year, which made him one of the most important officials in the Government. As mysterious as Rex himself is, I think, the fact that he was in Cape Town throughout Lady Anne Barnard's residence, and though she must have met him often, she never once mentions his name in her writings.

In 1804 Rex is said to have trekked to Knysna with sixteen wagons and a hundred slaves. There he acquired a large estate, upon which he lived until his death thirty-five years later. He lived like a well-born English squire. He possessed objects which inferred a prosperous English background, yet nobody knew anything about him, or of his life before he came to the Cape; and he himself observed silence. In later life, it is recorded that he developed the habit of walking about his garden at Knysna with his hands behind his back—just as George III used to do—pausing to address invisible generals and princes.

The story was subsequently spread, and is firmly believed by many in South Africa to-day, that George Rex was the eldest son of George III by a pretty Quakeress named Hannah Lightfoot. Some historians doubt the story; others believe it; the light skirmishers of history, the writers of Court scandals and so forth, have revelled in it. But none has ever been able to solve the mystery.

The first serious hint in print of an old love affair, when George III was the Prince of Wales, appeared five years before his death in the *Historical Memoirs* of Sir Nathaniel Wraxall, which are a mine of information upon the history of the Eighteenth Century. Wraxall, praising the old king for his blameless life, says (in a jovial boys will be boys manner) that stories were once " generally circulated " of " his attachment to a young woman, a Quaker ", and, though " probably well founded ", were, because of His Majesty's model character, nothing but " innocent gallantry ".

The only other reference during the King's life was in a little guide to Knole House, in Kent, published in 1817, in which the author, describing the portrait of a lady in white satin, says, " This is the fair Quakeress noticed by His Majesty when Prince of Wales ".

So that while the King was still alive two artless references were made to a romance of his youth with which it was assumed people were familiar.

But a suggestion that the affair was more serious than Wraxall had implied was delivered by none other that Dr Johnson's friend, Mrs Piozzi, formerly Mrs Thrale, then aged seventy-four. She knew Wraxall and had lived through the events he described, and she went through his book, annotating it and making her own comments in the margin; and these notes she delivered to her executors. They were published in 1861 by Hayward in his *Autobiography of Mrs Piozzi*, and they were so highly thought of that they are now incorporated in the best edition of Wraxall. Her note on the reference to George III and the Quakeress was just this: " Her son by him is yet alive ".

Mrs Thrale was one of the notable women of her time, and she knew the history of her age and its scandals as well as anyone then living. There seems to be no reason why she should have added that note unless she had good reason to know it to be true.

Ten years after the King's death the Hannah Lightfoot story blew up in earnest, not only in England, but in America. An amazing series of claims were made, generally by the underground movement of historical research, in books entitled *Great Passions*, and such like, that Hannah Lightfoot had been abducted by the Prince; that he had married her a few years before his marriage to Queen Charlotte; that she spent her entire life in not unhappy seclusion; that among the children of the marriage was the eldest son, George, who went to America and fought as a royalist in the War of Independence, and may be the George Rex who arrived later at the Cape.

To unravel this story is rather like trying to complete a jig-saw puzzle from which most of the key pieces are missing.

It would be profoundly interesting to know who George Rex really was, and I must say that Mrs Thrale's comment on Wraxall lingers in the mind. That Mr Rex lived a happy and abundant life at Knysna is well known. His descendants are still distinguished residents in the district, and many of his slaves, as the custom was, assumed their master's name.

When I was in a chemist's shop in Knysna, a little coloured, barefoot girl was standing at the counter with a piece of paper which was probably a prescription.

"What's your name?" asked the chemist.

"Rex," she whispered, with a roll of her great eyes.

§ 12

One night in the hotel Mr Fraser and I were talking about South Africa. He was saying that if a young man is ready to take off his coat and roll up his sleeves and work, well, there's nothing to stop him. What a country! What a grand country! He had come to it as a boy without a penny in the world and he had worked while others had played, and—well, well, what a grand country! . . .

Then, of course, we began talking about Inverness and the Fraser country and the Highlands of Scotland.

"My great-great-grandfather took part in the storming of the Heights of Abraham," he said. "I can tell you a story about it that you won't find in any book. . . .

"The Frasers, as you remember, were 'out' with Bonnie Prince Charlie in the 'forty-five. When it was over, my great-great-grandfather, like lots of other Highlanders, had to fly to France. Simon, Lord Lovat, our chief, was executed on Tower Hill, and his son, young Simon Lovat, was captured and put into Edinburgh Castle. Then the English, as they always do, began to make friends with their old enemies and the Highlanders began to creep back to Scotland as the chiefs of the clans were pardoned.

"Well, at this time the American war broke out and young Simon Lovat was pardoned and made a colonel in the British Army. He asked permission to go back to his father's estates —for they had not yet been returned to him—and raise recruits for the war. And, man, they let him go! Now just you imagine it. There he was, the Master of Lovat, the chief of the clan, back on his own land! Can you not imagine how they would come over the hills from every little but and ben to see him and shake him by the hand. Well, he unfurled the standard, and in a fortnight he'd enlisted fifteen hundred men!

And among them was my great-great-grandfather, who, as I've said, had been in exile in France.

" They called them the Fraser Fencibles, and they marched away with young Simon Lovat at their head, and they marched all the way from Inverness to Greenock and were shipped to Canada. Then they were with Wolfe at Quebec, and they had to storm the Heights of Abraham. It was at night and dark. Seventeen hundred men got into the boats and dropped down the St Lawrence to the place where they had to climb the cliffs. As they got out, and were getting ready to climb, Simon Lovat passed the word down that he wanted the man who stole a cheese from the Tower of Fairburn. Now, this was a tower near the Muir of Ord, very difficult to climb, where cheese used to be kept in old times. But the man who had climbed it and got a cheese was my great-great-grandfather!

" Simon Lovat told him to go first because a man who could climb the Tower of Fairburn could climb the Heights of Abraham. And he did! He led the way up the cliffs. And, d'ye know why the Frasers passed up so quietly, and went through the French sentries? Because my great-great-grandfather could speak French and knew the password! And that story I've often heard my grandfather tell, who had it straight from his grandfather. . . ."

CHAPTER FIVE

I go to Port Elizabeth, where I remember the 1820 Settlers. Here I am shown the snakes of South Africa. In Grahamstown I see a cathedral, a university, many schools, and a museum. At Bathurst I encounter South Africa's most English village.

§ 1

RAIN fell during the night, and in the morning the dust had been laid. A glorious South African day was beginning: the sky was clear of cloud, the trees were refreshed, the warm earth breathed contentment, and the mealies lifted their green leaves and took heart. Everywhere was that cheerful and inspiring South African light.

I left Knysna in the early morning, and travelled eastward along a road that was never far from the coast. After a time I saw around me the first hint of a more tropical land. There were ravines and gorges, and woods flickering with sunlight where monkey ropes were flung from tree to tree, and I saw forests so dense that the light hesitated and stopped in the first few yards and I gazed, as through the open west door of a great church, into dim, green naves. I saw wild bananas and wild grapes. There was a hill covered with pink Watsonia, and there were acres of gladioli.

Most spectacular of all South African flowers is the national flower, the protea, which in shape is rather like a giant fir cone, its petals vividly coloured. It grows all over the Cape and I believe its name refers to the wonderful variations shown by this family, for Proteus, the sea god, could change his form at will. The protea is unknown in Europe, but grows in South America and Australia, which gives colour to Wegener's displacement theory that millions of years ago Africa and South America were joined together and drifted apart like floating icebergs. I was interested to see that Dr Hutchinson of Kew believes in this theory and gives several maps in his *Botanist in Southern Africa*, showing how neatly the western coastline of Africa will fit into the eastern coastline of South America.

The Groote River was as dark as a Highland burn. It came sliding out of green gorges towards the sea. Then I came to the Blaauwkrans Forest and to a pass which went spiralling down with an airy nothingness on the outer edge. Far below were the distant heads of trees. Even a solitary aloe on the side of the road might have given some comfort, but there was nothing but a long drop. From that jungle, which smelt of hot, wet leaves, I climbed to a higher road, and away to my left the Tzitzikama Mountains were lying blue and smooth against the sky. Tzitzikama . . . What a word it is! A man at Knysna told me it is a Hottentot word which describes the sound of sparkling waters.

I passed through glorious and powerful scenery where dark pines and black firs were standing in great ridges and marching over mountains like the lances of Charlemagne. And when the road straightened, there was mile upon mile of bright pink Watsonia, just sheets of it, laughing in the sun. So I went through Humansdorp to Jeffrey's Bay and its vast sandy beach which slopes to the sea.

There were three native boys baiting fish-hooks with gory strips of octopus.

"What do you catch?" I asked them.

They grinned up at me.

"Kabeljou, baas!" said one.

"An' steenbras, baas," said another.

Then at my feet I saw a lovely shell. I picked it up and put it in my pocket. A few yards away was an even better one. I noticed that the tide, as it went out, left behind hundreds upon hundreds of shells of all shapes and sizes; and I was soon half a mile away, picking up these exquisite little things and rejecting them when I came across a better specimen.

Shell-gathering is the most insidious of pursuits. It is sheer acquisitiveness, because, at the back of your mind, you know perfectly well that the moment will come, either before you have left the beach or later on in the hotel, when you will abandon the lot. But how grand it was to walk on the firm sand, with the Indian Ocean and its line of surf only a few yards away. Sometimes a wave would come creaming in-shore and catch my feet with a sudden access of energy, and then, retreating, leave behind some superb specimen, for which, who knows, conchologists would give their ears.

And what a pity it seemed to me that certain young people far away in England, who would so highly have applauded my actions, were not there to share that innocent dissipation and to urge me to still more intensive saturation.

§ 2

I had a room in a large seaside hotel at Port Elizabeth, or " P.E.", as everybody in South Africa calls this town. Look-ing from the window I could see tram-cars passing and re-passing along the front, the Indian Ocean beyond, and nearer the pendulous nests of weaver birds hanging like coconuts from the branches of trees on the hotel drive.

These birds are small and finch-like, and the nests they weave so exquisitely, and hang so skilfully in order to be out of the reach of snakes, are entered from underneath, and some have a small entrance hall or neck which projects from the base for an inch or so.

I had often seen such nests elsewhere in the Cape, and had accepted them as part of the landscape until I found an English translation of *The Soul of the White Ant* by the Afrikaans writer, Eugene M. Marais. The author, writing about the instinct of birds and animals, says that once a pair of weaver birds were taken into captivity and denied any weaving material. They were evidently distressed when nesting time arrived, but made the best of it and hatched chicks without a nest. The same thing happened for several generations. Then weaving material was introduced, and the first thing the birds did, although many times removed from a weaving generation, was to weave a nest and suspend it!

It was fascinating to watch those active little architects entering and leaving their snake-proof houses.

Port Elizabeth is a thriving and energetic town. The Edward-ian town hall and the main street are so English that I felt I had often seen them before. Every one in " P.E." is proud that the history of the town goes back for a century and a quarter. And look what we have done in that time, is the implication. And it is astonishing to reflect that the bustling life of a first-class port and an expanding manufacturing town has grown up in that short space of time. As recently as the eighteen eighties prints showed passengers coming ashore at Port Elizabeth on the backs of natives, and now there are magnificent docks which can take the largest merchant ships of to-day.

Port Elizabeth flings itself with energetic gaiety over five and a half miles of Algoa Bay. There are factories. There are sites for new factories. There are native locations and coloured locations and housing schemes. There are suburbs, golf courses, parks, and bathing beaches. There are more than a hundred and thirty-five thousand people living in Port Elizabeth, half of them white, the other half black, coloured, and Asiatic. And this began with the landing of the 1820 Settlers. Who were they?

As the three-masted ships sailed down the Thames on those icy December days in 1819, the settlers, old and young, wrapped in their overcoats, their shawls, plaids, and blankets, gathered upon the decks to say farewell to England. Upon such a moment the heart is filled to overflowing, and though it may have seemed that the land they were leaving did not need them or offer them a future, few eyes could have been dry as the ships moved away from the sights and sounds of home.

The England they were leaving was the England of Robert Owen and William Cobbett, of Wellington, Peel, and Canning, of Wilberforce and the humanitarians, of James Watt's separate condenser and Hargreaves' " Spinning Jenny "; the England in which George Stephenson was designing locomotives, but had not yet made the *Rocket*; in which the Royal Mails were carried in gleaming red coaches drawn by glossy teams of four; the England of the new Regent's Street and the Brighton Pavilion; of the Prince Regent's waistcoats; of Beau Brummell, Grimaldi, and Vestris; an

England in which poor old George III, deaf, blind, and white-bearded, was cut off by years of gentle madness from a changed and bewildering world.

In this England high society numbered about six hundred, and the great mansions round the park were still served by powdered flunkeys in plush knee-breeches, while coaches with footmen mounted behind drew up before their exclusive portals. There were nearly fourteen million other people in Britain, but only about one hundred and sixty thousand had a vote. Power was in the hands of the few, and society was a rigid pyramid of caste.

It was the London of the Corinthian and the Bow Street runner; the London in which Tom, Jerry, and Bob overturned night watchmen's boxes, attended sanguinary prize-fights, explored low drinking-dens in their well-cut riding-coats and tall hats, standing among a hideous but unmalicious assembly of cut-purses, chimney sweeps, and sluts; an England of brilliant salons and squalid slums, of exclusive clubs and thieves' kitchens.

Old London Bridge still opposed the bulk of its mediæval piers to the river's flow, causing frosts and frost fairs; the Fleet Prison was still full of debtors, but public hangings were no longer witnessed at Tyburn and gas lamps were still a novelty in the Strand. A new and classical London in stucco had arisen from Piccadilly to Regent's Park, but one step from the columned terraces led to a warren in whose cellars the high-waymen of the last century were still remembered with affection. Something like country air still blew through London. Thousands of cows were milked in the capital every day, and milk was carried round from door to door by buxom girls in kirtled skirts with a yoke upon their shoulders.

Beyond the wealth and poverty of the capital, and the queer mixture of town and country that it was, stretched the roads upon which the indignant Cobbett rode, leading to rural villages and mansions and to red brick towns whose factory smoke drifted through the autumn woods. Trout were caught in those days, and pheasants shot, within sight of factory chimneys, as the new world gained stealthily upon the old. In some country houses old men lived who still wore wigs and knee-breeches and enjoyed Virgil and Horace in Latin; in others were to be found the new squires, who counted their wealth, not in cattle or in crops, but in machinery and production.

Two Englands lived side by side: the old England of church, mansion, and cottage, where men still stood awed and respectful before bloodstock, and the new England of coal, iron, and cotton, whose inhabitants, no longer rooted to the earth, were projected by the still novel art of reading into violent discontent. The sound of their riots and the noise of smashed machinery penetrated to the capital, where the Lords and Commons were reminded of those old cries of Liberty, Equality, and Fraternity which England had fought for twenty years to silence.

How strange and incalculable it was, with Napoleon, dressed in civilian clothes, safely stowed away on St Helena, that peace and plenty and the expected return to the good old days had not come. In 1819 England was learning that peace following a long war is more difficult to understand and to bear than war itself. Factories were closed. Prices were high. The unemployed multiplied. The veterans of Trafalgar were joined on the kerbstones by the veterans of Waterloo. The whole balance and harmony of life, as it had been known in agricultural days, were gone. The violent mechanics and artisans of the time were unrecognisable as the sons of the docile cowmen and carters of a previous generation.

It was natural that an age which still fled in any physical ailment to leeches and blood-letting should have considered emigration. The population had doubled itself in sixty years. The country was too small for it. Get rid of people! Reduce the pressure! Send some to Canada, some to the Cape! And all over Britain humble people, who could see no future for themselves and their families, and others who did not like the signs of the times, began to think of taking up their roots and becoming colonists.

The 1820 Settlers were part of a larger scheme of assisted emigration. So many people were fleeing to the United States from the post-war depression in England (in 1819, two hundred a week), that the Government decided to direct the flow to countries within the Empire. Canada and the Cape were then the only suitable places. It was rather cynically pointed out by the Cape enthusiasts that a block of British settlers was urgently required on the eastern frontier as a defence against the Bantu, and men like Wilberforce, who were already the keepers of the English conscience, were given hair-raising and exaggerated accounts of the Dutch cruelty to the Hottentots in a successful attempt to gain their powerful support.

Glowing descriptions of the Cape as a land of golden opportunity raised the spirits of thousands of poor and discontented people all over Britain. Cruikshank took a more cynical view of the scheme and drew a couple of ferocious cartoons, in one of which the settlers were being eaten alive by savages, with the assistance of cobras and a boa constrictor! But this did not daunt the spirit of the emigrants.

So many applications were received by the Colonial Office that the Government decided not to give free passages to single individuals, but only to parties of not fewer than ten. Each party had to be recruited and organised by a leader, known as " the head of the party ", who was responsible for discipline, finance, and so forth. Every individual had to hand over ten pounds, which would be returned to him in South Africa. The Government offered a hundred acres of land to each person.

Groups were recruited all over the country, many of them much larger than the minimum. Some leaders were peasants and mechanics, others were ex-officers and discontented gentlemen who wished to try their fortunes in a new land. Among the gentry were some who had recruited as members of their group their own servants and retainers, so that they moved out as a self-contained country house unit on the old English pattern.

The majority of the settlers came from London and the cities, though there was a good sprinkling of farm workers, craftsmen, and artisans. That many of the settlers were not agriculturalists probably did not matter in 1820, when most people were only a generation or so removed from the land. Over eighty thousand British people applied to go to the Cape, but only three thousand, four hundred and eighty-seven were selected.

So the 1820 Settlers sailed through the ice and sleet of a hard winter and away from a troubled land. They were departing from it at the precise moment when the curtain was falling upon the Eighteenth Century. The riots and the cries for " radical reform " were not, as the Duke of Wellington may have thought, the sound of approaching tumbrils: they were the first rather unseemly sounds of the English Middle Class.

Although no one knew it, nor would they have believed it in that time of confusion, the future was really quite well planned. As the ships stole out of the Thames that December, there was already, in Kensington Palace, " a fine healthy child " of seven months named Victoria, and there were two school-boys, one aged fifteen at Walthamstow, and the other aged ten near Liverpool. The first was an exotic boy called Benjamin Disraeli, and the other was William Ewart Gladstone.

The voyage was not too bad. There were one or two accidents at the outset. One ship went aground on the Good-wins, but was refloated just in time; another went ashore opposite Greenwich Hospital. Off the Cape Verde Islands a ship had the distinction of being mistaken for a pirate and received a shot in the carpenter's cabin from a shore battery.

The settlers were more than three months at sea. There were outbreaks of measles, whooping cough, and smallpox, and there were a few deaths. There were also several births. A small party of Irishmen enlivened the voyage with violent quarrels; in another ship the dissension, though equally violent, was theological; and it was perhaps only natural that in others people from a country that was seething with argument, discontent, and class hatred should have rebelled against their conductors and have wished to regroup themselves under different leaders.

But there were happy, unforgettable days too, days that the Settlers must often have remembered in the future, when drought had wiped out their year's work, or when rains had washed away their huts, or when someone's corpse had been found gashed by assegais and torn by wild animals. Those were the days when the ships rode becalmed upon an enamelled ocean, and from little boats fishermen dropped their hooks into sunlit water. Those who had never left London must have seen with amazement the island of St Jago riding upon the sea, whose natives were willing to barter for an old coat two hundred oranges, twelve coconuts, and a goat and her kid.

The voyagers drew nearer to reality as ship after ship, at intervals of days or weeks, came into False Bay, and the settlers gathered on deck to gaze appalled at what seemed to them the wild and barbarous mountains of their new home-land. After taking on water and food, the ships sailed round to Algoa Bay and to the hill above a beach which was not yet Port Elizabeth.

From their anchorage in the bay the Settlers looked ashore to a canvas camp. There were tents and Highlanders from the fort, ox wagons, Hottentots, and Boer farmers. The first to land were towed towards the surf in lighters, then carried ashore on the backs of sturdy Highlanders or natives. Waiting to greet them was a bereaved, kindly man, Sir Rufane Donkin, the acting governor, who had assembled every spare tent he could put his hands on for their accommodation. He was then forty-seven years of age, and only two years previously had lost his young wife, Elizabeth, from fever in India.

Among those who landed at that time were some who were to give their names to South Africa's history—Ayliff, Bowker, Daniell, Chase, Cock, Currie, Godlonton, Southey, Scanlan, Shepstone, and Shaw.

So it happened that in the first months of 1820 South Africa received her third injection of good European blood. The Dutch had brought with them the intolerance of the Seventeenth Century and their own innate republicanism, the Huguenots had brought religious fervour and a French liveliness and intelligence, and now from Britain, well meaningly disguised as agriculturists, came men of commercial energy and enterprise who brought to their new home the love of a man for his wife, while, in the secret places of their hearts, lived the loyalty of a man for the mother who gave him birth.

§ 3

Among the most interesting of the 1820 Settlers was Thomas Pringle. He was the son of a Roxburghshire farmer and, because of an injury in childhood, was a cripple and walked with the help of crutches. He was a poet, journalist, and writer. He was temperamental and subject to religious melancholy and to equally powerful attacks of cheerful enthusiasm. Walter Scott, who was his idol, considered him conceited; but then Scott was a Conservative, and Pringle was full of the cocky Radicalism of the new age.

Pringle was thirty when he set sail for South Africa as group-leader to a Scottish contingent of ten, which included his wife, his father, and his brothers. They settled on a grant of land in the valley of the Baavians River, and called it Glen Lynden, a name which it bears to this day.

Pringle was the first South African poet, and though some may consider his poetry badly haunted by Sir Walter, his verses have considerable vigour and charm, due almost entirely to their unusual inspiration. He was also one of the founders of the South African Press; for it is extraordinary to realise that no independent Press had been allowed at the Cape from 1652 until Pringle's time. His best work, however, is *A Narrative of a Residence in South Africa*, in which he described the experiences of the 1820 Settlers in the most graphic and interesting manner.

The camp at Algoa Bay must have been a surprising sight. Boer farmers with their ox teams and wagons had been provided to take the settlers to their locations, and Pringle conveys in the most admirable way how strange it was for the Londoners and others to go off into the unknown to the creak of wagons, the crack of whips, and the wild shouting of the Hottentots. He gives one or two fine little glimpses.

"The boors", he writes, "unslung their huge guns (or *roers*, as they called them) from the tilts of the wagons, and placed them against a magnificent evergreen bush, in whose shelter, with a fire at their feet, they had fixed their place of repose. Here, untying each his leathern scrip, they produced their provisions for supper, consisting chiefly of dried bullock's flesh, which they seasoned with a moderate *zoopje*, or dram, of colonial *brandewyn*, from a huge horn slung by each man in his wagon beside his powder flask. . . . The Dutch-African boors, most of them men of almost gigantic size, sat apart in their bushy *bield* in aristocratic exclusiveness, smoking their huge pipes with self-satisfied complacency."

Such references to the Boers in Pringle's narrative are interesting. Not only are they a welcome change from the intolerance of such writers as Barrow, but they show how ready the Boers were to offer the hand of friendship to the British newcomers. There are several other excellent descriptions of the well-to-do patriarchal Boer, with his flocks and herds and his family prayers, which both slaves and Hottentots attended; and the impression given is that of a race of frontier warriors who, with a Bible in one hand and a gun in the other, had built up an aristocracy in the wilderness.

Pringle's description of the foundation of his own little colony is full of interest. They experience the perils of the wilds, they encounter the savage extremes of the South African climate, they learn the frontier ways, and it is good to add that, unlike many of their compatriots, those Scots eventually prospered.

Within two years Pringle left them for Cape Town, where he became sub-librarian to the Public Library. He wrote home to invite his friend James Fairburn to join him, and the two friends produced South Africa's first newspaper. Four years later Pringle, having fallen under the strong spell of Dr Philip, whose influence was so great upon the Colonial Office, returned to London, where the rest of his life was spent in the noble cause of the abolition of slavery.

The most interesting thing about the 1820 Settlers is the speed with which they began to look about for commercial openings, as though some of them had immediately summed up the situation and knew that if there were a future for them at all, it was in trade. There exists a notable document of the time called *The Diary of Harry Hastings*, in which the writer shows that the very same year they landed, stray Englishmen were trading not only with the native, but with the Boer. It is fascinating to read this early manifestation of the spirit

L

of enterprise which has led to the eminence of Port Elizabeth.

" This evening our company came together for the purpose of hearing from Robert Trumpet the news about his trip amongst the Dutch," writes the diarist. " ' Well,' said Bob, ' I am unable to tell you how anything can live up there, for there is no grass, and yet the sheep and cattle are very fat. . . . When you go to the place of the farmer, you go straight to the house, the farmer comes to the door and gives you permission to outspan. They always are willing. You then begin to loosen the oxen from the yoke, at which the Dutchman always comes to assist. When this is done you go in again, and the farmer's wife sends you a basin of tea—they call it " tea water ". Then commences the work of trade. You have a large mat and you spread all the wares on the mat. When this is done the whole of the family comes out to purchase. You first hear the price of the cattle, sheep, goats, soap, etc. As they select the goods you tell them the price. They take it, and it is booked in your memoranda book. After the purchase is made you generally make a present to the daughter or to the mistress. After this there come the slaves and the Hottentot servants, and they, too, purchase a good deal, for I have found on this journey that these black people have got lots of fine cattle, horses and sheep amongst the Dutch. . . . These Dutch people, I find, said Bob, are very religious, for as soon as the work is done the whole family have prayers, and the same in the morning before daylight. You get as much as you can eat and drink without paying, and after eating a hearty supper of fine fat mutton, you have a large soup plate full of milk and bread, as white as snow and as sweet as a nut. I do assure you they are a very good sort of people, and I think that those who trade amongst them will make a good thing of it.' "

How revealing it is to know that slaves and Hottentots were rich enough to " purchase a good deal ", which hardly agrees with the stories which more influential observers than poor Bob Trumpet were spreading in England about the Boer farmers and their down-trodden victims.

The little trade boom that followed the initial hardships of the settlers was shattered on the eve of Christmas, 1834, when, without warning, the Kaffirs carried out a cleverly planned war upon Albany. They attacked the settlement along its whole front from the Great Winterberg to the sea, burning and killing everything in their path. That was the Settlers' first taste of real frontier war, but not their last, thanks to the perverted sympathies of the Colonial Office. Nevertheless, in spite of all those trials and perils, the 1820 Settlers had struck root, not always in the soil of South Africa, but certainly in the towns; and to their courage and energy and that of their descendants, South Africa was indebted for a free Press, a more liberal Government, and a share in the commercial life of the future.

§ 4

I went to the hill overlooking Port Elizabeth to see the Donkin Memorial. It is a small brownstone pyramid standing side by side with a lighthouse. Sir Rufane Donkin, as a brass plate tells one, erected it as a memorial to Elizabeth his wife, " one of the most perfect of human beings ", after whom he named the town.

Elizabeth Donkin was the eldest daughter of Dr Markham, Dean of York. She was twenty-five when she married Donkin, who was forty-two, and on his way to take up a command at Madras. They went out together, but in three years Elizabeth died of a fever, leaving her husband with a son seven months old. This loss completely shattered him. He had his wife's heart removed and placed in an urn.

He was invalided to the Cape and was still on sick leave when he was asked to take over the Government of the Colony during Lord Charles Somerset's absence in England. South Africans of British origin will always think of him with affection because of his thoughtful and kindly welcome to their ancestors. He spent his retirement in London, and there he wrote several books, which can be found to-day in the Library of the British Museum. He became one of the original fellows of the Royal Geographical Society, and at the age of fifty-nine married again. His health broke down when he was in his late sixties, and, sad to say, he committed suicide at Southampton, and was buried in old St Pancras churchyard, in London, with the heart of his first wife, Elizabeth. This graveyard is now a small public garden and most of the bodies have been removed. A granite tombstone was erected here by Cecil Rhodes in memory of the Rhodes family, whose ancestors are said to have farmed land in the parish.

So Port Elizabeth owes its name to a woman whose bones lie in India and whose heart is in London, about whom nothing is now known except that she inspired an undying grief in her husband's breast. His little pyramid is merely a footnote now to her fame, for in the name of this town the memory of Elizabeth Donkin has been carried all over the world. To look down upon the port and to reflect that only yesterday, as time is counted, it was a lonely beach, is to understand the drive and power imparted to South Africa by the Settlers. Where their ancestors were carried pick-a-back through the surf, the modern Elizabethans have made a great harbour which thrusts an arm far out into the bay, and for miles around the once desolate landscape is covered with factories and pleasant suburbs.

Wool was the foundation of Port Elizabeth's fortunes. Ten years after the landing some enterprising settlers seized the chance that had been neglected by the Cape in the previous century and were soon exporting wool, not in large quantities, neither was it first-class wool, so they re-introduced the merino sheep. Then came mohair. The local goats were not good enough, so the silky Angora was procured.

Boots and shoes, motor-cars, chocolates, cement, wheat and flour milling, chemical laboratories, electric-light globes . . . so it goes on.

On the outskirts of the town an enormous area has been reserved for future factories. I motored over it with a man who already seemed to think they had been built.

" Pickles ! " he said, waving a hand towards a stricken mound.

" Tyres ! " he cried, indicating several empty acres.

" Electrical ! " he said, setting the car at a piece of waste ground. " I tell you this is the coming town of the Union.

Nothing can stop it! We've got everything! Labour! Electricity! Water! Transport! . . . Everything!"

He now charged a slight hill and pulled up.

" Come back in five years, and you won't recognise this spot!" he cried. " It's going ahead, and what's more, it's going to solve a heck of a lot of our troubles!"

" I always love to hear of troubles which can be solved," I said. " How is this?"

" Well, take the Poor White Problem . . ."

And as he told me all about it, I knew why it is that Port Elizabeth has grown, and continues to grow. We then went to several of the native and coloured housing estates. Everything in South Africa, from a cactus to a plumber, casts a black shadow. A white builder sometimes has three or four black shadows; a carpenter usually one, which carries his saw; a plumber one, which carries his bag; and so on. Cities, towns, and villages each cast their black shadows, known as " locations ", or places where the natives are located for the purposes of sleep.

Most of the locations seemed to me to exhibit great earnestness and forethought on the part of the municipality, which was wisely spending a great deal of money in converting black slums into clean encampments.

We next went to a boot and shoe factory, which at first sight was supremely uninteresting: I might have been in Northampton. But a manager in white overalls told me a good story. Long ago, it appears, Port Elizabeth used to make comfortable but primitive velskoens for the farmers. During the first World War supplies of imported boots and shoes ceased, with the result that Port Elizabeth built up a shoe industry which has made South Africa independent of European shoes. The industry jumped from velskoens to glacé kid in one bound. The most modern machinery and English technicians were imported, and the result is obvious to anyone who glances into a shop window in South Africa.

The machining work was done by girls. They sat in rows, running the uppers of boots and shoes under little sewing-machines which would sew one side of an upper in a single angry burst of needlework. All the girls were white. Beyond a door, however, were coloured girls. The desire for segregation was apparently mutual. There were coloured men at stamping machines. A foreman with a Northampton accent brought me the millionth pair of Army boots.

§ 5

Many South Africans refuse to admit that they have ever seen a snake. When hard pressed they may possibly say, " Oh well, I believe there was a puff adder in the garden years ago, but the ' boy ' killed it "; or, " When Jim was cleaning out the shed a long time ago he killed a snake with a niblick ". Anyone who has read *Snakes of South Africa*, by Mr F. W. Fitzsimons, will suspect that the whole country crawls with the most loathsome and venomous reptiles; and in Port Elizabeth there can no longer be any doubt about it!

Port Elizabeth is snake headquarters, and its Snake Park is famous all over the world. The present Park was built in 1936 to replace one opened in 1906 by Mr Fitzsimons, when he was director of the Museum.

I walked under a pleasant pergola surrounding a sunken garden. Gazing down into the plants and shrubs, I saw a fair selection of South Africa's snakes, enough anyhow to make you think twice about walking in the garden after dark! There were long, lithe, active snakes and fat, somnolent ones; there were black, green, and brown snakes; some were asleep, some were awake, and a few were swimming like eels in the water-trench that surrounds the pit.

While I watched fascinated, a Basuto, wearing goggles, a khaki uniform, leggings, and thick gloves, entered the pit and began to stroll about among the serpents. Some writhed away and threaded themselves into the reeds and bushes, but one like a small cobra, named a ringhals, erected its hood and, lifting itself a foot from the ground, spat repeatedly towards the man, lunging forward each time with a thin hiss.

Mr J. A. Pringle, the present director, told me that this snake can project venom, often towards its victim's eyes, for a distance of four to five feet. The Basuto's name was Freddie. There was a senior snake man named Johannes.

" How do you train these men to do this kind of work? " I asked.

As I asked this question, Freddie was strolling round casually, picking up snakes from here and there until he held a writhing fist full. Finding that he had more than he could conveniently carry, he draped one round his neck.

" It's not easy," replied Mr Pringle. " When the park was first opened one of the native cleaners in the Museum was trained to handle and exhibit snakes. All went well for a time, but one day he was bitten. The shock was too much for him, and he resigned. Then Johannes, another cleaner, came forward and volunteered for the job. That was twenty-six years ago, and he has been going strong ever since."

" But has he never been bitten? "

" Oh yes, with great frequency! He has been bitten over twenty times by poisonous species, and he can't count how often by the mildly venomous ones. Yet, in spite of all these bites, Johannes is not immune. He has not been bitten regularly enough! "

" And Freddie? How is he getting on? "

" Freddie has been doing this work since 1945 and has been bitten several times. It takes about nine months to train a native to handle snakes properly. They fear them as much as anyone, and the fear can be overcome only by training. If a boy gets a bite in the early months of training, it's generally all up. He just vanishes! It's not an easy job. Fear and familiarity are equally dangerous."

Freddie had now festooned himself with snakes. He advanced towards us like a dusky Medusa, with several coils round his neck and black tongues flickering round his face. When he fancied a particular snake that was lurking in the bushes, he would suddenly drop one of those he was grasping and, dragging the other one out by the tail, would add it to his handful.

Mr Pringle pointed out the various snakes to me. We saw the loathsome puff adder, which may easily be trodden on because it is too somnolent to get out of the way. A female puff adder produces anything from thirty to seventy young during March and April!

The Cape or Yellow Cobra is the commonest of the five kinds of cobra found in South Africa. They are all dangerous, and Mr Pringle added that, with the exception of the mamba, they are more feared in South Africa than any other snake. Unlike the venom of the puff adder, which is a slow poison, the cobra venom is rapidly absorbed, and a bite can cause death within twenty minutes.

Then there was the boomslang, the tree snake, that lives on chameleons, lizards, eggs, and young birds. It has black fangs and, although I was told it rarely bites, its venom acts on the blood and contains an extra toxin which causes hæmophilia in human beings. Until 1914 it was believed to be a non-poisonous snake, but in that year a native boy called William was bitten in the Park by a boomslang and, neglecting the bite, very nearly died.

Among the commonest snakes are the night adders. They hide all day and come out at night in search of frogs and toads. I had no idea that snakes are so fastidious about their food. While the night adder will eat only cold-blooded creatures, the puff adder will eat only warm-blooded ones. There are snakes that live entirely upon eggs. Only the cobras and the ringhals seem to be omnivorous.

I was then taken to see the most deadly of all South Africa's snakes, the mambas, which are kept in large glass compartments. These sleek and terrible snakes are sometimes fourteen feet in length. The black mamba haunts hillsides, and the green mamba, which is as bright green as spring grass, haunts forests. They are not found in the Cape, but in Natal and the Northern Transvaal.

" If you get between a mamba and its hide-out," said Mr Pringle, " or if you cross its path suddenly, it has been known to attack."

" And the venom? "

" It can cause death in ten minutes."

" What do you do when an attendant is bitten? "

" Give an instant injection of snake serum. It can't be done too quickly."

By this time my horror of snakes was replaced by a fascination for them as poison laboratories. The story of anti-snake serum is a remarkable one. I was interested to learn that as long ago as 1894 Calmette began to experiment with snake venom at the Pasteur Institute in Paris. His method was to inject a horse with increasing quantities of Indian cobra venom until, at the end of two years, the animal was immune. From its blood was prepared an antidote for Indian cobra venom, but not for that of any other snake.

Since then research in France, the United States, Brazil, and at the South African Medical Research Institute in Johannesburg, has been a search for a general antidote. It was found that there are two general types of venom in South Africa, the blood-venoms, as in the puff adder, and the nerve-venoms, as in the cobra and the mamba. The present serum, which saved so many lives during the War, is produced from the use of both these venoms, and it is effective against the bite of any South African snake.

Snakes are " milked " for venom in Port Elizabeth, and the poison is sent up to the Research Institute in Johannesburg. It is collected about once every fortnight during the feeding season, November to May.

I was shown how a snake is " milked ". Freddie, or some-one equally courageous, grips a puff adder or a cobra behind the head with his left hand, while he swings its body under his left arm-pit. He then takes a large glass like an ice-cream bowl and brings it up to the snake's nose. The snake then strikes, and the venom drips into the glass. About fifty snakes are " milked " at a time, in order to get sufficient venom. After each snake has discharged its venom, its mouth is washed with disinfectant to prevent the spread of any mouth disease.

" The collection of venom is a slow process, as you can see," said Mr Pringle. " Each snake yields only one two-hundred-and-a-fiftieth of an ounce of dried venom a month. Venom is measured in grammes. I went on two circular tours by car during the War, and took with me a trained native and a bag of live snakes ! At each farm we let loose our snakes and demonstrated how to catch them. We also offered three times the normal price for snakes, and the result was that we received cobras and puff adders by the hundred ! "

" But what did the Post Office or the Railways say? " I asked.

" Ah," said Mr Pringle, " you've asked a question! Most of our snakes are sent by rail, and the railway authorities demand that boxes containing snakes shall be securely closed. It's quite natural, I suppose! But farmers send in the strangest collection of old tins and boxes, so that now and again accidents happen. On one occasion a ringhals gave birth to a family en route. As I've told you, the young of a ringhals vary from thirty to eighty! Well, the little ones wriggled out of the container into the guard's van. Long before the train reached Port Elizabeth, I received an appeal for help from the station-master. I went down to the station and met the train, and had to catch all the youngsters, and declare the train free of snakes, before any of the railway employees would touch the guard's van! "

" Opening your post must be fairly exciting."

" We have a special room for it, because a box may contain anything from a lizard to a mamba. After the name and address of the sender has been recorded, the box is opened, and the attendant knows at the first glance how to deal with the contents."

Puff adders and cobras are bought by weight and pythons by the foot. A fair price for a python is anything from one shilling to three shillings a foot. A good large mamba will fetch two pounds ten. The snakes have been locked up since a small, barefoot native boy was in the habit of climbing into the pit in the dark, capturing a snake, and selling it to the Curator in the morning. Instead of punishment, surely he should have been given a job on the staff and a medal for valour!

Mr Pringle taught me a lot about snakes. Until I went to the Snake Park I did not know that snakes have no external ears and cannot hear sounds, so they are unaffected by the flute of the snake-charmer. Their sight is so poor that they are unable to distinguish a stationary object, but their tongues are so developed that some experts think they may hear, smell, and taste by means of the tongue. Snakes feed only for seven months of the year, November to May, and fast for the remaining five.

But the most surprising thing about them is their appalling fertility. It is really difficult to believe those South Africans who say that they have never seen a snake! Perhaps they have never looked.

§ 6

Leaving Port Elizabeth one afternoon, I was soon upon the road to Grahamstown.

This is not the most beautiful road in South Africa, but it is an interesting one. The lines of the hills, the scrub, the groups of natives beside the road, all gave me the impression that I was approaching something different from anything I had yet seen. Like many parts of the world which have been the scene of bloody strife, this bush country, streaked with muddy strips of water such as the Bushman's River, still wears an air of alertness not unlike that of the Scottish Border.

From Cape Town to Port Elizabeth the traveller sees thousands of Cape Coloured, but of Zulus, Basutos, and Xosa and the other formidable invaders of South Africa he sees practically nothing. But upon this road he is definitely moving into Bantu country. The faces he passes are not the sharp, complex, yellowish faces of the Cape, but are dark, gentle, childlike faces, possessing an attractive good humour. Driving donkey-carts along the road, or advancing barefoot, strumming upon guitars slung across their shoulders, or waiting in a waving group at a bus stop, these dusky inhabitants of South Africa awaken curiosity and interest and drive away that vague feeling of embarrassment induced by the Cape Coloured. But the much publicised pictures of native South Africa—lines of bronze maidens bearing water-jars upon their heads, and dark Apollos in leopard skins—are not yet realised. The natives are clothed in odds and ends of European garments; and I was pleased to see that the good old brown batter-pudding felt hat, that has been sat on and kicked about for years, has achieved immortality here as it has in the country districts of Ireland.

I was told that I should find Grahamstown " very English ", and coming to it in the heat of afternoon, I saw an austere stone town—or I should say city—where every sun-blind was down. A brown cathedral stood in the centre of an enormously wide main street which was lined on either side by Corinthian banks, offices, and two storeyed shops in which it was possible to buy anything from an American refrigerator to text-books on chemistry. But in appearance I did not think it English. It reminded me of Scotland, and, had it been raining, it might have looked like St Andrews.

At the hotel a young native boy in white ducks seized my luggage which, among several loose parcels, numbered a frail cardboard box containing a stuffed puff adder which I was taking to a child in England. Like a French porter, a native boy will completely festoon himself in suit-cases and parcels until he can just move. It seems to be a point of honour that, as long as the human frame is able to advance behind a breastwork of luggage, the move must be made in one journey and not two. This poor boy loaded himself with everything I possessed, keeping the puff adder for the last, and holding the box in position against his chest by keeping his chin on the lid.

Upstairs, in disentangling himself, the lid came off the box, and the boy saw a close-up of an enormous puff adder coiled in repose, and, just allowing everything to drop from him on the floor, he fled with a low moan of fear. I was sorry to have frightened him and went out to find him, but he had vanished. Then I saw his faced looking up from a bend in the stairs, his eyes like two black marbles in the centre of two white saucers.

" Dead ! " I said reassuringly. " The snake's dead ! "

" No, master, no," he crooned, " bad snake ! "

" Yes, I know it's a bad snake," I said, " but it's dead ! "

He shook his head and shivered and smiled at the same time. I went into the room and came back holding the puff adder to prove that it was stuffed, which was the most unfortunate thing I could have done, for, with one terrified leap, he sprang down the stairs and disappeared and I never saw him again.

I placed the puff adder in its box and hid it on top of a wardrobe ; for it occurred to me that should it have the same effect on every member of the staff, my stay in Grahamstown would not be comfortable.

As I wandered round Grahamstown, I was charmed by its dignity. It has the cosy look of a solid, early Nineteenth Century British town. Although everyone in the Union knows it as the " Settlers' City ", Grahamstown was founded eight years before the Settlers came out, when Colonel John Graham sited his dragoon barracks there and made it a frontier post. The 1820 Settlers helped it to grow from a village into a town, and in this place, and on every hill and valley for miles around, they strove shoulder to shoulder with their Boer comrades and with the British garrison to hold back a long series of Bantu invasions. If it is difficult to imagine Port Elizabeth as a desolate strand a century ago, it is even more difficult to imagine this serene and academic city of Grahamstown as the centre of border war, as indeed it was for something like fifty years.

Grahamstown is one of the great educational centres in the Union. Rhodes University College houses about a thousand students. There is St Andrew's College, which is the Eton (or Harrow) of South Africa, the other being Bishops at Cape Town, which is the Harrow (or Eton). There is also St Aidan's College, managed by the Fathers of the Society of Jesus.

There are other preparatory schools, colleges, convents, high schools, primary schools, diocesan schools, a training college founded by the Anglican Sisterhood of the Community of the Resurrection, and St Paul's College, which is the only Anglican theological college of its kind in South Africa. There is also an art school and a technical institute.

In the headmaster's room at St Andrew's College is preserved a telegram from a father who served with the Boer Forces during the South African War. It was despatched from Potchefstroom on September 29, 1899, on the eve of the war.

" Leave for front to-morrow," it reads, " have wired twenty pounds your credit my son's school fees next quarter don't let him leave unless you have my signature for it further school fees will be safe best regards."

" What happened to the boy? "

" He remained here happily at school throughout the campaign, and when the war was over his fees were paid!

Incidentally, the boy rose to high rank in the Union Defence forces."

South Africa must be the only country in the world where you send your son to school with the enemy—and on tick!

§ 7

In one of Grahamstown's many shops I bought an adequate box for the puff adder, then, feeling easier in mind, I paid a visit to the Cathedral of St Michael and St George.

Among those delightful improbabilities which rejoice the traveller's heart, Grahamstown Cathedral must occupy a high place, for it is the work of that prolific architect, Sir Gilbert Scott, the father of St Pancras Station and the Albert Memorial, and goodness alone knows how many churches, parsonages, mansions, and monuments throughout Great Britain. It is a brown, Gothic church which might have been designed for any large parish in England. Its bell tower houses eight London-made bells, and from it rises a slender spire.

The church inside is cool and dark. The nave columns are of black Belgian marble streaked indelibly by an attempt to polish them with oil after erection; the lectern is a smaller copy of the pelican feeding her young lectern which Gilbert Scott reconstructed for Durham Cathedral, and the pulpit, carved in Lichfield, shows the appearance of Jesus to His disciples, four of whom have been given the features of the first four Bishops of Grahamstown.

The south aisle still carries part of the old wooden gallery of the 1820 Settler church which formerly stood on the site. The verger told me that from time to time there is talk of pulling it down, and, although that bit of Georgian woodwork looks decidedly odd in Scott's Gothic church, it would surely be a pity to demolish it. It is the oldest piece of English church building in South Africa.

The first church was built with remarkable speed, for which the Settlers had to thank Lord Charles Somerset. In 1821 he was on leave in England, and took the opportunity of approaching the Society for the Propagation of the Gospel for a contribution towards a church in Grahamstown. He succeeded, as he put it, " in squeezing out of them £500 ". More funds were forthcoming, and the church was started in 1824 and completed in 1830. This was just in time. In 1834 the Kaffirs came over the frontier again and another bloodthirsty war began. The church was then a central refuge for the women and children, and the most convenient depot for arms and ammunition.

The old gallery is a precious link with the days when the English in South Africa were undergoing their baptism of blood. One can fancy the women in their high-waisted dresses, shawls, and poke bonnets, the frightened children, the nave cluttered with old firearms, the quartermaster sitting at the Communion Table writing in a book, while the clerk stands within the rails and hands over muskets and bayonets; the scene which the Reverend J. Heavyside saw when he looked in before Christmas in 1834. In that shabby old gallery in Grahamstown the Boer and the Briton shake hands.

I went to see the Roman Catholic Cathedral, which is dedicated to St Patrick, and this also is an interesting church. The building was erected by Roman Catholic soldiers of the garrison stationed in Grahamstown in the forties, and I suppose, from the dedication, that some of them were Irish.

At the upper end of the High Street is a fine old white gateway with sentry boxes on each side and a lamp above the central arch, which leads, not to a barracks, but to the buildings of Rhodes University College. I was told that it had been built by the South African hero, Piet Retief, in the eighteen thirties, with other buildings now demolished.

I spent what was left of the afternoon roaming about the sunny streets and strolling past the arcaded shops, thinking that this was a most pleasant and delightful place; in fact, the sort of city in which one could retire and settle down happily and become either hopelessly lazy or very industrious. Finding myself at the town hall, I went in, and was richly rewarded by the sight of that mythical creature, the Cape Tiger, on the coat-of-arms of the Mayoral chair! Everyone who has read the accounts of early travellers in South Africa must have noted how often they speak of " tygers ", which, of course, have never existed in South Africa. They mean leopards.   The Cape Tiger is a joke, but, joke or not, there he is, a genuine Bengal tiger, as a supporter to the Grahamstown arms.

The streets became filled with young men and young girls. The men strolled together with books under their arms, slow-moving, hatless, and flannelled, as if they were at Oxford or Cambridge, and the girls fluttered about with tennis racquets, like butterflies let loose; and the old town seemed to take on a new meaning and interest.   They were good-looking specimens, those young South Africans, and I listened with interest to stray scraps of conversation about exams and papers, for it was getting near the end of term.   It was interesting to hear some of them break out of English into Afrikaans.

And only a hundred and thirteen years ago—which is not long enough for a family to be anything but alien in an English parish—only a hundred and thirteen years ago, this city, with its cathedral and university, its libraries and museum, its swimming-pools, tennis-courts, and cricket fields, and its population of assured young people, was a frontier post at war with savages!   And the descendants of those savages carry up your luggage, clean your boots, and empty the waste-paper basket.

South Africa is indeed a remarkable country.

§ 8

After dinner my host led the way into his library and we sat down to talk.   I could see the inevitable query trembling on his lips, and at last it came.

" What do you think of the native question? "

" When I have completed my fiftieth year in South Africa, I'll tell you."

" Um," he said, disappointed.   " Very sensible."

It was now my turn.

" What do *you* think of the native question? "

" Well," he said eagerly, " of course the native isn't given a fair deal.   I'm one of those people who believe in the native and would like to see him given a chance.   In theory he can be educated, but in practice there are few opportunities for him. When he qualifies professionally, what is he to do?   Then, so far as the labouring native goes, his whole standard of living must be raised. He must be given a decent wage and, some day, the vote."

He argued that fear was at the back of the European attitude towards the native, but that there was nothing to fear. He at least was not frightened. The black man had to be helped along like a sick person, until he could stand on his own feet.

We talked of many other things, and then I asked him:

"What would you expect to find if you could come back to South Africa in a hundred years?"

"I should expect to find a coffee-coloured race rather like the Portuguese," he replied. "It seems to me inevitable. It will happen from the bottom up. It is, to a certain extent, happening now, mainly from economic reasons. Only the other day in Cape Town I met a young European employed by a 'bus company. He told me that he had just married. 'Is she English?' I asked. 'No, coloured,' he replied. 'Why have you married a coloured girl?' I asked. 'Well,' he said, 'I couldn't afford to keep a white one on my wages. The first thing she'd expect would be a servant to do all the dirty work for her. But my wife doesn't expect that; in fact she wouldn't have it, and you ought to see my home.' That," concluded my friend, "is how it will happen, in my opinion. Oh yes, I think there can be very little doubt about it!"

"But you don't like the idea, do you?"

"No, of course I don't. I hate it. But I deal in facts."

We talked about something more agreeable.

"Why is Grahamstown called the City of Saints?" I asked.

"Some people say that we have more than our share of churches, but there is another story. They say that about 1846, when the Royal Engineers were here, they were held up for want of building tools. A message was sent to Cape Town asking urgently for a vice to be sent from the Ordnance Stores. The reply came back, 'Buy vice locally.' To this, the Royal Engineers replied, 'No vice in Grahamstown.'"

I walked back to the hotel feeling depressed as I recollected the earlier part of our conversation. It was the first time I had encountered that point of view in South Africa.

M

§ 9

If you would like an idea of the old Kaffir frontier, go up to Signal Hill and look down upon the magnificent sweep of country that lies to the skyline and Natal. It is not difficult to imagine how the sparks would burn from hill to hill during a night alarm, as the beacon fires were lighted far away from the Fish River drifts, getting nearer and nearer, warning the lonely farmer and the little garrisons in fort and blockhouse.

Upon a distant hill named Governor's Kop stands a fire-tower, a solid stone structure of two rooms, one above the other. The door is half-way up the wall and is approached by projecting ladder stones, and the windows are narrow loopholes. It was from this tower that Signal Hill and Grahamstown received the alert.

Few of us in Europe realise how near this frontier life still is to the South African. No other white colonists in the world were pitted against a more valiant and dangerous foe, or one more numerous. Only the merest handful of white farmers, Boer and Briton, and a few British troops, held back a tidal wave that might have swept on and overwhelmed even Cape Town.

I made a note on Signal Hill to ask the next octogenarian I met—and South Africa is full of them—what first-hand stories he had heard of the frontier. That very evening my wish was answered, not by an octogenarian, but by a charming woman, my hostess at a dinner-party, who was the daughter of a missionary.

"When I was a small child," she said, "I remember hearing the Kaffir war drums. Do have some pineapple?"

"The drums?" I pleaded.

"You'll want some sugar. . . . Oh, the drums! Yes, I shivered in my bed and listened to them thudding, thudding, a quite indescribable sound. No one who has ever heard it can ever forget."

An enormous warrior entered, bearing a silver tray with coffee upon it. She said something to him in his own language, and he inclined his head, respecting her for speaking this language.

"Quite indescribable," she continued. "Like this!" And she rapped on the table.

The warrior re-entered and respectfully placed before her a silver box of cigarettes.

§ 10

The Albany Museum, like the Drostdy at Swellendam, is what a local museum should be: it illustrates the life of its own district and has not allowed itself to be cluttered up with old tusks and mummies and irrelevant things which have nothing to do with the town. Here you can read letters and proclamations, diaries and deeds, see pictures and objects of every kind, all of them dealing with the life of Albany in the Nineteenth Century.

I was interested to see a letter from Piet Retief, whose murder by the Zulus was perhaps the most dramatic event in the history of South Africa. It is a pathetic letter, dated Sept. 10, 1835, begging the Civil Commissioner for ammunition.

There is another letter from the Reverend F. Owen, the missionary who saw the murder of Retief and his followers, dated March 16, 1838, and addressed to D. Coates, Esq., Church Missionary House, London. This was the covering letter that accompanied Owen's *Diary*, since published by the Van Riebeeck Society. "On the 6th of Feby," he writes, "a scene took place which can never be effaced from my recollection . . . the murder of 60 Dutch farmers before my own eyes and the subsequent massacre of 250 individuals at break of day in the Dutch camp."

Owen's *Diary*, which he posted a bit at a time to London, is now one of the treasures of the Cape Archives. South Africa owes its possession to Sir George Cory, the historian, who, when visiting London in 1922, went to the London Missionary Society to see if by any chance the document still existed. After a search it was found where it had been lying, dusty and forgotten, for over eighty years. Having "feasted his eyes" upon it, as he said, Sir George ventured to suggest that the *Diary* would be of greater interest to people in South

Africa than to those in England; and in a few days it was given to him.

Another pathetic relic proves, rather surprisingly, that the first white woman to die in the Transvaal was an American. She was a Mrs Jane Wilson, the wife of an American missionary, Alex. E. Wilson. She died of fever in September, 1836, at Mosega, in the present Marico district. The mission to which the Wilsons belonged had sailed from Boston in 1834, and after various adventures was split up. The Wilsons with three other missionaries penetrated into the Matabele country, where Mzilikazi, the chief, gave them permission to settle, but afterwards turned against them. When Jane Wilson died, her husband buried with her a small stone with the following words on it.

" Her spirit was called away to join ye assembly of ye just in Heaven soon after she commenced her toils in this land. Her flesh sleeps till ye resurrection, when it will rise up to testify ye benevolent desires of her husband and those connected with him to impart ye blessing of ye Gospel to ye natives of Africa."

The stone was not discovered until 1912, when it was turned up during some digging operations and fell into the hands of an English farmer, a keen antiquarian, who gave it to the Pretoria Museum. The Grahamstown relic is a plaster cast.

So only in 1836 the Marico district, which is now on the main line from Johannesburg to Kimberley, seemed like the very depths of the Congo to the people of that time. Near the place where the stone was found, the Martha Washington Club of Johannesburg has put up a memorial to the " first white woman to lay down her life within the Transvaal ".

In the museum I was delighted to find more work by that wonderful man Thomas Baines, who is not yet appreciated as he ought to be in South Africa. It seems to be the fashion to smile at the vivid colouring of his paintings, but I think the time will come when everything from his brush—and what a lot there is—will be valued at its true worth. At his best he was a magnificent painter of animals, and, working on the spot, often with third-rate colours and materials, his success in depicting the atmosphere of South Africa is amazing. One of his pictures shows the 1820 Settlers landing in open boats on a rough sea, a spirited picture, and another is a painting of David Hume's wagon, loaded with ivory and skins, in the Grahamstown market. There are, by the way, two more pictures by Baines in the Grahamstown Art Gallery: " Church Square, Grahamstown, 1850 ", and a fine picture, which badly needs some restoration, of Malays beaching a boat on the shores of Table Bay.

Baines was an attractive, unworldly little man, always poor, always full of courage and hope, painting anything and everything to earn a few shillings. He was the son of a skipper of King's Lynn, in Norfolk, and came to the Cape in 1842, when he was twenty-two. He was self-taught, with a natural gift for painting. His first big task was that of artist to the British Army in the Kaffir War of 1848. He then went to Australia, where his work earned the special thanks of the Government. Back in South Africa in 1858, he became artist to Livingstone's Zambesi expedition.

Livingstone, and particularly Livingstone's brother, Charles, treated him most shabbily, there was a quarrel, and Baines left to join up with Chapman, who was also bound for the Victoria Falls. It was at this period that he painted the many splendid pictures of the Falls—some of them are now in the Cape Town Public Library—which caused such a sensation at the Crystal Palace. The best were sent down to Windsor to be shown privately to the Queen and the Prince Consort.

One would have thought that this might have put poor Baines on the highroad, but apparently it had no effect on his career or his bank balance. Again he turned up in South Africa, a middle-aged man, still poor, but full of enthusiasm and still painting. This time he was really going to make money! He took charge of an expedition to study the gold-fields of " the Tati ", now in Bechuanaland, and in the course of this journey gained material for one of the best books written at that time about South Africa, *The Gold Regions of South-Eastern Africa*. But, as usual, poor Baines had no luck with his gold. He returned from that long and expensive journey to find that the company which had sent him there was unable to pay his expenses. So, back to the paint-brush !

His industry was prodigious. In Kaffirland he painted the pictures—has anyone ever counted them?—which are to be found here, there, and everywhere in museums and art galleries. Then the dream of gold returned—that wonderful, infectious South African dream—and off he must go, almost alone, to the far north, with a small quartz-crushing machine, to make his long-delayed fortune. He arranged his outfit in Port Elizabeth, hired his wagons, and then, on the very eve of the great journey, died in Durban of dysentery, aged fifty-five.

David Hume, whose wagon Baines painted in Grahamstown, is another explorer who has never been given the credit due to him. He was one of Benjamin Moodie's Scottish emigrants. He arrived in South Africa in 1817, at the age of twenty-one, and, like the canny Scot he was, left the land and began trading in the interior, not towards the Fish River, but northwards into what eventually became the Free State and the Transvaal, and beyond.

He was one of the first white men, perhaps the first, to have any dealings with Mzilikazi. In 1829 he was escorting the Reverend J. Archbell to the Matabele chief when he met Dr Moffat, who was also on his way there under the guidance of two traders, Schoon, an Afrikaner, and McLuckie, evidently another of the Swellendam Scots. So far from being utterly unknown country in those days, the northern provinces seem to have been scattered with all kinds of stray adventurers and traders, men shooting elephants, looking for legendary gold, and missionaries in search of stations.

In 1830 Hume, in the course of a remarkable journey to the north of the Limpopo, was the first white man to travel to the Macloutsie River. On his return he crossed the site of Pretoria. From there he made his way through Mosega to Kuruman, where he had established a trading-post. This journey was one of the great explorations of central South Africa, and the territory he travelled through north of the Limpopo was not seen again by a white man for fourteen or fifteen years, until Gordon-Cumming and other hunters went there.

Hume was known to every hunter and trader of the time. There are many references to him in the *Matabele Journals of Robert Moffat*, so romantically discovered in an old ironbound pine-chest in a Cape farmhouse in 1941. Hume was the first white man to be seen in the Bamangwato country in 1833, now the Bechuanaland Protectorate. No one can look at Baines' picture of his experienced ox-wagon loaded with ivory and skins and feathers without feeling a warm glow of admiration not only for him, but for all those solitary pioneers and hunters who blazed the trail into the unknown north.

I was taken to an old house in Grahamstown which was once the house of Bishop Ricards, who was Roman Catholic Bishop there about ninety years ago. The house itself is an antiquity. The Bishop's library, lined from floor to ceiling with calf-bound books of the Eighteenth and Nineteenth Centuries, is just as he left it when he died. It is a haunted room, and you would not dream of sitting down at the desk, in case the owner came in and found you there.

I was shown a framed piece of window glass upon which the Bishop had scratched his initials, with this inscription. "Initials of the Rt Rev James David Ricards, cut with the first Diamond discovered in South Africa. 1867."

This was the diamond that led to Kimberley and to all sorts of other things. It was found by a child on a farm on the banks of the Orange River near Hopetown, and was seen by a farmer named van Niekerk, who offered to buy it from the child's mother. She said, "It is only a pebble; you may keep it if you want it." It then passed from van Niekerk to an Irish trader named O'Reilly, who decided to have it examined. Dr Atherstone of Grahamstown was then the foremost geologist at the Cape and so the diamond came to him. The Doctor declared it to be a diamond, the Bishop wrote his initials on the window, and the stage was then set for a new South Africa. While the Bishop was writing on the window-pane in Grahamstown, there were already two significant invalids in the world. One was a dreamy-looking parson's son of fourteen, named Cecil Rhodes, at Bishop's Stortford Grammar School, and the other was a man of forty-two, who had recently broken his left leg when his mule cart overturned in a dry ditch—Paul Kruger. . . .

There is an interesting pendant to this story in the *Graham's Town Journal*. It appears that an acute gentleman in

London, named Harry Emanuel, sent to South Africa a geologist named Gregory to spy out the land. Mr Gregory came to the remarkable conclusion that there were no diamonds in the Cape, and that those already found had been dropped by ostriches or had been planted on purpose to increase the value of land!

While Dr Atherstone was contradicting Mr Gregory in the *Graham's Town Journal*, the discussion was interrupted by the same Mr van Niekerk with something really large, for which he had given a half-caste shepherd boy five hundred sheep, two oxen, and a horse. This was the Star of Africa!

Things then began to happen. What Mr Emanuel said to Mr Gregory, when he arrived back in Bond Street, is not, alas, on record, but in South Africa to this day any tall story is still " a Gregory ".

§ 11

I explored the country south of Grahamstown and saw the village of Bathurst, which I commend to anyone who is looking for South Africa's most English village. Many of the families round about are those of 1820 Settlers, and the churchyard is full of good old English names. I met Chris Dell, aged eighty, who keeps wicket for Bathurst and grows acres of pineapples. He has never been to England, does not call it " home ", and has no family stories about it. The road goes on to the coast at Port Alfred, and when the wind is not blowing, it is one of the prettiest seaside places anyone could wish to see.

I also explored the country to the north and travelled for miles along the old front line, coming at length to Fort Beaufort, where I saw a recruiting office for natives who wish to enlist for work in the gold mines. But the most interesting thing about Fort Beaufort is a fantastic love story.

About 1840 a girl named Ann, her surname is unknown, who lived in an English fishing village, lost her lover, a youth named John Marvell. She believed that he had run away to sea, and, with the idea of finding him, she stole her brother's clothes and signed on as a steward in a ship called the *Abercrombie Robinson*. In 1842 this ship sailed to the Cape with the 91st Regiment, and was wrecked in Table Bay, fortunately with no loss of life. Ann, however, was among the few casualties, and in hospital she was found to be a girl.

One of the officers' wives, possibly the wife of Lieutenant-Colonel Lindsay, took a fancy to her and engaged her as nursemaid to her children. The regiment moved up to Fort Beaufort, where the sailor-nursemaid became a great favourite of the family. She had told her mistress the romantic story of her search for John Marvell. Returning from a walk with the children one day, she seemed pale and upset, and confessed that she had seen her lost lover on sentry duty outside battalion headquarters!

In order to satisfy her the names of the guard were produced, but no John Marvell appeared among them. Ann persisted, and eventually a certain young man admitted that he had enlisted under an assumed name and that he was indeed John Marvell! To his amazement the missing lover was then introduced to his old sweetheart. They became engaged again, but were fated never to marry. When returning from Grahamstown shortly before the wedding, John Marvell tried to ford the Konap River and was drowned. Nine months later Ann married Troop Sergeant-Major Moffat of the 7th Dragoon Guards, and they had two children. She died about 1851, and was buried at Peddie, on the main road from Grahamstown to East London.

This extraordinary story is told in a manuscript found in Canada in 1936, and acquired by Mr A. Gordon-Brown. It has since been published by the van Riebeeck Society as *The Narrative of Private Buck Adams*. (Surely it should be " Trooper ", for Adams was a Dragoon Guardsman?) It is a fascinating document, revealing frontier life in South Africa as observed from the ranks. In his retirement Adams kept a sweet-shop in Tottenham, and died, aged eighty, in 1910. There is a masterly restraint in his description of the story of Ann and John Marvell as " somewhat romantic ".

The document is a good example of the shrewd outlook of an observant ranker who could see as clearly as British settler or

Boer farmer how South Africa at that period was ruled not from Cape Town, but from Whitehall. He referred acidly to " the old ladies of Exeter Hall ".

This was the celebrated meeting-place in London of the religious and philanthropic societies of the time, whose influence upon the Government, and consequently upon the affairs of the Cape, were so powerful. I wonder how many South Africans know that they are living on the site of this building when they stay in the Strand Palace Hotel.

CHAPTER SIX

*In which I travel through the Ciskei and the Transkei, where I see
the native with his flocks and herds. I go through King William's
Town to East London. I fall in love with Port St Johns and go
north through tribal lands to Umtata and Kokstad, and on the borders of
Natal I recall the story of the Voortrekkers.*

§ 1

THE traveller in South Africa who, as most travellers do,
wishes to see the Bantu-speaking native in his primitive
tribal conditions, should motor from Grahamstown
through the enormous territory which is divided by the River
Kei into the Ciskei and the Transkei and stretches for hundreds
of miles north to the border of Natal. This native territory,
a tract of country the size of Holland, includes the tribal
territories of the Xosas—the original Kaffirs—the Tembus
and the Pondos.

A twelfth of the land area of the Union has been set apart for
the occupation of the Bantu, yet this is not sufficient to support
its population. The native reserves, as such parts of the
Union are called, are closed to European settlement and
are administered through the Ministry of Native Affairs in
Pretoria by European magistrates and their staffs, who have
under them hereditary native chiefs and a chain of authority
which descends to an ubiquitous old man with a stick who is
known as the village headman. Witchcraft, magic, the most
primitive form of agriculture, a prehistoric attitude towards
cattle and ancient tribal custom and lore, may be studied
in this vast black South Africa, much of it hardly influenced
by European civilisation. Mission stations of the various
Christian churches are scattered over the enormous area,
traders' stores dot the landscape at a distance of five miles
one from the other, but apart from these, and away from the
main roads, the " raw native ", as he is called, may be seen
dressed in his blanket.

There are nearly eight million Bantu in the Union. Two million are said to work on the white man's farms and another million work in his cities and towns, so that much more than half the Bantu population is still to be found in the reserves. Thousands of young natives are always in transit between the reserves and the gold mines of the Rand. They enlist for periods of nine months or so and then return to their villages. One of South Africa's greatest problems at the moment is the tendency of the Bantu towards detribalisation and a consequent drift to the cities.

The Native Problem is not one in which an unqualified stranger should dabble. Long residence in the country is absolutely necessary for its understanding. It is not the familiar problem of a repressed minority, but the more puzzling one of a vast majority on a lower plane of development which, if given privileges, might swamp its masters and imperil the future of a painfully built up civilisation. This problem was difficult enough in a more settled world, but to-day in an age of revolution when numbers count more than quality and licence is sometimes confused with liberty, it is not difficult to understand the South African fear. On the other hand many liberal minded South Africans admit that the native should have better educational opportunities, better housing, higher wages and a less restricted field of labour. More conservative thinkers fear that the attempt to grant privileges too quickly may have a disastrous result on the future of the country. It must occur to any visitor that could South Africa's two million white people be increased to ten million, and the deadening ban on white manual labour removed, perhaps the Native Problem would change overnight.

The impression sometimes spread abroad that the South African cares nothing for the native is fantastically wrong. It is a problem that is rarely out of his mind. It faces him on every hand. It even invades his home. And never has so much intelligent interest been shown in the Bantu. Study groups in the universities, race relationship organisations and other bodies are showing a constructive interest in the future of the native, and it might be true to say that some of these students envisage a future South Africa in which, without imperilling or questioning the supremacy of the white man, the black man would be given a new deal.

At this moment the political rights of the native consist in the election of three European representatives to the House of Assembly and four European members to the Senate. In addition native members are elected to a Native Representative Council with the Secretary for Native Affairs as chairman.

As I set off to motor through the native territories, I came right on the frontier to an interesting and surprising introduction to the primitive land of huts and blankets. Near a small town called Alice I visited the most celebrated native school in the Union, Lovedale, where Scottish missionaries train more than a thousand native boys and girls in European subjects. Not far away is Fort Hare, which trains the native up to University standards.

It was interesting to remember those young natives, all so studiously European in appearance, as I went on into the Ciskei and saw the hillsides dotted with native huts and cattle kraals, and met upon the roads the Xosa women, who had drawn circles of white paint round their eyes, giving themselves a clown-like appearance. Some had whitened the whole face. Many were dressed in voluminous skirts and saffron-coloured blankets, and wore cloth turbans twisted round their heads. Some of the young girls, naked to the waist, had the grace of wild animals as they ran and gesticulated, or looked up startled by the sound of a car. With a slow, gliding motion a woman would pass for a moment against the sky, carrying a water jar upon her head; a mother would come along, the little black face of an infant peeping from the fold of a shawl at her back; a commanding, incredibly wrinkled old woman would stand grasping a stick, looking like the Witch of Endor. Even at a first glance the absence of young men was noticeable. They were away in the gold mines at Johannesburg, earning money to pay the poll tax and to buy cattle which, in their turn, buy wives.

Pictorially the Ciskei was grand; agriculturally it was a tragedy. Everywhere I looked the earth was split and seared and the top soil had gone. Thousands of miserable cattle and goats roamed everywhere, making tracks that would some day form cracks which successive rains would open into gullies and dongas. Soil erosion is one of the tragedies of the reserves. Much of the land is the best in the Union, but it cannot bear its weight of men and particularly of cattle. To the Bantu, cattle are wealth. They mean wives and power. Because of the monstrous over-stocking and the primitive conception of agriculture that goes with it, hundreds of square miles of South Africa must bleed to death.

§ 2

Towards King William's Town the country began to look like a shaggy compromise between Dartmoor and the South Downs. Stretches of more barbaric country came in between, where the road winds among rocks and mountain gorges and where rivers the colour of cocoa carried away into oblivion the soil of South Africa.

When a land is as large as South Africa and many a long name on the map turns out to be merely a few tin sheds, one approaches a town with a feeling of cheerful anticipation. And King William's Town looked to me a pleasant haven from the red dust of the road, with churches, public buildings, and banks, rising head and shoulders above the rest of the place.

In most South African towns there is a building which a visitor from ancient Greece would assume to be the temple of Apollo. It is the branch office of the Standard Bank of South Africa or of Barclays. In a country whose universities and schools have practically abandoned Greek and Latin, the branch banks of South Africa are like a glowing brochure on the advantages of a classical education. There is a huge square in King William's Town where ox-wagons once out-spanned with their loads of wool; now motor lorries perform the same task.

I was taken to the Museum to see a famous South African personality, now, unfortunately, stuffed, Huberta the Hippo.

From 1928 to 1931 this appealing creature was perhaps the most exciting non-political event in South Africa. Deciding to trek from her distant home in far-off Zululand, Huberta came south, a vast but gentle intrusion, encountered by night in towns and hamlets calmly cropping the grass or making a midnight meal of municipal herbage. Town clerks and councillors surrounded her, shining torches in her face, and she gazed calmly at them, sometimes yawning enormously, before vanishing into the darkness. Upon one occasion she stopped a train. The whistle of the engine failed to awaken her as she lay dreaming on the metals. Only after the locomotive had prodded her respectfully once or twice did she arise and, with a mild, reproachful glance at the busy and restless world she had invaded, quietly depart.

" Huberta became like a serial story," says Mr Wells in *South Africa*. " On Johannesburg tram-tops men thrust evening papers at one another and began ' I see old Huberta's been . . .'; office girls chuckled at her doings over five o'clock coffee in Cape Town cafés; children all over the Union demanded to be told stories about her before being put to bed. Britain and America began to follow her doings and she was featured in such diverse papers as *Punch* and the *Chicago Tribune*."

Her end was sudden and tragic. A farmer who could not read, and was therefore not one of her fans, saw Huberta bathing in the local river. He lifted his gun and fired a shot that reverberated throughout the Union of South Africa and echoed sadly in other countries where the death of Huberta was mourned. Her death was mentioned in the South African Parliament. She was called a " famous national character ", and the unfortunate man who shot her was summoned for shooting royal game without a licence and fined.

And in the museum in King William's Town Huberta stands to-day, wearing an expression mild and bewildered, as of one whose motives have been tragically misunderstood, whose benevolence has been rebuffed, whose curiosity misinterpreted.

From King William's Town to East London I travelled through country which was the scene of the most fantastic event in South African history, the great " cattle-killing ". It took place in native territory when the Xosa had been defeated in the Kaffir Wars, and the frontier, although enjoying an unusual lull, was clearly due for some new trouble.

This strange business began one morning in 1856 when a Xosa girl of fourteen went to draw water from a stream, and returned to report that she had been in touch with the spirits of the dead. She took a relative to the stream, where he also met and spoke with the spirits, who said that they were the inveterate enemies of the white race and wished to see all white men driven into the sea. They promised, if the Xosa would obey them, to return at the head of a great army containing all the tribal heroes, and regain for the conquered tribes all their former possessions, and more. But they would do so only on the condition that the tribes slew all their cattle, emptied their grain-pits, and left the land untilled. The dead cattle would be replaced by great herds of celestial cattle, the grain-pits were to be miraculously replenished, and the land would be covered with splendid crops.

The news of this revelation spread like a bush fire. Other prophets arose and began to say much the same thing. The madness spread to neighbouring tribes, and for months the cattle-killing went on, together with the destruction of all food and crops, while the deluded people began feverishly to build new kraals to contain the celestial beasts and new grain-pits for the heavenly grain. The Government tried to stop the race suicide, but were powerless.

As in all these outbreaks of fanatical delusion, a day was appointed as the resurrection day when the prophecy should be fulfilled. It was February 27, 1857. The sun was to rise blood red; some visionaries said there would be two suns, followed by a tremendous hurricane which would herald the arrival of the supernatural host. In a land piled with the carcases of dead beasts, a land of gorged vultures and fanatical human beings, the great day was awaited with intense excitement. Some people shut themselves in their huts in order not to be blown away by the hurricane; others sat up all night waiting for the rising of the two red suns which would herald the white man's destruction.

When nothing happened the tribes were appalled. They gave way to despair, and thousands advanced upon the Colony not as conquerors but as famished people begging food, which was not denied them. But it is said that sixty-seven thousand natives perished. The power of the Xosa was shattered for ever. They had committed suicide.

It has been suspected that the " cattle-killing " was inspired by chiefs who believed that by reducing the race to despair—in effect, by burning their boats—they might be able to fling their armies upon the Colony in one final and victorious battle. If this were so, it would be interesting to know why they had made no military preparations when the great day arrived.

§ 3

East London is another of those remarkable towns which only a hundred years ago were bush and hillside. Now it stands, a monument to the energy of its founders, with expanding industries and great ambitions, the one South African port on a river mouth.

My admiration for the 1820 Settlers grew with every mile I travelled eastward from Grahamstown. It required no effort of imagination to visualise what this frontier looked like during the intermittent Kaffir Wars to those everyday folk with their wives and children, who were suddenly projected from village and town life in England to the perils of the front line.

East London was nothing but a desolate shore upon which the Buffalo River discharged its waters when John Rex, the son of George Rex of Knysna, sailed a brig into the river mouth in 1836 with a man called John Bailie, one of the 1820 Settlers. Bailie was struck with the possibilities of the site and planted a Union Jack on a pole upon the hill at the river's mouth. Port Rex was the first name given to the place, and it seems that Rex was in the habit of going there by ship and trading with the natives. There is a story that friendly Kaffirs made a stone seat for him on the hill, where he used to sit enthroned during his transactions with them.

N

It was not until ten years later that the place grew into a settlement which shared to the full the troubled history of its hinterland. But Bailie had proved to be right, and East London's fortunes grew with the agricultural advance of the district and the industrial and mining enterprises with which the century closed.

There is a seemingly endless main street named Oxford Street. I noticed also a Fleet Street and a Drury Lane. At the top of Oxford Street is a museum in which East London keeps its famous fish. This is the cast of a bright blue fish of majestic size—it is about five feet long—with the face of an aged and ill-tempered salmon. It is known as a Coelacanths, and its claim to fame is that it has no right to exist to-day. Until 1938, when I believe it was rescued from a slab in the fish market, scientists assumed that the last specimen had died about fifty million years ago.

Glancing through the East London telephone book, I came across many German names, as well as names like Mendelski, Kaschula, Saltzwedel, and Waberski. These people are the descendants of the Germans, Poles, Flemings, and Bohemians who fought with Britain in the Crimea. After the Xosa suicide in the great cattle-killing, vast tracts of Kaffraria became vacant, and the Cape Government was only too glad to welcome the hardy and industrious peasants who wished to emigrate from Germany.

The first to arrive were members of the German Legion, who, to the disappointment of the colonists, were mostly unmarried. South Africa had learnt the lesson that woman is the secret of successful settlement. A bachelor, as everyone knows, is a restless, homeless creature, often dissolute, always grumbling, and a nuisance to everybody! But a married man is a model of virtue and responsibility, who never wishes to wander or, at any rate, is rarely able to do so. In a moment both romantic and practical, King William's Town raised some money and in 1857 brought out a shipload of nice girls, mostly Irish, who in the twinkling of an eye converted a fortunate proportion of the roving bachelors into steady, self-respecting members of the community.

The main body of settlers followed afterwards, and this time it was arranged that most of them should be married. A shopkeeper who has lived for thirty years among the farming community told me what wonderful settlers the Germans have been.

"Among the first to come," he said, "were many who sailed from England and were allowed to bring English brides with them. I have heard old people describe how the couples were married in a church porch somewhere in the south of England and then married again later in their own churches here. Lots of them became engaged on the ships."

The German settlers were at first as poor as the Huguenots and the 1820 Settlers. They set to work at once to support themselves on their small holdings. Too poor to buy coffee, they grew chicory, too poor to buy sugar, they kept bees; if they could keep a pig, they were well off with their own pork, their own mealies and vegetables. While the men worked on the land, the women kept house and marketed the vegetables. Every farthing was saved, then gradually those frugal and hard-working folk were able to add a cow to their possessions, or a horse, which trotted into the distant market between the shafts of a home-made cart.

The neat stone farms round East London to-day are a tribute to the courage and thrift of those who gave the fourth great injection of good European blood to South Africa.

"When Hitler came to power," said the shopkeeper, "he spent a lot of money in this part of the world, hoping that all the Germans here had kept their children 'German'. Battleships and boats used to come along and treat us to free beer. The farmers used to come along in hundreds and listen to lecturers who, in the guise of parsons, travelled about the country. But they had no luck. When our regiment marched out, the names of the German settlers in it proved that!

"They say that when a young farmer went into the recruiting office to enlist, they asked him his name. 'Deutschmann,' he said. They asked him where his home was. 'Berlin,' he replied. The Deutschmanns are a well-known family in Berlin, near King William's Town!

"Of course we've got a lot of the old 1820 Settlers round here too. There are the Mountforts on the West Bank. Their ancestors fought at the Battle of Hastings. There's an old stone in a churchyard in England that proves it. Then there's Mrs Venables, who still lives in the original homestead built by her grandfather. . . . Oh yes, you could easily write a whole book about East London."

Upon the promenade—for all South African ports are also seaside resorts—I visited a fascinating place; an aquarium filled with fish from the Indian Ocean. There were beautiful little coloured fish like flowers which floated up, made mouths at me, and disappeared. There was a glazed eye behind a rock, and behind the eye a sinister intelligence that moved a tentacle. There were small, hurrying, transparent fish which wheeled and manœuvred as if drilled by a group will.

I saw the pine-cone fish that, because it lives in the black depths of the ocean, has been given luminous organs on the lower jaws. There was an electric ray which paralyses its victim with an electric shock and, having done so, has to retire to recharge its " batteries ". There is a hermit crab which goes through life with a stinging anemone on its back to protect it. The anemone is willing to do this in return for the movement it receives, and the better feeding conditions. When the crab grows out of his old shell and finds another one, he carefully removes and reseats his old friend on the new abode before he moves off.

§ 4

I was met at East London by an official of the Transkeian General Council—the native Parliament of the Transkei— with whom I motored all day through the most fantastic deathscape it has ever been my misfortune to see. Nothing can exaggerate the melancholy spectacle of soil erosion. It is horrible to see a fine country bleeding to death.

The countless herds, having grazed the land to the bone, go drearily like Pharaoh's lean kine vainly seeking some blade of herbage left over from yesterday. They never appear to chew the cud, but are always on trek in search of something to eat. The grass can never seed and renew itself. The rain slides off the hard earth and runs off in rivulets, seeping into the cattle runs and the goat tracks, forming cracks which split open and widen into trenches which in their turn grow into gullies, and so the soil pours away. You can see this all day long for mile after mile.

The sharp hoofs of the goats—animals which are invaluable as bribes to a headman or a wizard—cut into the earth and mark out new areas for erosion. Their omniverous jaws devour every shoot of green.

Every time I saw a hut I had a fancy to enter, or a native I wanted to talk to, we stopped and plodded over the landscape. The pattern of life was much the same everywhere. Women were doing most of the work. Young boys were herding cattle and driving plough oxen. Old men sat about doing very little. The young men were away. The great social event of the Transkei, as of all native territories, I gathered, is what is called " a beer drink ". Upon these occasions natives gather from near and far and steadily drink Kaffir beer—a mild, thick brew made from maize or kaffir-corn—sometimes for days on end. If you would like to know what goes on behind the apparently placid surface of the native reserves, I would recommend *Reaction to Conquest* by Monica Hunter. Two other books which will help the stranger to understand the native problem, and, what is more important, to refrain from expressing any opinion about it, are *Race Attitudes in South Africa* by I. D. MacCrone, and *The Bantu in the City* by Ray E. Phillips.

Some of the women working in the fields appeared to be breaking the earth with mallets, others were gently scratching the soil with hoes. From far away—water always seems so far away—black maidens ascended a hill with pots on their heads, slowly, gracefully, in hieratic attitudes, reproducing upon a sunny hillside in South Africa the same lines that you may see by the light of tapers in the tomb of Pharaoh. Here indeed was spread out on every hand the native South Africa of the photograph and the publicity booklet. But it was much better. No photograph has ever caught the exquisite grace of a native girl as she moves like a brown faun in the sunlight, and no publicity brochure, with its " age-old " this or that and its " quaint " and

" picturesque customs ", has ever described the feeling that comes over you of sympathy for these fine-looking human beings with their basic niceness (" The old red native is one of Nature's gentlemen," was my friend's frequent comment), combined with perplexing thoughts of their place in the future.

We called on our way at agricultural schools where European and native teachers were expounding modern methods; and we went to " betterment areas " where a whole village had been persuaded to fence its land and kill off half its cattle with encouraging results. Once, descending a mountain miles from anywhere, we came to a tin shed in which a native girl in nurse's uniform, a very brave girl I thought, lived alone and administered a clinic. She told me with a merry laugh that her most frequent patients were men suffering from knife wounds for, as she said, " they are great fighters ".

We took the long and very beautiful road northward to Umtata, and I could readily understand why many people think the Transkei is the most beautiful part of South Africa. You can see for enormous distances where hill lies against hill, the native huts like clumps of mushrooms planted on the high places, the sky blue above, the aloe and the prickly pear rising from the side of the road. From various points of the compass, women converged on the villages with firewood or water, while children drove the cattle towards the kraals for the night.

It was strange to hear so much about malnutrition in a land which can hardly bear the weight of its beef and mutton. But the native, although surrounded by meat, rarely eats it except on ceremonial occasions. His staple diet is a porridge made of maize or mealies.

§ 5

Umtata, a diminutive city with a little Gothic cathedral and a see about the size of Wales, is a pretty place in grand mountain country, hot, well built, and far away from any-where. Blanketed Pondos and Tembus stroll about its arcaded streets, bringing a breath of the tribal wilds with them as they gravely examine the shop windows. In the memory of men still living, Umtata was a remote post on the banks of a river, where a few adventurous traders had persuaded a chief to allow them to build their huts.

Those of the white population of some two thousand who are not engaged in trade and commerce are officials of the Transkeian General Council, South Africa's interesting experiment in native Government. The Bantu Parliament meets in a fine white building which has been described as a pocket edition of the Australian Parliament Building at Canberra, but unfortunately it was not in Session when I was there.

My hotel might have been in the West End of London, except that the food and the service were better and belonged to the old pre-war world. After dinner I wandered about the warm streets as fascinated by the shop windows, full of spangles and snow with the approach of Christmas, as two mighty Pondos were with a little toy train. They were enchanted by it. They laughed at it. They tore themselves away from it only to return to chatter and laugh again and point out its details to each other. Although I could not understand a word they said, it was obviously in their eyes the little brother of the train which took one away to the mines of " Goldie "!

I went to bed that night to the sound of the crickets in the bougainvillea, but beyond lay the immense silence of hundreds of square miles where native huts stood on the hillsides and the land of the white man was a remote fantasy. From Umtata it seemed an incredibly long way back to Grahamstown and the old front line. . . .

One morning my friend of the General Council took me down to the coast, a distance of about fifty miles, through lovely hill country where successive ranges shouldered each other to the sky. It may have been the light, it may have been my mood, but I thought that, apart from the immediate surroundings of Cape Town, this was the finest looking bit of South Africa I had seen. It was the South Africa of the early aquatints; the South Africa of Latrobe, Burchell, Barrow and Gardiner. The circular thatched huts sprouted out of the landscape as naturally as the fungi which they so much resembled. Women crossed the landscape, big, bold-eyed creatures tinkling with bangles, bearing huge cargoes of firewood on their heads; girls drove ox-drawn sledges across the downs, also piled high with the wood, and boys clothed only in a flapping sack guarded the cattle and were only too glad to leave them and run shouting beside the car, waving their sticks.

We came down to sea level through hot, lush vegetation and to the banks of a deep river called the Umzimvubu, which led to a place which I shall always think of as a glimpse of an earthly paradise. Its name is Port St Johns. Mountains covered with trees rose above the estuary and the Indian Ocean broke in spray beyond a lagoon where children were playing. A few houses and an admirable hotel stood facing the lagoon, and the whole place was steeped in peace, contentment and warmth.

Here for the first time I smelt semi-tropical South Africa. All resemblance to the Mediterranean had vanished. Papaws grew beside the road. There were mangoes and avocado pears, and pineapples were threepence each. In a luscious green lane I saw Zulu cattle for the first time, beasts with wide-spreading horns, their hides strangely flecked with black and white like cattle pictured in the tombs of Ancient Egypt.

At night I could hear the Indian Ocean steadily pounding on the sands and in the morning, when a barefoot native girl came in and, with the almost touching gracefulness with which these people perform minor services, gave me a cup of tea, the sun was already up. I went for a walk with one of those dogs who waylay strangers and, having led them to the beach, blackmail them with wistful expressions to fling stones into the sea. I managed to escape when he wasn't looking and return in time for breakfast. The breakfast papaw had been grown in a near-by garden. This fruit is like a cross between a melon and a marrow, and is eaten all over the Union with sugar and a slice of lemon.

We went to an entirely lovely place not far away called the Second Beach. There was nothing in sight but a sandy beach enclosed by rocks and rock pools, where Bantu girls were prodding for shell fish with spiked sticks. A man and a woman appeared through the trees, shed their wraps and ran across the hot sand into the waves.

Port St Johns was the most exquisite place I have seen for years. I could have stayed there for months, perhaps for ever.

§ 6

In the course of the next few days I travelled slowly up from Umtata to the borders of Natal. I entered many a native hut and found each one as neat and clean as a Dutch kitchen. I met a noted witch-doctor who fertilises the earth with charms before the sowing season. I saw natives and their wives as raw as you could find them, and the more primitive they were the better I liked them.

At Libode, a little town full of native convicts in striped jerseys, swinging picks under gum trees, I attended a native court where a white magistrate sat beneath an oleograph of Queen Victoria: at Lusikisiki I saw one of the *Grosvenor*'s guns in the hotel garden and heard the story of the most famous wreck in those parts—it happened in 1782—when an East Indiaman ran ashore and the passengers, including a number of white women, were never heard of again. Some people believe that three million pounds worth of treasure, including the old crown jewels of Delhi, went down with this ship, and many attempts have been made to find them.

As I went north I advanced into the mouth of a furnace. At times the temperature was over 100 in the shade. One day I saw a huge screen of remote blue mountains to the west. It was Basutoland. I travelled into splendid, heroic looking country and at the foot of a long hill came to an oasis of European life slightly canted on a hill slope, with Mount Currie at the back, and the name of this town was Kokstad.

Like Umtata, it was an unexpected gleam of civilisation in the wilderness, a small, go-ahead place of some two thousand white people, well built, well run, with a street of fine shops and roads of pleasant houses, and an hotel which gave me a bedroom and a bathroom which would have done credit to any hotel in Europe or America. In the dining-room about twenty travellers and residents, in appearance like any crowd you might find at Eastbourne or Bournemouth, sat down to dinner beneath electric fans while native boys in white garments served pea soup, fish, roast lamb and green peas, and a vanilla ice.

In this hotel I met a fiery little Englishman who was not well pleased with the " age of social justice " at home and had toured the Union looking for somewhere to settle. He was not easy to satisfy.

" It's a grand country, but what's its future to be ? " he asked. " If they pander to the native, as I suppose they will, and give him the vote someday, then there'll be nothing for it but to pack up. Have you been in the Free State? Well, go there. Those Dutch people may not like us, but I tell you they've got the right ideas. No nonsense about equality about them. I wish a few of the British South Africans who talk to me about social justice and the rest of it would go home and have a dose of it ! "

" So you're not going to settle out here ? "

" I can't make up my mind," he replied. " Has it occurred to you that this country is like England was in the Nineteenth Century: a small established aristocracy with a huge labour force just beginning to feel its feet ? "

" Yes, but . . ." I began.

" There's no but about it at all, sir," he said sternly. " We've handed our country over to the mob and it's happening all over the world. When people lose faith in themselves and forget how to rule, it's bound to happen ! "

What else he might have said I shall never know, for at that moment a middle-aged Englishwoman whom I had noticed at dinner entered the room and came towards us.

" Here's that poisonous female again," growled my acquaintance. " I must go ! "

He left the room and she came and sat down at my table.

She had come out to the Union to visit relatives.

" Such a lovely country," she said. " Such a lovely country to live in if only one could close one's eyes to the misery around one. Yes, I mean the dear natives. They lead such hard lives, don't you think ? "

In the morning I motored into Natal, and at Ixopo, where the temperature was 110 in the shade, the petrol evaporated in the feed pipe and I was stranded on a shadeless road. At last I walked to a native kraal and managed to make a girl understand that I wanted a bucket of water. She carried this on her head to the car without spilling a drop, and when I had soaked rags in it and cooled the feed pipe, I managed to continue my journey. I had often been held up by snow and ice, but never before by heat.

§ 7

I found Pietermaritzburg sweltering in heat. Indian waiters were serving iced drinks to men in palm beach suits. The whole city—it is the capital of Natal—vibrated to the snapping of the cicadas in the gardens.

Having now left the boundary of the old colony, my thoughts turned to the central fact of South African history, the creation of the other three provinces and the story of the Voortrekkers, two of whom are commemorated in the name of Natal's capital—Gerrit Maritz and Piet Retief.

I have said something about the creation of the Boer frontiersman who early in history began to wander away from Cape Town with his cattle. Until the eighteen-thirties his trek took him eastward and parallel with the sea, along the coastal grasslands, but he did not attempt to cross the mountains into what are now the Free State and the Transvaal. That region was known only to missionaries and hunters.

At the time when the 1820 Settlers were cynically thrown into the front line, the Boer trek had been met and halted by the Bantu trek moving in the opposite direction, and the result was the Kaffir Wars. From that time a solid wall of Bantu barred further movement, and if trekking were to continue it would have to be over the mountains to the central plains. And that is what the Boers decided to do. Suffering from grievances of many kinds against the British Government, they decided to remove themselves from the jurisdiction of the colony and to seek new lands where they might live in peace under their own laws. They did not dislike the British settlers. Briton and Boer who had fought side by side in Albany against the Kaffirs were the best of friends; indeed, several 1820 Settlers who had married Boer girls took part in the Trek, notably John and Thomas Montgomery, whose diaries and reminiscences have just been edited by Professor C. J. Uys of Bloemfontein. It was the remote control from Whitehall that the Boers could not tolerate, and the knowledge, which cannot be glossed over, that from the earliest times of the British occupation some missionaries had slandered the Boer and had pictured him to their subscribers at home as little better than a cruel savage. Perhaps the final straw was Lord Glenelg's surprising dictum that the Kaffirs had been right when, with one stroke of the pen, he wiped out the hard-won gains of fifteen months destruction and bloodshed and ordered the Governor of the Cape to restore the frontier as it had been before the Kaffir War of 1835–6. That was the breaking point, and the Boer decided to leave a colony in which he despaired of receiving justice or understanding.

Though the Boer had been unaffected by the French Revolution or the Industrial Revolution, the fires of the Reformation still glowed in him. Almost his only reading for a century had been the Old Testament. And as this vigorous race of frontiersmen moved out of the Colony in Biblical formation, with their flocks and their herds, their man servants and their maid servants, their hearts were uplifted by the conviction that they were God's Chosen People.

The pace of their exodus was that of their oxen. Many full spans of sixteen drew the heavy wagons over the grasslands, loaded with the earthly possessions of their owners. An American would have recognised in this scene a companion picture to the trek of the covered wagons to the West.

The Boer wagon was as truly a creation of the frontier as the Boer himself. It was the heavy European farm wagon adapted to Africa. This ship of the veld was small—only twelve feet in length—and it moved on four heavy wheels shod with half-inch iron. Rising from its body, upon semi-circular hoops, was a tilt of canvas, part painted to resist the rain and part unpainted to admit the air. In spite of its

massive build, a trek wagon could be taken apart, as sometimes happened on the mountain passes, and reassembled on
the other side.

It was driven by a man who sat with a long whip upon the
front box, or kist. He drove more with his voice than with
his whip, for he knew the temperament and name of every ox
in the span. The two most powerful beasts were placed on
either side the disselboom, or wagon-shaft, then the team were
yoked two by two, and led by the two most intelligent or most
experienced oxen. In order to keep them straight, a voorloper, or walker in front—generally a small Hottentot boy—
led them, grasping a leather thong attached to the horns of the
leaders. The sight that gladdened the frontier heart more
than most things was a well-matched span.

Inside the wagons were the older people and the young
children. At a pace of two or three miles an hour, every
young person would be riding or walking, and engaging in
the hundred and one tasks of the caravanserai. There were
enormous numbers of cattle and sheep to be herded and kept
on the move. These animals ate wide brown paths through
the grasslands as they slowly advanced. Horsemen trotted
ahead, scouting or hunting, but the main body would ride
near the wagons, flintlocks at the saddle.

When there were hundreds of wagons on the move, widely
spaced to allow the flocks and herds to graze, the trek must
have looked an apparently unwieldy migration. But the
organisation was intensely sensitive. Many years of frontier
fighting were behind it, and the defensive system of the laager,
whereby the wagons were wheeled into a circle or a square
and made into a fortress, was well known and was to become
an almost automatic military manœuvre. Let a couple of
scouts signal on the skyline, and instantly the trek would
observe a changed pattern and be ready for danger. The
Boers soon learned to react to peril like a hedgehog.

Strict domestic discipline was kept on trek. Children were
not allowed to have a glorious holiday, but at the frequent
halting places had to attend open-air schools, and one pupil
testified in later life that the rod was not spared.

Once they had forded the Orange River Drifts, the country

into which the trekkers climbed was the southern end of Africa's immense high plateau, whose mean level is higher than the top of Table Mountain. It is tilted towards the west, so that all its rivers flow into the Atlantic. They saw a country dotted with hills that levelled out as they went north into enormous plains where the birds flew over miles of grassland. As they were looking for pasture, this land must have seemed a goodly sight. It had only one disadvantage: it was still too near Cape Colony.

It was a land of eerie emptiness and desolation. The hand of Death had only recently been lifted from it. What is now the Free State, the Transvaal, Natal, and Rhodesia, had been practically depopulated during Bantu tribal wars in which, it is believed, no fewer than a million and a half natives perished. Instead of the hundreds of tribes who might have barred their way, there was nothing but a vast, deserted battle-field. For something like forty years a great native war of extermination had been going on behind the iron curtain of African distance. It was waged by the Zulus, then far beyond European influence, and the devastation it brought to such enormous areas would seem to contradict that picture of the idyllic world in which the native lived before the coming of the white man.

§ 8

Did the trekkers know where their Promised Land lay, or were they moving at random?

Some years before the Great Trek, scouts had been sent to spy out the land. At much the same time two parties left the Colony bound for the north, and made incredible journeys. One party was massacred by natives; the other, decimated by fever and its cattle killed by tsetse fly, descended the hair-raising precipices to Delagoa Bay, from whose malarial shores a few survivors were eventually rescued by sea.

The real Great Trek was started in 1835 by a man named Hendrik Potgieter. With about two hundred people he went up into the Free State, where he was joined by other farmers, including the Krugers, who had with them a boy of ten named

Paul, who was to become a future President of the Transvaal. They travelled on slowly month by month, living upon the country, taking note of everything they saw, and riding out on long exploring expeditions. Although the country was depopulated, it was still patrolled by war bands of the Matabele from the north. One day a roaming band surprised a party of trekkers and massacred fifty-three men, women, and children.

The Boers knew that they would return in stronger force, so they sought a commanding position, now called Vegkop, and at the foot of a hill placed fifty ox-wagons in a circle, lashed together with chains and the openings closed with thorn trees. In the centre of the circle they placed four wagons for the women and children, roofed with planks and hides to catch the falling assegais.

The Matabele army which was sent against these fifty Boers is said to have numbered five thousand. Out of range of the Boer guns, they sat down for hours round the laager and slew eighty oxen, upon which they feasted. The little garrison waited for the attack which they knew would soon come. The guns stood cleaned. Hundred of bullets had been cast. The women were ready to reload, and any young boy who could fire a gun had a place in the line.

All night the Boer sentries watched the camp fires of the five thousand gleaming in the darkness. One morning they heard the hissing and the shield-beating of a Matabele advance, and successive waves of warriors dashed themselves against the wagons and thorn bushes and even managed to wrench the wagons out of alignment. The Boer bullets bored holes through the mass formation, but with reckless courage the Matabele, even though shot at with elephant guns at point-blank range, tried to mount the wagons and tear their way inside. After three hours they gave it up and retired, leaving four hundred and thirty dead piled round the laager and over a thousand assegais inside it.

Potgieter's brother was stabbed to death, also another man. Those were the only two deaths among the Christians.

As the native army went off, it drove in front of it all the Boer cattle. A fortnight later, far away in the north, an

English traveller and big-game hunter, William Cornwallis Harris, who had been up in the Matabele country, encountered a great army of warriors who were driving enormous herds of cattle. They surrounded his wagons as if they would have attacked him. They were dressed in fur kilts made of monkey tails, tippets of white cow tails hung round their shoulders, while their knees, wrists, elbows, and ankles were ornamented with a single ox tail. Many of their shields, he noticed, had been drilled by musket-balls. He continued to meet large straggling parties of this army throughout that day. They were the defeated host from Vegkop.

This fight was the first step towards that control of the north which added the Free State and the Transvaal to the map; and from that moment one can begin to think, not of Cape Colony, but of South Africa. But the Boers, although victorious, were an army without transport. With the decaying corpses of their enemies all round, they were forced to move, and had to yoke their horses to the wagons. But help was near, for a second party had crossed the Orange River under the command of a forceful man named Gerrit Maritz. They had a hundred wagons and were a mighty reinforcement.

Both parties now linked up in the neighbourhood of Thaba 'Nchu, a mountain rising two thousand feet above the plain, and there they stayed for the remaining months of winter, hunting and making plans. Could they continue the trek before they had cleared the country of Matabele? They decided to send out a Commando of a hundred and seven horse-men—a pitifully small force, it would seem—on an expedition two hundred and fifty miles away, in order to assert their authority and regain their cattle. How right they were is proved by Cornwallis Harris, who, during his visit to the Matabele chief, Mzilikazi, had heard whispers of the chief's determination to exterminate the white invaders.

The little Commando set off on the long journey to the north. They surprised the Matabele army at Mosega, slew over four hundred without loss to themselves, and returned, bringing back their lost cattle and accompanied by three American missionaries, including Wilson, whose wife was the first white woman to die in the Transvaal. The chief was not present at Mosega, so that the Boers knew they would have to fight a more decisive action at some future time.

The self-confidence of the Boer and his sure instinct in these matters are something for wonder and admiration. His trust in his gun and his horse, and his unerring eye for guerilla war, are only less remarkable than his contempt for natives in the mass. But reading his records side by side with those of Harris and the diaries of the great missionary, Dr Moffat, it is clear how intensely nerve-wracking from the point of view of Cape Town must have been those Boer Commandoes thirsting for the blood of natives who were nominally the friends of His Britannic Majesty.

The spring of 1837 saw the Christian men still encamped round Thaba 'Nchu, but no longer a happy band, for a bitter quarrel had broken out between Potgieter and Maritz. Both were strong men of different types, Potgieter a lean, tough old Pilgrim Father, and Maritz a more comfortable, sophisticated person who had been a prosperous wagon-maker. Whether the unity of the trek would have been threatened is unknown, for at a critical moment in April news came that an undeniable leader, Piet Retief, was coming up to them across the river.

Retief was liked and respected by them all. He was a man of affairs and consequence, and was probably also the best educated among them. Born of Western Province Huguenots, he had been a trader, a contractor, and a farmer. He was fifty-six years of age, a fine speaker and a disciplinarian. He came with a hundred and twenty men and a hundred wagons. In one of the wagons was his family, which included two sons and two girls, both so pretty that they had inspired the name of his farm, Mooimeisiesfontein—the Spring of the Pretty Maids.

Retief rode into camp ahead of his wagons, and was surrounded by an eager crowd who persuaded him to become Governor and Commander. Once or twice he modestly attempted to put aside the crown, but it was no good.

It was indeed an animated scene upon the plain that day, where flocks and herds, wagons, bivouacs, and camp-fires stretched for miles as people walked and rode in from great distances to catch a glimpse of the leader. It must have been

o

the strangest mixture of domesticity and frontier war : washing and petticoats hanging on thorn bushes, bearded guerillas sitting horses with guns at the saddle, cooking-pots and elephant guns, nursing mothers and old patriarchs, and wondering groups of Hottentot servants, many of whom had followed their masters into the unknown.

Hundreds of trekkers would press round the leader, and every wagon would be a grandstand. Pretty girls in high-waisted dresses, guarding their complexions with parasols or little masks of goatskin, stood upon tiptoe on the wagons, laughing and chattering. Spartan matrons in serge gowns, their severely parted hair concealed by sun-bonnets tirelessly tucked and ruched, men with smooth upper lips and bearded chins beneath vast straw hats with green linings, crowds of darting children, an outer circle of tall, shaggy Boers from the uttermost edges of Cape cattle-ranches, pipe in mouth, gun in hand, and sheath-knife at the waist, grandfathers and grandmothers, strapping youths and buxom wenches—all would gather to welcome Piet Retief.

And it may be that upon such an occasion the Sabbath garments came out of the wagon kists : carefully tended corduroys, rustling gowns of sprigged silk, special go-to-kirk kappies of flowered linen, maybe even muffs, for the more prosperous of the Voortrekkers carefully took away with them such emblems of their former lives, as you can see in any museum. It seems at least probable that from the pale blue wagon of Gerrit Maritz may have descended a figure resplendently crowned with a bell-brimmed topper, for in those days no Sunday, and certainly no republic, would have seemed quite right without that symbol of rectitude.

The excitement would die down and there would be the sound of psalms. Evening would come. The milkers would go to the cows, and the flocks and herds would be gathered for the night. There would be a smell of wood burning, of coffee and mutton; and the light of the setting sun would linger last on Thaba 'Nchu and go; and it would be starlight.

§ 9

Even the most ardent admirers of the Voortrekkers have never claimed that they were easy to manage. Like country folk everywhere, they had their prejudices, feuds, and suspicions: they were distrustful of everything, and not least of each other. Considering their background, however, their break with the past and their present circumstances in the wilderness, with the future still in hazard, they held together with remarkable success. They could certainly have given points to the Israelites, who in a similar situation afflicted Moses with very kind of abuse and complaint.

Upon the crowded modern stage of the early Nineteenth Century they suddenly become like people in a story by Homer. They might be Greeks in corduroy. They broke out of the modern world, with its machinery and its organisation, back to a time when individual prowess and the encounters of a few people achieved an extraordinary human value, as if Thermopylae were being fought again. It is this epic touch that makes their story so interesting. Fights like Vegkop and Blood River read like Greek history. Marathon and Thermopylae have made a great stir in the world, but were they not merely small, heroic engagements of this kind? Potgieter with his elephant gun and his stabbed brother is something out of Greek poetry: so is Piet Retief riding to his death down the Drakensberg.

Ten days after Retief had arrived, the trek moved on. It was now necessary to split themselves into five or six groups, separated by considerable distances because of the vast herds of cattle and sheep that needed pasture. Two things worried the trekkers. Where were they going? And when should they again attack the Matabele? As far as their destination was concerned, there were two promised lands instead of one—a most perplexing problem upon which, no wonder, they were divided. Retief wanted to lead them down the mountains into Natal, where they would have a port on the Indian Ocean. Potgieter's mind was made up for the Transvaal. Maritz sided with Retief.

At a place now called De Hartplaas, at Winburg, on the Little Vet River, they paused early in June to frame a constitution. Oaths were taken and it was decided to call themselves the " United Laager ", and the land to which they were going was to be the " Free Province of New Holland in South East Africa ", a clumsy name in which we can see the childhood loyalty of the Reverend Erasmus Smit, a rotund little unordained Dutch ex-missionary who was the only person resembling a churchman on the trek.

Hardly had this been done when the camp was invaded by the breezy self-confidence of Piet Uys, who joined them with a fourth party of many wagons, bringing the total number of trekkers up to between three and four thousand. Among his wagons was one in which an old man, his father, Jacob Uys, sat clasping a large Bible which had been given to him by the British settlers as the wagons had passed through Grahamstown. They had expressed regret at losing their friends and wished them luck in the land they were seeking.

Piet Uys soon plunged into local politics and began to quarrel violently with Maritz. Meantime the trek slowly crept across country through the winter months of June and July, so severe a winter that great numbers of sheep and cattle died by the way. Retief was still determined to go to Natal, and sent horsemen riding to the Drakensberg to see if a pass existed suitable for wagons. They left from a farm now called Brandhoek, west of Winburg, and returned in a fortnight's time with the news that there were five passes leading down towards the sea.

No decision upon the destination of the trek could be reached, and the winter months wore on and spring came, and with it Retief's determination hardened. Potgieter was still equally determined to punish the Matabele. So the United Laager became divided: Retief with a small following went east to the Drakensberg, and the others went north to make war on Mzilikazi.

It is said that Potgieter's Commando left between four and five thousand Matabele dead upon the battlefield. Mzilikazi fled with the remnant of his army into what is now Southern Rhodesia, where he founded Bulawayo. The Matabele never recrossed the Limpopo again, except as raiders; and so the Commando laid the foundations of the Transvaal Republic.

§ 10

While this was happening, Piet Retief rode on with a few friends to make a reconnaissance in Natal. Behind him straggled for miles the wagons of his followers, which halted some few miles from the pass, waiting for the messengers to return with news of the Promised Land. They waited for five weeks, enjoying a holiday in beautiful country. It was October. The veld was covered with gay spring flowers; down the mountain sides the rains of winter still fell from rock to rock, and dark gorges led ever upward into a solitude of peaks. Meanwhile Retief rode down into Natal.

Strange as it may seem, in view of the indignation with which the Voortrekkers left home, cordial letters were passing between Retief and the Cape authorities. He had recently written to the Governor assuring him of his friendly feelings towards " His " Majesty's Government—for he did not know that Queen Victoria had just come to the throne—and a later letter told of his intention to explore Natal. At that time it was an unknown land where about thirty English traders lived with the consent of the Zulu tyrant, Dingaan. Retief wished to contact these men at Durban to make sure of their attitude; and he also intended to visit Dingaan's kraal and ask the Zulu for a grant of territory.

The explorers climbed into the mighty Drakensberg, where blue summits touched the sky, and around them they saw evidence of a country startingly different from the level plains upon which Potgieter's heart was firmly set. It was a land of richer vegetation, of brighter birds, and of strange flowers never seen in the Cape. Through the darkness of mountain forests and the bleakness of a sterile world of rock, their path led upwards to the Berg, and then Retief saw what he believed to be the Promised Land. Far below it lay, rounded hill upon hill to the very sky and the ocean.   It was the fairest prospect he had ever seen.

Round about Durban Bay in those days, living in shacks and huts, were those few Englishmen whose adventures would make Robinson Crusoe's seem a tame story.   They had gone there to trade in ivory and anything else they could find.   Groups of unattached natives had squatted near, and looked up to these white men as their chiefs.   In the district were also the American missionaries who had sailed from Boston in 1834, the party which had included the Wilsons and two others who were found by Potgieter at Mosega.

The little band of English traders welcomed Retief with open arms and appeared to be delighted to think that he might establish a republic in the district.   They had been petitioning the Government for years to do something about Natal, and it seemed good to them that at last some Christian men would colonise it.   As in the old Colony on the Zuurveld, British and Afrikaner, with no Government to frustrate them, were the best of friends because they were thinking, not of economy or policy or philanthropy, but of South Africa.

It was agreed that it would be necessary for Retief to see Dingaan, the chief of the Zulu nation.   This individual was a fantastic monster whose word was life or death.   Inflicting suffering, such as burning a hole with a sun-glass in the bodies of his attendants, was one of his more playful occupations.

They set off for " the Place of the Elephant ", Umgungundhlovo, a hill some sixty miles to the north-east, on the other side of the Tugela river.   Leaving the wagons at the river, they crossed with their interpreter, Thomas Halstead, an Englishman.   They saw a large town composed of hundreds of thatched bee-hive huts arranged in rows with military precision, in an oval formation that covered the hill-top.   Huts higher than the others were built for shields and war gear, to keep them out of the way of ants and the larger vermin.   In this place lived Dingaan with a hundred wives, surrounded by a mighty and magnificent army corps of Zulus, each regiment with its own quarters and its own distinctive war dress.

An adjoining hill was known as Hlomo Amabuta—the place of execution—a Golgotha above which the vultures circled hopefully all day long. Not far off were some new huts just occupied by the Reverend Francis Owen, M.A., of St. John's College, Cambridge. Recently a curate at Normanton in Yorkshire, the missionary call had led him and his gallant wife, his sister and a serving-maid, to this ogre's den in Zululand.

Dingaan kept his visitors waiting; and at the end of two days they were solemnly conducted into his presence. Against a background of black concubines they saw an enormously corpulent Zulu sitting in a chair, with a red veil over his eyes. There was a long silence until the autocrat spoke. Retief's anxiety for his people was such that he seems to have been willing to read more hope into his interview than either Owen or Halstead did. After criticising Retief's appearance, for he was not a typically tall Boer, the chief charged the trekkers with having stolen some of his cattle. This Retief denied, and suggested the thief was a minor native chief. Well, then, replied Dingaan, get them back and come and see me again. His grant of territory was conditional, and it was not even clear that it was not land already given to the English. Nevertheless, Retief felt himself obliged to comply.

During the negotiations Retief had written several enthusiastic letters to his comrades, with the result that the wagons came pouring down the pass of the Drakensberg into Natal. The pass, although steep on the Natal side, was not dangerous, and only one wagon capsized with the loss of a set of chains. A lion, attracted by the noise, took a cow. Eventually a thousand white covered wagons came creaking down into Natal, and the host spread itself out upon the west side of the Tugela, where the Bushman's River meets the Blaauwkrans.

Retief rode back to his people and organised a Commando which went off after the missing cattle. Some two months after his first meeting with Dingaan, Retief with a large company set out to clinch his bargain, driving the recovered cattle before them. It was now the end of January, 1838. Sixty-six Europeans, with Halstead as interpreter, and about thirty Hottentot servants, rode out from the laager and took the road to Umgungundhlovo—the " Place of the Elephant ".* Several

* Or "the Secret Conclave of the King ".

small boys, including Retief's son, had begged their parents to let them go to see the King of Zululand, and these children were given a holiday and set off, one may imagine with what pride and excitement, with the cavalcade.

The Boers fired a volley to announce their arrival and were given a camping site on a hill-slope outside the town.   Enormous crowds of Zulus in war dress had been arriving for days, and these pressed round to see the Boers.   Dingaan wished his visitors to " dance on horseback ", whereupon they formed up and went through a Buffalo Bill act. The Zulu warriors then treated them to dances.

On the following day Retief and a few of his chief officers had a long conference with Dingaan.   Now that his cattle had been restored, the chief said he was willing to complete his share of the bargain and accordingly made his mark on a document ceding territory to the Boers.   Retief placed this document in his hunting-pouch.   The next day was one of merry-making and preparations for departure.   The Boers sat in the kraal and saw in the sunlight, as on a great arena, regiment after regiment of young warriors dance with cattle, threading their path between them, in and out, each regiment dancing with differently marked beasts.   The first regiment danced with four hundred hornless cattle, the next with four hundred black, a third with four hundred white oxen.

Dingaan plied his visitors with questions and boasted of his greatness.   As a finale—a most unfortunate one, it might be thought—Retief gave a display of mounted action in which the Boers exhibited their skill in firing from the saddle.   Dingaan had not seen anything like this before; but he had heard about it.   That was the sort of action that had ruined his fellow Zulu, Mzilikazi, and had made him a fugitive beyond the Limpopo.   The Boers, having finished their display, formed up and trotted away to their camp to off-saddle and cook the midday meal.   After this, as they were preparing to go, a messenger arrived from Dingaan, asking them to delay their departure until the next morning, when, after more dances and a drink of Kaffir beer, they might go in peace.   It was decided that it would be tactless to decline his invitation.

Many people knew by this time that there was something in

the wind. The Reverend Francis Owen in his mission station overlooking Dingaan's kraal—missionary and chief were always watching each other through telescopes—was clearly bewildered and unhappy. It is said that he warned one of the Boers to go that night because something was " brewing " and the Zulus were "peculiar". There were other warnings. But it seems that Retief would not be convinced of Dingaan's treachery. On the morning of the next day two of the Boers went over and had breakfast with Owen. The missionary asked what they thought of Dingaan. They said he was " good ".

Shortly after breakfast Dingaan sent one of his generals to the Boers to say that everything was ready. Leaving their horses and guns in their camp, as they had been requested to do, they walked on foot to the great kraal where Dingaan was waiting for them. His chair, carved from a solid block of wood, had been brought into the open, and seated on this, with Retief by his side and the rest of the Boers sitting on the ground some little way off, Dingaan gave the sign for the dances to begin.

Two regiments had been ordered to dance, the White Shields and the Black Shields, and, as the Boers sipped Kaffir beer and the little boys who had come with them drank milk, the warriors, without arms, began to chant and to gyrate in the movements of the native dance. Behind, watching, were two regiments in war dress armed with spears and knobkerries. As the dance reached a climax and the chant rose louder, the bulky form of Dingaan suddenly rose from the throne and in a voice of thunder he shouted:

" Hither, my warriors! Kill the wizards! "

Before the Boers realised what was happening, the Zulus had flung themselves upon them. Thomas Halstead cried, " We are finished! " " Treason! " " Help, O Lord! " were other cries, as the seized men fought savagely with knives. Several Zulus were killed and others, maddened by knife-wounds, broke the command that no blood must be shed in the kraal as they clubbed some of the Boers to death on the spot. The rest, fighting and stabbing, were over-powered and dragged away to the Hill of Execution. Above the screams, the howls, the chanting, and the rattle of spears against shields, was heard the great voice of Dingaan ordering the murder.

Just before this happened a Zulu knocked at the door of Owen's mission station with a message from Dingaan. He bade Owen not to be frightened, but he was going to kill the Boers. Owen, who had been afraid for days, was wondering how he might risk death by warning the Boers, when some-one in the room shouted, " They are killing the Boers *now*! "

" I turned my eyes and behold! an immense multitude on the hill," he wrote in his *Diary* that evening. " About 9 or 10 Zulus to each Boer were dragging their helpless unarmed victim to the fatal spot, where those eyes which awaked this morning to see the cheerful light of day for the last time, are now closed in death. I lay myself down on the ground. Mrs and Miss Owen were not more thunderstruck than myself. We each comforted the other. Presently the deed of blood being accomplished the whole multitude returned to the town to meet their sovereign, and as they drew near to him set up a shout which reached the station and continued for some time. . . . At this crisis I called all my family in and read the 91st Psalm, so singularly and literally applicable to our present situation, that I could with difficulty proceed with it! "

The Boers died fighting hopelessly to the last. Retief was made to witness the death of his son and his followers. The young boys were killed with the others. The bodies were piled upon the hill of death, and over them were the bodies of the grooms and attendants. The heart and liver of Retief were removed and taken to Dingaan so that he might look upon them. Over sixty Boers, one Englishman, and numerous attendants lay dead in the sunlight of that morning in February, and the vultures of Hlomo Amabuta came down from the sky.

Within a few days Owen and his family fled from Dingaan, fearing until the very last that they might also be murdered. He remained in South Africa for another three years, and then returned to England to become vicar of a parish near Sheffield.

The discovery of Owen's *Diary* has put to rest for ever the terrible rumours, natural perhaps in that time of grief and anxiety, that the Boers had been betrayed by their English friends. In the days that followed practically the whole English settlement in Natal was wiped out in battles with the Zulus.

§ 11

The moment the Boers had been slain, Dingaan selected three of his crack regiments, numbering about ten thousand, to exterminate the laagers. The plumed warriors, armed with throwing and stabbing assegais and knobkerries, were ordered to move swiftly and silently, seeking the cover of ravines, and to surprise the Boers as they slept.

By this time those Voortrekkers who had come down into Natal were spread out over a wide stretch of country. Their tented wagons could be seen for miles, outspanned upon the banks of the rivers that flow into the Tugela. Some were in family groups, some, more prudently, in laager. By the night of February 16th, ten days after the massacre, thousands of Zulus had crept up to within rushing distance and lay waiting for darkness to fall.

The Zulus stormed the encampments during the night. In the morning the grief-striken Boers counted the dead bodies of their friends and relatives. Forty-one men had perished, fifty-six women, eighty-five children, and two hundred and fifty coloured servants who had served their masters faithfully to the end. That was the Blaauwkrans Massacre.

The Boers knew that there could be no future until Dingaan had been defeated, but they had to wait for ten months—until December—before they were able to destroy him, and in that interval Maritz died. Under the leadership of a great Afrikaner, Andries Pretorius, who subsequently gave his name to the Transvaal capital, they formed a Commando of four hundred and sixty-four men and set off to face an enemy who was numbered by tens of thousands. They took with them sixty-four ox-wagons. On the way they begged God to help them and vowed that if they were granted victory they would build a church and for ever keep the day of their triumph as a

Holy Sabbath.   Professor Uys tells me that while this vow was made, the laager was guarded by Englishmen.

The Commando made contact with the enemy near the Zulu capital and formed laager with a river at their back.   In the morning the Zulus attacked and the Boers held their fire until the enemy was ten yards off, then a hail of elephant ball and buck-shot poured from the wagons.   The battle lasted three hours and the Boer guns were smoking hot.

Then came the moment in the plan of a Boer battle which above all others rouses admiration.   Bart Pretorius, the brother of the General, put himself at the head of a small body of horsemen and galloped out, the men levelling their hot gun-barrels and firing from the saddle.   In the last of three charges the Boers managed to split the Zulu army.   Seeing this, Andries Pretorius took command of three hundred horsemen and came galloping out of the laager.   He rode straight into the gap between the Zulus, and then one section wheeled left, and the other right, and each began to press back and drive the now demoralised enemy in front of them.   The rout became a headlong flight.

When the Boers rallied and assembled, and came back to the laager with their hot guns and their spent ponies, they saw that the river was red with Zulu blood; and its name on the map to-day is Blood River.   If one sometimes suspects upon reading of these Homeric contests, that the casualties must have been estimated on a classical basis, there is at least firm authority for the statement that the Zulu dead at Blood River, which were carefully counted, numbered some three thousand.

Pretorius then pushed on to Dingaan's capital, which he found in flames.   Dingaan fled into Swaziland and was buried in a grave which was unknown until only a few months ago.*   The Boers went to the hill of execution, where they recognised, by scraps of clothing, the sheaths of knives, and such like, the bodies of Piet Retief and his men, which had been lying there for ten months.   It was the law at Umgungundhlovo that nothing was ever touched upon Hlomo Amabuta.   The valley was strewn with copper and brass armlets and other

* In the Ubombo range overlooking Gollel in N. Zululand.

objects of adornment, but no native would dare to touch them. The hill belonged to its guardian deities, the vultures.

In the pockets and round the bodies of the murdered Boers were found all the personal possessions they had been carrying at the time of their deaths. From the hunting-pouch of Retief was taken the document signed by Dingaan, ceding Natal to the Boers.

Two strong impressions remain after reading this chapter in Boer history. One is the singular resemblance between the Boer leaders and Cromwell's Ironsides; the other is the military prowess and the personal courage of the Zulus. Dingaan was a monster, but was probably no more cruel or fantastic than many another black or white uncontrolled human being. He was also a Zulu patriot. In an attempt to keep the white man out of his country, he had added guile and treachery to the magnificent military machine inherited from his predecessor, Shaka.

The Boers fulfilled their vow. At Pietermaritzburg, which became the capital of the republic in Natal, they built a church; and to this day December 16, Dingaan's Day, is a solemn day of remembrance throughout the Union.

§ 12

The place that interested me most in Pietermaritzburg was the Church of the Vow, now the Voortrekker Museum. It is a modest little building, devoted to the relics of that not so far off day.

I saw the only organ used on the trek, which I suppose came down the Berg with Erasmus Smit. There is the footrule used in laying out Pietermaritzburg in 1839. There are several early Nineteenth Century dresses, which show how charming the mooi meisies must have looked on Sundays. Then there are some fine and impressive waistcoats, wedding veils, and, in an inner hall, a complete trek-wagon.

To me the most interesting object in the Museum is a dark green glass flask found on the body of Piet Retief. In raised relief on one side is an American eagle and a wreath containing the initials, "J.K.B."; on the other side are a number of

Masonic emblems used in England and America during the early part of the Nineteenth Century. Such flasks, which are not common, are a puzzle to Masonic antiquaries. Although the Museum calls it a " water bottle ", I believe most authorities believe that these bottles originally contained gin or whisky. The double of Retief's bottle, bearing the same initials, which are those of the maker, is to be seen in the Grand Lodge Museum in Freemasons Hall, London, and other specimens are known to exist in the United States.

The Director of the Yale University Art Gallery tells me that these " J.K.B." bottles are believed to have been made at the beginning of the Nineteenth Century at Keene, New Hampshire, a time when discussions on Masonry had reached a peak in America. " J.K.B." is thought to be a combination of makers' marks at the Keene works.

Who gave this American flask to Retief, I wonder? So far as I know, he was not a Mason. The problem is confused by a picture of an entirely different flask with silver mountings illustrated by Dr Godée-Molesbergen in his *Zuid-Afrika's Geschiedenis in Beeld*, who says that this was given to Retief by the Freemasons of Grahamstown and that it is in the Pretoria Museum. He wrote in 1913. But it is not there, nor, so far as I can find out, was it ever there! Where is it? The Pietermaritzburg flask was presented by the Theological Seminary, Stellenbosch, and there is no reason to question its genuineness, but it would be interesting to know how this mysterious object came into Retief's possession. It is possible that the American missionaries who were established near Durban at that time gave it to him. But if he already possessed one from the Freemasons of Grahamstown, why should he have been given another?

It must have gratified the Voortrekkers to know that their hero went to his death with the American eagle in his pocket.

Pietermaritzburg is a fine-looking city which wears its air of grace and quality with becoming ease. The summer heat can be like that of an oven and there is no relief from it at night, when the semi-tropical trees stand in the thick air and one longs for a breath of wind.   The inhabitants refer to the city as " sleepy hollow ", and make jokes about their indolence that are contradicted by the number of shops which sell tennis racquets, golf clubs, polo sticks, cricket bats and footballs.

There is a fine City Hall which is called Renaissance, but is really a massive bit of pure Edward VII, a distinct little period in architecture and dress.   I was taken to the much finer Provincial Council Building, where the Parliament of Natal assembled before the Union.   It was a strange sight to see the shadow of Westminster falling so far from home.   In an airy, classical chamber I was shown the bar of the House, the division bell, and, in a glass case, the ruffles, mace, cravat, and sword of Black Rod.   There is also a war relic of Westminster in the form of a stone from the Houses of Parliament.

Not unnaturally in a young country, public statuary in South Africa is an expensive civic indulgence which has as yet produced few masterpieces, and I was therefore impressed by the Natal Volunteer Memorial of the South African War, which stands in a little garden.   I thought it a notable piece of allegory, crowned by a lovely figure of a Winged Victory in the act of sheathing her sword.

Every evening as dusk begins to fall you will hear the sound of wings over Pietermaritzburg.   From every point of the sky flocks of birds are seen flying towards the city.   Some come in formation like duck, others come in enormous flocks, like starlings, and they settle among the trees in the Bird Sanctuary.

A five acre lake in a well planted park has been devoted to the birds, which might be classified as permanent residents, such as the water-fowl and the stately cranes, and more numerous lodgers, like the egrets, who fly off every morning to earn their keep in distant fields.   It is fascinating to watch their home-coming in the evening.   I was reminded of Trafalgar Square, where much the same thing occurs when the thousands of starlings come home to roost round the National Gallery and St Martin-in-the-Fields.   Here in Pietermaritzburg the egrets return in their hundreds of thousands, but more gracefully and with better manners than the London starlings.

The egret is the cow's little white companion, whose patient, statuesque figure is one of the memorable sights of the South

African countryside. He is called the tick-bird, and, having adopted a cow, his life is spent in standing beside it all day long, seizing insects disturbed by the animal's feet and, it is said, in picking up the gorged ticks which fall from its body. Sometimes an impatient egret is seen standing upon its cow.

It is as a lonely, devoted individual that you think of the tick-bird, a creature seen in ones and twos throughout South Africa. As you observe his little upright figure in the fields, it occurs to you that perhaps he accompanies the object of his devotion to bed. But this is not so. In the Bird Sanctuary it is proved that the tick-bird is as gregarious as the swallow or the starling. Each one belongs to a flock. As it grows dark, each tick-bird says good night to its cow and joins the great homeward flight, which settles like a snowstorm upon the trees round the lake.

On my way to Durban I paused to admire the Valley of a Thousand Hills, which is, after Table Mountain, perhaps the most talked of view in the Union. It is a view of Natal that may be seen by any casual visitor to Durban with an hour or two to spare, and it is indeed a panorama of green mountain country stretching away to Zululand that is not easily forgotten.

DURBAN

CHAPTER SEVEN

I go to Durban, hear of Dick King's famous ride, enter Zululand, attend a native dance, and pass through the country where the Isandhlwana Massacre occurred and where the Prince Imperial was killed. I spend a few days in the Game Reserve at Hluhluwe, where I encounter a charging rhino.

§ 1

A LINE of gleaming buildings, that reminds the traveller of Miami in Florida, rises from the sea and shines in the hard sunlight. The waves pound upon sandy beaches, the tide rises and falls in a great lagoon which is one of the finest harbours in Africa. And from a hill above the town at night you can look down and see the lights of Durban sparkling for miles.

There is an air of musical comedy or of a film set about this place. The light is just a little too strong and white to be sunlight, the flowers are a little too bright to be real, the flamboyant trees seem too exotic to be genuine, yet against this sunny, lotus-eating background the tramway system operates, motor omnibuses run to time, people go down to offices and earn their living, typewriters tap, cables are sent off to every part of the world; and in a huge municipal palace the mayor sits in an air-conditioned parlour, with several cooling pictures of New Zealand on the walls, and administers the affairs of what is, in spite of everything, a real city.

Like all South African ports, Durban is a delightful mixture of business and fun. Its streets are always filled by residents and visitors, so that in saying that the girls of Durban at once strike the observer with their charm and beauty, one is paying a compliment to the womanhood of the Union, for one may have been gazing with admiration upon the maidens of Pretoria or Bloemfontein. And where else in South Africa can you see a more provoking mixture of white and brown and black and yellow? You leave the main street and find yourself looking at a mosque or a Hindu temple. You see Moslems wearing the fez, and Indian women, in youth as frail as spectres, drifting along in clouds of mauve chiffon. Then in the next street you come to the more earthy Bantu market, where huge bronze-skinned native men are putting back municipally brewed Kaffir-beer with enormous heartiness. And on the wayside, a few steps from a spotless chemist's shop in which a man in white overalls will make up the most hieroglyphic of prescriptions, a native wizard sits offering for sale the paws of monkeys and the fat of the hippopotamus.

Among the tramcars, the motor buses, and the American limousines, stands the barbaric figure of the Zulu rickshaw "boy". Upon his head topples a fantastic structure of bull's horns and feathers, coloured beads hang about his fine body, and with a rhythmic, leathery sound of bare feet he trots between the shafts—the oddest-looking human taxi in the world.

Durban Europeans have their yacht club, a country club, and polo, swimming, golf, and cricket, and some are fortunate enough to live in imperial Roman villas upon hills where, between the snowy columns of their pergolas, they can watch the distant Indian sea. Great showers of brick-red and blue bougainvillea droop from the white pillars. In the still gardens, which have a warm, snapping, crackling life of their own, lizards bask and flash. The earth is ochre-red, and from it spring hot-looking flowers. Jacaranda trees hold bunches of blossom as blue as Kew in lilac time, and the Flamboyant, lit with its great red stars, is sometimes taller than an elm. In these exotic gardens I would come to a row of hollyhocks and a border of delphiniums with the feeling that I had been handed a glass of cool spring-water.

The first evening I was in Durban, I was invited to dine in a restaurant. The electric fans were working, for was it not December? There were mangoes with the dessert. My host, addressing the Indian waiter, said:

" It's a long time since I've seen you. How have you been keeping? "

The Indian at once adopted an expression of the utmost

misery. He cast down his eyes and said that Fate had been cruel to him, for he had lost a son. My friend said how sorry he was, and asked if he had any other children.

" Now," replied the waiter with an air of lugubrious loneliness, " I have only sixteen."

§ 2

It is not easy to surprise Durban in that slipshod, half-awake condition so familiar to the early riser in London and Paris. When seven o'clock strikes in the morning the place is fairly humming with activity: by eight o'clock not only can you buy almost anything, but you can also ring a man up at his office. By nine o'clock you begin to seek the shady side of the street and to understand why Durban begins its day so early.

An institution which gave me a great deal of pleasure is Durban's large and beautifully run Museum. What the Stone Age, the Bronze Age, Celtic, Roman, Anglo-Saxon, and so on, are to us, animal life is to the museums in South Africa. The bewildering variety of life on wings, crawling on its stomach, and walking on all fours, fills one with astonishment.

The South African birds which you begin to know very quickly are the egret, or tick-bird, the secretary bird, the big eagle, the lammervanger, who is sometimes seen sitting on a rock brooding, or more often gliding about the sky on unmoving wings, the cranes, and wild duck; but the great number of smaller birds remain unidentified until you go to a museum of this kind. One of the strangest birds I have ever heard of is the Honey Guide. It is not much larger than a sparrow and is greyish-brown in colour, with a spot of yellow on each shoulder. Its habits were described by Andrew Sparrmann in 1772, but no one believed him.

This bird, which is found in many parts of Africa, guides men and animals to bees' nests, and, when they have taken the honey, the bird expects to be left a portion of the comb as a reward, preferably a piece containing larvae.

" When I was trekking in South Rhodesia some years ago on a collecting expedition," the Director told me, " I noticed a small bird following me and obviously calling to attract my attention. One of my natives told me it was a bird that led people to honey. I decided to follow it. It would wait until I came close, then it would fly on and wait for me, calling to me all the time. This continued for an hour or so, and I began to think of giving up!

" Soon, however, instead of continuing its flight, the bird began to fly round in a most excited way giving an entirely different cry, and I noticed that bees were leaving and entering a hole in the ground. I had the nest dug out and left the comb containing the brood, which the bird immediately claimed. The natives say that should you leave nothing behind for the Honey Guide, the next time it will lead you to a cobra, a puff adder, or a mamba! "

The Director told me the story of a friend who was led by a Honey Guide on a long chase which, to his irritation, ended near the starting-place, but on the far side of a ravine. When he had taken the honey, he decided to go the short way back, but found it impossible. After several attempts, he realised that the Honey Guide had taken him along the only possible route for a human being.

One of the most interesting objects in the Museum is a skeleton of that extraordinary and now extinct bird the Dodo. I was told it was bought about thirty years ago from a French naturalist of Port Louis, Mauritius, the island on which the Dodo used to be found. Durban's Dodo is more complete than those possessed by the British Museum, the Cambridge University Museum, or the Natural History Museum in Paris, and a feathered reconstruction of the skeleton shows what a poor, fat, silly, and entirely delightful bird it was.

It was really an ancient type of pigeon that settled on Mauritius in prehistoric times and, taking to the ground, lost the use of its wings. It was as large as a turkey and became heavy and duck-shaped, with little, useless wings and an absurd tail-tuft; at the same time its pigeon's beak was enormously exaggerated, while its eyes remained the same size, so that the poor Dodo became an object of ravishing unloveliness. The Portuguese called it the Dodo, from doüdo, a fool or simpleton, and the Dutch used to chase it about Mauritius and club the poor creature to death with pistol-stocks or anything else, just for fun, apparently, for the Dodo was not good eating. The Dutch called it the nasty bird—walgvogel.

Those Dodos which survived the Dutch in the Seventeenth Century were exterminated when dogs and cats and other animals were introduced on the island. The poor creature was not fitted for modern life, and you can see him sitting up in his case in Durban Museum wearing a placid expression, as though entirely in favour of extermination.

§ 3

The Old Fort at Durban was built by British troops in 1842, but is now such a rampagious tropical garden that you can only with difficulty follow the line of the earthworks. It has been planted with trees and flowers by the Durban Light Infantry Old Comrades Association, who have settled a number of old soldiers and widows of others in the barracks.

The garden enshrines a number of early Durban memories. The first white men round the bay were British adventurers and ivory traders who, under two naval officers, Farewell and King, managed to make friends with the Zulu tyrant, Shaka, and obtain from him a large grant of land. That was in 1824, thirteen years before the Voortrekkers appeared in Natal. The little group of Englishmen was in the heart of enemy country. What is now the Transkei was then a wild and hostile native territory which separated them from white civilisation at Grahamstown. The gallant adventurers hoisted the Union Jack and repeatedly, but vainly, begged the Colonial Government to make Natal a British possession.

An alert young Jew, Nathaniel Isaacs, who was with them, has left a fascinating and vivid account of the rough Robinson Crusoe–Swiss Family Robinson life round Durban Bay in those days. By the time Retief arrived in Natal both Farewell and King were dead and Shaka had been assassinated by his half-brother Dingaan. In the forays with the Zulus that followed many of the original English settlers lost their lives, and after Blood River the Boers established a Voortrekker republic of Natalia, with its capital at Pietermaritzburg.

The Colonial Government, at last roused by these stirring events and alarmed by the idea of a state on its borders with a sea coast, sent troops to hold Durban. A clash between these troops and the Boers in 1824 led to the famous ride of Durban's hero, Dick King, to get reinforcements from Grahamstown, six hundred miles away, through wild and hostile country. King was the son of an 1820 Settler and at the time of his ride was a young man of twenty-eight. He knew the country well and had spent his life driving ox-wagons and collecting ivory from the Zulus for the traders. He completed the six hundred mile journey in ten days.

His famous ride is a good example of the room for disagreement about an event which occurred only a century ago, for hardly two accounts agree in all details. Some say that he started from the Old Fort, or from the bottom of Gardiner Street, where his fine mounted statue is to-day, or from elsewhere; some say that he rode a white horse, others say a bay; some claim that he rode the same horse all the way, others that he frequently changed horses at mission stations.

What is unquestioned is that he followed the coast for the first hundred miles or so, then struck inland and on the last hundred and fifty miles passed through Morley, Ibeka, Butterworth, and King William's Town. Of the innumerable rivers, some, presumably, he could ford in the saddle, others he had to swim. Sometimes he hid by daylight and pressed on in the night.

I do not know whether any similar feat of horsemanship has ever been recorded; if Dick King rode the same horse for six hundred miles—which hardly seems credible—there is nothing with which to compare it. The greatest ride in English history, so far as I know, is Sir Robert Cary's four hundred mile gallop from London to Edinburgh to tell James I that Queen Elizabeth was dead. Cary left London at about ten in the morning on a Thursday and was kneeling by the royal bedside in Holyrood Palace on the Saturday night, telling James that he had succeeded to the throne. His four hundred miles had been completed in three days, but he was not in dangerous country, he had a relay of horses, and there were no rivers to ford.

Dick King saved the garrison in the fort. Reinforcements immediately embarked and were sent to Durban by sea, and the little Republic of Natalia was forced to submit. So Natal became a British Colony in 1843 and, like everything else in South Africa, its story is so surprisingly recent. It was the year Nelson was placed on his column in Trafalgar Square!

Even those historians who may consider that Natalia would in any event have ended in bankruptcy, or in disagreement and more trekking, admire the men who made it and their efficiency in action. The achievement of the Boers in clearing within four years so vast a territory as that between the Orange River and the Limpopo, and the Province of Natal, for white settlement is surely one of the great romances of colonial history.

§ 4

I left Durban early one morning and passed through smiling suburbs to the road that leads northward into Zululand.

The approach to this native sanctuary was unlike anything I had expected. I might have been in India or Trinidad. All the way out of Durban I ran through little townships and villages which swarmed with Indians and their enormous families. Hindu temples and mosques were to be seen in what presumably had once been white towns. The Indian traders and merchants who stretch down the east coast of Africa culminate in Natal with a tremendous population of some two hundred thousand. Once the lowest of the low in their own country, they now dominate many branches of trading and some, I was told, have made large fortunes. That they can undersell the European, have a lower standard of living and, when rich, wish to live side by side with the Natalians, constitutes part of what South Africa knows as "the Indian Problem".

These people were imported in 1860 to cultivate the sugar, tea, and other crops in Natal, and they continued to be brought

into the country until 1911. When their period of indenture
ended, many were allowed to stay on as market gardeners,
hawkers, and domestic servants, and, together with traders
who arrived from India, multiplied and increased, as they
obviously continue to multiply and increase.

I went on through the sugar country and came at length to
the town of Stanger, which was once a great centre for the
ivory hunters and traders on their way back from Zululand.
Standing in a little garden just off the road is a memorial
erected by the Zulu nation to the Bantu Napoleon, Shaka.

The creation of the Zulu military state is surely one of the
most remarkable events in the history of South Africa, and
one wonders how it came about. Legend says that towards
the end of the Eighteenth Century a chief named Dingiswayo
went into exile and wandered about for years, coming eventually to Cape Colony. There he was impressed by the sight
of European soldiers drilling in uniform.

Zulu tradition recounts how one day Dingiswayo returned to
his people riding upon a horse and grasping a gun, the first
horse and gun seen in those parts. But more interesting still,
he is said to have been accompanied by a white man whose
identity is one of the enthralling mysteries of Africa. Who
was the white man who helped to launch the Zulu nation
upon its career of conquest, and what happened to him?
This unfortunately we shall never know.

Dingiswayo, who had assumed the chieftainship, began to
organise the tribe on a military basis. He introduced con-
scription and imposed discipline, forming his men into
battalions on the European pattern. When he launched his
well-trained warriors upon the surrounding tribes, his victories
followed one another, but during one of his expeditions he was
captured and put to death. He was followed by the terrible
Shaka. That was about the year 1818.

Shaka was a born conqueror and despot. His nation, like
Sparta, was now an armed camp. Every boy went into
training and was eventually admitted into the army, and no
man was allowed to marry until he had washed his spear in
blood. Regiments, which numbered about two thousand
men, were split up into companies, and each one was distin-

guished by a special uniform and a name. Some wore skins of otters, some of leopards, some had crests of ostrich feathers, others wore the plumes of the blue crane and the feathers of the Kaffir finch. The cow-hide shields were either red, white, black, or spotted. Certain regiments of proved valour were royal regiments and formed a Praetorian Guard.

Zululand was now covered with military kraals, each one the station of a certain regiment. After every engagement there was a ghastly ritual, when those who were said to have shown cowardice in action were put to death upon the command of Shaka. Upon one occasion a whole battalion which had not distinguished itself suffered the death penalty, each man having the point of a spear thrust beneath his armpit until it pierced his heart.

One of Shaka's first innovations was to limit the number of assegais carried into battle and to force his troops to rely upon a short stabbing-spear. His plan of battle was the pincer movement of modern mechanised warfare. The Zulu army advanced in the form of a half moon, and when the right and left wings had surrounded the enemy the main body advanced and delivered the attack. While the battle was in progress a large body, the reserve, remained seated with their backs to the fray.

The memorial at Stanger is placed upon the site of Shaka's great military kraal, Dukuza—the Labyrinth—where Farewell and King, Fynn and Isaacs visited him. It is possible to gain from these observers a clear idea of those great military camps, where the king lived with a host of concubines and surrounded by thousands of mostly celibate Janissaries.

Thousands of beehive huts spaced with military precision formed a circular band round the kraal, and each group of huts were the quarters of a particular regiment. Like a queen in a hive, the Zulu monarch was the central figure, accessible to his subjects, and on occasions only too visible in transports of ungovernable rage. He exercised absolute power over the lives of his people. The organisation of the Great Place was perfect. At a moment's notice the army commanders could call out whole regiments in full war-paint to dance, to display cattle, or to go off to war or to hunt. Everything the King said was formally approved by thousands of yes-men shouting in chorus. That Shaka saw through it all is perfectly obvious, but he throve on a reputation for inhumanity and based his power on fear; in which, of course, he was not alone in the ancient or the modern world.

When Fynn saw him first, Shaka was wearing a turban of leopard skin from which a crane's tail-feather rose two feet into the air, cubes of dried sugar-cane were let into the lobes of his ears, his shoulders and his body from waist to knee were covered with a fringe of twisted monkey skin, and at his arms, elbows, and knees were bunches of white hair from the tails of oxen. He was over six feet high, muscular, and active.

Isaacs tells how every morning the king would bathe and then rub his body with balls of pounded raw meat. Sometimes he would spend most of the day reclining in his hut surrounded by the royal girls, who knelt on mats. At night he would curl up on a reed mat and place his head upon a wooden neck-rest. Anyone who asked for an audience had to comply with etiquette as rigid as that of a European court.

His cruelty took extravagant forms, such as his massacre of thousands who did not appear to him to show sufficient grief when his mother died, a slaughter that was ludicrously extended to calves, so that the cows should appear to join in the universal lamentation. Once, suspecting infidelity, he made a clean sweep of the whole harem. His judicial functions seem always to have ended in the wretched defendants being hurried away, their necks broken by a sudden sideways jerk in transit, and their bodies beaten with knobkerries.

The white men were a great pleasure to Shaka. He did not know enough about them to fear them, as Dingaan did. To him they came at a time when life was boring, when a million Bantu had been slain in war and there were no new worlds to conquer—when in fact there was nothing to do but to gloat over the cattle and spend days in the company of a tedious harem. These white visitors were new and exciting, so were the stories they told of a brother monarch named George far across the sea, in whom the Zulu chief took the keenest interest.

The few years before his assassination were brightened by the gifts of macassar oil and purgatives, by a razor—a bold gift to offer him—and a mirror. With flawless logic he argued that if one pill were good, twenty must be twenty times as good, so that his court frequently suffered from overdoses of popular remedies. The muse of history would have been in one of her most playful moods if Shaka's desire to travel across the sea and meet his fellow monarch in London had been gratified. One wonders what George IV would have made of him, and he of the First Gentleman of Europe! George's tastes were catholic, and they might have got on famously. It would also be delightful to be able to report a subsequent attempt to recreate the Brighton Pavilion upon the hills of Zululand!

But Shaka's life was cut short by the assegai of an assassin, and he was buried where his monument now stands. Rising upon a series of stone plinths is a tablet surmounted by a draped urn that might more fitly commemorate John Wesley.

§ 5

My surprise grew as I approached the capital, Eshowe, for this was not a bit like my idea of Zululand. I was prepared for something lush, tropical, and threatening; in other words, Congo country. But instead there were gentle downlands, rounded hills, long sweeping valleys that reminded me now of Dorset and again of Devonshire, sometimes of the Yorkshire Moors and often of Scotland.

It was surprisingly green, and less congested than the Transkei. Huts dotted the hills and the slopes, different from the white mud-walled huts in the other reserves; these were made of plaited basket-work and thatch that came down almost to the ground, giving them the appearance of old-fashioned bee-skeps.

The natives also were different. The men looked infinitely finer and taller, and I thought more young men were visible than in the Transkei. I passed them marching across the land or resting beside the road, and those not dressed in European clothes had skins that shone as if polished with blacklead. The women were performing the same eternal tasks, carrying burdens and drawing water; and they too, I thought, looked slightly more vivacious than the Xosas and the Pondos: in grace of movement, however, there was nothing to choose between them.

Eshowe is another of those beautiful onomatopoeic words— perhaps the best of them all—which describes the wind passing through the forest. The town stands high and is surrounded by forests. It is fairly cool, and within twenty miles of the sea. You could go there and see little except the excellent hotel, a trader's store, and a few shops, but scattered all round about are many buildings which if brought together would form quite a respectable little township. There are at least four churches, a court-house, a hospital, a police station, a swimming-bath, an agricultural college, and a building in which the *Zululand Times* is printed.

Confidently expecting by this time to be lost in darkest Africa, I found myself instead in a sophisticated little hotel full of people who would have fitted into the background of Boscombe or Ilfracombe. There was even the same elderly woman knitting the same ambitious garment whose progress I have been watching all my life. Lunch included Scotch broth and the best steak-and-kidney pie I have encountered for years. When I asked the manageress whether the cook was English or Scots, she replied: " Oh no, he's a Zulu. Would you like to meet him? "

In the kitchen outside a rotund little bearded Zulu was introduced to me, wearing on his head a peculiar cone-shaped chef's hat like a dunce's cap. His name was Mzwayi. When I complimented him upon the pie he was pleasantly modest, and said that years ago he had been cook to a " most particular English missus " who had taught him how to make it.

I was lost in admiration for that unknown woman. Are not such women the true standard-bearers of civilisation? Posterity bestows its laurels upon people who have never done anything half as useful as teaching a Zulu to carry a perfect steak-and-kidney pie into the future. I thought I would like to have met Mzwayi's " most particular missus " and to have congratulated her upon her contribution to civilisation.

I was so tired that I went to bed at nine o'clock. The next moment, it seemed, a Zulu maid was gently finding room for a tea-tray on the bedside table, the sun was invading the room, and the usual South African bird was saying "Ho-ho" from an adjacent tree; for no one has taught these birds to sing.

§ 6

Sixty-five miles away to the north-west of Eshowe are Isandhlwana and Rorke's Drift, and the place where the Prince Imperial was killed. I wonder how many people in these days could give off-hand an account of Isandhlwana? Yet it is only eighty-six years since that disaster horrified our great-grandparents and created an outcry in Press and Parliament.

It happened thirty years after Blood River, when the Zulu nation had recovered from its defeat and under a new military patriot, Cetewayo, was ready to fight the white man again. The Government, finding war inevitable, sent out an army from England in all the splendour of European military pageantry. There were lancers with fluttering pennons, brass bands, and gun teams with pipe-clayed drag-ropes. It is clear that the folly of fighting a frontier war in the European tradition was obvious to Boers like Kruger and Joubert, who warned Lord Chelmsford, the commander, that the only way to fight Zulus was to put scouts out ahead, form laager and wait. But that was not the way things were done at Aldershot.

So the army marched into Zululand with bands playing, and one of its columns was surprised by a force of twenty thousand Zulus, who massacred eight hundred British soldiers and five hundred native auxiliaries. The tents were discovered still standing as if nothing had happened, and all round lay the disembowelled corpses of the defenders, the dead horses and oxen, and the rifled stores and ammunition boxes. That was Isandhlwana.

Cetewayo was eventually defeated at the battle of Ulundi, when the army formed a square, as at Waterloo, which was in effect a living laager with the cavalry in the centre. As at Blood River, the square opened at the critical moment and the cavalry rode out. This battle broke the military power of the Zulus and Cetewayo became a captive.

I would like to have seen the place were the Prince Imperial died. I am told that there is a rough stone cross erected by Queen Victoria in " affectionate remembrance of Napoleon Eugene Louis Jean Joseph, Prince Imperial, to mark the spot where he, while assisting in a reconnaissance with the British troops on 1st June, 1879, was attacked by a party of Zulus and fell with his face to the foe ".

The Prince Imperial, son of Napoleon III and the beautiful Empress Eugénie, was an embarrassing addition to Lord Chelmsford's troubles in South Africa. He was a young man who, at the tender age of fourteen, had been taken by his romantic parent to witness the triumph of the French army in 1870 and, instead, he was returned to his mother before Sedan. His father was now dead, and as Prince Imperial he had already heard the intoxicating cry of " Vive L'Empereur ! " rising into the English air from the throats of French royalists; for to them he was already the Emperor Napoleon IV and the hope of the Third Empire. He was thus a heavy responsibility for any commander-in-chief, especially in a country where any patch of tamboekie grass might conceal an assegai.

He was twenty-three, romantic like his father, headstrong and brave, and it was natural for him to see in the Zulu War an opportunity to distinguish himself as became the son of Napoleon Buonaparte's nephew. Might not a brilliant career in South Africa end amid fluttering handkerchiefs, the tossing plumes of cuirassiers and the blare of fifes and trumpets in the Champs Élysées? Where but on a battlefield might a Napoleon reach a throne—and Zululand at that time was the only available battlefield.

The British Government, with the Isandhlwana despatches newly in the files—for the Prince came out with reinforcements after the disaster—firmly opposed the young man's wishes. But his mother went to see the Queen. That entente was irresistible.

" I did all I could to stop his going," said Disraeli after the tragedy. " But what can you do when you have to deal with two obstinate women? "

The Prince had passed high in his class at Woolwich—too high at least for a prince—and no one knew quite what to do with him. Little jobs like sketching and mapping were found for him, but the great thing was to keep him away from dongas and patches of mealies.

One morning in June he rode out with Lieutenant Carey, six troopers, and a Kaffir guide to inspect a camping site. While they were making coffee, a party of Zulus hidden in a donga opened fire. The horses plunged, and only five of the horsemen managed to scramble into the saddle. Two horses broke loose and two men ran about to try to catch them. The Prince Imperial, who was riding a mettlesome grey standing sixteen hands high, could not get his foot into the stirrup-iron. Hearing the other horses galloping past, the grey plunged and swung round, attempting to follow them, the Prince made a desperate effort to leap into the saddle with the help of a holster, which snapped and flung him off his balance so that he fell to the ground. His excited horse trampled on him and galloped off after the others.

He was now alone. The two unmounted troopers had been stabbed to death. He scrambled to his feet, drawing his revolver, and faced fourteen Zulus. Later that day a cavalry patrol was still able to recognise the naked body of the young man who, to many Frenchmen, was the Emperor Napoleon IV.

In April of the following year a strange procession moved through Zululand and picked its way carefully over the rough country that leads to Itelemi Hill. An escort of some twenty Natal Mounted Police surrounded a civilian spider driven by General Sir Evelyn Wood. Behind rode a groom with a led horse saddled for a lady, and farther back were baggage-wagons and a vehicle in which the startled faces of ladies' maids gazed out at the grim landscape. When they reached the place where the cross is now, Sir Evelyn Wood gave his arm to a lady in deep mourning whose lifted veil revealed the lovely face that for a little time had smiled in the sunshine of the Second Empire. What Eugénie thought as she knelt at her son's grave will never be known. She had been Empress of France. It must have seemed to her that the glittering adventure, begun so long ago in Corsica, had ended for ever in this lonely grave in Zululand, slain by the assegai of a black Napoleon.

§ 7

The Chief Native Commissioner had kindly arranged a Zulu dance for me at a kraal far over the mountains. We set out in the afternoon, and travelled for a long way until we came within sight of a mountain top which I was told was four thousand feet above the sea.

The kraal was evidently a large one, but we lost sight of it as we turned off the road and began to ascend a steep track. As we came in sight of it again, it was clear that we had been observed, and a large group of Zulus was gathering to welcome us. Even at that distance, seen against the sky, I could tell that they had put on their war-paint. I could see tossing headdresses of feathers, and I was reminded of the descriptions of Nathaniel Isaacs as he approached the Great Place of Shaka.

This was, of course, nothing like Shaka's vast military town, but it was nevertheless one of the largest kraals I had so far seen in Zululand. A stockade of thorn bush and cactus enclosed several acres in which stood perhaps thirty or forty huts. They were all of the old-fashioned beehive type with the thatch touching the ground, and an entrance so small that you would have to enter on hands and knees. Within the main enclosure was a smaller cattle kraal constructed of wickerwork, where the milking was done and where the cattle were kept at night.

As we drove up into the entrance a crowd of some hundreds of Zulus, men and women, surrounded the car. I did not see one old hat, football jersey, or pair of trousers. The sight reminded me of the African village in some exhibition I had seen when a child. While I was admiring the fearsome and barbaric assembly, an old Zulu dressed in a white overall, riding-breeches, brown leather gaiters, and a sun helmet

ZULU WOMEN AND CHILDREN

strode up in a stately manner and saluted the Commissioner, then, taking off his hat, he uttered the royal salute, " Bayete eZulu ! ", which was echoed by all his followers. He was the chief.

He led the way into the cattle kraal where the dance was to be held. A few chairs had been placed for us, and no sooner had we taken our places than three cows were driven into the kraal. The chief made a speech to the Chief Commissioner, who rose and critically examined the beasts before selecting one. The chief then presented this cow to the Commissioner, who expressed his thanks in Zulu and returned the gift to the chief. The animal was driven away and immediately killed and flayed. All this, I thought, was running remarkably true to type! I began to wonder which of the onlookers would be hurried away to a Hill of Death!

The dancers, a startling sight, gave me a good idea of the scene witnessed by our ill-fated men at Isandhlwana as the impis swarmed towards them. From caps and rings of leopard skin, tall black plumes waved like the ostrich-feather bonnets of a Highland regiment. Their necks and shoulders were covered with leopard-skin corselets, which hung down in front of their bodies in a V shape. The tails of animals hung from their waists, and some wore bushy tufts of white hair above the elbow and below the knee. Each man carried a shield—some of them small dancing-shields—and everyone carried a blunt stick.

The same atmosphere of anti-climax and hiatus, which is also inseparable from any Arab ceremony, then pervaded the enclosure, and the dancers drifted off in ones and twos until I began to wonder whether anything would happen. Leaving the Chief Commissioner and the chief in earnest talk, I took a stroll into the village. The delay, I gathered, was caused by the women dancers, who were not ready. They were sitting outside their huts clothed only in beads and bands of beads, busily engaged in greasing one another's legs and bodies until they shone like oiled bronze.

I had been told that the old chief possessed twenty-one wives and I wondered whether the dancers were young wives or elder daughters. With such a domestic establishment, it

Q

was obvious that what I had assumed to be a village made up of many different families was really only one family, and that most of the population must be the sons and daughters of the old man in the sun hat.

No woman preparing for a presentation at Court could have taken more pains before her mirror than the dancers as they crouched on the earth greasing themselves, seeing that every bangle and bead was in place, and especially that the elaborate hair-dressing was properly arranged. They were not wearing the high Nefrititi-like mud-pack of the married Zulu woman, but had arranged their hair in thin plaits, each plait ending in a bead or a charm, and the whole fringe falling round the face in front as well as back. At last they arose and, giving a final pull to necklaces and hip-bands, walked slowly towards the cattle kraal.

The dancers now formed up in a wide half-circle, the women in the front row, and began shuffling and stamping their feet to the sound of a low, mournful chant. The warriors brandished their sticks and knobkerries and waved their ox-hide shields and, as the dance progressed, the chanting became sharper and louder. A little old woman beating a tin can ran rapidly in a crouching attitude in front of the dancers, shrieking a word or two at them and inspiring them to greater stamping and shuffling.

This dance was called the Inkondhlo, and is one often performed at weddings and on other festive occasions. It was monotonous, and once having started there seemed no end to it.

The old chief, whose name was Nkantini, sat in state with the Chief Commissioner, facing the dancers and occasionally pointing with his stick to anyone who in his opinion was not giving of his best. I heard an amusing explanation of the name Nkantini, which is, of course, a corruption of the word canteen. This man's father, Siteku, had taken part in the attack on Isandhlwana, and after the battle took possession of a canteen, or quartermaster's stores, in which there was a large quantity of paraffin. Mistaking this for whisky, Siteku and his followers drank so deeply that some of them are said to have died. The effects of paraffin so impressed Siteku that he called his young son Nkantini to commemorate the event!

When the dance petered out I went for another walk round the kraal, and was delighted by the dignity and good manners of the people. They were in a very happy mood. The beast that had been slaughtered was ready to be roasted, so that everyone was looking forward to the feast which would begin as soon as we had departed. Outside one of the huts I saw two young married women helping one another to build up the peculiar cocoa coloured head cone, the *isiChola*, which is as distinctive of Zululand as the women's white eye paint is of the Transkei. First, the woman's hair is drawn up to its full length and plaited with grass into long spikes which stand upright from the crown of the head. The hair is then built up with certain fibres and treated with fat and red ochre. The finished effect bears a close resemblance to the high crown of Akhnaton's queen, Nefrititi.

We had a tremendous send-off, and the inhabitants of the kraal departed hastily to prepare for their feast.

§ 8

Among those sights which have impressed most travellers in South Africa from the earliest times until well into the Nineteenth Century were the enormous herds of game which roamed all over the country. Nothing like it had ever been seen elsewhere in the world. The great herds of bison in North America, impressive as they were, could not be compared with the variety of wild life to be seen in South Africa.

When the white men first landed, hippopotami and lions roamed round Cape Town, then, as man and his guns advanced, the animals retreated, but even in the first few decades of the Nineteenth Century there were gigantic herds of migratory buck mixed with zebra, ostriches, and all kinds of other animals in regions now cultivated and settled.

A vivid idea of the sights seen by Nineteenth Century hunters may be gained from the illustrations in two accessible books which once had great popularity in England, Cornwallis Harris's *Wild Sports of Southern Africa*, and *The Lion-Hunter of South Africa*, by Gordon Cumming. The frontispiece in Harris's book shows a horseman galloping beside a great herd of antelope, wildebeeste—or gnu—zebra, and ostrich, while in the distance other herds are calmly grazing, undisturbed by the tumult. Gordon Cumming shows a man firing from the saddle into a herd composed literally of thousands of blesbok.

What has happened to the once vast animal population of South Africa? A mass slaughter took place in the Nineteenth Century, as the heads and horns in castles and mansions all over the world, and in the glass cases of natural history museums, prove, and, as the human invaders pushed their towns and their railways forward, the game retreated, and might by this time have been almost extinct if South Africa had not established game reserves.

Large tracts of land have been set apart in many districts throughout the country, where the game are allowed to breed in natural conditions. No one is allowed to shoot them and Nature is encouraged to establish its own balance, as in the days before the coming of the white man. Lions and leopards are allowed to prey on buck, zebra, and giraffe, with the result that the species are kept strong and healthy. The two most famous reserves are the Kruger National Park in the Transvaal, celebrated for its lions, and the Hluhluwe Game Reserve in Natal, celebrated for the black and the elsewhere extinct white rhinoceros.

South Africans love nothing better than to spend a holiday in the rest camps at these reserves, where they sleep in huts and go out by day to see the wild animals in their natural surroundings and shoot them with a camera. Nearly everyone in South Africa has some startling story of a lion met face to face in the Kruger Park, or of a rhino that charged them in Hluhluwe.

When Mr D. E. Mitchell, the Administrator of Natal, offered to drive me up to Hluhluwe for a few days with the rhino, I accepted with alacrity, for there could be no better guide.

We left Eshowe after lunch. The journey before us was one of a hundred miles to the north into the more desolate coastal regions of Zululand. We passed through beautiful green hill country, where the beehive huts had the mournful look of lonely cabins in Connemara. Sugar-cane grew on each side of the road, and once we had passed through the little town of

Empangeni the road stretched ahead devoid of town or village for mile after mile.

Hluhluwe—another lovely word—means "Sweet waters", and you can hear them lapping if you pronounce the h's as l's. At first sight unpronounceable, this word may easily be rendered correctly, as in Zulu, by any Welshman, and indeed by anyone who can say Llewelyn. Mr Mitchell told me that the Hluhluwe Reserve covers sixty square miles of country, and it is the only place in the world where you can see the South African white rhinoceros, for the white rhinoceros of the Uganda is a sub-species.

We crossed the Black Umfolozi River on a long, rickety bridge and saw, far below, a trickle of warm brown water flowing eastward to St Lucia Estuary, where crocodiles and hippopotami are to be seen and where men go to catch sharks. The country now became wilder than ever. A place that looked quite important on the map turned out to be a trader's store with a petrol pump and a few chickens pecking round outbuildings near a cactus hedge.

As we went on, I saw another aspect of Nature's attempt to turn South Africa into a wilderness. Here was a problem of land degeneration almost as difficult to fight as soil erosion. It is called bush encroachment. We passed through mile after mile of recently good grassland, but now bush country in which nothing can grow. Between this point and Swaziland to the north there are tens of thousands of acres of good land degenerating into bush. You can look back and see the grass like an outgoing tide.

We passed imperceptibly into the Game Reserve, where I saw a glorious wild land of green rounded hills and dense valleys, and far off line after line of blue mountains. There is a profound difference between wild country, no matter how desolate, in which man is living, and utterly primitive country that has never known his fires, his huts, and his ploughs. The Hluhluwe Reserve was primitive Africa, incredibly primitive pre-Bantu Africa. I could have imagined that any rock near the road concealed the pigmy people, who, according to Zulu tradition, were an older, smaller race even than the Bushmen. Then there was a sudden gallop, a frisk of tails, and right

across our path streaked a dozen zebra like fat, painted ponies.
The grass grew high beside the road and I saw a movement in
it. We stopped the car. One by one several melancholy
snouted faces appeared, and then, bounding on their knuckles,
turning every now and then towards us, a family of baboons,
the little ones bringing up the rear, crossed to the other side.

We came to a dell as green as any wood in Surrey. The
trees arched overhead and the watchful stillness of woodland
lay all around.

" Look ! " I cried, " the animals I've been longing to see—
springbok ! "

" No," said Mr Mitchell.   " Impala."

And almost before we had had time to watch, six exquisite
red-brown bodies had curved like divers through the air across
the road, six bodies with curving horns, six deer-like muzzles,
each with a little white mark near the eye ; and they vanished
noiselessly, like a dream, into tall grass.

We came out of the wood to the shoulder of a hill. A
notice-board stood there as surprising and laconic as
" Unexploded Bomb ". It just read : " Danger. Rhino."
We scanned the hillside eagerly, but could see nothing.

§ 9

The rest camp at Hluhluwe stands upon the top of a hill.
There are a number of circular white rondavels standing in
lines upon grass, a welcome and cheering sight. There is a
smell of wood smoke as Zulu servants fire the stoves for hot
water. The huts are civilised places ; mine had a small
kitchen and a bathroom and also electric light.

About eighty visitors can be housed in the camp, and they
must bring their food with them. The camp provides beds,
bedding, cooking utensils, cutlery, crockery, firewood, and
large, silent, competent Zulus, who do the housework and the
cooking. Like so many things in South Africa, I thought the
price—four shillings a night—amazingly cheap.

After a bath we went off to dine with Captain and Mrs
Potter, the Game Conservator and his wife, who live at the far
end of the camp in a house among trees. The Potter

mansion touches the highest point of improbability. Standing upon a hill in Zululand, surrounded by many strange African trees and shrubs, it has the air of having flown straight over from Sussex. It is one of the houses advertised every week in *Country Life*: solid, stone-built, leaded casements, and all modern conveniences. One expected the door to be opened by a London stockbroker.

Upon a parquet floor covered with lion and zebra skins stood Captain Potter, wearing a safari shirt and khaki trousers, tall, lean, brown, and observant—just the type you would choose if you were writing a play or a film about life in the back of beyond. The things that worry so many people —stocks and shares, money, the deplorable state of the world —meant nothing to him in this solitude. More important than Russia and America and anything else was the sick rhino calf in Umfolosi.

Captain Potter was born about sixty years ago in Staffordshire, although, like so many South Africans of sixty, he looks no more than fifty. When he was a schoolboy at Berkhamsted, he remembers seeing Lord Rothschild emerge from the gates of Tring Park behind a team of zebras; but he had no idea then that his knowledge of these animals was later to become more profound than that of his lordship. He came out to South Africa, where eventually his love of animals and solitude led him to Hluhluwe.

We had dinner as if we were in a house in Cape Town, the well-trained servants in white jackets moving noiselessly over the lion skins. The talk was all of wild animals—of rhino, buffalo, zebra, buck, but always back to rhino, the pride of Hluhluwe. I gathered that the average visitor arrives by car and spends his time looking for rhino, generally with a camera. He can go in his car along the few roads that traverse the reserve, where he frequently meets these animals round a corner, or he can go on foot, but should he do this, he must take a game guard with him.

It is not uncommon for a visitor to be " treed " during his visit, and this has happened to many distinguished and dignified persons; for when it sees you, the rhino will either lumber away or instantly charge. Two policemen upon a recent visit to the reserve had been forced to spend a night in a tree while a rhino patrolled beneath.

There are a hundred and fifty of the ordinary black rhino in Hluhluwe and two hundred and fifty to three hundred white rhino, mostly in the adjacent Umfolosi Reserve, the only remaining white rhino in the world. The difference between these animals is in size and habit, not colour, for the white is much the same colour as the black. But he is, after the elephant, the largest of land mammals. A good-sized male will stand six feet six inches at the shoulder and may weigh about five tons. White and black rhino have two horns, the larger of which is between four and five feet in length.

" How can you tell a white from a black rhino? " I asked.

" The white rhino has a square lip, and the black has a pointed, prehensile upper lip," I was told.

I asked if there are any other signs that might be observed from a greater distance.

" Yes. The white rhino lives on grass and carries his head so low that it almost touches the ground; the black rhino lives on the leaves of trees and bushes and carries his head higher."

The white rhino, although larger than the black, is not so aggressive. Both animals have such poor sight that they can see nothing farther away than about thirty paces, but the senses of smell and hearing are highly developed. The black rhino never utters a sound. When angry, his grunt can be heard only for about ten yards, but the shout of the white rhino can be heard for half a mile. Both white and black rhino calve only once in three years.

During the day-time the rhinoceros often sleeps, and feeds at dusk and in the early morning. He is so frequently met with at night that visitors are cautioned to arrive at the reserve in daylight.

§ 10

It was not yet five on a sharp, chilly morning. Mist lay in swathes in the valley. There was utter silence. I shivered as I put on a bush shirt, but I knew that in two hours it would be almost unbearably hot. Just as I had loaded a camera, I heard the sound of a car outside. Mr Mitchell and Captain Potter were looking keen and resolute.

The road from the camp winds steeply down into the reserve, passing round a tall hill; the ground falls away on the left to grassland dotted with bush; to the right is the steep hillside. As we turned a corner, Mr Mitchell braked and brought the car to a stop.

" Look! " he whispered. " What a bit of luck! "

Forty yards away, right in our path, a female rhinoceros and her calf were asleep on the road, snuggling into the hillside. We had the sun behind us and it shone on them.

" I say, Potter, she's big, isn't she? " whispered Mr Mitchell.

" Yes, she is pretty big," said Captain Potter.

I thought she was colossal. She lay in the road like a broken-down tank. Her body was elephant-grey with a hint of pink, and the immense mass heaved slowly as she breathed. The calf was the size of a big pony. I had not yet seen a rhinoceros move, and was feeling fairly courageous. I suggested that I should get out and take a photograph.

" Be quick," said Mr Mitchell, " for we may have to reverse if she charges."

Taking a few steps on the road, even though accompanied by Captain Potter, my heroism began to ebb. The rhino's main horn was at least four feet long and her sharp little ears were like the knot in a handkerchief which people make to assist memory. As we tiptoed towards her, those small ears twitched independently, and suddenly, with a stupendous lurch, she was on her feet looking at us. It was a most surprising movement. The calf rose, too, and stood beside its mother. I decided not to bother about a photograph and went back to the car.

" We'll just creep a bit nearer," said Mr Mitchell, slipping forward yard by yard.

Having heard us, smelt us, and now having seen us, the rhinoceros moved to face us squarely. She lifted her head with its two horns and watched us. The sun shone in her eyes, lighting up two spoonsful of black malice. As we slowly advanced, she stood her ground squarely. We were now about thirty yards away. I looked round to see if Captain

Potter had brought a gun. He had not. I looked back and thought it would not be easy for us to reverse uphill at a sufficient speed. I already saw the engine of the car speared on her horn and began to wish that Mr Mitchell's nerves were not so good.

" Look out," whispered Captain Potter.

" It's all right—I'm watching her," whispered Mr Mitchell.

The malicious vegetarian lifted and lowered her head as if scenting us, and made a slight stamping motion with a foot.

" Here she comes! " said Mr Mitchell, putting the car in reverse, as the ponderous mass came lightly towards us, then as suddenly swerved off the road into the bush, accompanied by her calf.

She paused when a hundred yards away and again faced us as we continued down the road. At the next bend, we encountered a small car puffing up the hill towards the camp, packed with a laughing family party, who waved to us and shouted cheerfully as they went past. Little did they know what game we had flushed from their path!

After breakfast we motored off again in search of rhino. We repeated the process after lunch. We counted twenty-seven rhino in the course of the day, which I believe is almost a record bag. We saw also kudu, impala, inyala, buffalo, bush buck, zebra, wart-hogs, and monkeys.

I noticed that every one of our twenty-seven rhino carried a red sore about the size of a saucer on its body. Captain Potter told me that these sores appear only during the breeding season, and his theory is that they are musk glands.

" If you returned here in two months time," he said, " I would give you a fiver for every sore you could find. They will all have healed up. If you should examine the body of a young rhinoceros, you would see on its side an indentation where the musk gland will develop in adult life. You will not find this theory advanced in any zoological work. It is my own theory, based on observation and contact with these creatures. Also, during this time of year I can smell the rhinoceros musk."

We spent an enchanted afternoon among hills and valleys, coming suddenly upon pastures where zebra and wildebeest grazed together. With a tribe of monkeys running, stooping, and turning before us, we climbed hills and came to cool forest paths, full of furtive movement as buck hid from us, all save one, a tall kudu bull who stood beneath an arch of leaves and faced us eye to eye. The only movement in his body was an inquisitive trembling of velvet nostrils until, the engine starting up, his resolution snapped and he was gone, with nothing to show that he had ever been there but a waving bough.

The great thrill of our day was waiting for us, unsuspected but not unsought, at the top of a hill as we were returning to the camp. We came slowly up the hill and, turning a corner, had just changed gear for the flat when we saw a rhinoceros charging at full gallop, with his horn aimed at us. Automatically Mr Mitchell pressed his foot on the accelerator, the rhinoceros pulled up at a small bush on the side of the road and worried it with his horn, and in that second we were past him!

It happened so quickly. There was no time for alarm.

"Well, did you ever see anything quite like that?" said Mr Mitchell. "That old Punyana heard the car and was waiting for us at the top of the hill, and—if it hadn't been for that bush he might have got us!"

The Punyana is a slightly smaller type of rhino, bad-tempered and savage, as we saw only too well. The extremely clear impression I had of him was that he was moving with the speed of a horse and was attacking us out of sheer ingrained malice.

The following day we set off by car from Hluhluwe and were in Pietermaritzburg in the evening.

CHAPTER EIGHT

*In which I leave Natal for the plains of the Orange Free State,
visit Bloemfontein, the Central City, and go down to the Karoo, where
for a week I live in a civilised desert.*

§ I

I TRAVELLED along the fine mountain roads from Natal
towards the Free State. At Chieveley, where a lonely railway line crosses a green plain, I saw the spot where war correspondent Churchill was captured by General Botha during the
South African War. At Ladysmith, which takes its name from
the Spanish wife of Sir Harry Smith, a gallant soldier who
played a great part in the mid Nineteenth Century history of
the country, I saw relics of the siege—old Lee Metfords, a
drum, cavalry muskets and so on—which to anyone who has
been in an air raid seem like something left over from Waterloo.

I turned towards the Drakensberg and spent several days in
the Natal National Park, where a superbly sited hotel offers in
the wilderness all the ease and comfort of Durban. By the
worst of ill luck it rained most of the time I was there, an
unusual patch of bad weather I was told, so that I was unable
to climb the Berg as I had hoped to do. During a storm of
thunder and lightning I caught a Loch Leven trout in a
tributary of the Tugela.

Entering the Free State, I stayed at Harrismith, a town full
of cheerful people who are interested in polo, woollen blankets,
and an annual race to the top of a mountain called the
Platberg.

Rain again blotted out everything the day I went to the
World's View, to see the place where Retief's party waited
while he went down into the Promised Land. I was told that
on a clear day the view down towards Natal is one of the fairest
on earth. All I could see that day were rocks and drizzle.
Upon one of the rocks pretty Deborah Retief had inscribed
her father's name in green paint, and there it is to-day, with a

glass case over it, the only inscription, so far as I know, left by the Voortrekkers.

I continued my journey across a flat, attractive landscape with enormous views to the horizon, a plain where green koppies broke the distance, where farms stood among trees, where aluminium water-wheels were revolving in the breeze, and where churns stood ready for the creamery lorry. I came to Bethlehem—named by the Voortrekkers—a pretty place with a beautiful bird sanctuary and a reservoir like one of the smaller Cumberland lakes. Then I crossed a lovely tract of country and entered a pass called the Golden Gates—Basutoland always at my elbow like a mixture of Wales and Switzerland—and in the evening, drawing nearer to the mountains, I crossed out of Union territory at Maseru, the capital of Basutoland.

Basutoland does not belong politically to the Union, but, like Swaziland and Bechuanaland, is administered by the Colonial Office. Many people in the Union think the time overdue when these High Commission Territories, as they are called, should belong to the Union politically as they do geographically.

On the following day I continued across the great plain through some of the finest looking farming country I had seen, and as darkness fell I arrived in Bloemfontein, the capital of the Free State. I saw long, well-lit streets, and in front of the post-office a coloured fountain which was sending up cheerful plumes of water, now red, now blue, now orange. It was a pretty reminder that the name of Bloemfontein is the " Fountain of Flowers ".

A friend called upon me after dinner and suggested that we should go for a drive to the top of Naval Hill, a tall koppie round which the city is built. In a few moments we had left the street lights behind and were mounting a road that curves for five miles to the summit of the hill. As we turned a corner a large animal bounded away from our headlights into the bush that lies on each side of the road. It was some species of buck. A few yards further on we had to slow down to allow a couple of zebra to cross the road. They were tamer than New Forest ponies.

When we came to the summit we left the car and walked forward to a spur of rock from which we looked down at the city below us. We could see the whole of Bloemfontein and its southern suburbs outlined in sparks of light. Miles of streets and cross streets glittered in parallel lines, and beyond lay the dark loneliness of the veld. We watched the glow-worm train miles away approaching the Free State capital and, as we looked, another left the station and went north to Johannesburg.

§ 2

I went out in the morning to find my way about Bloem-fontein, which was not difficult, for the city is not large and is well designed. I was at once struck by its air of quality, its dignity, and its assurance. There is a vitality and a fresh-ness about Bloemfontein which I think are due to two things: the altitude, which is four thousand five hundred feet above the sea—or a hundred feet higher than the top of Ben Nevis—and the good fortune it has had with the architectural pro-fession. Indeed there is no public building of note that is not both distinguished and pleasing.

The harmony of Bloemfontein is in a great measure due to buildings erected in the proper style for South Africa. The perfect little Raadsaal gave me great pleasure. To me it means something. It is not a great Semitic ziggurat, but a little fragment of the clear classical world in blossom upon the High Veld. Two other buildings of distinction are the Supreme Court and the Court of Appeal.

What South Africa would have done without the ox and the wagon, one cannot imagine. The ox wagon, as I have already said, is a truer emblem of South Africa's history than anything else, and its influence extends even to town planning. When the first dorps were built, the streets were made sufficiently wide for a full team of oxen to turn round in them—a necessary provision—and the result is that when a village grew into a town, and a town into a city, there was plenty of room for buildings, and it was unnecessary first to clear from the site acres of crowded habitations, as it is in Europe.

The city is the legal capital of the Union and its court is

the highest appeal court in the country. Many people believe that some day the two capital system will be ended by common consent and that Bloemfontein, as the central city, has the best claim to be the capital of the Union. With Naval Hill as its Acropolis, this city could indeed become a splendid capital.

Bloemfontein might also claim to be the astronomical capital of the Union. Michigan University has its observatory on Naval Hill, and so clear is the atmosphere of the Free State that Harvard Observatory has removed itself from the Andes in Peru to Mazelspoort, a few miles from Bloemfontein. I was told that one of the largest telescopes in the world is being installed at Mazelspoort, which will then become the most important observatory in the Southern Hemisphere.

The debt which South Africans owe to tree planters and gardeners from the time of van Riebeeck and van der Stel onwards has many times been acknowledged, but I wonder whether South Africa is also aware of the gratitude she owes to the manufacturers of refrigerators and the constructors of swimming-pools. Indeed, I cannot imagine how the vast quantities of meat consumed every day were kept in good condition before the invention of the refrigerator, unless, of course, the answer is that it was not eaten fresh but as biltong. And no town in South Africa is too small, too remote, or, what is more remarkable, too short of water, to deny itself a public swimming-pool of the latest design.

Bloemfontein has a fine pool in the city which, when flood-lit at night and seen from Naval Hill, looks like an oblong emerald, but the pool everyone talks about is some miles off at Mazelspoort. Here the admirably named Modder, or Mud, River, magically filtered, flows sparkling and white into what may well be the longest swimming-pool in the world; I have never seen a longer one, even at the bioscope. On days when the sun grills the Free State and the celebrated air appears to be flowing from the mouth of a steel furnace, family parties go off to Mazelspoort to swim, to take trips on the river, and to sit beneath the trees, never out of the sight and sound of water and as delighted with this as were the Moors of Granada with the Alhambra.

I spent a perfect afternoon and evening with two charming families at Mazelspoort, and after the children had bathed and had fallen in and been comforted, we sat beneath the trees and watched the stars come out, and ate that cold banquet which South African women prepare so superbly.

King's Park in Bloemfontein lives up to the city's name. It is one of those places, and I have seen many, which makes a gardener long to grow flowers and shrubs in South African soil, to get busy with pencil and measuring tape and to spend unforgettable hours with the nurseryman's catalogue. If you have ever known the sense of frustration which often attends such a selfless act as, say, the planting of a mulberry tree in England, South African gardens, with their almost instantaneous maturity, their thick hedges and their dense shrubberies, all of a few years growth, fill you with envy. Provided you have plenty of water, to be a gardener in South Africa must be bliss.

Bloemfontein's zoo is celebrated for an animal, a cross between a lion and a tiger, known as the liger. New York's Zoo, which I think is the only other zoo which possesses them, calls them tiglons. This animal might be described as a lion coloured tiger, and I studied it, as I have sometimes studied the children of dear friends, searching vainly for some glimpse in them of those characteristics I admire so much in their parents.

There are many fine schools and colleges in this city, as well as one of the finest museums in the country. But the institution which all English visitors should see, one which may possibly call for an unusual amount of understanding, is the Anglo-Boer War Museum, where many relics of that deplorable struggle are perhaps too carefully preserved. The South African War was in two parts, a short war fought before the discovery of gold, and a three years' war fought afterwards.

The first South African War began in 1880, three years after Britain had annexed the Transvaal, which at the time was bankrupt and encircled by native problems. To this war belongs Majuba Hill, where the British forces were surprised and defeated by the Boers. When peace was restored, the Transvaal was again recognised as the South African Republic.

THE RAADSAAL, BLOEMFONTEIN

A few years afterwards the discovery of gold on the Rand had two results: the arrival in the Republic of thousands of fortune seekers, mainly British, and the enrichment of a previously impoverished state.

Paul Kruger, the Boer President, who was opposed to change, resolutely declined to give way to the civic and other demands which those who had so profitably invaded his state considered a due return for the taxes they paid. Cecil Rhodes and several important persons in Cape Town and London contrived an armed raid into Transvaal territory led by Dr Jameson, who was neatly captured by the Boers with his five hundred troopers, and put in prison. The tension increased, and the struggle between the modern world, represented by Rhodes, Milner and Joseph Chamberlain, and the old world, represented by Kruger, reached a deadlock which was broken by war. The story of the tragic struggle is accessible in many forms from history to reminiscence.

The feature of the war which still provides ammunition for the anti-British politician in the Union was the policy of burning down farms and sending the homeless Boer women and children to often ill-equipped and badly run concentration camps. Deaths from dysentery, measles, and other complaints reached the appalling total of twenty-six thousand.

One English voice was raised in protest and indignation, that of Emily Hobhouse, a member of a well-known family. She went out to South Africa, worked in the camps, and carried her criticisms to the House of Commons and the Press. Unknown in her own country, she is a heroine in South Africa. When she died in 1926, her ashes were taken out to be interred in the most sacred plot of land in the Union, where a giant obelisk near Bloemfontein marks the burial place of President Steyn of the Free State and General de Wet. Probably the most moving speech of his career was made on that occasion by Field-Marshal Smuts.

" As a very small people that has suffered much at the hands of history," he said, " we are prone to exalt the virtue of patriotism above everything else. Let us not forget Emily Hobhouse. She was an Englishwoman to the marrow, proud of her people and its great mission and history. But, for her,

R

patriotism was not enough. When she saw her country embark on a policy which was in conflict with the higher moral law, she did not say ' My country, right or wrong '. She wholeheartedly took our side against that of her own people, and in doing so rendered an imperishable service, not only to us, but also to her own England and to the world at large. . . .

" More than anything in our history the example of Emily Hobhouse reminds us that we are not merely citizens of South Africa, but that we belong also and above all to the greater city of God."

§ 3

I went up to Naval Hill one morning, and met a man striding briskly down, twirling a stick and singing.

" Good morning! " he shouted.

" You're English," I said.

" How did you know? "

" I should say Bradford."

" Not bad," he replied. " At least only a hundred miles out. I'm Burnley, but I've lived in London for years."

" But Yorkshire sticks."

" Aye, ba gum, lad, it does that," he replied mockingly.

He was hatless and was wearing a blue flannel jacket with gilt buttons, as if he were on holiday at Scarborough.

He said, suddenly quite serious, " What a glorious country this is! "

" Why do you say that? " I asked, for his change of manner was startling.

" Well, I'll tell you. Six months ago I was half dead with asthma. I used to spend nights in a chair, sitting up with my arms on the back trying not to wheeze. Then I'd have a bad go and get no sleep, and I got worse and worse. The doctor said to me, ' You'll never get better until you go to a high, dry climate.' Well, what's the use of saying things like that to chaps like me! A high, dry climate, when you're due in Leadenhall Street every morning at nine. Might as well say, ' Go and live on the moon.'

" Then I got even worse. I thought I was going mad.

No sleep. I got so bad I had to give up my job, and then my missus and I sat down and said, 'So what?' Well, as nothing could be worse than the mess we were in, we scraped up every penny and decided to come to South Africa.

" ' Bloemfontein's the place for you,' the doctor said. I'd never heard of it before.

" And the moment we came out here I began to get better. The asthma went. I feel young again. I can sleep."

He threw out his chest and took a couple of deep breaths.

" Look at that! " he cried. " Not a wheeze! The old tubes as sound as a bell! That's what Bloemfontein's done for me! "

" How lucky you were to be able to come out," I said.

" I can't afford it," he admitted frankly, " but I'm so well now that I'm going to take on a job, and I shall be able to struggle on."

" Not much struggle about you, if I may say so."

" How right you are! " he said. " No more struggle for breath. I feel like a two-year-old! "

And with a twirl of his stick he wished me good morning and strode off down Naval Hill.

§ 4

I went up to Naval Hill just before midnight and looked at the white sheet of stars overhead. Not only were the stars brighter than I have seen them anywhere else in the world, but the air was so clear that I had some conception of stellar distances.

More mundane matters maybe have caused people to overlook the long and productive stellar history of South Africa. It is an aspect of history with no bitterness in it, a history unaffected either by materialism or racialism. No argument has ever arisen in this history which could not be adjusted by a few amiable old gentlemen with the aid of a telescope and mathematics.

As soon as Europeans came to the Cape, scientists were eager to observe the South African sky. The first to do so were French Jesuits on their way to Siam, who were allowed to put up their instruments in the Governor's summer house—now Government House—in Cape Town.   Then in the middle of the Eighteenth Century the Abbé de la Caille went to Cape Town, and lived in Strand Street while he was compiling his catalogue of southern stars.

When the Royal Observatory was founded in Cape Town in 1820, a number of interesting and distinguished men followed one another to South Africa.   It is strange that South Africans never mention them, while they perpetuate the country's association with dozens of less celebrated individuals.

Astronomers should be a source of inspiration to ambitious boys and to parents with unusual children, for so many have been poor boys who by chance have taken a glance through a telescope that has altered their lives and led them to fame. For instance, Fearon Fallows, South Africa's first Astronomer Royal, was the son of a poor weaver in Cumberland; Thomas Henderson, one of his successors, was the son of a Dundee tradesman; and the great Sir David Gill was the son of an Aberdeen watchmaker, who studied science in his spare time in a little laboratory which he made at home.   Perhaps the most interesting of the Cape's astronomers was Sir John Herschel, who for four years, from 1834 to 1838, studied the stars there and wrote a book which is one of the classics of astronomy.

The lives of most South African astronomers contradict the popular assumption that a star-gazer must be a man with no earthly interests, for they were all vividly aware of the world around them.   South African lighthouses owe much to Sir Thomas Maclear, Astronomer Royal in 1833, whose name is perpetuated in Cape Maclear.   He was also interested in exploration and taught Livingstone how to use a sextant. Sir John Herschel found time from his study of stars to redraft the educational system of the Cape, and Sir David Gill was interested in social and political problems.

I had been invited to visit the Michican University Observatory at midnight.   The dome rises like a large ribbed melon above everything on Naval Hill, and I could see it clearly by the light of the stars.   I rang the bell, but the place appeared deserted.   At last I heard approaching footsteps and the door was opened by the professor, who was wearing a thin shirt and a pair of white flannel trousers, for it was still warm.

" Come in," he said abstractedly; " I think I can show you one or two things to-night. . . ."

I forget which star he said was rising, as we hurried down a long passage and entered the room beneath the dome.

When my eyes became used to the darkness of the circular room, I could see that a section of the dome was open, revealing a slice of sky burning with millions of stars. Directed towards the sky was an object which looked like an anti-aircraft gun. I mounted the iron ladder at the back until I was high enough to sit and focus the eye-piece with my right hand. It was so finely adjusted that the slightest touch put everything out of focus and turned the whole sky into a whirling mass of comets.

The professor climbed up and swung the barrel of the telescope to a different portion of the sky.

" Now look," he said; " those are nebulæ."

I saw a cluster of bright pin-points.

He pressed an electric switch and the roof began to revolve slowly with the throbbing sound of a refrigerator suddenly picking up at night. He climbed up to me and focused the telescope again.

This time I saw a match-flame burning with a steady light.

" That is the top star of Orion's Belt," said the professor, and there followed statistics of time and distance.

" The total number of stars in the universe," wrote Sir James Jeans in *The Mysterious Universe*, " is probably something like the total number of grains of sand on all the sea-shores of the world. Such is the littleness of our home in space when measured up against the total substance of the universe."

Although Sir James Jeans had a life-long experience of astronomy, he never forgot the terror which a first inspection of space can inspire in some minds. " We find our universe terrifying," he wrote, " because of its vast meaningless distances, terrifying because of its inconceivably long vistas of time which dwarf human history to the twinkling of an eye, terrifying because of our extreme loneliness, and because of the material insignificance of our home in space—a millionth part of a grain of sand out of all the sea-sand in the world."

" And now," said the professor, " look at that star with the naked eye first, then look through the telescope."

I saw a small isolated pin-point of light, then the telescope magnified it into a whole galaxy. I looked again, hardly believing that it could be the same object.

The professor moved the telescope, and this time I saw what looked like a little golf ball lying neatly inside a curtain-ring. It was the prettiest, most spectacular thing I had seen that night.

" Saturn in his ring," said the professor.

I climbed down from the lonely and awe-inspiring observation post and we began to talk about ordinary things. It was easy to understand why so many astronomers have been men of the world. Lacking some mundane hobby, an astronomer would go mad. And all over South Africa that night, I thought, telescopes were pointed to the stars and men were quietly probing the outer spaces of the universe.

§ 5

While I was in Bloemfontein, I received out of the blue an invitation to spend a week on the Karoo and—as the invitation put it—" see how we live in this civilised desert ". This meant doubling back towards the Cape, but the chance was too good to be missed.

The Karoo—a Hottentot word which means " dry place "— is an arid plateau lower than the plains of the Free State, lying within the Cape Province. The first Dutch settlers viewed this desert with something of the abhorrence reserved by the Englishmen of Dr Johnson's day for the Highlands of Scotland : but Walter Scott made the Highlands romantic and Balmoral made them fashionable, and something of the same kind has happened in South Africa. It is now fashionable to admire the Karoo, its sunsets and its silences, and I had often been told that if I failed to see this desert I should miss one of the most memorable regions in the Union.

I set off from Bloemfontein early one morning to travel south. It was such a hot day that, remembering the vaporised petrol in the Transkei, I took the precaution of carrying a bottle of water and some rags. I do not know for how long there had been a drought, but the land was parched and brown and quivering with heat. Now and again I met a pathetic herd of cattle, their ribs visible, hungrily trekking on in search of grass and nosing as they went the barren khaki rocks for some stray blade of herbage.

The beasts were driven by a few natives powdered from head to foot in dust, but once I met a white man following in a cart, and I stopped and spoke to him. He was a sad-looking man who spoke English with some difficulty, and his clothes hung on him as if upon a scarecrow; a different person from the sleek, happy farmers I had met hitherto. When I said what a cruel drought it was, he looked at me with dull, miserable eyes. His cattle were dying, he said, and he was trying to save the remainder. He had heard there was some grazing over there—he pointed with his whip—and he would have to pay so much per beast for it.

Behind his eyes I could see a money-lender or a mortgagee. I could see his furniture piled up in the sunlight and people bidding, and someone laughing as a poor little possession came under the hammer; and I could see him in his shabby clothes, probably with a wife and many children, taking a step downward towards those unhappy regions where the landless men live with just a fence of prickly pear separating them from the native location.

Water. That was all he needed. Perhaps just a few nights of rain, maybe a few hours, and his whole life would change. But there had been no water for months—nothing but this cruel yellow quiver on the land, the dying grass, the gritty dust, and the dying beasts. There are times when even genuine sympathy has the ring of a false coin, and I could find no reply in answer to the pain at the back of his eyes as we parted.

From sky to sky the land lay yellow in the sun, sheep stood in the glare, finding goodness knows what upon the grilled surface of the earth. I would see a clump of trees far off, and the road, straight as a sword, would lead into a little red-roofed town, where there would be a Dutch Reformed church, an hotel, and a petrol station, then the road would leave this tiny oasis and dive onward into the heat.

The bitter dust was blown in on the warm air. I could taste it and I could smell it. Thinking longingly of the sound of ice against a glass, I resolved to stop at the next town and drink something cold.

There was a patch of shade beneath a gum tree for the car, and opposite was the door of the hotel. There was nobody inside the bar but a young pot-boy, who was sitting in front of the stupefying selection of drink, tier on tier, which is to be found in even the smallest bar throughout the Union. The young man, I noticed, had a typical Irish face. I sat on a stool while he took my drink out of a refrigerator. While he was doing this, a man came in and asked for a bottle of beer, and they had a long and animated conversation in Afrikaans. The pot-boy evidently spoke this language as perfectly as he spoke English. When we were alone again, I asked him what life was like in such a quiet little spot. I had evidently touched a raw nerve.

" Hell ! " he said, " that's what it's like—just hell ! If you want to find out what petty-mindedness is, what nosey-parker-ism is, what tale-telling is, and what a dirty, filthy game politics are, just come and live in a dorp like this ! I come from "—and here he mentioned a town in the Free State— " and this dorp makes me sick ! "

He took up the empty beer-glass, rinsed it, and began to polish it savagely.

" But I don't give a damn," he said, " I'm out of it in two weeks. I'm off to the Merchant Navy ! "

" Surely you're Irish ? " I asked.

" No," he replied, " I'm not. But my dad is Irish. And he's been to Ireland and seen where his family came from. He went there in the War—not this last war, but the one before."

" Why do you dislike life here so much ? " I asked.

" Politics are the curse of this country ! " he cried, and banged the tumbler down on the bar.

I couldn't help smiling, for I have often heard men with his face and voice say exactly the same thing about Ireland. Leaning his elbows on the bar and lowering his voice, he adopted the typical confidential Irish manner.

" This is the way it is," he began. " I'll tell you. The

other night a great big mouth called Mr. S.—he's one of our local Nats.—came in here and asked for cigarettes and matches. We hadn't any matches and I said so in Afrikaans, which I can speak better than I speak English. When I said that, what did he do but throw the cigarettes back at me. ' Well, then,' says he, ' I'll buy my cigarettes where I buy my matches ! ' Then says I in English, because I knew it would annoy him, ' We haven't got any matches.' Says he, ' I don't understand your language ! ' ' Oh yes, you do,' says I, ' but you won't speak it.' ' All right, then,' says he, ' I won't speak it.' ' Then,' says I, ' I won't speak Afrikaans to you.' ' Oh, won't you ? ' says he. ' Then come outside and speak to me ! '

" I go outside. We are standing on the stoep just there. Suddenly he ups with his hand and gives me a backhander across the face. Then my Irish blood gets up and I give him one like this—not straight, but a twister—and he ends up on his tail in the road. . . . Yes, politics are the curse of this country—but I'm off ! "

§ 6

Bridges were marching across stony river-beds.

There was a town, neat and clear-cut in that fine air as a model in a toy shop window. The aluminium water-mills had ceased to turn, waiting for a breeze. The heat had closed down upon the town like a brass lid. The gum trees drooped despondently, and in their shade a few natives lay stretched asleep upon the ground.

It was like Spain in midsummer, and the voice of the parched earth was a background of insect noises, of whirring wings, of snapping wings, a steady tick and beat of invisible life like the crackle of thorns in a fire.

A long girder bridge was casting its reticulated shadow into an oily swirl and eddy of brown water far beneath ; and this was the Orange River. It looked as though the rich red earth of South Africa had melted in the heat. The bridge was so high, and the river so low, that it was like crossing Clifton gorge.

Colesberg was a little white town built between two clusters of ironstone koppies, a town definitely of the Cape, a place of age, charm, and character. There was a large Dutch church and a small English one. In the free library I admired a painting by little Thomas Baines called " Colesberg, 1850 ". The museum is not Colesberg's strong point, but when I had found the key, I unlocked an upper room and found myself in the midst of a wonderful collection of unrelated objects: old bandoliers, stuffed birds, an Uhlan's helmet, stones, and fossils. There is a piece of glass bearing the initials " D v P " (or N), scratched with van Niekerk's first diamond, the same significant stone which scratched the glass in the Presbytery in Grahamstown. I should like to see those two inscriptions together in the Cape Town Museum. They are the first marks made on the world by South African diamonds.

It needed resolution to walk down Colesberg's hot main street and take a look round. The few people who watched me from the shadow of stoeps and the shade of gum trees probably thought I was mad. I thought so myself. On the right hand side of the road I found a little graveyard with the sun beating upon its split slate gravestones and its mouldering tombs. It cannot be nice to live in Colesberg, conscious that this pathetic forgotten acre exists in the very centre of the place. One flag day, even in little Colesberg, should produce enough money to plant some trees and seal up a few of the tombs.

Many of the epitaphs on the gravestones are illegible, other stones are split and cracked. Major Dugald Ducat, 91st Regiment, who died in Colesberg in 1843, aged forty-five, " deeply lamented by his brother officers ", is commemorated by a stone erected by his "disconsolate widow". Josiah Billingham was only twenty-seven when he died in 1849. He was the son of Joseph and Martha Billingham of Daventry, Northamptonshire. William Hannay of Wigtonshire, Scotland, who died in 1850, lies beneath a stone for which his two brothers had composed the following :

> *And brother laid in lonesome grave*
> *Shall sleep in Death's dark gloom*
> *Until the eternal morning wake*
> *The slumbers of the tomb.*

Robert Gibbon, who was born at "Basham West", Norfolk, in 1793, died at Colesberg in 1869. And how delightful it was, six thousand miles away from dear old Norfolk, to come across this touch of local pronunciation, for "Basham West" is Barsham West, near Walsingham, but to this day the old people still omit the "r" and pronounce it as it is spelt on this tombstone in far-away South Africa.

The sun was sinking upon the Karoo.

I could see the road running ahead, disappearing for a while and emerging again upon the face of the greyish-brown plain, which was dotted with small peppercorn bushes like a Hottentot's hair. Its flatness was broken by shining, wet-looking iron-coloured koppies which rose from a base of scattered boulders. Upon the edges of the sky, etched in blue, were mountains with flat summits like Table Mountain, every one decapitated at the same height above the plain.

As I continued my journey, I searched the sky-line in vain for some human habitation. Where was I to sleep that night? In what strange surroundings would I find myself? The Karoo had the look of a drained aquarium. As far as the eye could see there was no bush, much less a tree. It was a land peculiar and unique, and so ancient that Nature had inhabited it with a specialised form of life: queer objects with long tap roots, plants with water-storing leaves, prickly plants which might lie quiescent for months and then spring to life in a drop of rain. Nature has spent many a century of careful thought upon the Karoo. Each square yard was a miraculous essay in the art of self-preservation.

The sun went down. A hush deeper even than the normal silence lay upon the world. The far hills became the colour of purple heather. For miles around the bushes were touched by the last rays of the sun, as waves are tipped at sea; then came a grey light in which near objects rose, sharp and black, in a silence now so deep that a man, it seemed, might shout to the horizon and be heard. Darkness had not yet come. Clouds of red, gold, and pink rode into the western sky to hang like banners in vast splendour. In the important hush of that

brief moment I seemed to see St Anthony upon his knees in a
desert place: it was the short time between day and night
when a way seems open between heaven and earth.

§ 7

My week on the Karoo was in some ways the most unusual
experience that had yet fallen my way in South Africa. Had
I been asked beforehand to describe what a Karoo farm would
be like, I should have drawn a picture of Olive Schreiner's
African Farm, something rough and crude and close to the
hard and bitter earth. And I have an idea that I should have
been right. I was upon the golden edge of the Karoo. Had
I taken a horse or a wagon and gone out into the brown,
blazing distance, I have no doubt that I should have come at
length to Tante Sannie and Bonaparte Blenkins. But that
was not the Karoo I saw.

I found myself in a spacious house full of old silver,
mahogany, pictures, books, rose-tinted candlelight on the
dinner-table, a silver epergne piled with peaches in my bedroom, and life well organised, pleasant, and easy, running to
a pattern once well known in the country houses of England.
I am aware that this is not typical of the Karoo. It could not
be. The wonder is that it can exist at all. The transition
from the desert to the belt of trees and the water pumps which
enclosed this establishment was as sudden and as strange as
anything in *Alice in Wonderland*.

My host was a Scot who from his birth had spoken Afrikaans
like an Afrikaner. His charming wife, who bore a maiden
name well known in Cape history, spoke English like an
Englishwoman. What a happy union! Could it be repeated
upon a national scale, what a happy South Africa!

Seen from afar, this farm was a dark patch upon the Karoo,
like a ship at sea. As I approached it, I saw that the trees
were firs and gums and that in their shade shone a white
house with a stoep all round it burdened with bougainvillea.
Set back from the house were the stables, the barns, and the
farm buildings. Among more trees was a dam like a small
natural lake, and upon its banks and at various points round

the farm were water-mills which revolved over underground springs and made life possible. As those wheels turned, their clicking and whirring was accompanied by the sweetest sound in the Karoo: the spurt of spring water falling into a tank.

After dinner we retired to a library where magazines and periodicals were laid out title by title as if by some careful butler, and there we talked of the Karoo, of race-horses, which thrive there, of cattle, and of sheep. All the time I was conscious of the intermittent ringing of a telephone bell.

"No, it's not for us," said my host, noting my glance towards the sound. "All the farms in this district are on a single line to the exchange, which is in the railway station fifteen miles away. Each farm has a different call. Ours is two long and two short dashes. We don't hear the others!"

This was literally true. They talked unconcernedly through the frequent ringing, but the instant the bell gave two long and two short rings my host was on his feet and upon his way to the telephone. He returned to say that two friends on their way to the Cape by car had had a burst tyre somewhere and were in a ditch. They would be arriving to spend the night.

His wife just asked what time they would be likely to arrive and went off to draw the blinds of the spare room which is always ready in South Africa.

"I daresay you'd like to hear the English news," said my host and switched on the wireless. A voice from London filled the room.

Before we went to bed that night two weary and dusty men arrived. They brought with them the atmosphere of Johannesburg. We listened to their talk of stocks and shares and Jews and millionaires, and what to buy and what not to buy; and it was like news from another world.

As I lay in bed that night, listening to the crickets and the thump of the electric light engine, it seemed to me that this oasis in the Karoo had a close kinship with the succulents which surrounded it. What were my host's pumps, with their tubes descending into the earth towards some streak of subterranean water, but the long tap roots of the Karoo bush; what were his tanks of galvanised iron and concrete, the big lake itself with the wild duck and the geese upon it, but another version of the water storage of the ice-plant? There is only one law of life upon the Karoo: if you can store water, you can live.

§ 8

I was roused at five o'clock by the sound of a bell. For a moment, half asleep as I was, I thought I must be in some Greek monastery, but I quickly realised that this bell did not possess the resonance of a Greek bell. It was the bell which hung in the tall white arch, like the slave bell of Groot Constantia, and it was ringing to summon the coloured farmworkers from their huts on the hillside.

At six o'clock a coloured maid came into my room like a brown mouse. She carried a silver tea-tray and said, "Morning, master." She snapped up the blind, and I saw a savage slash of sunlight across the stable wall. To everything I said, she replied, "Yes, master" or "No, master"—not an exhilarating conversationalist, but one whose humility searched my conscience. "Sir" is one thing, but "master" is another. I looked at her as she drifted noiselessly about, putting my shoes here and folding a towel there. What infinite grace there was in her silent ministrations! I asked her if it were going to be another hot day, just to hear her reply, "Yes, master."

I walked in the garden before breakfast and admired the mass of petunias round a fountain. There was a bank of cannas; there was a rose garden with a pergola covered by a crimson creeper: but on the other side of the wall the Karoo began. The scattered metallic stones shone like brown glass in the sun, the immense distances ran away to sky and mountains. One step from the garden, and you were in the desert.

It was the same from the croquet lawn. Beyond the hedge lay more Karoo: brood mares were cropping the low bushes, wild geese were flying towards the dam, and far away was a thin moving line of dust with something twinkling in it— springbok.

By the time breakfast was over the day's work was in full swing. The lorry was setting out upon its twice weekly journey to the railway station to collect the mail, stable-boys were at work, stockmen were with the cattle, the old gardener was hosing the rose-garden, a coloured carpenter was making a stable door in the carpenter's shop, the laundry-woman was rubbing clothes on a stone under a pepper tree, the barefoot maids had washed up and were polishing the mahogany; and my hostess was showing me her modern kitchen with its refrigerators and her store-room full of bottled peaches and nectarines. In a range of buildings near the house was a dairy and a meat store. In one the morning's milk was cooling, and a whole sheep was hanging in the other.

We walked round the garden. The irrigation channels had been opened, so that tinkling streams of water were running in all directions. Bright birds perched in the trees, and beyond the great tent of shade in which the house stood the blazing picture of the Karoo lay, mile upon khaki mile. These words of *Isaiah* came into my mind: " The wilderness and the solitary place shall be glad for them; and the desert shall rejoice and blossom as the rose."

The Karoo hills are brown by day and blue in the evening. They are clothed with low bush and they remind anyone who knows Palestine of the hills of Samaria. How easy it is to understand the readiness with which the Boer farmers, who had read little but the Bible, recognised in the country around them all the natural features of the Holy Land: the dry water-courses, the wilderness with its wild animals, the brazen sky, the lack of rain, the water-pools, the oasis, and the rare life-giving rivers. The purity of the Karoo is that of the Sinai desert. Its spiritual voice is that of the " desert place " of the Gospels, which in all ages and in all climes has led men's thoughts to God.

I loved to walk out into the Karoo during the full blaze of afternoon heat. I would open a gate and leave the oasis behind. Wild geese, ducks, and storks would rise from the waters of the dam at my approach and fly a little farther off, coming down again upon the water with loud cries of alarm and indignation. A hare would get up from its form almost at my feet and go racing off into the miniature forest of low bush.

A silence wrapped itself round me like a cloak, a vast silence

which matched the vastness of the sky and the open spaces:
then I noticed that the Karoo had a thousand little voices of
its own, brittle insect sounds, whirring, clicking, chirping
sounds which filled the air with small, powerful vibrations.
My footsteps would set up a glassy tinkle among the millions of
ripe Mexican poppies; then some insect would tick like a
metronome and, as I tried to find it, would sound farther off in
another direction and stop as suddenly as it had begun; and
the silence would be deeper than before.

The Karoo, which looks so flat, is really a series of undulations, and when I had walked a quarter of a mile the farm with
all its fine trees had sunk into invisibility.   The koppies which
rise above the plain gave me the idea that I was watched from
excellent cover by keen, hidden eyes.   Men's eyes?   Perhaps
not.   Baboons, a panther maybe, possibly the ghost of a Bushman.   But when I reached a koppie, I would find it deserted
except for lizards lying with palpitating throats upon the rock.
I would go about seeking for some boulder not too hot to sit on,
and, having found one, I would take out my sandwiches and
eat them with my eyes on the sky-line.   Then I would drop
my eyes to the ground in front of me and notice that the
fallen crumbs were moving away over the sand and through
the bushes in slow but determined procession.   The ants, as
they carried away the crumbs, looked like native bearers in a
Congo expedition moving in single file through jungle.

What a teeming, intense life goes on down there.   What a
terrifying experience it would be to find oneself no larger than
a fly in that Karoo bush, encountering at every turn some prehistoric monster, some green and fearful dragon, some loathly
winged worm.   The human race in past ages has encountered
no creatures as fantastic and nightmarish as those a man would
meet, were he small enough, in any single yard of the
Karoo.

The ant has a fairly free hand there.   Apart from Man, who
uses the cement-like hills as ovens and pulverises the dust as
floor covering for huts, and the ant-bear, an animal as secret
and nocturnal as our badger, which breaks down the hill and
thrusts his tongue inside, the ant has few enemies; and none
that seriously threaten his fertility.   I saw hills that the

PEDIGREE AFRIKANDER BULLS, KROONSTAD

ant-bear had broken down, many of which had been sealed up again and reconditioned by the insects.

The vegetation of the Karoo has a charm of its own. Each square yard is a little botanical curiosity which possesses the delicacy of a Japanese garden. Many of the greyish-black bushes are perfectly shaped little trees. The variety of these bushes, and the way they grow apart at certain distances one from the other, as if by agreement, are fascinating to one who has never seen them before. There is the bitter Karoo bush, which has a yellow flower, and the vaal Karoo, which is a greyer version of the bitter; there is the kapokbos, which in seed-time sheds soft, fluffy wool; the ganna, which is loved by sheep; the Turkish fig, which looks like heather; the brack-bosch, which is bluey-green; and countless more, some invisible beneath the earth waiting to rise in resurrection at the first transforming whisper of the rain.

The Karoo bushes have a herbal, dusty smell. The horses and the cattle roam slowly over the plain nosing out those which they prefer, and their shining, plump bodies prove that, odd as it may seem, the Karoo provides rich and luscious pasturage.

Every afternoon, or late evening, clouds appear above the desert, and the farmers look at them and wonder. The clouds gather upon the distant mountains and advance to lie over the plain. Then a wind springs up, the water-wheels revolve violently, all the clouds are blown away, and another suffocating evening closes down upon the thirsty earth.

§ 9

Early one morning we went off to a sale of farms and live-stock. Every ten or fifteen miles or so we saw a cart-track leading from the road across country to a clump of trees, and among the trees would be another patch of European life, with its water-wheels, homestead, a rose garden maybe, and farm buildings. Some of these farms were well-to-do, some not so well-to-do, and in some no doubt a man was waging a bitter fight with the Karoo, with drought, with pests, and with the bank manager. English and Afrikaner are more or less evenly spread over this wide land, but no matter what their origins

s

or their political views, they possess a community spirit as Karoo dwellers.

We were motoring along a straight road when my host cried, " Look ! " and stepped on the accelerator.

To our right, and perhaps a mile and a half away, a wisp of Karoo dust was travelling at speed in a direction that would cross the road ahead of us.

" Springbok ! " he said. " We might be in time to see them cross the road ! "

The car rushed forward, and it became an exciting race to get there first. As we drew nearer, I saw the lovely sight I had longed to see—several hundred springbok travelling flat out ! They were running in a long line, never anywhere more than three or four deep, led by the swiftest and ending perhaps with the youngest or the less fleet of foot, if such a term may be used of any springbok. I could see the fawn and white bodies, the neat, pretty heads, and the beautiful little horns like curved V's, and when they became aware of the car approaching they did not increase their pace, for that would have been impossible, but it seemed to me that they showed an increased tendency to leap and vault.

Sometimes from the centre of the herd two or three, one after the other, occasionally several at the same time, would spring high into the air and leap over the backs of those ahead and come down on delicate feet apparently at full gallop. Some would leap with downward heads and legs close together, others would fling back their heads towards their tails and fling their legs forward; it did not seem to me that this leaping increased their pace, but I may be wrong.

We were now so close that the herd gave the impression of a news reel taken at Tattenham Corner. We could not see the flickering legs, but the brown and white bodies glided forward out of the funnel of brown dust. The springers came up like flying fish out of the sea. And now the leading springbok were on the road—and across it—and we were still fifty yards away !

" They've beaten us ! " laughed my friend, as he slowed to a standstill.

As they came to the road we had a magnificent view of them. Some cleared it with one graceful leap, indeed they would have cleared the roof of the car had we been there, and with a few feet to spare. In a few moments they were far off on the other side, visible merely as a spurt of dust with a brown and white twinkle in front of it.

We journeyed on until we came to a track leading to the farm where the sale was to be held. We had not met a soul since we had started out, neither had we seen another car, yet, turning a corner, we came upon the really astonishing sight of about three hundred gleaming American limousines drawn up in a car park. Where had they come from? How amazing that this desert could produce so much expensive urban smartness!

We walked to the homestead—a delightful house with fine stables and outbuildings surrounded by a shady garden. Beneath the garden trees sat the ladies of the Karoo with their sunshades, obviously making a day of it. They did not seem to be interested in the sale, for they sat on a wall with their backs to the auctioneer. I gathered from the pretty dresses and the stylish hats that this was definitely an occasion.

While the ladies of the Karoo talked philosophy—for what else could they have been discussing so eagerly?—the men of the Karoo, in the heartless world of sunlight beyond the trees, were getting ready to bid for farms, farm implements, and livestock. Here I saw what a fine, big-boned type of man the Karoo produces. I should say that six out of every ten men present, English and Afrikaners, were six feet high. Some were in khaki shorts, some, wearing tweed riding-coats, sat on shooting-sticks, and among them, making no concessions to the climate in their black Sunday clothes, were many Boer farmers.

The auctioneer, in a silk shirt and a pair of tussore trousers, fanned himself with a catalogue as he announced and described each lot in English and then in Afrikaans. Six great sheep farms, each of several thousand acres, were sold—one of them fetched £6,000, which seemed a very moderate price —then came the livestock.

Native herdsmen took huge and resisting Afrikander bulls into a cattle kraal and led them round, and it was a fine sight to watch them tossing their wide horns, raising the red dust and pawing the ground, while a ring of intent faces gazed at them, noting each point. You had only to watch the men as they ran their eyes over a bull to realise how early anyone would have to rise in the morning if he hoped to get the better of a Karoo farmer in a cattle deal!

While all this was going on in the dusty, lowing, bleating, bellowing sunlight, the ladies sat with their backs to it, drinking tea in the shade. What a picture it was: the brown distance, the flat-topped mountain on the sky-line, the water-wheels, the sudden solitary flowering of green and colour in all that wide-open landscape, the sheep nuzzling and bleating between hurdles, the red bulls with their broad, flat foreheads and their startled eyes, the farm wagons in a line, a young man examining a rifle and aiming it at the blue sky, the masculine crowd, watching, whispering, laughing, the auctioneer red in the face, and in the shade the ladies beneath their parasols, interested only in those things which interest ladies on the wide-open spaces of the Karoo. It certainly was not " one wool press, three sorting tables, three mowers, three rakes, and one Hobson Leveller ".

The moon was rising. It was a foot above the horizon, and as it rose into the sky, a silver haze spread over the Karoo and each bush stood in a thin shadow. It was the time the bats come out to flicker round the eaves as they do at home, the time the ant-bear stirs in his mysterious den and decides to make a raid, the time the panther stretches himself and yawns at the moon and begins to think of baboons and buck.

That strange, strong land was silent now and silver, and locked in night until to-morrow's sun should leap into the sky. I was sorry to be going away, for I could have stayed there for a long time, perhaps too long. It is a dangerous place. Many a man, having seen it, has gladly left the world for it, and many a man will do so again.

CHAPTER NINE

I see diamonds at Kimberley and go on to the Vaal River diggings, where fortune hunters are at work. I see the new goldfield at Odendalsrust, stay on a farm, and spend Christmas at Potchefstroom.

§ 1

A HUNDRED miles of bleached country dotted with ant-hills six and seven feet high lie between Bloemfontein and Kimberley. The veld looks as though hundreds of lorries have tipped piles of cocoa haphazardly about the countryside. These hills are as hard as steel, and I would be interested to see how an ant-bear tackles them.

Wherever there are ant-hills there is a delightful-looking little animal called a meerkat, a cross between a weasel and a squirrel. He sits bolt upright, his small front paws hanging loosely against his stomach, watching the road with two large eyes ringed with black fur and set in an inquisitive snouted face. He is the greatest gossip and watcher in South Africa: the whole veld is his stoep.

When you draw level with him, the meerkat flashes into his burrow, but he does not go very far, for when you look back, you notice that he has returned, accompanied by all his friends, to sit up and wait for the next traveller. There are two kinds of meerkat, the grey, which has a thin tail, and the waaierstert, or fantail, with a bushy extremity which he uses as a parasol, and may often be seen sitting up in the shade of it! In this part of the Free State the meerkat is as common as the rabbit used to be in England.

The neat, inquisitive meerkat sitting beside an ant-hill; the secretary bird moving like a lord chamberlain across the veld; the widow bird's wavering, embarrassed flight; and the sudden heavy lift of wings as the big eagle, the lammervanger, rises from a gatepost, are for me the unforgettable spirits of the veld.

And upon this road there was another South African, a bird

known as the korhaan, or knorhaan, the "scolding-cock", and a good name it is, for I think the meerkats employ him as a watchman! He is a large ventriloquist, with a harsh and irritating "kruk-kruk-kruk" as he flies off to warn every living thing upon the veld that danger is approaching. His voice, as you try to spot him, sounds now here and now there, and all the time he is hiding almost beneath your feet.

As I went on, I came to a bare gridiron of veld where a little ramshackle farm drooped in the shade of a few gum trees. I wondered in what excess of optimism anyone could have believed it possible that this stony earth would have rendered him a living. The ant-hills had advanced into what had once been a front garden. The out-houses were tumbling down, and the sun quivered over their corrugated iron roofs. I knocked at the door and asked the way to Kimberley.

The woman who came to the door was pale and thin, and her startled eyes, when she first saw me, were those of one who has given up expecting good news. She expected me to thrust a summons into her hand or to ask why something had not been paid. In her relief that I had not come to ask for anything, she invited me to enter, and led the way into a dark front parlour. There was a harmonium in the corner, a table, a few horsehair chairs, and some startling pictures of the Pyramids executed in blue and green stencil.

She went out, and her husband entered, a big quiet Afrikaner in his shirt sleeves and with the same strained look on his face. I explained myself in detail, and he relaxed. Perching himself on the tiny harmonium stool, he sat there like someone in a Greek tragedy, with his huge hands on his knees and his eyes every now and then gazing out of the open door to the brassy heat which sat as firmly on the land as a lid on a saucepan.

Ja, it was a terrible drought! Verskriklik! All the mealies were withered, and there was some kind of worm in them as well. All the cattle had gone on trek. Some farmers had been forced to sell up and go to the town to look for work. He moved uneasily and unhappily on the stool.

The wife came in with glasses of tea on a tray, while three gloriously dirty little barefoot boys with bright flaxen hair, three little Huckleberry Finns, stood shyly behind her. We sat sipping the hot tea and no longer talking about the battle of endurance which was going on under the galvanised iron. I wondered for how long would it go on? How long could they stand the siege? Would it be days or weeks before they would hear the drums of the relieving armies thudding on the galvanised roof?

I went on my way reflecting that with many people farming in South Africa seems to be not a way of earning a living, but an hereditary habit. And all the time the real wealth of the country is not on the earth, but underneath it. Could I have had a wish that afternoon, I would have wished a couple of Cullinans in that poor fellow's garden which would have brought de Beers buzzing round there before breakfast.

§ 2

Kimberley is hot, brown, and rambling. It still looks like a mining town. Its streets were not laid out for the turning of sixteen span of oxen, but by diamond-diggers in a hurry, who put up little tin shacks here, there, and everywhere. The shacks have gone, and modern buildings have come in their place, but they still stand huddled together like a crowd of miners discussing a find.

Visitors go to Kimberley to stand awed upon the brink of the Big Hole—the workings of the old Kimberley Mine—and to fling stones and wait for the sound of their arrival far below. What makes the Big Hole so uncanny is that you would expect so great an excavation to be balanced by an equally large pyramid. But of the earth which came from the Big Hole there is no sign. Every bucketful was scrutinised, washed and disposed of by those who found it worth while to dig it out.

From the Big Hole and other chasms round Kimberley have come suites at the Ritz, enormous motor cars, diamond tiaras, Crown jewels, insolent butlers, champagne in rivers, racing stables, yachts, mink coats, houses in Park Lane, expensive families, heart attacks, suicides, disillusion. Yet you would never imagine that such a quiet, unpretentious place has been responsible for so much. The only thing that has never happened to Kimberley is a millionaire who said, " Now that I have made a million, I'm going to settle down in dear old Kimberley and spend it all there!" It has the look of a bran-pie after the children have gone home from the party.

But Kimberley also has an atmosphere which is not exactly Bohemian, neither is it hearty nor happy-go-lucky, but is possibly born of all three, and might be described as warmth of heart. Even in a country of kind hearts, the people there are remarkable for their generosity and their affability. It may be possible to see in this a legacy from those extraordinary personalities who founded the town, men who, no matter what this apprehensive, conscious-stricken age may think, were at least full-size human beings with an immense vitality and a colossal zest for life. The most romantic of them all was Cecil Rhodes, the most acute was Alfred Beit, and the most fantastic was Barney Barnato.

It is perhaps curious that South Africa was called on to face two of the great Nineteenth Century movements in an extreme form: social reform, represented by the missionaries, and materialism, represented first by the diamond diggers and then by the gold mines. A people who had been cut off from Europe for centuries were asked to assimilate those violent and indigestible manifestations of western life within a century. The rush of diggers to the Vaal River not only from England, but from North and South America, Australia, the Dutch East Indies, and every corner of South Africa itself, was some-thing entirely new in South African life. The money motive had entered South Africa, and in one bound she was right in the middle of the modern world.

Many of the Boers were as eager as any uitlander to pick wealth out of the river-bed, but others, less modern maybe, or perhaps more deeply aware of the Ten Commandments, were only too glad to sell their farms to the speculators and trek away from the wild and greedy men who were about to dig the biggest hole in the world in search of money. De Beers is a name everybody knows. It suggests to most people stocks and shares and brokers. But the original De Beer was a Boer farmer (perhaps not unlike the men I had met upon the burn-ing veld on the way to Kimberley), whose barren farm had suddenly revealed the diamonds which lay beneath it. The farm, called Vooruitzicht, was owned by two brothers, Diederick Arnoldus de Beer and Johannes Nicholas de Beer, who had paid fifty pounds for it. They sold it to the diggers for six thousand guineas, and before they had yoked their oxen to trek away, five hundred men were burrowing there like moles! It is said that since that day ninety million pounds worth of diamonds have been taken from the mine.

The De Beers were not the only farmers who sold their land. What had been bare veld, covered with karoo bush and dotted with mimosa trees, was soon a heaving mass of thousands who had swarmed up to the dry diggings from the Vaal River. That diamonds should be found on dry veld and beneath koppies seemed at that time incredible, for until then it was believed that they were only to be found in river gravel. So overnight Kimberley sprang up on the fiery veld.

The town takes its name from a tiny hamlet near Wymondham in Norfolk, where the Wodehouse family have lived for centuries. A member of this family, Lord Kimberley, was Colonial Secretary when the diamond fields were annexed to the Cape, and possibly to save the Colonial Office the ordeal of pronouncing Vooruitzicht, he gave his own name to the town of diamonds.

The youthfulness of South Africa's first millionaires is an astonishing fact. Cecil Rhodes was only eighteen when he arrived at Kimberley, so was Alfred Beit; Barney Barnato was only twenty-one. All three were millionaires long before they were thirty.

I think it will be agreed that the tall, brooding presence of Rhodes at Kimberley gives tone to what would otherwise have been a disorderly rabble. The ascetic side of his personality seems to have been much in evidence in those early days, if his biographers are to be trusted. They say he read the classics in the mining camp; but he was making money as well. This boy of eighteen soon wrote home to tell his mother that he was turning over a hundred pounds a week. Then he left the saloons, the tents, and the shacks of Kimberley, the crowds of rough diggers and the gambler's life, for the peace of the cloisters of Oriel College, Oxford. And this astonishing undergraduate would interrupt his study of Roman history to buy a pumping engine and direct it to be sent out to the diamond mines! He returned to Kimberley more idealistic and more materialistic than ever.

Then little Alfred Beit, physically timid and financially courageous, who admired in Rhodes all that he lacked in himself, also had a mother in Hamburg to whom he used to write. They say his only ambition when he first arrived in South Africa was to make enough money to give his mother a thousand a year and a carriage.

Barnett Isaacs was a different type. He was a Whitechapel Jew who had toured the East End music-halls in a juggling act with his brother, Harry. They called themselves the " Barnato Brothers " because they believed all high-class juggling acts were Italian, and Barnato seemed an adequately southern version of Barnett, or Barney. Calling himself Barney Barnato, Isaacs arrived on the diamond-fields with a fund of Cockney humour, a straight left, and forty boxes of dubious cigars for sale on the diggings. At first he acted in a circus, then he saved a few shillings and persuaded diggers to let him re-sift gravel, in which he found a few miserable overlooked stones, and so, bit by bit, but with astonishing speed, he became a diamond expert and a buyer, then a digger and, eventually, a millionaire.

The early years at Kimberley were a chaos of individual miners. The thousands of men who had rushed there from all parts of the world each bought little claims and began to sink shafts. Soon they were working in a hideous honeycomb whose narrow roads, now far above them, often caved in and came crashing down, killing them and obliterating their mines. The deeper they went, the more dangerous it became and the more costly it was to haul the diamond earth to the surface.

Hundreds of diggers were glad to exchange their claims for shares in a mining company, and soon dozens of companies replaced thousands of individual miners : then the companies began to swallow each other until only two great groups remained, the De Beers combine, under Rhodes, and the Kimberley Mine combine, under Barnato.

Now the strange thing about the diamond is that it is not really a precious stone in the sense that an emerald is precious because of its rarity. If all the diamonds in South Africa, especially round the Alexander Bay region, which is sealed off, were mined and put on the market, the price of diamonds would collapse. It is only by limiting the supply of diamonds that the price can be kept up. Rhodes saw that if his combine and Barnato's remained in competition, it would be impossible to regulate the diamond market.

His argument, which was delightfully and typically Rhodesian, was this: that in Europe and America were sufficient young men willing to spend four million pounds a year on diamond engagement rings. Therefore, in order that all those pledges of love, so painfully excavated in Kimberley, should render a due profit to the mining industry, he was determined to make certain that the market was not flooded with stones. The only way to do this was for De Beers to acquire the Barnato interests. The battle between the diamond kings was eventually won by Rhodes, and De Beers became, as it is to-day, the controlling factor in the diamond trade.

Among the stories told all over the Union is that of Rhodes, Barney Barnato, and a bucket of diamonds. As told to me dozens of times, it seemed pointless to the verge of inanity.

The story is that during the negotiations, Rhodes, wishing to flatter Barnato, told him that he had always longed to see a bucket full of diamonds. Barnato, glad to show that his mines could easily produce such a sight, turned up with a bucket filled with diamonds to the brim. Even such a good biography as that by Basil Williams gives this improbable story, and adds that Rhodes plunged his hands into the bucket and " lifted out handfuls of the glittering gems ", which is surely odd, because uncut diamonds do not glitter, but look like bits of soapy glass.

But the point of this story is to be found in the book by Rhodes' secretary, Gordon le Sueur. Here it is said that at a point in the negotiations, when Rhodes was particularly anxious for the market not to be flooded with diamonds, Barney Barnato had sorted an enormous stock, and threatened to put them on the market unless Rhodes agreed to his terms. Rhodes went to talk things over, and found Barnato placidly smiling, master of the situation, with thousands of diamonds all neatly sorted and labelled on a side table.

In the middle of the discussion Rhodes strode quickly to the table and said: " Barney, have you ever seen a bucket-full of diamonds? *I* never have. I'll tell you what I'll do. If these diamonds will fill a bucket, I'll take them all over from you at your own price."

Then, before Barnato could do anything, he swept the diamonds into a bucket that was standing near—which they did not fill!—and left the room. He had got the delay he needed, and " as Barnato turned to face the astonished gaze of those seated there he only then realised that he was no longer a factor in the negotiations, as the re-sorting of his diamonds for market meant a matter of weeks ".

If this story is true at all, that version surely has the ring of truth. As for Rhodes diving his hands into diamonds like a pantomime Ali Baba, that is highly improbable.

§ 3

Twenty silent men sit facing the light of windows, as they neatly pick up with tweezers what appears to be fused glass. Some of these lumps are the size of beans, other the size of peas, and many are smaller.

So all the shouting and the tumult, the drinking and the fighting, the wasp-waisted barmaids, the dusty mule teams and the weary ox-wagons from Port Elizabeth, the grinding of the winding-gear, and the rocking of ten thousand gravel-washers, has boiled down to this quiet room, where solemn men adjust green eye-shades and pick up one little bit of soapy-looking glass from a pile here, to arrange it in a row with others on white paper over there.

" You see a quarter of a million pounds worth on the tables," said my guide.

Surely much more was visible. I saw hundreds of engagement rings for girls who at that moment probably had no thought of getting married. But De Beers would be ready for them! I saw the diamonds which thousands of men had yet no idea they were going to give to women! I saw tokens of

devotion, expressions of manly remorse, sordid bribes; I saw
elderly gentlemen popping into Cartier's feeling not a day older
than fifty; I heard female voices in a variety of accents and
languages saying, " Oh, but you *shouldn't* . . ."; and I saw
clever people escaping from revolutions with small hard little
packets sewn up in chamois leather. All this was clearly
visible on the sorting tables at Kimberley. It was like watching the Fates spin their webs.

I asked the experts to define a diamond, and this is what they
said:

" A diamond is a mineral formed of carbon subjected to
certain temperature and pressure."

But the precise reason why carbon should become a diamond
rather than coal or any other mineral is apparently unknown;
and no one has yet been able to make an artificial diamond.
The stray bits of crystallised carbon are deposited, with all
kinds of other eruptive matter, in the pipes of volcanic craters
and nowhere else. The early diggers believed that the stones
were only to be found in river-beds because they had discovered there the diamonds which had been washed out of the
volcanic pipes during centuries of soil erosion and carried by
rain into the rivers. It was a great surprise when, for the first
time at Kimberley, men found, not stray washed-away stones,
but the actual source of supply, which was the pipe itself.

I was taken to the Du Toits Pan Mine, where I changed my
clothes and put on overalls and a crash helmet. We went
down in the cage to a depth of about a thousand feet and
stepped out into a large lime-washed hall where a crowd of
black men, naked to the waist, were waiting to go up to the
surface. They were Basutos, Pondos, Xosas, and others, and
having seen their native lands and villages, their wives, fathers,
and grandfathers, it was interesting to see them in these
remarkable surroundings. Like the mine-boys of Johannesburg, they are all recruited from the reserves for a stated
time, but, unlike the coal mines, the diamond mines keep their
natives in compounds throughout their service and do not let
them go out.

This segregation was a scheme started originally by Rhodes
in an attempt to stop the theft of stones and to save the natives

from drink.   Life is made as comfortable as possible for them in the compounds, they are well looked after and well fed, and they return to their villages, it is happy to relate, having had practically no contact with the corrupting West.

We set off at a brisk walk down the long white tunnels, and stood aside now and again to let a noisy train of cocoa-tubs go rumbling past, full of the precious blue ground.   We were moving about in tunnels made in the great volcanic pipe which millions of years ago had shot up its engagement rings and solitaires into the veld.   And at last we arrived at the face, where a white miner was supervising several black labourers who were hacking at the rock and loading it into tubs.

It was not unlike the cleaner kind of mining everywhere, and by no means as unpleasant as some coal mines I have explored.

On the surface again, I saw the diamond earth, having been pulverised, passing over pulsators, which were really mechanical riddles, or sieves, which sorted out the various kinds of little stones found in the rock, most of them more attractive in appearance than the diamonds; then the process of washing and sifting goes on until you come to a machine where one or two diamonds are lightly held in a bed of grease.

Everyone in the diamond mines is blessed with good eyesight.   White and black know exactly what to look for and, if it is there, they will see it in a flash.   Natives still try to get away with diamond thefts, but it is not so easy as it used to be.   Medical science has been enlisted to make sure that the departing Basuto is not returning home with a tiara in his stomach.

§ 4

Fifty years ago a young Irishman from Killarney's lakes and dells decided that he was not cut out to be a priest, so he left the monastery in which he was studying and went off to South Africa.   Arriving in Kimberley, he was given a job as night guard in the old West End compound.

" And to think," says Mr A. M. Duggan-Cronin, " that after nine years at college and two in a monastery I was to be a night watchman at De Beers with nothing to do but keep awake! But never mind, it all turned out for the best! "

To-day the Duggan-Cronin Bantu Gallery is one of the sights of Kimberley, indeed of Southern Africa, for it is the most complete photographic record in existence of the domestic life and tribal customs of the Bantu. A few years ago Mr Duggan-Cronin gave his four thousand photographs to the city of Kimberley, which has now housed them in an attractive mansion and has installed Mr Duggan-Cronin as curator of his own collection.

The pictures are hung in tribal sequence, and a room is devoted to each tribe. Leading from the Matabele room is the Zulu room, then the Swazi, and so on. Here we can see how the tribes looked before they came in contact with the West. Here are the Xosas as the Zuurveld Boers and the 1820 Settlers saw them; here are the Zulus as seen by Dick King, Farewell, Isaacs, and Gardiner. Every passing year will make the Bantu Gallery more valuable. Even to-day it is not as easy as it was only twenty years ago to take a photograph of a native who bears no traces of European influence.

Mr Duggan-Cronin was first attracted to the Bantu by the varied tribal types in the mine compounds. Beginning his work with a twenty shilling box camera, he soon decided to make a record of the Bantu against the background of tribal life; and this meant long expeditions every year into native territory.

I asked him if photography is more difficult now than it was twenty years ago.

"Yes," he said, "I find it harder every year to get the primitive dress. Once a native dons a piece of European cloth, it's there for good! Changes of custom have not been so noticeable. It is difficult to say how long it will be before the Bantu gives up his dress and customs. As long as natives remain on their reserves and do not come into town locations, the old way of life will continue."

With the help of the Carnegie Corporation of New York, many hundreds of photographs from the Kimberley gallery have already been published in a fine series of books entitled *The Bantu Tribes of South Africa*. A new volume will deal with the Pondo and Pondomese tribes.

There was something distressingly logical about the remark of a chief to Mr Duggan-Cronin.

" What is the use of trying to civilise us," he asked, " if you want to photograph us in our leopard skins, which we have already thrown away? "

§ 5

I found myself for some days in a sunny little dorp not far from the Vaal River, in a landscape flat, red and fiery and pitted for miles, as if by moles, with the burrowings of departed alluvial diamond diggers.

The dorp was small, its population perhaps a thousand white inhabitants and twice as many black, and it was full of clear-cut individuals many of whom were violent Nationalists who hated England on principle. Knowing Ireland, I felt quite at home there! My chief impression of this dorp was that Ireland and Scotland had become inextricably confused in it. On Sunday it became indisputably Scottish. The average Afrikaner has no idea how Scottish is his background, due to the recruitment of Scots ministers for the Dutch Reformed Church in the Nineteenth Century. Many predikants who regard themselves as dyed in the wool Afrikaners have such names as Barrie, Murray, and Nicholls.

In the morning, from the stoep of the small hotel, I would see and greet all the town notabilities: the cheerful attorney plump with the profits of a litigious countryside, striding in an alpaca coat on his way to an office plastered as thickly with the brass insignia of insurance companies as a veteran's chest with medals; the sombre old school master and the rebellious young one, just out of the Army and once a prisoner at Tobruk; the post-master; the predikant; and various old farmers who would come driving in through the dust in Cape carts.

There was a hopeful individual digging for diamonds behind the hotel in what had been the garden of an abandoned chapel. He sat under a shelter watching like a hawk while three natives dug trenches.

" No, not yet," was always his reply when I asked how things were going; then he would point to the tottering chapel and add, " *That's* where they are! "

One morning Mr Smit, the diamond buyer, invited me to go round the alluvial diggings with him, and we were soon speeding along a sandy road. On either side of it were telegraph wires, brown grass, anthills, meerkats, and far off on the edge of the sky a black necklace of railway coaches plodding on over the veld.

As we went on each new mile continued to reveal the same monotonous expanse of sand and scrub from horizon to horizon. There was not a cloud in the sky. The ants and the meerkats had this country to themselves.

It is a queer bit of South Africa. For eighty years it has been a shaggy Monte Carlo, beckoning with alluring promises to the gamblers who, from the discovery of van Niekerk's stone until to-day, have flocked to the Vaal River in the hope of making a fortune. The individual diggers are scattered not only round the banks of the Vaal, but far inland wherever diamonds have been found. They are of all ages and of all types. Upon the news of a lucky " strike " the district is immediately invaded by " stiffs ", " mugs ", and " old birds ", which, I gather, are the three categories into which the alluvial diggers are divided.

" And they do find stones? "

" Well," said Mr Smit, with a smile, " I find it worth while to go round twice a week! "

" What is the biggest price paid for an alluvial diamond? "

" Let me see! There was one at the diggings outside Pretoria about five years ago which was sold for seventy thousand pounds! So, you see, it isn't all a mug's game."

We came to a stretch of devastated country which looked as though it had been shelled and bombed for years. Its stony hummocks and dips stretched to the sky. Every square yard had been dug up, turned over, and sifted.

" I can remember when twenty thousand men were working there," said Mr Smit. "Not one left now! That's what happens. A district is proclaimed, thousands rush to it, tear it to pieces, and go."

An old man passed in a mule-cart.

" See that old man? He's got a farm round here with diamonds on it. When times are bad, and during a drought,

T

he digs for diamonds, and manages to make enough to carry on.   There are dozens like that round here, half farmers and half diggers! "

We turned off the road on to a narrow track which petered out among rocks.   We left the car and started to walk over rough, churned-up country covered with mimosa trees and with an adhesive bush called the wag 'n bietjie—the wait a bit—which possesses thorns like salmon hooks.   There was a gorgeous yellow shrub called the bird of paradise, which I remembered having seen in a garden at Swellendam, but no one there could tell me its name.

Beneath the shade of a tree we came upon a tall man with a white beard, who sat at a rough table.   He was wearing a dirty sun-helmet, a bush shirt, a pair of shabby trousers, and his bare feet were thrust into a pair of velskoens.   His eyes never for a moment left a group of half-naked natives who sweated and swung their picks in a gravel pit below.   He could hardly bear to look away for a second in case they slyly pocketed a diamond while he wasn't looking.

" Have you got down to it yet? " asked Mr Smit.

The man rose slowly, and as he did so—for movement is revealing—I recognised him as a gentleman of an old vintage.

" Hardly," he replied in an Oxford accent, " but I'm getting precious near it."

He looked enquiringly at me, and Mr Smit introduced us. He shot me a frosty gleam of blue eyes.

" How d'ye do? " he said, and somehow I felt there were still hansoms in the Strand.

They walked round the pit together, whispering knowingly and pointing to the gravel.   I wondered who on earth he was. As we left, he said solemnly, with a nod that was almost a bow, " Good day to you," and turned again to bend those icy blue eyes upon his minions.

" He's an old bird," said Mr Smit.   " He made his pile and spent it.   He went away to England for ten years, perhaps fifteen, but one day he turned up again, just the same, but a bit older.   Speaks to nobody, tells nobody anything, lives in that wooden hut over there, does all his own cooking and—well, he's just an old bird."

We travelled on until we came to the bank of the Vaal River, which that morning looked a milky blue. We embarked upon a chain ferry worked by two chanting natives who turned a wheel and so drew us slowly across the smooth water to the opposite shore. The land everywhere appeared to have been picked up, examined, and thrown away. As I looked at it, the resemblance which had evaded me all morning suddenly came to me. The Vaal diggings look like the ruins of Babylon! The diamond diggers searching for treasure, and the Arabs searching for antiquities, have produced the same landscape.

With the midday sun bearing down upon us and the panting earth lying helpless and inert, we came to a deserted place named Holpen, where a small building called itself the Queen's Hotel. All was silent. Round us stretched another Pompeii of the Vaal. We knocked and hammered, and at length the door of the hotel was opened and we stepped into a scene which ought to be preserved as an ancient monument.

The hotel, with its tap-room and bar, its high stools, a disillusioned-looking poker table, a picture of the Battle of Trafalgar, another of Waterloo, stands just as it did during the diamond rush of 1880, when the now desolate mounds which encircle Holpen were covered with swarms of men. The iron bar which fits into slots across the door after closing time is the thickness of an arm, and is now the sole remaining tribute to the determination and thirst of the men who once strove so mightily in that place.

A few miles away we came upon a scene of noisy, rattling activity. Three or four claims were being worked within sight of the Vaal River. All kinds of gear had been erected on the hummocks, and the white masters sat beneath trees or under wooden shelters, each one watching the movements of his own gang of natives like a lynx.

The earth and gravel from the claim was first thrown into a wooden frame on swing rockers fitted with meshes of varying size. As a native rocked the frame, which is called the "baby", a stream of water helped to break up the deposit as it was shaken through the grid. I naturally thought the name of this contrivance referred to its likeness to a cradle, but this was not so. An American with the appropriate name of

Babe arrived on the diggings in the eighteen seventies and introduced this machine, which was already in use on the Australian gold-fields. They used to say that he was the only Babe who had ever rocked his own cradle.

When the deposit had been cradled, it was placed in a sieve and carried to the digger. This is the exciting moment! The digger takes the sieve, dips it in water, and with a neat movement perfected by long practice tips the whole sieve-full upon a sack. Should there be a diamond, it will probably lie on top of the wet and glistening pile of tiny red, blue, and green stones. Seeing nothing, the digger takes a piece of slate, with which he swiftly cuts the pile of gravel, then he spreads out each little pile flat upon the sack, and if he finds nothing the whole lot is thrown away and the process is repeated.

This goes on all day, month after month, sometimes year after year. And there is, I suppose, a queer and awful fascination in it. It is not difficult to understand the call of the diamond diggings. Once a man answers it, it must be almost impossible for him to free himself from the spell of a monumental inactivity presided over by Hope. Every sieve comes along like a golden question mark. Every time he tips it over on the sack Fate may have decided to smile upon him. Each sieve-full is important for precisely six seconds. So he goes through life, sitting in the shade of a mimosa tree, watching and watching, and rooted to the spot perhaps for a lifetime by that thrilling series of minute optimisms.

Although I watched for nearly an hour, I saw only one diamond discovered, and that was so small that I should not have thought it worth keeping. But the digger solemnly pounced upon it and put it in a match box.

" I suppose you've never come across a woman digger? " I asked.

" Yes, we're going to see one now."

We bumped off the road towards a distant farm. A native boy pointed into the heart of the blazing afternoon when Mr Smit asked in Afrikaans where his mistress was. Walking across the veld, we came to a familiar scene: gravel-pits, the rhythmic creak of the " baby ", the swish of muddy water and the sound of picks. Some way off we saw Mrs van Aswegen, wearing a large kappie or sunbonnet, in the act of tipping a sieve out on a table. She was young, slim, good-looking, sunburnt, and wore a print dress and a pair of black worsted stockings. She handled the sieve like a man. She could not speak a word of English, and I had an impression of laughing blue eyes, strong wet hands, and arms muddy to the elbows. She walked back to the farm, where she had some diamonds for Mr Smit. We sat in a dark room crowded with furniture, and the lady returned in a few moments with diamonds and coffee.

I thought Mrs van Aswegen the most sensible digger I had seen that day. She had the whole thing sized up. For her there was nothing romantic about it, no spell or fascination or glamour: it was just plain business.

I asked Mr Smit to find out what she would do with a fortune. She replied that she would put it in the bank, buy a new herd of cows, and shut down the digging and never bother with it again. I asked her to say honestly if she did not find romance or excitement in it. No, of course not, she said. Romance in all that gravel and mud! "But men . . ." I began. Oh men! Men are mad enough for anything, especially lonely men without women, living in huts and being cheated by natives and living on tinned sardines!

We said good-bye to those clear and sensible blue eyes, and went on to spend a fantastic moment with a man who was knee deep in a digging beside a main road and within a few yards of the church! Pausing for tea at Bloemhof, Mr Smit spread out the result of the day's work upon a sheet of note-paper. It was amazing that so much all round effort should have produced so little to admire.

What can happen in an irrigated South Africa may be seen at a little town named Christiana, where I looked down on what might well have been the Thames Valley. Lines of poplars fringed the river banks, great fields of corn and lucerne, mealies and potatoes were growing, and seven hundred miles of concrete channels carried water from the Vaal Dam—a river dam sixty miles in area and deep enough to float the *Queen Mary*—transforming a desert into an Eden.

They say that Africa is a land of contrasts. I thought that no greater contrast could be seen than the thirsty land where the bemused seekers groped for their diamonds and this noble spectacle of Nature responding to the intelligent hand of Man.

§ 6

Travelling eastward from Bloemhof across the Orange Free State, one crosses a plain whose outline never varies: a low koppie, miles of grass, wilting mealie patches, a sleepy little dorp among gum trees; and the road goes on into the distance, puffing into red clouds with the approach of a farmer in a mule cart.

Then you come suddenly to a dorp which is filled with the sound of hammering. Builders on ladders are at work on a little shack called the Commercial Hotel, there is an air of excitement and alertness about the place: a brand new estate office has been erected on the outspan, or village green, and as you stop in front of the hotel, you find many expensive cars drawn up there, and from the building emerge not farmers and their friends, but men from cities, journalists who can be spotted a mile off, and press photographers. The name of this dorp is Odendaalsrust, the centre of the new Free State gold-field.

A few months ago no one had ever heard of this dorp; now it has appeared on the front page of the world's newspapers and is known on every Stock Exchange. There is an extraordinary air of " country boy makes good " about the place. Everybody is smiling—or almost everybody. The old man standing at the corner is almost certainly counting his chickens, and the young man in the general store no doubt already imagines himself another Stuttaford.* People stroll about the old dorp and look at it with new eyes. They look at tin shacks and see concrete skyscrapers. They look at the old dusty road and see electric tramcars and motor buses. Bewildering memories of their first sight of Johannesburg come to them as they watch the lorries struggling through the red sand with

* A noted South African store.

mining machinery; for the good fairy or the bad fairy—as you will—has waved her wand over Odendaalsrust as she did over Kimberley and the Rand.

Sometimes a newspaper turns the limelight upon a puzzled individual who has won a sweepstake and been swiftly translated from poverty to wealth. This has happened to a whole dorp! Some people have already cashed in and have sold property previously worth twenty pounds for tens of thousands; others hold out for wilder profits.

I went into the little hotel bar which was crowded with uitlanders in city suits. They were chaffing the young German proprietor who stood behind the bar with his sleeves rolled up, while the placid faces of native workmen appeared through holes in walls and between new timber partitions, as they enlarged the building to suit its sudden rise in the world. A man whispered to me that the proprietor had refused an offer of a hundred thousand pounds for his little hotel.

" Man," he said with a sigh, " if only it had been offered to me ! "

Odendaal, I learnt, was the name of a man who had farmed land on the site a generation or so ago, and "rust", or "rest", refers to his grave, which is in the neighbourhood.

I walked over to the little estate office on the outspan. It was only a three or four roomed bungalow, but already it represented the powerful modern world. I had to give my name to a receptionist, and there was a clatter of typewriters from an inner office. As the manager unrolled maps of the district and told me of the great prices already paid for land, I began to wonder whether I was not perhaps moving in history. When you have seen Johannesburg and its skyscrapers, it is fascinating to read the accounts of men who only eighty years ago passed that way and saw a bare ridge with a few tents upon it, where the first miners were gathered. As I looked out of the window at Odendaalsrust a herd of cattle were being driven over the sandy road, and the future metropolis was still definitely a dorp.

But where were the gold mines? I was told that they were scattered about the veld three or four miles away. I found the offices on a shadeless plain. A young engineer motored me out in a shooting-brake to Shaft Three of the St Helena Mine, which, I understood, was the first to be started. There was a power-station, pit-head gear, and a crowd of sweating workmen at the top of a huge inclined shaft which looked very similar to the entrance of an underground railway station. The gold was four hundred feet below.

" But how do you know it's there? " I asked.

The engineer then explained boreholes, drilling operations, and the science of geophysics, from which I concluded that the discovery of a new gold-field is not unlike the discovery of a good Stilton cheese. In those days, which some of us remember with pleasure, before the king of cheeses became extinct, you would go at Christmas-time to the grocer who, taking a thin silver probe, would thrust it firmly into the heart of the cheese, and withdrawing it would offer for your sight, smell, and taste, a specimen of its interior. I only hope the Free State probings will be as memorable.

I sped on into the Free State reflecting that everything is firmly organised these days. No longer do thousands of men arrive on new gold-fields with picks and spades. Scientists make their probings, companies acquire land, and the one person no longer present in a gold rush is the digger.

§ 7

The farm house in which I was staying was built among trees on a slight koppie, and the ground fell towards a spruit which ran through my host's land. Beyond the spruit the Free State stretched in level distances towards a sky-line dotted with ridges which looked within walking distance in that clear air, although they were twenty miles away.

Every afternoon at the same time enormous clouds would gather, and the chief topic of conversation would be—will it rain? The immense skyscape darkened until it became indigo shot with jagged spears of lightning, and while thunder was tossed about the sky, we would sit on the stoep and watch ripe blue clouds open and send their rain shredding down on a distant mile of parched earth. It was extraordinary how, day after day, the same kind of storm would assemble in the afternoon and how the rain would fall all round us but never upon us.

Sometimes these storms would rumble over the Free State for hours and would last until the night, but always when I looked out of the window in the morning, the sky was wiped clear, the heavens were intensely blue, and the sun was already growing warm upon white walls.

My host was one of the most likeable people I had met in South Africa, and that is high praise. He was an Afrikaner, a great reader, an enthusiast for the Afrikaans language, a classical scholar, and a farmer. I shall call him Meneer Jan Bruin. He had the usual Boer characteristics: height, a rural outlook, and penetrating opinions upon every subject under the sun. He had handed over the management of the farm to two fine sons, one of whom had recently returned from the war, and he would sit regally on the stoep and issue commands to his sons and to various Basutos, which were instantly obeyed. A second throne on the stoep was occasionally, but not as often, occupied by his wife, a woman with a great sense of humour and a fine match for him; her rule inside the house and in the kitchen was as absolute as his was outside it.

Occasionally Meneer would step from his throne and, followed by an eager Dobermann Pinscher and hounds of less recognisable origin, would go to the garage nearby; selecting an old and experienced car, he would disappear down the dip and across the spruit to the veld, where, regardless of anthills and other obstructions, he would drive at forty miles an hour behind a herd of wildebeest.

" Look at them! " he would cry at these moments, " look at the action, look at the way they put down their heads and frisk along! What beauties, aren't they? "

Then he would turn homeward, and setting the car at the water splash with a loud cry of " Thalassa! Thalassa! ", he would dash into the spruit and go tearing up the opposite bank!

He had been closely in touch with Scotsmen at some time in his youth and had great powers of mimicry. He could imitate a Scot to the life, and his knowledge of Scottish idiom and slang was first rate.

He had a wonderful way with children. It was amusing to go with him on to the veld with two little boys who were staying on the farm. He had a story about every animal and bird we saw, and every time we came across a peewit standing red-legged and tufted in the grass, he would call:

> *Kiewitjie, kiewitjie, wats jou naam ?*
> (*Little peewit, little peewit, what's your name ?*)

And both the little boys would shout together at the top of their voices:

> *Basie, basie, rooi beentjie !*
> (*Little master, little master—red legs !*)

But Jan always pretended to be horrified by this response.

" No, no, no ! " he would say in Afrikaans. " You must not say it like that. Look at the kiewitjie! See how neat and prim he stands on his little red legs, nodding his little head to you. You shout, Piet, you shout, Hans, like bad little boys! That is *not* how the kiewitjie speaks! He speaks in a kiewitjie voice, like this."

And raising his voice to a high treble he would croon, " Basie, basie, rooi beentjie ! ", and the two little boys, instead of laughing, would suddenly become silent and awed and point out that the peewits were nodding and bowing their heads in reply.

We would walk over the veld watching the guinea-fowl, the tarentaal, pour away into the mealies as if on rails. In the hot afternoon, with a storm overhead, we would see in the sudden bursts of sun each of a thousand holes upon the veld occupied by a snakey head, still as stone, as the sun lizards gazed out; the ou'volk, Jan called them, and the boys would creep up to see how near they could get before the heads flashed down into the earth. We heard the korhaan lifting his sore-throat voice in warning from the stones, and we would come softly down to the spruit in time to see a heron lift himself slowly on blue wings and a kingfisher come flashing up the stream. Then a few warm drops of rain would fall and roll like quicksilver from the mealie leaves, and we would rush for home, to be greeted from the stoep by the voice of motherhood, which called for no Afrikaans dictionary:

"What have you been doing with those boys? Just look at them. They're dirtier than ever!"

§ 8

We went to bed at nine and were up at five o'clock in the morning. When darkness fell the dogs took up their positions round the farm, and some of them slept under my bedroom window. Generally at about two o'clock there would be a great outcry and they would go tearing off into the night. I would get up and look out of the window and see the veld silent and silver in the moonlight, the outhouses standing in sooty shadows, the trees like black cardboard. The South African watch-dog is a fine natural policeman, and I wonder how anyone has the courage to visit a farm after dark!

At five o'clock the sun would be up and the sky clear. Basuto girls with milk-pails on their heads would come slowly from the native quarters to the farm and disappear round the corner by the kitchen. Presently arrived that moment I enjoyed so much. There would be the sound of bare feet on the cool tiles outside and a rap on the door. Jan would enter in a dressing-gown, holding a tray with two cups of coffee upon it and a box of cigarettes. He generally began the day with a quotation. It might be Horace or Virgil, or even Wordsworth. Placing the tray on the table, he would seat himself at the foot of the bed and say solemnly:

> *You yet may spy the faun at play*
> *The hare upon the green.*
> *But the sweet face of Lucy Gray*
> *Will never more be seen.*

"How does it go on? That's how I learnt English when I was a little boy. The *First English Reader*! How well I remember it. And we little Boers would stand up and say poems in chorus, over and over again, until every word was engraved upon our memories for ever."

I asked him why he never wore slippers in the morning.

" It's most important," he replied solemnly, " to charge the body with electricity. Everybody ought to walk about on the earth with bare feet in the morning. Have you never heard of that before? *Ex Africa semper aliquid novi !* "

Lighting a cigarette, he would continue.

" ' The gowan glitters on the sward, the laverocks in the sky, and Colley in my plaid keeps ward, and time is passing by.' Now that's another voice from the past! I know what a plaid is—and you notice I don't pronounce it playd!—but tell me what a gowan is and what laverocks are! "

Then, becoming serious, he would take a topic—it might be Russia, it might be the Native Problem, or it might be General Smuts or Dr Malan or the future of South Africa—and he would hold forth in a most agreeable and interesting manner.

" When I was a little boy," he said one morning, " it seemed as though the Boer was going to lose his language. Then— may I make a little joke?—Dr Jameson struck a great blow for us and Afrikaans was firmly launched. What Europe doesn't know, and quite a lot of English South Africans don't know, is that in the last forty years Afrikaans has developed so quickly that it can now maintain itself as a medium of thought against any European language. I wish you understood it, because I could tell you stories much better in Afrikaans. It is more direct—stream-lined. In a sense, it's like American.

" Tell me, what do they know in Europe of the language of the rough and simple Boer? Nothing! I thought so. Well, it may be that some day Afrikaans will be taught and spoken in European universities. ' *Ex Africa !* . . .' I must tell you that modern Afrikaans is as different from the Taal, which is the dialect the Boers used to speak in the country districts, as modern English is from the English of Chaucer. The way our language has grown and strengthened itself and become a first-rate literary language in my life-time is perhaps the most interesting thing that has happened in South Africa. It has fed on all the best-known literary vitamins. It has done in half a century what English did in many centuries; but then we live in different times! English used the ox wagon; Afrikaans has used the air!

"Afrikaans has naturalised into its idiom all the best selected thoughts and ideas of English, Dutch, and German literature and popularised them in simplified language. Let me put it like this. It took a straight branch of knowledge, so to speak, pulled off all the little protruding branches and leaves, scraped off the bark, sand-papered and polished the remainder, and formed it into a very serviceable walking-stick. I hope you get the idea as it strikes me. Is it a poetic language? Oh yes. . . . Listen to *Die Vlakte* by Jan Cilliers, who was one of the great pioneers.

> ' *Ek slaap in die rus van die eeuwe gesus,*
> ' *Ongesien, ongehoor,*
> ' *En dof en loom in my sonnedroom*
> ' *Ongèwek, ongestoor.* . . .' *

"Isn't that a beautiful language? And doesn't the metre remind you of Shelley's *Cloud*? But why should I be talking so much on this beautiful morning? We have no coffee! Let us go to the kombuis! "

He would pause on the way and say:

"Now that's an interesting word! Seafaring Dutchmen turned their backs on the sea and became farmers, but they still called their kitchens by that word ' Kombuis ', which is the ship's galley of a Seventeenth Century East Indiaman. And here's another relic of our seafaring past. If a dance or a party has been a success, we say ' Goed afgeloop '—it went off well. But originally that phrase was used in Dutch ship-yards—' Goed van stapel loop '—which literally meant that the ship left the scaffolding well; but as slipways and scaffolding have no meaning for farmers, we've discarded the word, but we still use the old shipyard phrase. Come along, let's get some more coffee. . . ."

The kitchen at that time in the early morning, as Jan bustled in on bare feet, was always an interesting picture. A plump Basuto matron would have fired the stove. The kettle would be boiling. Two or three young maidens would be sitting on the floor, waiting for Mrs Bruin's arrival to galvanise them. We would pour ourselves more coffee from

* See Glossary.

the pot on the hob and go out of the kitchen door to drink it in the sunlight, looking out over the dip of land and across the spruit to the veld, where the cows were trooping from the milking-kraal to the grazing grounds.

§ 9

Two notable features of life in the Free State are the stoep and the gate. Let us take the stoep first. In Holland most of the old houses are tall buildings approached by a fairly long flight of steps to the front door. Beside the door at the top of the steps you will find a little seat on which it is pleasant to sit in the afternoon and watch the ships and barges on the canals. The Dutch took this little seat with them to South Africa, and the Boers carried it with them into the wilderness, and although their single storey farms had no flight of steps, they continued to call the place where they sat the stoep. This word now includes the whole of that space round a Boer house or farm which we should call a verandah.

When you are living on a farm the first thing to do is to discover, and this will not be difficult, which is your host's chair on the stoep and which is his wife's. Having done so, the next thing, even under pressure of the most cordial invitation, is to refrain from sitting on them! The Boer's seat upon his stoep is as sacred as the Englishman's chair by the hearth, and just as it would be sacrilege for any stranger to occupy many a chair in England, so there are thrones upon the stoep to which no stranger should aspire.

The stoep might be likened to the quarter-deck of a warship. It is the place where the captain and his commander are most often encountered in public, and where they greet their visitors; it might also be compared to the bar parlour of an English inn, because it is the true Parliament of the country. There is hardly a stoep in South Africa, certainly in the Free State, without its resident politician.

Stoeping can become almost a profession, certainly a calling. The spell of the stoep is tremendous. Once you have your own seat there, it is difficult to be anywhere else. I can only compare it to spending a day in bed. As soon as you arrive, someone is almost certain to bring you a cup of coffee. And you sit on watching sunny South Africa, content to be in the shade (" Yes, I will have another cup of coffee! "), and postponing the effort of going forth into the white fire of the afternoon.

Then gates. Nowhere except in Ireland are there so many different kinds of gates as in the Free State. The motorist off the main roads is always stopping to open and shut them, often several times within a hundred yards. Few of these gates are ever the same. There is the gate fastened with chains as if it were some kind of a puzzle; the gate that opens inwards and the gate that opens outwards; the gate that suddenly swings away from you when released and the gate that has to be carried, ploughing up the earth as it goes. There is even the gate that attacks you. They call it the bekslaner hek, which means the smack-you-in-the-mouth gate.

No penny was ever better spent than the coin which is so often tossed through the car window in South Africa to the little piccanins who are sometimes—but, alas, not always—the guardian spirits of those varied obstructions.

When you are on the veld it is never a good idea to admit that you may be a good shot, for it is certain that you will be invited to shoot. The Boers have a belief, which dates back to days long before the South African War, that no Englishman can shoot straight; and it is unwise to undeceive them. Should you do so, your reward will be this. You will be given a .22 rifle and told that you can wander where you like over the veld and shoot guinea-fowl.

This may seem too easy. It may seem rather like going into a barnyard and taking a shot at the turkeys. But should you fall for it, you will soon discover yourself embarked upon one of the most impossible and desperate of adventures. The guinea-fowl, which appear so large and static to an unarmed man, become to a sportsman a disappearing target of almost incredible efficiency. They live in fairly large flocks on the veld, and the moment they see a man with a gun they melt away into the nearest mealie field or patch of cover, not in panic or excitement, but with a smooth, inevitable motion, and they know the effective range of shot-gun or rifle to within a few yards.

If you take a boy and a dog with you, the result will be the same, only quicker. The guinea-fowl will wait until they see in what direction they are to be beaten, and then they will pour off in the opposite direction like so many beads of spilt quicksilver.

§ 10

In company with Jan I visited many neighbouring farms. They were all enormous according to European ideas. In addition to flocks and herds, most of the farmers took pride in herds of such wild animals as springbok, blesbok, and wilde-beeste, and one of them even owned a small herd of English fallow deer.

The Boer farmer reminded me in many ways of the English landowner of the Eighteenth Century, and much the same unjust things have been said about him. The hereditary principle was still in being, and many a farm was already owned by the grandson of the first owner. But one farmer lamented to me about the drift away of the young Afrikaner from the land.

"What was good enough for my father and me is no longer good enough for the young men of to-day," he growled. "Young men want to go into the cities and make their fortunes."

"That's true," put in Jan. "That's one of the new things in South Africa. It's the new trek: the trek of the young Afrikaner from the land into commerce, business, and industry."

"I wanted my sons to take over the farm," said the first man, "but they have no love for it. One is in a Government office in Pretoria and the other is going into a manufacturing business in Port Elizabeth. Old ideas are breaking down!"

"And it's right that they should," said Jan. "We Boers must not be old-fashioned and think exactly as our fathers thought."

There was upon every farm a Basuto village where the farm labourers lived with their wives and families, their hens, ducks, and stock. I went into many huts, which were similar to those of their compatriots which I had seen in Basutoland. In addition to a small monthly wage, the natives were given rent-free houses, firewood, their own mealie and vegetable patches, and the use of their master's stud animals. One native foreman ran his own horse and trap. As far as I could judge these farm workers were well off and well content, and the relationship between employer and man was obviously, in very many instances, that of master and old family servant.

I was surprised by the absence of horsemen on the farms. There were plenty of horses, I even watched wild colts being broken in, roped to a tame horse, but the only people who ever seemed to ride were the natives.

" I expected to see horses hitched to every post on your farm," I told Jan. " What has happened to the Boer pony? "

" The motor car has happened," replied Jan, with a smile. " Young men to-day don't ride: they get out the car even for the shortest journey, and between you and me, if a Boer Commando were ever called out again, I expect it would probably have to be mechanised! "

Another Boer custom which has vanished, except, I was told, maybe far off among the poorer inhabitants of the backveld, is the picturesque and pleasing custom of the *opsit-kêrs*—the sitting-up candle. In the old days a young man who was looking for a wife would put on his best clothes and, saddling his stallion, would ride forth to visit the lady of his choice. One glance at the cavalier, at his brushed hair and shaven cheeks and special clothes, would tell the girl that the visitor had come a-courting, and so after the family had retired to rest the young man and the maid would sit up and talk by the light of a candle. If the young man were favoured, the candle would be a long one and the talk would last as long as the light, but should the girl not care for him, she would produce a short candle and he would know that his chances did not appear to be too good.

I wonder if this custom came from Holland. Dutchmen tell me that they have never heard of it, and D. J. van der Ven in his book on love-making among the Dutch peasantry does not even mention it. Yet oddly enough E. V. Lucas refers to something similar in his *Wanderer in Holland*. "When a

U

young man thinks of courting," he wrote, " he first speaks to the parents, and if they are willing to encourage him he is asked to spend the evening with their daughter. They then discreetly retire to bed and leave the world to him. Under his arm is a large cake, not necessarily of gingerbread, and this he deposits on the table, with or without words. If he is acceptable in the girl's eyes she at once puts some more peat on the fire. He then knows that all is well with him: the cake is cut and Romance is king. But if the fire is not replenished he must gather up his cake and return to his home."

This is surely very similar to the old Boer custom.

" Nowadays," said Jan, " among the middle and wealthy classes motor-car drives and the bioscope have been substituted for the *opsit-kêrs*."

§ 11

It is five o'clock on a still summer morning. The wide Free State stretches to the sky, a bird is calling " Piet-my-vrou . . . piet-my-vrou! ", and the red cows, casting long early morning shadows, stream over the ridge towards the open veld.

There is a heavy dewfall on the thin grass, the sun lizards are all at the doorways of their holes and the swallows are dipping under the wooden bridge across the spruit, threading in and out and up into the morning sky. The day's first task is to assemble and yoke the plough oxen, which stand in a massive red group in the kraal where they have spent the night. Basuto herd boys move about shouting " Voorman! Voorman! " and " Aasvoël! ", and at the sound of their names two big oxen lumber out, the velvet-soft keelvel at their throats shaking as they move, and go down from the kraal towards the ploughs.

Six ploughs stand on the veld—six South African ploughs with the furrow wheel larger than the other—and in front of each plough, stretched far out on the grass, are the chains and the yokes of the team. Fourteen oxen go to each team, and eighty-four will be needed for the six ploughs.

The animals know what is expected of them. Most of them, certainly the older ones, even know their own places in the team.

As with men, some are eager, while others hold back until the last moment and have to be driven to their work with cries of " Hoy, hoy, hoy! " When at last the fourteen animals stand near the yokes they are lined up in the place they will occupy in the team, two by two. They are now standing with their tails to the plough. First a leather throng, or riem, is taken and attached to the forehead of the off-side ox. The wooden yoke is lifted and placed across the necks of the first two oxen so that it lies easily and cosily in front of the skof, or hump, and then the loose reim is taken from the forehead of the off-side beast and bound to the horns of his companion. And so it is continued until seven pairs of oxen are inspanned and the plough is ready to be sent off to the fields.

They are a grand sight: a tremendous power for so small a plough, but the earth is brick hard in the summer drought. The Basuto boys dart here and there, speaking all the time to their animals, quickly adjusting a riem, resettling a yoke, and putting the last touches to the span.

Each ox has a name and knows it: Stormberg and Aasvoël; Very Nice and Appel; Kommandant and Soldaat; Pontak and Sinkkwas; Wapad and Wiegman; Voorman and Carpenter; Vuilbaard and Sweetveld.* The ploughman takes a last look at them and lifts a tall whip. He bends back for a moment and there is a flick of the lash in the air and a crack.

" Kom! kom! kom! " he cries.

The slack trek-chains are pulled tight, the red heads go down, the team wheels to the left with a click of horns like boys fencing with sticks, and the plough moves off, absurdly light and toy-like behind the fourteen great Afrikanders.

" Troei! troei! troei! " shouts the ploughman.

The plough strikes the furrow and the share comes down, no longer a toy but something hard to drive through the resisting earth. So it passes across the field, the oxen bowing to the yoke, a thin dust rising, the whip cracking; and a voice clear on the morning air urging on the great red beasts.

" Trek, Wiegman! Trek! trek! trek! . . . Pontak, Pontak! Trek . . . trek . . . trek . . . !"

The next plough moves off, the next and the next, until

* See Glossary.

eighty-four oxen are slowly crossing and re-crossing the field, the wide horns clicking, the dust rising higher; and as I go away I hear the voices growing fainter in the morning air. " Trek . . . trek. . . . Ver-ee Nice! . . . Trek! "

As I approach the farm the smell of coffee and eggs and bacon comes down the hill to meet me.

§ 12

Which brings me to food.

The great and noble art of cookery, as I have already suggested, is appreciated in South Africa, and in that country, it is good to relate, a woman is rightly admired and revered for her excellence in the kitchen. South Africa is the home of certain noble dishes which every traveller should insist upon tasting; indeed no one can be said to have visited South Africa unless he can speak intelligently about bobotie, biltong, sosaties, melk tert, and, slightly more esoteric, mebos.

Bobotie is an admirable curried dish of minced meat flavoured with dried apricots and a bay leaf. The name is believed to be a Malay word, and it is certain that this dish arrived at the Cape with the Malay slaves, or was composed there under an eastern influence.

Biltong is dried meat and is commonly eaten grated on toast or bread. It may be made of beef, mutton, buck, or ostrich. I have tasted beef, mutton, kudu, and springbok biltong; and I would unhesitatingly vote for the springbok. Like many farmers' wives, Mrs Bruin makes her biltong every year, but it was not the right season, otherwise she would have given me a demonstration. The time for making biltong is July, when there are no flies about.

The meat, having been cut and trimmed to the required size, is well rubbed with coarse salt to which a small quantity of brown sugar has been added. The pieces are then placed in an enamelled dish (not a galvanised one) and are left from twenty-four to forty-eight hours according to thickness. They are then taken out and rubbed down with a cloth dipped in vinegar and then hung up outside to dry in the shade. The curing continues until every piece of biltong is dry, and if properly cured it will keep almost indefinitely.

Sosaties—another Malay word—are a popular and delicious grill which can be as simple as veal or mutton cutlets sprinkled with curry powder and roasted on a skewer over a clear wood fire, or as complex as pieces of mutton or pork soaked in wine and vinegar, spiced with coriander, pepper, tumeric, and tamarind, and grilled in the same way. This is a more ambitious version of kébab, the skewered roast meat eaten all over the Near East and sold on Turkish railway stations.

Melk tert is a grand custard tart flavoured with almond essence. It is usually made with puff pastry and, as a gesture to departing civilisation, I will give a recipe for puff pastry in favour in the Free State. Take one pound of flour, one pound of butter, salt, and one wine-glass of brandy, and add a tumbler of water.

Mebos is not common. Here again we have something that came to the Cape from the Far East. Some believe that the word is derived from the Arabic mushmush, an apricot, but others, and this is more likely, from umeboshi, a Japanese word given to preserved plums. Mebos is made of ripe apricots, dried, salted and sugared, and the taste is an acquired one, for it belongs definitely to that " sweet and sour " order so palatable to the Chinese. People brought up in China tell me that plums salted and sugared like mebos are still popular there, and it is fairly certain that this unusual sweetmeat came to South Africa in early times by way of the Dutch East India Company's factories in China and Japan.

I said good-bye to my kind friends in the Free State one hot morning in December.

" ' Will ye no' come back again ' and . . . tot siens ! " said Jan as he wrung my hand. And when I stopped to battle with the first gate, I looked back and saw him standing waving to me from the stoep, waving me off along the roads of his complex and delightful country.

§ 13

It was now drawing near to Christmas. Every day the sun grew hotter; every day more and more dahlias, salvia, and petunias appeared in the gardens, and, as if to underline the strangeness of Christmas in summer time, the South African year threw itself into a frenzy of production. All kinds of ripe fruit appeared in the shops: pineapples, plums, peaches, melons, mangoes, and strawberries, figs, bananas, and apricots.

I detected in myself a desolating and harrowing home-sickness. I pushed it away during the day, but it would return at night when, alone, I listened to the hot African sounds in the gardens and watched the strange African sky. I began to think of cold misty mornings at home and to wish that I were there. There would be thin ice on the ponds in the morning maybe, and the trees would be bare; in the evening the rooks would come home against a blue and windy sky and people would be saying, "We shall have snow for Christmas".

It was going to be strange indeed to wake up on Christmas morning to a summer's day. . . .

The name of Potchefstroom, the oldest town in the Transvaal, perpetuates the memory of that tough old Voortrekker, Hendrik Potgieter. It is a town whose pleasant suburbs wander over miles of gardens and where the Mooi river comes dreaming under willow trees. It is a great educational centre.

Upon Christmas Eve I found myself there in the heart of a kind and friendly family. I arrived after nightfall, but I could see that the house stood in a fine garden; and later on as I went to bed the scent of flowers came through the open window and there was a bowl of red roses on a table. It was exceedingly warm—for Christmas Eve! At this moment at home, I told myself, they would be creeping up chilly stairs to hang stockings beside bed-posts, frosty stars would be snapping in the winter's sky, and the waits, their breath visible in the cold air, would be singing " Hark, the Herald Angels Sing ". . . .

" Hark, the Herald Angels Sing ! " There it was ! I could hear it ! One of the boys had switched on a wireless somewhere in the house and it was Christmas morning. " Hark, the Herald Angels Sing " from Johannesburg! Just think of that.

I went out into the garden, where the first thing I saw was a swallow curving through the summer sky. There were dahlias in beds and borders, cannas, hollyhocks, salvia, petunias, red-hot pokers, French marigolds, roses, syringa, bougainvillea. I had never seen such a garden upon Christmas Day.

Through the deep hush that lay over Potchefstroom in the morning we went to kerk. How like Scotland it was : the same group of uneasily garbed children wearing gloves in the church-yard; young men and women in their Sabbath garments; then the older people, mostly in black. The pews curved in semi-circular tiers from the pulpit; the elders entered in their frock coats and white ties, then the minister in his gown and white bands. Although I was unable to understand Afrikaans, I could follow the service with ease, so closely did it appear to follow Scottish procedure. Afterwards I met the predikant in the vestry and I was introduced to the elders, or Kerkraad, who in their uniform frock coats and white ties concealed such varied callings as that of soldier, merchant, farmer, and so on.

Arriving home, a stupendous feast was ready. Whoever had told me to expect nothing resembling an English Christmas was very far out. Upon a positively Dickensian table, a turkey, roast pork, a superb pie, a plum pudding, and ice cream followed one another massively, while the hot day swung into a sweltering afternoon. There was nothing for it but to retire like a boa constrictor into a darkened room and listen to the cicadas snapping.

In the early evening, the Christmas sun still hot upon the garden, the young people dived and swam like seals in a great cistern of water. Then came dinner, dusk, and the arrival of friends, who sat out on the stoep and discussed all those problems which perplex the South African soul. Perhaps the most significant thing about the Afrikaner is that in a world which has lost its nerve, he is not afraid to be a master.

§ 14

Boxing Day began with a great banging of tin cans, and we went out into the road to watch a band of native boys dressed in fantastic garments dancing convulsively for pennies with much hand-clapping and laughter.

We drove out some miles to a fine farm where an immense and cordial farmer who, like my host, had fought against us in the South African War, welcomed us with open arms. I had been warned to keep away from this unhappy topic when in the company of Afrikaners, but I found it unnecessary. Not only was it possible to discuss the miserable origins of that fratricidal strife, as with any educated persons, but I found them only too ready to give their reminiscences. Like soldiers everywhere who have been in action, they were free from rancour. It is odd that it should be only the civilian, and notably the civilian who has never heard a shot fired, who perpetuates expired animosities the world over.

In the very depths of the Transvaal, in a house embowered in trees, I met a veteran of a different kind, the Afrikaner poet and scholar, Dr J. D. du Toit, who has played an historic part in the birth of the Afrikaans language and in the great work of translating the Bible into that language. He occupies much the same position in Afrikaans intellectual life that Douglas Hyde and Yeats occupied in the Irish revival. I discovered with a mournful sigh that we both share precisely the same views of the modern world.

Hurrying back to Potchefstroom, we arrived at a tea-party whose merriest members were predikants.

" There is a lot of good-natured rivalry between the Free State and the Transvaal," one told me. " We in the Transvaal say that the Free Stater is a boastful, talkative fellow. Well, two Transvaalers were fishing one day in the Vaal, which, as you know, is the boundary, and when they had caught a fish one man said, ' Is it a Free State fish, do you think, or is it a Transvaal fish ? ' ' Open its mouth, man,' replied the other, ' and if it's a big one, it's a Free Stater.' "

Then I heard another story. There was once an old Boer

farmer away out in the backveld who had never been able to
master the mechanism of his car.   Unable to stop it, he used
to drive round and round the veld until the petrol ran out.
One day the first aeroplane which had been seen in those
parts flew low over the house.   The native girl rushed into the
kitchen calling to her mistress: " Missis, missis, come quick
and see where the old baas has got to now! "

And here is a third.

A farmer took on a native who had appeared out of the blue
and asked for work.   The native was a terrific worker.   He
finished his tasks in half the time the farmer had expected and
turned up to ask for something else to do.   The farmer was
amazed, for he had never met a native like this one before.
He gave him so much work, which the man got through in
record time, that by the end of the week the farmer thought he
ought to give him an easy day.

" See that pile of potatoes," he said.   " All I want you to do
is to pick out the seed potatoes and throw them on that pile
and put the other ones over there."

Returning at the end of the day, the farmer was astonished
to find that the native had done nothing at all, but was sitting
as he had been left earlier in the day, looking at the potatoes.

" What on earth's happened? " asked the farmer.

" Baas," replied the native, " the anxiety's killing me! "

When we returned to my host's house, native servants were
building a fire in the garden.

" We're going to have a braaivleis! " I was told.   As it
grew dark the guests began to arrive, until the lawn looked
like a nocturnal garden-party.   Women in light summer
dresses with their husbands and fathers encircled the fire,
watching the preparation of this typical South African occasion
as the best part of a butcher's shop, it seemed, cut into chops,
steaks, and cutlets, was placed upon a grill and on skewers.
Soon the smell of sizzling meat had conquered the night scents
of the garden.

What a vegetarian does if invited to a braaivleis, I dare not
imagine!   It is a feast in which the carnivorous instincts of
South Africa are seen at their best.   You roll up your sleeves
and, approaching the fire, seize a chop or a cutlet and eat it

in your fingers.   For some odd reason meat cooked and eaten in this way tastes better than upon any plate, and the quantity of meat consumed at a braaivleis under the kindly cover of night is quite extraordinary.

South Africans love above everything to camp out or eat food out of doors.   Perhaps the story of the Great Trek has given these acts a sacramental significance.   However that may be, a braaivleis, especially to anyone from a country where meat is rationed, remains long and frequently in the memory.

CHAPTER TEN

*I see Johannesburg and its mines and Pretoria. I go to Barberton in
the Northern Transvaal and to the Kruger National Park, where I see
lions. I fly north to Bulawayo and the Victoria Falls.*

§ 1

IN remote ages to which no period can be given, a great
river flowed southward through Africa into a lake which
covered what is now the Rand. It carried with it
particles of gold which had been washed out of rocks. These
particles, settling down at the bottom of the sea, became
covered with mud, sand and gravel, which in time turned to
shales, quartzites and conglomerates. Then the sea dried up
and its bed, containing the layer of gold, became warped and
tilted in some geological disturbance so that, instead of lying
flat, its rim became visible on the surface and then dipped down
into the earth. So a golden sandwich was hidden in the
Transvaal.

" Now here," we may imagine Fate saying, " is a nice
piece of trouble. This shall be concealed from the Chaldeans,
the Babylonians, the Phoenicians, the Egyptians, the Greeks,
and the Romans, and it shall lie there protected on the north
by mosquitoes and everywhere else by mountains and sea
until a remote and distant time. . . ."

And of all places on earth this, the richest gold-field in the
world, was the place chosen as grass land by simple farmers
who were flying from the hated modern world and wished
only to have nothing further to do with it! So the Promised
Land turned out to be El Dorado, the earth opened and out
sprang the most agile and powerful of all modern demons—
Gold!

Johannesburg is a big modern city with skyscrapers, service
flats, bus companies, tramways, crowded streets, Neon lights,
miles of shops, thousands of limousines driven by men without
mercy, or without brakes, which is the same thing in the long

run; and at the end of many of the streets you can see golden pyramids shining in the sunlight. These are the goldmine dumps.

So golden are they in certain lights that children seeing them for the first time might imagine they were the veritable gold dust on which this city is founded. In other lights they turn a dirty white, grey, sometimes almost blue, and on sunny evenings you can see them so sharply in that clear air that every erosive wrinkle which furrows their flanks stands out sharply pencilled in blue shadow. The Cornish miners who went to Johannesburg a generation ago must often have been reminded of the china clay dumps which dot the landscape round St Austell.

Those mine-dumps compensate the city for the lack of any great architecture. They are its hall-mark. They are unavoidable and compelling, drawing the eye to them all day long. They are what St Paul's is to London, what Table Mountain is to Cape Town, what the Acropolis is to Athens: the landmark that all eyes see and know to be a symbol of the city, its true coat of arms.

The extraordinary thing about Johannesburg is its youthfulness. Only sixty years ago there was nothing to be seen but a bare, treeless ridge and a few tents. A generation is only just dying which can remember when Johannesburg went to bed under canvas. If you go to the wonderful Africana Museum on the top floor of the Public Library, you will come to a room where the whole history of the city is shown in photographs. In 1886 there were about fifty miserable-looking tents, three years later a few more and a tin shed or two, some ox-wagons standing on unmade roads, and crowds of men—women apparently had not then arrived —gathered in dusty groups, wearing billycock hats. That was Johannesburg sixty years ago.

The people who fill the streets to-day hold your attention. There comes surging towards you a crowd that is both black and white. You see natives from all the tribes of South Africa, you see the Englishman, the Afrikaner, the Jew, the Latin, all of them living more or less in water-tight compartments. You go to a shop and are served by a Scot; in the next shop you are served by a Jew, in the next by a Greek, in a fourth by an Irishman; a native boy sells you a newspaper; a smiling old native, whose grandfather probably hurled his assegai at the white man, takes you up in a lift. You wonder whether a more cosmopolitan population has filled the streets of a city since the days of ancient Rome.

I took a taxi at the General Post Office and told the driver to take me anywhere. He was an acidulated Englishman who had come out to South Africa twenty years previously. Every time we came to a traffic block he turned to give me information, usually of a gloomy kind.

" There's a murder a day in this place," he said. " Shocking, isn't it? Yes, natives. We call them Amalayita, which means toughs. Don't you go wandering about at night, Guv'nor! Knock you on the head as soon as look at you."

At the next stop he turned again.

" Uncivilised, that's what they are. Did you see in the paper about that man and his girl who were knocked out in a car last night? I tell you straight, this place isn't safe, and it's getting worse. You go out, if you've got time, and have a look at the native locations. Detribalised natives, thousands of them! That's our trouble here. . . ."

At another block he stopped again.

" Look at 'em! " he cried, nodding towards the crowds on the pavement. " It's a paradise for white women! They don't do a stroke of work."

In company with this cruel and destructive critic I went to some of the suburbs, which are perhaps even more interesting than Johannesburg itself. What was so recently treeless veld is now covered with trees and houses, each house standing in a pretty garden. The bus routes leave these inner suburbs for outer ones and continue towards a chain of satellite towns. Nothing gives a more impressive idea of the wealth of Johannesburg than such suburbs as Houghton, where a ridge and its slopes have been covered with expensive houses, each one an example of Spanish Colonial, Cape Dutch, Tudor, or what Mr Osbert Lancaster has called " Brewers' Gothic " and " By-pass Variegated "; and each one has its garden, its garage, and its gate posts, round which the Zulu house boys drape themselves in picturesque indolence in their off moments.

"Know what you'd have to pay for one of them?" asked the driver, nodding towards the houses. "Twenty thousand quid!"

In the bright sunlight the suburbs of Johannesburg have a Californian luxuriance, and I knew that with the help of the languid, black individuals in their spotless white garments, a pleasant domestic life goes on there amid the flowering shrubs, the pergolas, and the swimming-pools.

Life would be intolerable in Johannesburg were the city not six thousand feet above the sea. But lifted as it is to an altitude two thousand feet higher than the summit of Ben Nevis, the sun, which would otherwise be tropical, is tempered and tamed. When the Johannesburg gold-miner has driven his shafts to the great depth of six thousand feet, he is only just on the level of Table Bay.

Sometimes the sultry summer afternoon storms turn into extraordinary bombardments by enormous hail stones. Lumps of ice often the size of walnuts come crashing down and can stun men and animals and smash roof tiles. Watching one of these storms, I could hardly believe that a warm day could in a few seconds have deposited on my window-sill enough ice to fill a bucket.

Johannesburg is one of the noisiest cities in the world. This is caused by innumerable cars fitted with the loudest procurable klaxon horns and by natives who never talk in a conversational tone in the street, but shout, laugh, and sing at the top of their voices. As most of the hotels are situated in the midst of this racket, sleep is not easy. The babel tends to lessen at midnight, but begins again sharp at five o'clock in the morning with a noise like sheets of tin being hurled from roof-tops to the sound of laughter and gaiety. A glance through the window will reveal mule-drawn municipal dust-carts collecting the contents of rubbish bins.

§ 2

It is fascinating to travel along the sixty miles of the Rand, from thriving, go-ahead Krugersdorp on the West, to Springs on the East, and to see mine-dumps, pit-head gear, and town after town, like a golden chain linked to the gigantic locket of Johannesburg. The Rand is a gold-mining entity just as the Rhondda Valley in South Wales is a coal-mining one.

Only a little over sixty years ago, just before gold had been discovered, the Witwatersrand was a desolate tract of country dotted with a few farms, all of which might have been acquired for ten thousand pounds. Hopeful individuals went about picking at the rock here and there as they wandered, over land that was soon to be worth untold millions. When gold had been found and part of the area had been proclaimed a goldfield in 1886, the big diamond men rushed over from Kimberley and began to buy out the farmers at prices from a few thousand to seventy thousand pounds. Even at the highest prices their future profits were reckoned in millions.

One company, which had spent twenty thousand pounds in buying farms, produced over two and a quarter million pounds worth of gold within five years, and it is known that Cecil Rhodes, who was soon on the spot, was in ten years time receiving four hundred thousand pounds a year from his investments in the Rand.

Some of the farmers demanded to be paid in gold, and upon one occasion Rhodes counted out twenty thousand sovereigns on a farmhouse table.

Many of the old farmers, suddenly endowed with great wealth, took good care of their money, as Mr S. D. le Roux tells in his *Pioneers and Sportsmen of South Africa*. A certain gaunt and well known old Voortrekker named Willem Prinsloo, who stood six feet eight inches high, sold out to the gold speculators for a hundred and thirty thousand pounds. This he banked with the Standard Bank at Johannesburg until he heard of a bank crash in the Cape. Instantly inspanning his wagon, he trekked seventy miles to Johannesburg and demanded his money in gold from a startled cashier. The bank manager argued in vain with six feet eight inches of determined Boer, and at last the fortune was placed in the ox wagon in canvas bags, each one containing a thousand pounds.

Prinsloo kept his fortune in a large chest on his farm, and in order to protect it concealed loaded rifles and elephant guns at strategic points. Upon one occasion, it is related by an eye-witness, his son came to see him on the eve of a journey to Pretoria.

" Have you enough money? " asked Prinsloo.

" Yes, father."

" You may want more."

" No, I think I have enough."

" I say you may want more," roared the old man, and, going to his chest where the hundred and thirty thousand pounds were kept, plunged in both hands and shovelled a stream of uncounted sovereigns into his son's satchel.

Faced with the problem of moving his gold when the time came to go down to the low-veld in the winter, old Prinsloo decided, after much pondering, to make use of the bank again. But he could not be persuaded to deposit his money in the normal way. Making sure that the strong rooms were adequate, he hired one of them and paid storage on his gold for three years!

What extraordinary adventures came the way of those old Rand farmers! Prinsloo was only too glad to sell his farm and trek away from the pit-shafts, the new townships, the smoke, the noise, and everything that he detested, but, having fled from the site of one of the world's richest gold mines and seeking only peace and quiet, where should Fate lead him but to the site of the now famous Premier Diamond Mine, near Pretoria, where the Cullinan diamond was found!

§ 3

I saw a number of interesting places in Johannesburg: the beautiful Anglican Cathedral; the Art Gallery; a railway station with a main hall like the interior of a gigantic mosque;

JOHANNESBURG FROM THE AIR

a Stock Exchange which resembled a Byzantine basilica; two wonderful Colin Gill murals in the new Magistrates Court; and a hospital, surely one of the largest and most modern in the world.

In the entrance hall of the Witwatersrand University I was shown one of the Portuguese crosses erected by Diaz in the Fifteenth Century, and the most ancient European relic in the country. It was recovered from a sand hill at Kwaai Hoek in the Cape. It had been shattered in five thousand fragments and was put together on a sand bed like a jigsaw puzzle. Among the prehistoric remains in the museum I saw some bones which anthropologists believe may be those of the first men who walked the earth. Professor Robert Broom, South Africa's veteran anthropologist (who was nevertheless born at Paisley!), has drawn the attention of the world to the likelihood that Africa was man's first home. The African "missing link" was evidently a creature with hardly any forehead and a long snout, who must have been even uglier than the Piltdown Man.

A region of Johannesburg strange almost beyond belief is that part of the town which is frequented by the mine-boys. Like the sailors in the London docks, who rarely get farther west than Aldgate Pump, the mine-boys do not flock into the main streets of Johannesburg, but mostly stay in their own quarter. They have given it an atmosphere of its own. Here on a Saturday afternoon you may observe young Africans dressed in what they imagine to be the height of European fashion, having their portraits taken by a kerbside photographer against a ducal background of columns painted on the wall.

The most picturesque place in Johannesburg is the Mai-mai Bazaar, where the mine-boys go on their half-days to shop and to drink municipally brewed Kaffir-beer. It is a large market divided into streets of little native shops and workshops rather like an Arab souk. But, unlike the town Arab and the Egyptian, the Bantu is a grave and dignified person who never pesters you for baksheesh. Although you will not see a white face in the whole of the Bazaar, you can walk through it for hours and rouse no comment or vulgar curiosity.

x

It is interesting to see this place after you have been through the native reserves, for not only are you able to recognise types of the many tribal natives who keep shop there, but you notice what is entirely lacking in the reserves, native handicrafts. Although I had travelled for hundreds of miles through purely Bantu country, this was the first time I had seen natives making things out of leather, wood, and metal, and offering them for sale to their fellows. I went into the shops where the natives, smiling broadly, were only too delighted to show me how they made the brilliant leather belts studded with metal, which the mine-boys love, and the gaudy chests in which they pack their belongings when they leave the mines and start the long trek back to the reserves.

In addition to the row of shops I have mentioned, there is a Harley Street in the bazaar where you can buy anything in the Bantu pharmacopœia: skulls of monkeys, bits of dried python, puff adder, baboons' teeth, preserved frog, dried porcupine, hares' feet, eagle and ostrich eggs. Growing in pots outside the shops are all the best known and most prized native herbs.

In some of the shops can be bought the whole regalia of ancient Zulu war-dress. There are collars of leopard skin, tanned until the skins are as soft as chamois leather, kilts of jackals' tails, garters of buffalo hair, shields, and miniature assegais. These objects are bought by the mine-boys for the mine dances that take place in the compounds on Sunday.

§ 4

You see one side of a city when you live in the best hotel and hire a car, and another side when you learn to use the tramway cars, the omnibuses and the suburban railways.

In a mean semi-manufacturing district, where Johannesburg is seen flaming against the sunset like an American advertisement for steel and concrete, I spent an instructive evening with Poor Whites. Some lived in the shabby pillared houses of the magnates and mine managers of long ago and some lived in tenement houses reeking of the usual slum smell, places where the banisters were broken, the windows smashed, and where fair-haired children screamed round concrete areas and chased each other up and down long flights of stairs. I must say it was surprising to see a native maid of all work emerge from one of these hovels and peg out the washing! Many a poor white, it seems, is not too poor to retain that symbol of aristocracy.

I had a long talk with a woman who described her father as " one of Queen Victoria's soldiers ". Her mother had been an Afrikaner. We sat in candle-light, for the house had no electric light or gas, in a room which was neat and tidy, for this woman also, poor as she was, had a daily maid! Her husband earned £4 a week in a sweet factory. She had several children, boys and girls. She forbade the girls to go out after dark and was afraid every time the boys went out that they would get into a knife fight with the coloured people who, she said, were invading the district.

Many other families had much the same story to tell. Some of them referred ironically to the City of Gold. Compared with them, the most rabid negrophobe would appear comparatively liberal-minded.

Then I spent several days in the native locations at Pimmville, Orlando and Sophiatown, all of them a short railway journey from the city. Thousands of natives have overwhelmed these districts since the war, and in the absence of new building the overcrowding has become frightful and the slum atmosphere is in several places appalling, notably in Shanty Town, where hundreds of natives were living in shelters made of tin, rags and cardboard.

There is no doubt that the increased crime on the Rand is due to the war-time overcrowding and the bad housing conditions in these locations. But what a problem it is. Where does the reformer begin? Like the European slum, the native slum presents the same spectacle of good and bad humanity inextricably mixed, but with this difference. In the European slum an individual may climb out among his own people, but the African slum dweller has collapsed between two civilisations and he seems to belong to no one.

I met a number of literate natives, most of them the product of Lovedale and other missionary schools, from whom I heard a lot of grievances about the Colour Bar, the pass system, whereby every native has to carry an identification card (they were astonished to see mine!), the police pick-up vans and so forth.

When I mentioned to friends in Johannesburg that I had been to these locations, they were surprised. Not one of them had ever been there. Yet is this surprising? How many Londoners who live in Kensington have ever been down to Stepney?

§ 5

Should it be your fate to go down a gold mine, let me give you a piece of advice that may save you from pneumonia. No matter how hot the day may be, insist upon taking down the mine with you a winter overcoat and a muffler. It is going to be violently hot down there and it is also going to be bitterly cold. You may notice round about the mine compound solid blocks of ice. These are on their way down to the cooling plant a mile or so below the surface of the earth, where air will be pumped over them; and you will encounter these cold currents later on when you least expect them.

When you arrive at the mine buildings you will sign the usual form stating that you go down at your own risk, then you will be taken to a dressing-room where you are issued with khaki overalls, a sweat-rag for your neck, and an acetylene lamp.

The first lift drops four thousand, nine hundred feet in a few seconds. I stood in an iron cage side by side with my guides and several Zulu police boys, and the cage just fell into the dark. I stepped out into an electrically lit, whitewashed cave where a shift of labourers was waiting to go to the surface. They sat patiently on their haunches like miners the world over, and their strong teeth and the whites of their eyes gleamed in their dark faces. There were Basutos, Bacas from Griqualand, Machopis from Portuguese East Africa, Mzingili from North Zululand, Pondos, men from the Ciskei and the Transkei. They all had the air of docile automatons. Most of them were young, physically fit, and their dark flesh shone with good feeding.

The second lift dropped down to seven thousand, three hundred feet, and somewhere on this drop I came level with the distant waters of Table Bay, for six thousand feet below Johannesburg is just sea level. Here was the same kind of white cave with tunnels leading from it. It was now perceptibly warmer. I could hear the tinned air coming iced from the great fans, and as we walked on we passed in turn through temperatures that were tropical and Arctic. Then came the worst journey of all—to the mine bottom. This was accomplished in a wet steel tub on an inclined rail.

I made myself as small as possible and crouched inside it. Someone's boot lodged in the nape of my neck, as more and more men crawled in, until the last man slammed the steel lid into position and off we shot downwards, clanking and swaying into the hot bowels of the earth. We stepped out eight thousand five hundred feet below Johannesburg, and started to walk along tunnels, or drives as they are called, all of which lead to the reef. It was now very hot indeed.

As we walked along, there came a warning shout from the darkness ahead, just as in a Welsh coal mine, and a train of tubs went clattering past loaded with ore. The scene in the mine, the method of carting away the ore, everything but the infernal heat, were strongly reminiscent of the Rhondda Valley. At the working face, or stope as it is called, we saw a typical glimpse of Johannesburg's important and profitable underworld. Two white miners were examining the timbers which held up a great ledge of rock, while a group of native labourers were attacking the ore with a pneumatic drill and shovelling it into tubs for transport to the crushing mills above.

Two of the men, I was told, had completed their service and were off home to the Transkei in a few days time. They were husky, cheerful-looking fellows and, having been in the Transkei, I could imagine them, as clearly as I could now see them, swaggering round the village store in their city clothes and boasting to the admiring women of their adventures in the city of " Goldie ".

If South Africa's economy is founded on gold, and if the standard of life and living would crash if the gold mines closed, then this sight of the Bantu mining gold is the most important sight in the Union. The tramcars, the buses, and the motor cars above ground, the fine shops in Eloff Street, the suburbs, and the big houses on Houghton Ridge, are all directly dependent upon this astonishingly organised industry, and upon the Bantu's willingness to leave the air and the sunlight and go down into the darkness of the earth to work for a few months and earn a wife.

What a contrast is formed by the two sides of Bantu life: on one side lassitude and as much idleness as he can obtain, and on the other a brief period of real hard physical work. One of the first slogans the Dutch are said to have spread among the Hottentots was the doctrine of " no gather wood, no eat bread ", and here was the same old slogan, " no mine gold, no have wife " !

I thought the prevailing Nineteenth Century atmosphere of our own coal-fields, and the inconceivably dreary lines of streets in the mining villages of South Wales and Lanarkshire, the appalling ugliness of the houses, was a far blacker picture than the scene in which the South African gold-mining native labours. Under this remarkable system of migratory labour the mine company accepts responsibility for the mine-worker in sickness and in health, houses him, feeds him, pays him, perhaps not as much as a white miner would be paid, but anyhow enough to make the work sufficiently attractive for him to volunteer to do it in no uncertain numbers. Having seen what happens to a native in Pimmville and Sophiatown when he is cut adrift from his own folk and cast up on the white shore, I looked at the natives working at the stope and thanked heaven they were going back to their own people and were not fated to swell the threatening black tide of de-tribalisation.

We were now all sweating as if we were in a Turkish Bath. The sweat was running down the naked black backs and down the white faces. Our khaki overalls clung wetly to our bodies. I could pay no attention to the statistics that are always pumped into a visitor at such a moment. I reflected that no women have been paid a higher compliment than the Bantu women whose men win them in such heat. I also reflected that gold, whose gleam has such a powerful effect upon the

eyes of Mankind, looks in the raw less attractive than coal.
A good gleaming seam of coal is a finer sight than a bit of the
reef.

I tried to ask the boys how much they had saved, and if
they were looking forward to going home, but I might as well
have attempted to get a clear statement from the Delphic
Oracle. All I got was the usual " Ja, baas! "

It was not until I had left the mine and found myself in the
refinery above ground that I saw the first gleam of the all
powerful metal. Here I was shown a gold brick, the same
shape and size as an ordinary brick, but enormously heavy
and worth £7,500.

It is surprising to know what a small quantity of gold is to
be found in a ton of rock. Take a ton of rock, grind it into
powder, wash it over inclined sheets of corduroy, take the
residue, pump it into tanks, refine it still further, and then
subject what slime is left to chemical action, and all you have
from that massive ton of rock is a button of gold rather smaller
than a trouser button! In order to make one gold brick
something like three thousand, seven hundred tons of rock
must be pulverised and refined.

Native dances are held every Sunday in some of the compounds. I was invited to attend one of these at the Consoli-
dated Main Reef Mine. It was a hot day and the sun beat
upon a stone-built arena designed by the mine manager and
erected by the natives themselves. There were nine tiers of
seats and the arena was half-covered with an awning of canes.
The ground was dusted with red sand. The audience was
an interesting assembly of natives, some clothed in sketchy
European attire, some wrapped in blankets, and some in little
else but their bronze skins. A native band was thrumming on
" Kaffir pianos ", instruments like large xylophones. The
ground trembled with the rhythm. Then into the arena
in single file came the first team of dancers, a team from
Portuguese East Africa. They wore white singlets and yellow
aprons, great tufts of sheepskin waved round their bare ankles.
They carried shields and short stabbing assegais. Their

leaders wore tall crowns of ostrich feathers. These " boys ",
who had worked an eight hour day in the depths of the earth,
were full of vitality. They were tireless. They advanced
and retreated, shuffling their feet and stamping. The music
throbbed and thudded. Three men dressed as girls faced
the dancers, working them to a frenzy of what seemed like
warlike energy. Then with a great shout they suddenly
relaxed and left the arena.

The next dance was much the same—the dancers were from
East Griqualand—then a third team of magnificently garbed
Zulus came in, a barbaric and splendid sight. They wore
girdles of leopard skin. White sheepskin cross belts lay on
their coffee-coloured chests and plumes waved on their heads.
They carried shields and spears, and their performance,
although I was told it was a marriage dance, looked like the
beginning of a war. These were men splendid in physique
and bearing. They moved like kings. Their muscles rippled
under their brown skins and they provided their own music,
a long, shouting chant. The dance went on for the best
part of an hour. Sometimes they would all sit down and I
thought it was ended, but after a moment they would rise and
start all over again.

It was a strange spectacle. These natives were in Johannesburg, but they were not of it. They were free to explore the
white man's world, but they preferred to stay in their compound, in their own tribal units, and among those who spoke
their own tongue and knew their background. Some of them
would perhaps be going home in a day, a week, taking with
them messages to distant kraals in Northern Rhodesia and to
remote mountain villages in Basutoland; and their places
would immediately be filled by friends and relatives from the
same tribes.

What an extraordinary arrangement this is—this mixture of
primitive and industrialised life, this introduction of people
who are by nature pastoral into one of the more arduous
branches of industry, without making them city dwellers,
without snapping their tribal customs or severing their loyalty
to some hereditary chief.

I looked at them, marvelling at their energy and their

vitality. I remembered the lower levels of the City Deep and the shift that was waiting to surface. Those white eyeballs in the electric light, those quiet, docile men. Could these be the same men, these gay and violent dancers in the sunlight of a Sunday morning? And I could imagine them, their term of service over, going back to their distant homes with nothing but a blanket or a pair of trousers to prove that for a year they had helped the white man to find that red metal which he loves as much as life itself.

§ 6

Pretoria is only thirty-five miles away from Johannesburg, and the road, dotted on each side with farms, gum trees, wattle, and wayside cafés, runs downward all the time. You leave behind the relatively cool Rand highlands and descend into a warmer landscape where the northern capital rises above its jacaranda trees.

The cities and the larger towns of the Union, with the exception of Cape Town, East London, and Bloemfontein, are named after persons: Johannesburg after Johannes Joubert; Port Elizabeth after Elizabeth Donkin; Durban after Sir Benjamin D'Urban; Grahamstown after Colonel John Graham; Pietermaritzburg after Pieter Retief and Gerrit Maritz; Kimberley after the first Earl of Kimberley; Potchefstroom after Andries Hendrik Potgieter; and Pretoria after Andries Pretorius, the victor of Blood River.

South Africans everywhere are rightly proud of Pretoria, and it is difficult, should you be in the country during the months of October and November, not to be swept by the force of public opinion towards the jacaranda trees which at that time of the year submerge the whole city beneath a cloud of blue. Only the victims of hay fever do not join in the national pæan of praise for the exquisite annual cloak which has been brought all the way from Brazil to the Transvaal.

Although I was well aware of the extremes of climate to be met with by a swift-moving traveller in South Africa, I was surprised by the difference in temperature between Johannesburg and Pretoria. I had left the Rand on a tolerably cool morning with a fresh wind blowing, and now, only thirty-five miles away but fifteen hundred feet nearer sea level, it was swelteringly hot.

If one could say that Johannesburg is the New York of South Africa, then one might say that Pretoria is the Washington. It is the city where talk of government and policy replaces talk of dividends and enterprises. There the Governor-General lives. There the Government offices, the civil service, the Diplomatic Corps, are to be found until that strange and expensive moment of migration arrives when they fly off like so many swallows to attend Parliament in Cape Town.

Pretoria is more interested in ideas and persons than in things. It is a place where men do not usually acquire enormous fortunes, but live on salaries and pensions. The fine University does in Afrikaans what the Witwatersrand does in English. Pretoria has also become the biggest steel-producing place in the Union without losing its look of a garden.

The long streets, where crowds moved beneath pillared arcades, were two avenues of shadow on each side of the burning roadway. With his back to a classical railway station, the work of Sir Herbert Baker, President Paul Kruger, whose spirit broods as firmly over Pretoria as that of Rhodes over Cape Town, stands upon a plinth of Peterhead granite clothed in a bronze frock coat and wearing a top hat.

Deneys Reitz says in *Commando* that he and his father once visited the old President, who showed them the sculptor's first design for this statue. Mrs Kruger entered with a tray of coffee and suggested that, as the monument served no useful purpose, the top hat might be made hollow and filled with water so that the birds could drink from it.

" My father and I laughed heartily on our way home at her simplicity," says Deneys Reitz, " but we agreed that it was decent of her to have thought of such a thing."

I have seen it stated by at least one noted South African writer that Mrs Kruger's wish was gratified and that the Presidential topper really is a bird-bath! I was, however, told by the highest authority—a man with a ladder who was cleaning the statue—that this is not so.

Upon the northern heights above the city is the great building erected to symbolise the union of the four provinces and to house the administration. As I looked at the Union Buildings I thought that Cecil Rhodes never invested money which brought richer dividends than that spent in sending the young Herbert Baker to Greece and Italy. All over the Union, in public places and in private houses, the result of that moment of Rhodesian clairvoyance are to be seen; and nowhere more impressively than in Pretoria.

The two great wings of the building, linked centrally by what is really a Greek open-air theatre, is a majestic conception and one perfectly suited to the landscape and the climate. Indeed the more I looked at Baker's work in South Africa, the more I realised how acutely conscious he was of that classic feeling in the air, that clarity and silkiness of which, from Cape Town onwards, I was daily and gratefully aware. The Union Building is as near as Baker could come to a Parthenon.

Baker says in *Architecture and Personalities* that the central amphitheatre, the great feature of his design, was at first criticised, but "was surely proved when a large crowd gathered there to welcome Botha back from the conquest of South West Africa; and a second time when Smuts returned victorious from the long campaign in East Africa. He told me that from the tribune he spoke to 8,000 people there, all of whom could hear.

"Was not the building of this open-air place of assembly prophetic in view of the development of loud-speakers, which have done much to restore the ancient practice by which leaders of the people spoke to them in person?"

In front of the Union Buildings the ground is terraced and planted with beds of gay flowers and there is a replica, as in Cape Town Gardens, of the Delville Wood War Memorial. I did not appreciate the fine symbolism of this memorial when I saw it first in Cape Town, but it was explained to me that the two male figures and the prancing charger represent the Briton and the Afrikaner joining hands over a war horse.

"Above the Twin Brethren", wrote Baker, "are two vacant pedestals. For whom? For a 'Romulus' and 'Remus', Botha and Smuts, who, though former enemies of England, went across the seas to fight in the ranks of the Commonwealth for the cause of civilisation.''

§ 7

President Kruger's house in Pretoria is one of the most interesting museums in the country. Everything remains as it was half a century ago, and it has the awesome atmosphere of a house whose inhabitants, though departed, might at any moment return. Mrs Kruger would be horrified by the looped back lace curtains full of rich dust, but Oom Paul would find his way about—with a few explosions of wrath, one imagines—to his battery of pipes and his vast brass spittoon and his chair.

The place is to all intents just as it was when the old President sat on his stoep dispensing the wisdom of Solomon, flanked by the marble lions given to him by Barney Barnato, one of the few Englishmen who knew how to tackle him. Rhodes he mistrusted and disliked, but " when Mr Barnato wants anything ", Kruger once said, " he always comes to see me himself and we talk it over ".

The fierce old man returned with stinging words the gift of a living lion from the Groote Schuur zoo made by Rhodes from the purest and most friendly motives, but he kept Barney Barnato's marble lions! What an interesting sidelight those animals are on the relationship between two men so dissimilar in everything except in the sadness and disillusion of their last days.

The house is a long, white one storey building. The covered stoep is carried forward on ironwork and is roofed, like the house itself, with sheets of corrugated iron. I was shown the old President's pipes, his razors, his dress shirt, his bed, his chair, and the pen-knife with which he severed his left thumb in the hunting-field after the explosion of a gun-barrel. I was shown a whole room full of wreaths. In the coach-house outside is the Presidential coach, made in Long Acre, and a trek wagon. The most beautiful thing in the house is a small seated bronze by van Vouw showing the old man with all the fierceness drained out of him at the end, tired and old and ready for his rest.   The most pitiful thing in the house is the photograph, taken I suppose during his last years in Switzerland, showing his strong face furrowed by grief and age.   It is the head of an old lion.

The only picture Europe has of Kruger is that of the old diehard President of the 'nineties, with his stubborn face, his fringe of whisker, his top-hat, and frock coat buttoned tightly over a stocky figure.   But in South Africa they remember him in his youth as a great hunter and an athlete possessed of exceptional strength and agility.   He was also a soldier of skill and courage.

Kruger's rigid moral principles were firmly rooted in Holy Writ.   He was subject to religious ecstasy and once when a young man he disappeared for days into the veld like a Hebrew prophet and returned to say that he had communed with God. He believed that the earth was flat, and it is told by E. J. P. Jorisson that during a voyage to Europe in 1877, he interrupted an astronomical discussion on board ship at night with the words: "Stop, Jorisson, stop! If what you are saying is true, I may as well throw my Bible overboard."

The Bible was always in his hands and on his lips.   It was the Old, not the New, Testament that he knew by heart.   As President, the Bible was always on his table; in old age, when he conducted the affairs of the State from the Presidential train during the South African War, the old man could be seen, spectacles on nose, studying Holy Writ as the train took him from place to place.   He was the most remarkable example the modern world has known of a religious Rip van Winkle.   For him, Science and criticism did not exist.   It was small wonder that men like Rhodes, Milner, and Chamberlain could not understand him.   On the other hand, the Puritans, who sang psalms as they charged, and the Scottish Covenanters, would have found him entirely comprehensible.   Cromwell would have made nothing of Rhodes, but he would have recognised Kruger as a man and a brother.   The Seventeenth Century mentality which runs through South African history reached in Kruger what, to his opponents of the Nineteenth Century, must have appeared exasperation point.

That Kruger should have visited Europe three times on

diplomatic missions, and on one of these occasions have gone up in a balloon, has a ring of fantasy, almost as though Abraham had attended the Grand Prix. It was at the Paris International Exhibition that he saw his first balloon and courageously ascended, apparently finding nothing in the Bible to deter him from defying the law of gravity. " High up in mid-air," he wrote in his *Memoirs*, " I jestingly asked the aeronaut, as we had gone so far, to take me all the way home."

It is equally surprising to know that the patriarch not only saw the first motor car to arrive in South Africa, but also witnessed one of the first moving pictures. Mr Napier Devitt says in *The Spell of South Africa* that the first motor car arrived at the end of the year 1896. It was a two-seater Benz with a one-and-a-half horse-power engine, lamps lit by candles, and front wheels smaller than the rear wheels. President Kruger arrived to see this car at Berea Park, Pretoria, accompanied by an escort of State artillery, but declined an invitation to take a ride with the words, " No, thank you. A dog might bark and the car would buck and throw me out! "

Kruger at the cinema is well told by Hedley A. Chilvers in *Out of the Crucible*.

" Let it not be imagined ", writes Mr Chilvers, " that President Kruger never saw a moving picture. He saw one of the first ever taken in South Africa—one which made a feature of himself going to the Pretoria Raadzaal. Arrangements were made to show it to him in his own house, and Edgar Hyman and Dave Foote of the Old Empire went to the Residency for the purpose. They were duly received by Mrs Kruger.

" ' We have come to show the picture of His Honour going to the Raad,' explained Hyman.

" The old lady waved them inside and gave them some coffee. They entered a large room (which had once been two rooms separated by a partition) and proceeded to erect the screen and to instal a piano; for it was felt that the occasion warranted a little music and Dave Foote was there to supply it. However, His Honour returned before the preparations were complete, and his eyes at once lit upon the piano. He fell into a violent passion.

" 'What is this godless thing doing in my house?' he demanded in Afrikaans. 'Take it away. I'll have the men thrown out who brought it here!'

" 'What is he saying?' whispered Hyman to a much-perturbed official.

" 'His Honour's going to have you all removed,' was the reply.

" Explanations followed; but the subtlest diplomacy failed to soften the good old Puritan's wrath, and the piano had to be shifted. When, however, the suggestion was made that an organ might prove a more seemly instrument and more in accordance with the spirit of the house, Oom Paul was somewhat mollified, and an organ was ultimately installed, which Foote played throughout the screening of the film. The little function was attended by the Executive of the Raad.

" His Honour, who usually read his Bible until eight or after and then went to bed, watched his own movements with interest until nine, then retired, leaving the Executive to see the film through."

It is interesting to explore the old house in Pretoria and to see the famous stoep which is the background to the many Kruger stories told all over the Union. Anyone was free to call on the President and ask his advice on personal problems. This was always given over Java coffee and tobacco. Wisdom, of course, does not depend upon learning, and Kruger was in every sense a wise man whose judgments were based on thought and upon a rather grim view of human nature.

" To what height his marvellous intellect, coupled as it was with indomitable will-power, would have risen, if it had been properly disciplined—it is difficult to imagine ", wrote Carl Jeppe in the *Kaleidoscopic Transvaal*. In the same book is my favourite Kruger story. It seems that when the lamentable war broke out, the President was anxious to go to the front. One day a visitor was told that the President was busy and could not be seen, but, persisting, he was at length led out to the yard at the back of the house. " Here he found the old gentleman, rifle in hand and girt with bandolier, practising mounting a horse again—an exercise which he had abandoned for years."

He had a pleasing gift of irony.   It is reported that when in Paris he hastily retreated from a ball with the explanation that he must have arrived too early " because the ladies were not yet dressed ", and Mrs Smuts assures me that the old man was, surprising to relate, a great wag.

He was a zealous teetotaller, and if he smelt drink on anyone's breath would instantly say, " You stink like a vat." Early Johannesburg, with saloons at every street corner, must have been recognised by him as the junction of Sodom with Gomorrah.

The old man died in Switzerland in 1904.   Germany, from whom he had expected so much in his fight against the British Empire, let him down and the Kaiser went away on a diplomatic hunting trip in order to avoid seeing him.   But many nations honoured him.   On great occasions his frock coat shone with orders of chivalry bestowed by France, Germany, Holland, Belgium, and Switzerland, and, as Mr C. E. Vulliamy points out in *Outlanders*, he " only narrowly escaped the offer of a G.C.M.G.".   His body was brought home, and the last of the great Puritans lies with his third wife in a peaceful cemetery a few yards away from the stoep, from Barnato's lions and the little Dopper church where he used to preach.

§ 8

After Winston Churchill's capture by Botha at Chieveley in 1899, the war correspondent was imprisoned with sixty British officers in the State Model Schools at the corner of van der Walt and Skinner Streets, Pretoria.

I went to have a look at these buildings, which are now called the Central Junior High School, and from the expressions upon the faces of the children in the classrooms, I gathered that the sight of curious visitors prowling round outside looking for the place where a lithe and agile Winston scaled the wall is quite a usual one.   The school stands at the junction of those pleasant looking suburban roads where so much of the real drama of life is played.   The building opposite, from whose dark hall the prisoners were in the habit of receiving morse messages by lamp, is still there.   Whether the wall is

PRETORIA FROM UNION BUILDINGS

the same which Winston climbed, I do not know. It still separates the school from a house which in 1899 belonged to General Lucas Meyer, into whose shrubbery the fugitive dropped on the night of December 12.

Mr Churchill has described his escape twice, first within a few days of his adventure, in *London to Ladysmith*, and then in an amplified form in *My Early Life*. Choosing a moment when the sentries' backs were turned, he swung himself up on the wall and dropped down into the darkness of the shrubbery to face freedom with seventy-five pounds in money and four bars of chocolate.

Readers of his adventures must have admired his punctilious good manners in leaving upon his bed a farewell letter for the Boer Secretary for War, Mr de Souza. The standards of courtesy in war have declined since that day! This letter was reconstructed by him from memory and is to be found in *London to Ladysmith*, but it is not, of course, the original text. I was much interested to find that the original letter has been carefully kept in the de Souza family and was shown to me by Mrs O. E. de Souza of Barberton, a daughter-in-law of the late Mr F. L. de Souza. It is here printed for the first time.

State Schools Prison,
Pretoria.

Dear Mr de Souza,

I do not consider that your Government was justified in holding me, a press correspondent and a non-combatant, as a prisoner of war, and I have consequently resolved to escape. The arrangements I have succeeded in making with my friends outside are such as to give me every confidence. But I wish in leaving you thus hastily and unceremoniously to once more place on record my appreciation of the kindness which has been shown me and the other prisoners by you, the commandant and by Dr Gunning, and my admiration of the chivalrous and humane character of the Republican forces. My views on the general question of the war remain unchanged, but I shall always retain a feeling of high respect for the several classes of burghers I have met and, on reaching the British lines, I will set forth a truthful and impartial account of my experiences in Pretoria. In conclusion, I desire to express my obligations to you and to hope that when this most grievous and unhappy war shall have come to an end, a state of affairs may be created which shall preserve at once the national pride of the Boers and the security of the British and put a final

Y

stop to the rivalry and enmity of both races. Regretting that
circumstances have not permitted me to bid you a personal farewell,

Believe me
Yours vy sincerely,

Dec. 11*th*, 1899.   Winston S. Churchill.

Was it wit or good manners, or both, which caused the
departing guest to mark the envelope with the " p.p.c." of
Victorian formality, letters which a less punctilious generation
may like to know stand for " pour prendre congé "—to take
leave ?

§ 9

One night I left Pretoria by train for the North-East
Transvaal.   When I lifted the blind in the morning we were
travelling through a hot, lush landscape, where mangoes and
oranges were growing in large plantations and where rounded
mountains rose in the morning light.   Though it was only six
o'clock the sun was already warm and, crossing a river, I
looked down and saw a native bathing in a pool, neat and
graceful as a black cat.

The train puffed into Nelspruit and rested awhile before
continuing its journey into Portuguese East Africa.   Nelspruit
was hot and semi-tropical.   Thirsty passengers went to a
booth on the station and returned to their carriages with bags
full of peaches, oranges, and mangoes at a shilling a dozen.

I was met by two people who had invited me to stay in
Barberton, and we set off to motor the thirty miles to their
home.   The road plunged into grand mountain scenery and
then, as if we had passed through rocky gates, we saw stretching into the distance before us one of the most spectacular
valleys in South Africa.   It lay below us for miles like a green
lake, and behind towered, in blue and paler blue, the majestic
skyline of the northern ranges of the Drakensberg.   At that
hour in the early morning, before the mists had left the low
veld, it was easy to understand why this has been called de
Kaap Valley, for nowhere else in the Union is a scene which
more vividly recalls the mountains of the Cape.   It seems that
at any moment one should come upon the ocean, and my

friends told me that before sunrise it is sometimes possible to see the whole valley lying beneath a Table Bay of motionless mist.

"Last week," I was told, "a black mamba held up the Nelspruit bus. The bus came round the corner just as the snake was crossing the road. It was so startled that it reared up ready for action, and the bus stopped until it glided off."

We paused on the way down into the valley so that I might climb up to the rocks beside the road and see clumps of Barberton Daisies growing in their native soil. These pretty and hardy flowers, which flourish in so many English gardens, are not peculiar to Barberton, but they were first named in this valley and from it the first specimens were sent to England in 1884.

We came down into the valley where the town of Barberton —the earliest gold-rush town in South Africa—snuggles cosily at the foot of the mountains. We drew up outside a stone-built house which might have come from Cumberland, but it was covered with semi-tropical creepers and surrounded by a garden that looked like one of the hot houses at Kew.

After breakfast I went out, walking on the shady side of the road, to look at a little town which only by an effort of the imagination can now be associated with a gold rush. It is typical of modern Barberton that the old stock exchange should now be the garage of the local hotel! People on the verge of eighty, and this climate appears to confer immortality once the critical seventies are passed, tell of a very different Barberton. They speak of it boastfully and with pride, as a reformed rake might, from the safety of his rectitude, refer to his unregenerate past. The Barberton of their youth was apparently a hard-drinking place that attracted all kinds of strange, eccentric fortune hunters, saloon keepers, and yellow-haired barmaids, who mirrored for a moment the shape of the Johannesburg to be, before they faded off towards the newly discovered Rand. It is difficult to connect those days— although only sixty years distant—with the modern Barberton of milk bars and tennis-club dances.

However, if anyone wishes to recapture the atmosphere of an early mining community in South Africa, let him go to Barberton and be introduced to the Barberton Club, which is to-day just as it was sixty years ago. It is a long bungalow with a trellised verandah. The walls are decorated with photographs from whose fading brownness gaze the whiskered faces of the tough generation which created modern South Africa.

Sometimes a motor car powdered all over with grey dust draws up to the veranda, and out steps a man who, in his khaki shorts and bush shirt, looks like a muscular lad of fifty, but will tell you with pride that he is seventy-five. He hangs his sun-hat on a peg and calls for a Scotch and soda. If any other men of his vintage are about, you will hear first-hand reminiscences from the last men who remember South Africa's pioneering days. Many of these old stagers remember Mr Rhodes—that "Mr" is a subtle South African title—and the opening up of Rhodesia. They come into Barberton to go to the bank or the railway station from large sun-smitten farms where they grow vegetables for Johannesburg in the winter, and in the summer mangoes, papaws, guavas, bananas, oranges, and passion fruit.

They told me that the success of two brothers named Barber caused the gold rush of the 'eighties, when a motley crowd converged upon Barberton. Prospectors accompanied by donkeys laden with picks and dynamite were always passing through the town on their way to the mines in the mountains at the back.

"You'd meet some queer characters in those days," I was told. "There was once a man from Port Elizabeth who got angry with his wife because his dinner wasn't ready when he arrived home. So he saddled his pony and trekked up to Barberton! He lived alone here for twenty-one years. Then a son turned up, then a daughter, and at last the old lady herself. And I'm dashed if the old boy didn't have a second honeymoon, and a third child was born who inherited a farm I could point out to you."

A man whose story I shall not easily forget is Mr L. E. O. Lowndes—the initials are appropriate—who had an almost miraculous escape from a wounded lioness about ten years ago. The animal sprang at him, seized one of his arms in its mouth, and was shot dead at a range of three yards by his native servant. The curious point about this story is that

Mr Lowndes claims descent on his mother's side from Sir James Gayer, Lord Mayor of London, who, in thanksgiving for his escape from a lion in the East, left a sum of money for the " Lion Sermon ", which has been preached in the Church of St Katharine Cree every year since the reign of Charles I. Mr L. E. O. Lowndes can surely tell the best lion story in Africa !

When I went to bed I noticed with some misgiving that there was no netting over the window, for I had been warned in Johannesburg that Barberton is in the malarial belt. But this is no longer so. The plague has been driven from the town, and indeed I slept with open windows all the time I was there. During the night a violent storm broke over the mountains. I was awakened by a crash as the curtains blew in and swept to the floor everything in their path. Lightning more vivid than any I have ever seen was followed by a tremendous cannonade of thunder that cracked like a series of field-guns and then broke into a roar which seemed to shake the very earth. Rain descended in a straight sheet, and when the roar of the thunder was stilled I listened to the rushing of innumerable streams and waterfalls and the voices of a thousand rejoicing frogs. In the morning the sky was innocent and blue, and the " Pietmyvrou ", having miraculously escaped drowning, was piping from a tree.

§ 10

I was driven by a friend into the mountains to see the dead mining town of Eureka. We had with us an old miner named James Hall, who long years ago had come out from Manchester. Hall was so deaf that it was almost impossible to communicate with him and we had to wait for his pronouncements.

" The Rand's like a sandwich cake," he shouted to me on one occasion, " but Barberton's like a plum pudding! "

" That's very true," explained my friend. " The gold on the Rand is in layers, but out here it's dotted about in the rock just like fruit in a pudding."

We had now left the orchards and the farms, where some

splendid looking natives were at work, and were steadily climbing into the green mountains. I thought that Barberton possessed some of the most majestic landscapes in the Union. To me the only disappointment was that the sea, which always appeared to be round the next corner, was at its nearest point a hundred miles away at Lourenço Marques, in Portuguese territory.

" If you smell onions, that's it! " said Hall.

I pondered this for some time and had to ask for help.

" What he means," said my friend, " is that when you smell arsenic, which is like onions, you are near gold in this part of the world."

The road twisted round to a hill-top which was four thousand feet above the sea, and upon that lonely eminence we looked about at the scattered ruins of the gold-mining town of Eureka. It was indescribably desolate and melancholy.

We walked from ruin to ruin. Every scrap of timber which had gone to the construction of this town had vanished— salvaged, I suppose, as firewood. James Hall looked round at the ruins and remembered them when they were alive with movement and voices, and animated by the ambition and follies of thousands of fortune-hunters. He pointed to one of the largest heaps of stone.

" The old Victoria Hotel," he said. " Old Jack Frazer used to live there."

We walked across to a part of the mountain where Nature had almost reasserted complete sway. An eagle perched thoughtfully upon a rock rose and flapped slowly away as we drew near.

" The race-course! " explained Hall.

" Yes, the race-course! " he repeated, seeing our disbelief, " and there used to be some fine old field days here, I can tell you! Oh, we've had some big do's here and no mistake."

Hall led us round the race-course and then back to the main mounds and tumuli.

" Oh, it used to be a lively spot, all right," he said, his eyes roving over the mountain top. " What with chaps coming up from the mines of an evening for their booze, and one thing and another. Cornishmen, all of them."

" Did they ever make any money? " I asked.

" Lively spot," he continued, " coming and going all the time. Some would save a bit of money and off they'd go with their picks and bundles and donkeys and tents, some to try their luck on the Rand and some to booze their money away down in Barberton. Coming and going all the time. . . ."

I felt that we had heard the epitaph of a gold-mining town. The eagle flew back to the race-course.

As we continued our journey towards a distant valley, Hall told us of a poor miner who had given up all hope and had fallen asleep on a certain hill, which he pointed out; awakening in the morning, he found that he had been sleeping on a great nugget of gold! I can imagine no more interesting place than this for the people of Johannesburg. Here among the lonely deserted hills they can see what the Rand might have been like to-day if the reef had not gone down deeply as it does.

In a steep valley we came suddenly upon an unexpected scene of life and activity. There was a mine-shaft, pit-head gear, offices, and compounds, and all the bustle of gold winning. It was the famous Sheba Mine, which is still producing gold.

We changed our clothes in the manager's office and descended this mine, which I thought had more atmosphere to the square yard than all the great organisations of the Rand put together. At a certain depth we had to go down perpendicular ladders, sticky with wet mud, to pitch-dark platforms where still more upright ladders descended to lower levels. Here were no electric lifts to the bottom of the mine: you had to climb down every foot of the way! Gingerly and carefully, our thick borrowed boots slipping on the rungs, we stepped down into the ghoulish underworld to flash our lanterns over the face of the Barberton " pudding ", over a vast cavern mined out of the hot bowels of the mountain and upon the wet, gleaming bodies of those who were moving about so far down in the earth.

" This place, sir, is a geologist's dream," said the enthusiastic public-school voice of a young engineer, as we stood with tepid water dripping down the backs of our necks and our lanterns wavering over the earth's entrails.

If anyone wishes to strengthen his leg muscles or reduce a waist measurement, I can recommend the Sheba Mine. But what defeats me about gold-mining is how anyone in his senses should ever have thought it would be easy money.

§ 11

No part of South Africa, and I do not except the loneliest portions of Zululand, gave me a more profound feeling of solitude and of being locked away with a mode of life dictated by the climate than the country between Barberton and the Kruger Park. It is an insinuating, attractive district, and the solitude is really an illusion. There are many lonelier places. The planters and farmers of this region are within easy reach of the simple pleasures of Barberton or the more complex amusements of Portuguese East Africa, yet, as you survey the miles of hot, jungle-like country which stretches on all sides, you feel that this has the atmosphere of a countryside right out of the ordinary world.

The Europeans live far apart (so that they welcome the sight of each other on all occasions), in houses netted against the mosquito and darkened against the sun. They plant shady trees round them and, when possible, build upon slight hills which afford a view to the horizon.

In the extraordinary brilliance of the sunny day, the loneliness of these farms and houses is not so apparent; it is when darkness falls and they are alone with the stars and prowling animals of the night that you think of them as so many little fortresses which have pulled up their drawbridges until the morning. This romantic conception is sometimes shattered when, invading such fortresses, you discover the garrison sitting in electric light listening to the chimes of Big Ben. Still, that does not alter the fact that a lion may have strayed from the Kruger Park and be crouched outside, also listening to the chimes!

I met people who had made money out of tobacco, cotton, mangoes, or what you will; others who were pleasantly playing at farming in their retirement; some who were waging the usual African struggle with farming, and some who were enjoying old age and looked good for another fifty years.

The great romance of Barberton is not really gold but *Jock of the Bushveld*, for this is the country of South Africa's classic. The " Jock of the Bushveld Road " runs from Barberton through the Kruger Park and over the boundary into Portuguese East Africa, and everybody in this part of the world knows Sir Percy Fitzpatrick's book by heart. Sir Percy, who died in 1931, was born at King William's Town, the son of a judge of the Supreme Court of the Cape. He inherited from his father a ready Irish wit and brilliance, and was educated at the famous Catholic school, Downside Abbey, Somerset. At the age of sixteen he became a clerk in the Standard Bank of South Africa, but after four years roved off in search of a more exciting career, becoming a storekeeper's assistant in Barberton and then a transport rider, travelling between the Barberton gold-field and Portuguese East Africa. During this time he met the band of pioneers described in *Jock of the Bushveld* and gained that intimate knowledge of South African wild life which is reflected upon every page of his book. He made his fortune later on the Rand, and the adventures of his dog Jock were first told to his children in Johannesburg. It was Kipling who, having recently written the *Just So Stories*, persuaded Fitzpatrick to put Jock's exploits into book form.

Jock was a real dog, and his adventures took place in the Barberton district when the whole of the lowveld teemed with game as only the Kruger Park does to-day. Colonel G. M. Bennett, who lives in a delightful house with the finest view in Barberton, knew the author and is a keen student of the book's topography.

" When I came to Barberton twenty-seven years ago," he told me, " all the old people remembered Percy Fitzpatrick and Jock, and all kinds of landmarks were pointed out as those mentioned in the book. I was shown at least three fig trees in different areas which were said to mark the grave of Jock. But Sir Percy told me himself that Jock is buried at Picene, in Portuguese territory.

" The last time Fitzpatrick came to stay with me was in 1924, and we talked a lot about Jock. He said that Jim

Makokel was still alive somewhere on the highveld, but so far as I know the only survivor of Jock's people to-day is that grand old warrior Colonel James Donaldson.   On the last day of his stay, Sir Percy asked for my copy of *Jock* and promised to make some marginal notes so that I should know where the various adventures described in the book had taken place. When I returned in the evening he apologised for having fallen asleep without fulfilling his promise.   He promised to do so upon his next visit, but failing health decreed that he should never again visit Jock's country.   So I lost the opportunity of possessing a unique copy of *Jock*.

" However, he did make a few notes.   On page 215, where Jim Makokel incites Jock to attack the Shangaans, the author wrote : ' This occurred about half a mile below the Barberton Hospital, on the road to the Queen's River '.   On page 454, where Jock is taken to a prospector friend, Sir Percy wrote the friend's name, ' Jacob Cloete '.   On page 455, where Jock is nearly run over, he wrote, ' This was outside the Barberton Club '.   What a tragedy it is for all of us who love *Jock of the Bushveld* that the author fell asleep that afternoon ! "

By the way, Colonel Bennett is himself of interest to South Africans.   It was his mother, a Miss Melville, who exclaimed " What a wilderness ! " when she was taken as a bride to the Wilderness, near Knysna, an innocent remark which posterity has elaborated into a romantic but fictitious story.

But to return to *Jock of the Bushveld*.   Most readers of South African books must have thought how remarkably fortunate those books have been in their illustrators.   Not only were the Boers, the Hottentots, and the Bantu beautifully pictured in aquatint from Barrow, Burchell, and Latrobe onward, but the infinitely more difficult feat of portraying the wild animals of South Africa has been vividly and triumphantly achieved in later books, notably *The Wild Sports of Southern Africa* by Cornwallis Harris, *The Lion Hunter of South Africa* by Gordon Cumming, and the less well known *African Hunting and Adventure* by Charles Baldwin.

It is more difficult to portray a herd of leaping springbok, galloping wildebeest, or a charging lion or elephant, than it is to stop this movement with a bullet, and I think the men who have caught the spirit and action of African game have not received their due tribute; indeed little or nothing is known of them.

No book has ever been more happily illustrated than *Jock of the Bushveld*, and there is an interesting story behind those brilliantly alive marginal sketches. Mr Edmund Caldwell, the artist, was a painter of animals who exhibited in London towards the end of the Nineteenth Century, and all his work was distinguished by acute observation and a genuine love for animals.

Mrs J. P. Mackie Niven, Sir Percy Fitzpatrick's daughter, who lives in the Cape, tells me that, although she was a small girl at the time, she has a vivid memory of her father writing *Jock of the Bushveld* on board ship during a voyage to England. He was worried about the choice of an artist, and set himself the weary task of going round all the London galleries to see if he could find an animal painter whose work he liked. After a long and discouraging search he saw one day a brilliant picture in oils of a kudu bull standing and gazing into the distance, by an artist named Edmund Caldwell. Sir Percy got in touch with him, and found an elderly man who had never been out of England. He had painted the kudu in the Zoo!

Mr Caldwell was persuaded to return to South Africa with the Fitzpatrick family, and spent many months there studying wild animals and making sketches.

"While Mr Caldwell was with us," writes Mrs Niven, " my father arranged for us all to go by wagon to the Bushveld and camp there. I have the clearest recollection of that trip. We camped somewhere near what is now Mr Hall's estate at Mataffin, Eastern Transvaal. My brothers and their friends collected specimens for Mr Caldwell to sketch, and he saw the animals living and moving around him."

Caldwell is described by one who met him in South Africa as " a genial old boy more inquisitive than informative and keen to be scrupulously exact about every detail of animal life. He was spare, grey-haired and active. One thing that filled me with wonder was that he was such an accurate artist, despite the fact that he had to use glasses of enormous thickness and had to take a close-up, peering look at everything he wanted to sketch. I often wondered how he would manage to get a picture of a lion in the wild!"

His task completed, Caldwell left South Africa and resumed his work in London. He kept in touch with the Fitzpatrick family for years and sent the children exciting Christmas cards, generally with a picture of Jock on them. His end was the most tragic that can befall an artist; he became blind, and died in 1930.

During the War all the blocks of Caldwell's illustrations were destroyed in an air raid, but Mrs Niven fortunately possessed the original drawings. These have been sent to London, and the first post-war edition of *Jock* will be illustrated from the original drawings. No marine artist ever suffered closer scrutiny from sailors than Caldwell's work did from South African naturalists and hunters. Everything he did was passed with full marks except his sketch of the dung beetle. He had drawn that insect in the act of pushing a ball of dung with its fore, and not its back, legs. The mistake was immediately put right when it had been noticed, but the dung beetle standing on its hind legs and pushing the ball with its forelegs is the treasured mark of a genuine first edition of *Jock*.

§ 12

The most sybaritic mode of travel in South Africa is a private railway coach complete with cook and steward. I have no idea what this costs, never having dared to inquire, but when I was invited to spend a night or two in such a coach and visit the Kruger National Park, I responded with alacrity.

Were I a millionaire, that is how I should like to travel all over South Africa and Rhodesia, wherever indeed my saloon could be attached to a train. There is no trouble about petrol or punctures, hotels or food. You roll smoothly through the country to a tinkle of ice and whirr of fans, delightfully insulated from the grittier realities of life.

This coach, which exceeded my most extravagant notions, was shunted into a railway siding at Nelspruit as if it were a common coal-truck. My host had arranged for us to go by car after breakfast to the Kruger Park, where we would motor about all day looking for wild animals, and while we were doing this the saloon was to be taken to a distant siding by the Sabi River, many miles away, where we would rejoin it for dinner.

We sped by car over the roads to the Kruger Park, and came at length to the entrance gates of the most wonderful game reserve in the world. This enormous expanse of wild South Africa was set aside as long ago as 1896 by President Kruger in order to preserve wild animals. It is an area about the size of Wales, bordering the Portuguese frontier, where the immutable and blood-red law of Nature is supreme and Man is merely a visitor with a pair of curious eyes.

Grouped at various points in the park are several rest camps in which motorists—and no one is allowed to visit this place on foot, bicycle, or horseback!—may spend the night, or longer. The only rules are : you must not shoot animals ; you must not leave the roads ; and you must not get out of your car. A guide issued for the use of visitors contains these useful hints.

DON'T bathe ; there are often crocodiles in the smallest pools.

DON'T become alarmed if lions stand and stare at your car. They have probably not seen one before, and are naturally overwhelmed with astonishment. They mean no harm and in fact are looking at your car and not at you. The lion's nose tells him at once that a car is not good to eat and only smells of petrol. Lions have not realised that human beings are inside ; if they did they would run away. If you find lions standing or lying in the middle of the road in front of you, it is not necessary to do more than slow down ; when you get close they will get up and move to the side out of your way, but

DON'T imagine because the lions are passive that they are therefore tame, and that you can go up and pat them. If you get out of your car in close proximity of lions you are courting trouble. Remember that a startled or frightened lion is just as dangerous as an angry one. A lioness with cubs, though she may take little notice of cars, is almost certain to attack a human being walking towards her cubs.

As soon as we were in the park we slowed down to about five miles an hour and, keeping a keen look-out on each side of the track, were soon lost in a jungle of low-growing bush and woodland. It was surprisingly exciting. I have never shot lions or elephants, or indeed any dangerous animal, therefore I cannot say how this watchful expectancy compares with the thrill of the hunter. If you think that the feeling of peril, which must form a large part of the thrill of big-game hunting, was absent, I can only advise you to go to the Kruger Park for the first time and analyse your feelings. For my part, I should have felt safer with a rifle. The car seemed a pitifully poor protection. It appeared to me fantastic that a pride of lions, seeing a few helpless juicy human beings slowly travelling along in a frail tin box should not take some offensive action.

"What happens if you get a puncture?" I whispered, for as soon as we had entered the park we had for some reason dropped our voices.

"Oh, that simply must not happen," was the reply.

There was a movement in the grass, and we were in time to see a family of warthogs trotting away, heads and thin, indignant tails erect. This animal, in my opinion the most amusing in the reserve, is a species of wild pig, large-headed, tusked, and greyish-black in colour. The young are delightful replicas of their parents, and it is the perky, erect line of their tails, each one at the same angle, which is so amusing as they busily retreat.

Turning a corner we disturbed a herd of impala as they were crossing the road. Our appearance filled them with move-ment and they melted into cover. The last comers sailed across the road in splendid leaps, but by the time we drew level they were just so many reddish-brown shadows in the spotted thicket. It is difficult to say whether even the famed springbok is more beautiful or more fleet of foot than the impala, certainly nothing could be lovelier than the sight of a herd of impala, some in the air, some landing on neat, slim legs, some gathering themselves for a forward leap, and all of them together in silent, velvet motion which seems like the very music of movement.

Zebra were so plentiful that we hardly looked at them. They grazed beside the road, or stood half concealed among the trees, shafts of light and shade exactly matching their stripes. A car came towards us and stopped. We exchanged the usual Kruger Park conversation.

"Have you seen any lions?"

"No, have you?"

" They told us at the rest camp there was a ' kill ' this morning."

" Oh, where? "

" We don't know. We thought you might know."

And so on. Lions are to the Kruger Park what the wicked, evil-eyed old rhino are to Hluhluwe!

We moved on and circled round a great rock on whose warm summit sat enormous baboons, and then more warthogs, zebra, impala, inyala, and a little red jackal who stood in the middle of the road and looked as though he were going to bark at us; and the Rest Camp at Pretorius Kop.

The camp is a collection of thatched rondavels surrounded by a stout stockade with gates which are shut after dark. There is a general store where you can buy knick-knacks and hear all the lion stories. Every visitor has to be within the stockade half an hour before sunset and no one is allowed to leave until an hour after sunrise.

I met a man who as far as I could judge devotes his life to the spotting of lions. He lives and works with the sole idea of spending every possible spare moment in the Kruger Park. He told me stories, and substantiated them with photographs of lions half asleep on the running-board of his car, or sitting on the road a few yards ahead like drowsy cats.

" They just don't associate a car with human beings," he said. " The smell of petrol puts them off, and if they're well fed and feeling lazy they like the sound of a running engine, and will come up and listen to it, just like an inquisitive domestic cat."

The late Warden of the Kruger Park, Colonel J. Stevenson-Hamilton, has a lot of interesting things to say about lions in his latest book, *Wild Life in South Africa*. He makes it clear— a point which I think every visitor should know—that danger may be expected not from the lion you can see, but from the one you cannot see.

" At Pretorious Kop in the early part of 1938 ", he writes, " a number of people were gazing from their cars at a pride of lions a few hundred yards away on the slope of Shabine Hill. It was nearing dusk, and the camp closing hour approaching; so the visitors began to start up their engines preparatory to moving off. At the same time the lions began to come slowly down the hill. As his car got into motion, one man discovered that he had a flat tyre, so, getting out, he detached first a roll of bedding, and then the spare wheel from the back of it, and laid them in the roadway. He was just proceeding to jack up his wheel when Ranger Wolhuter, who at that moment came along in his own car to shepherd the visitors home, saw a lioness lying flat in the grass only some twelve feet from the man and watching intently the proceedings. Wolhuter shouted, ' Get into your car or that lion will have you! ' The man made a spring, but so, almost simultaneously, did the lioness, and had she meant to bag him, no doubt, she could easily have done so; but what had apparently been intriguing her was not the man so much as his property. Grabbing the roll of bedding she dashed off with it at full speed into the long grass and apparently had afterwards thoroughly enjoyed herself, for the contents were found next morning rent into the smallest ribands. Rumour has it that the other party in the case was then in so great a hurry to leave, that he tried to force the jacked-up car into movement."

Colonel Stevenson-Hamilton says that unless wounded a lion does not rush at its prey, as most people imagine it does, but prefers to get behind it and come on it unawares. " A tourist, ignorantly or foolishly getting out of his or her car the better to get a camera snapshot of some lions down the road, should beware lest there is yet another unseen, watching from the shelter of a bush close at hand." The writer says that some amateur photographers have been horrified to discover upon a developed film not only the lion they had photographed, but another a few yards away that they had not noticed!

How a pride of lions forms and breaks up is not perfectly clear, says the Colonel. A pride is led by a big male who corresponds to the herd bull among antelopes. He always takes his siesta away from the pride. Young males who rouse his anger are driven off and form bachelor prides; sometimes the young of both sexes leave to form prides and hunt together. The lot of the younger animals is apparently not always a happy one. When a kill has been made, it is sometimes as much as a young lion's life is worth to attempt to eat before his elders have gorged themselves, and when they have done so there is generally little left.

It is curious to know that, after man, the worst enemy of the lion is the seemingly harmless porcupine. If a lion's paws should be punctured by the quills of the porcupine, its life becomes an agony and the end may be starvation and death, for the quills work their way into the pads and cause wounds that become inflamed and make hunting an impossibility.

The stories told at Pretorius Kop are of narrow escapes, of lions that refuse to budge from the road, and of " kills ". Many are the visitors who, quietly motoring along, have suddenly found themselves in the centre of a terrific turmoil of lions in the act of pulling down a giraffe, a wildebeest, a buck, or a zebra.

While we were listening to some of these reminiscences, a car dashed into the camp and an excited occupant shouted, " A big pride about half a mile down the Skukuza Road! " Not waiting to hear more, we ran to the car and were soon on the way. The road was bordered on each side by high summer grass and dwarf acacia trees. Having travelled for half a mile we began to crawl, keeping a keen watch, until someone suddenly said: " Stop! There they are! " Looking through the left-hand window I saw a lioness about fifty yards away. She heard us and saw us, and I could see her sharp ears pricked and her big round face turned in our direction. As I silently measured the distance which separated us, I thought she was the largest lioness I had ever seen. Not a whisker twitched. She just sat watching us with the alert expression of an interested cat.

" How many can you see? " someone whispered. " I can see six! "

Looking closely at the bushes, I realised that what had looked at first like patches of brown grass were nothing of the kind. I counted up to five, and then the sixth was pointed out to me, a big male with a dark mane, lying some distance away in the shade of an acacia and almost invisible.

Someone in the car placed a camera through the window and took a photograph. The tiny click of the shutter—a sound so minute and unimportant—was heard by the lions, and two

z

who had been lying on their sides slowly raised themselves and added four more pricked ears to the pride. It was, I thought, a moment as tense as that when, turning a corner of the road in the Hluhluwe Reserve, I had come face to face with a rhino and her calf.

I was amused to see that lions lie on their backs with their paws in the air—that ridiculous attitude so familiar to anyone who has been owned by cattus domesticus.

That pride was the only one I saw during my two days in the Park, and I was told by rangers and others that owing to the drought the animals had retired into the depths of the bush.

§ 13

Having seen enough bloodshed in the course of my life, I had no real wish to witness a " kill ", and was glad that upon our second day our attention was chiefly taken up with giraffes and hippopotami.

Of all the animals in the Park I thought the giraffes the most interesting to watch. We came upon them in family parties and in larger groups, but when they were standing motionless among acacia trees it was impossible to see them until you noticed, protruding from the topmost leaves, a face rather like that of an alert and good-looking camel; then, following the line downward, you saw the giraffe standing in dappled sunlight which matched his spotted hide. A really gigantic bull, whose diamond markings were almost black upon his pale-fawn body, was, I thought, the most striking creature we had seen.

I had the good fortune to watch one of these animals lower his neck to drink. In order to do this, he had to straddle his forelegs bit by bit in five or six jerky movements before his long neck could be lowered to ground level. It is worth going to the Kruger Park if only to see a herd of giraffes in movement. They gallop as if mounted upon stilts fitted with springs, the fore and hind legs of each side moving together, the long neck moving backwards and forwards, and the tail held over the hindquarters. It is a curious, powerful, lolloping movement, and I was told that they can travel at a speed of thirty-five miles an hour over short distances.

This inoffensive vegetarian who would appear to be such easy prey is, I was glad to learn, well defended. His hind legs have a kick like a steam hammer, his vital parts are protected by a hide an inch thick, and his neck is the best watch tower in Nature; even the lion treats him with respect.

We came to a broad river in which about ten hippopotami were submerged save for the tops of their heads and their little, sharp, terrier ears. Now and again one would sink to reappear in a few moments for air. They spend their days floating, or sinking to the river-bed where they are able to walk about. We heard them giving voice with a sound which was something between a grunt and a roar. They were intensely curious animals. Whenever we whistled or called to them, heads emerged and the water was broken by little black ears.

I made a list of the animals we had seen: lions, giraffe, hippo, zebra, warthogs, water-buck, impala, inyala, wildebeest, monkeys, jackals, kudu, and many birds whose names I do not know. We did not see one snake, although, as Colonel Stevenson-Hamilton says, " the Sabi Bush is notorious for the number of mambas it holds, and there are certainly more to the square mile there than in any other part of Africa with which I am acquainted ".

I wonder how many visitors think, as I did, that the chief attraction of the Kruger Park is the glimpse it gives of a world ruled by Nature. The law of the survival of the fittest, which Man alone in all Nature has defied, is seen in full operation. In this blood-red world the beasts of prey are the instruments whereby Nature maintains the species at their highest perfection. Man slays the strongest, Nature slays the weakest.

In *Wild Life in South Africa* the author examines that extraordinarily delicate balance of life in the jungle whereby laws are at work regulating the birth rate of different species, the age to which certain animals live, the sex of those born, and the proportion of beasts of prey to those preyed upon. He points out that a jungle without lions and other flesh-eaters would soon become a wilderness.

" Therefore by their constant weeding out of those animals

which, inferior to their companions in physical powers or in intelligence, offer themselves more easily as prey, they ensure the general health and strength of the species being kept keyed up to the highest possible level; and by pulling down sick animals immediately their illness causes them to lag, if ever so little, behind their companions, they do much to restrain the spread of contagious maladies. Under natural conditions, without the aid of the predatores, overstocking, followed by destruction of the pasture and outbreak of disease and starvation, would occur, in a few years the country would be a sterile desert requiring years to recover and again sustain larger mammalian life. Thus the beasts of prey benefit no only the fauna, but indirectly the flora also. . . .

" The same stern law of survival of the fittest governs also the existence of the carnivorous species, any member of which, incapacitated for some reason from catching the prey necessary to maintain its life, must die miserably."

The saloon carried us through the hot mango country. The electric fans whirred. In the morning we awakened in Johannesburg.

§ 14

The Victoria Falls, which are in Southern Rhodesia, are one thousand, eight hundred and fifty miles from Johannesburg. I discovered that this long journey is made easy by an air service which leaves Johannesburg twice or thrice a week, arriving in Bulawayo four hours later, and that a night train from Bulawayo reaches the Falls early the next morning. I decided to go. I was full of misgiving, for it is unfortunately true that more often than we care to admit great natural phenomena are more impressive in books than in reality.

Two things about the Victoria Falls seem to me remarkable : that this gigantic cascade, whose roar can be heard for miles, was unknown to the geography books until only ninety-odd years ago, when Livingstone parted the leaves and gazed with awe upon it, and that Cecil Rhodes never saw the greatest natural wonder of his own Rhodesia. The Falls are caused by the Zambesi River, at this point a mile in width, as it

PART OF THE MAIN FALL, VICTORIA FALLS

suddenly descends into a chasm three hundred and sixty feet in depth.

I spent the day or two before my departure reading the description of Livingstone's discovery and the accounts of the first few white men who saw the Falls. It seems that Livingstone's claim to be the first white man to do so has been challenged at various times, but Mr Servaas D. le Roux, whose admirable little book, *Pioneers and Sportsmen of South Africa*, I have already mentioned, writes: " I have no hesitation in saying, after many years of careful investigation of the claims of all possible visitors to the Falls before Livingstone, that there are no grounds whatever for believing that anyone but Livingstone was the first European to see them ".

The next white man to see the Falls was the bloodthirsty little William Charles Baldwin, the lion hunter. In the course of one of his destructive forays he found his way to the Falls in 1860, and was the first person to measure them with approximate accuracy, for Livingstone's attempt to do so was inadequate. Then two years after came Thomas Baines with his pencil and his paint-box, and he sat down, suffering from fever and waving away tsetse flies, and became the first artist to paint the Falls in all their colour and majesty.

The first white woman to see the Victoria Falls was the Afrikaner wife of the hunter, George Westbeach, who was there in 1875.

The aeroplane deposited me upon a hot aerodrome at Bulawayo. The grass was brown and shrivelled; the earth was baked hard, and heat palpitated over the flat land. It was ninety-seven in the shade, but appeared to be much hotter. The Bulawayans, who were dressed in tropical suits and sun helmets, agreed that it was very hot indeed and said that it would remain so until the rains came.

I suppose in a country where an oak tree becomes a sapling in ten years and a peach tree in the same period is a fruit-bearing bush, one ought not to be surprised by the lightning growth of such cities as Bulawayo. But how extraordinary it is to see that a place described in our own time as a few tents and tin sheds has developed into a large, well-planned modern city. I saw fine public buildings, enormously wide thorough-fares, shaded by lavender-blue jacarandas and brick-red flamboyants, fine shops, a statue of Cecil Rhodes, a swimming-pool that suggested Hollywood, and flying everywhere in uncomplicated solitude brand new Union Jacks, so different from our old and tattered specimens at home.

The heat, which had been violent enough earlier in the day, became malicious in the afternoon. The air was actually hot on my eyeballs, my mouth was upholstered in baize and my teeth were turned to felt. Fortunately there was no shortage of lime-juice and soda.

I left by train in the evening. When morning dawned we were two hundred miles away, and plodding across the great Wankie coal-field, which is said to be four hundred square miles in area and to contain sufficient coal for the whole world for many generations. When the sun rose there was no gradual warming up: the world was instantly and violently hot. A tropical landscape wilted in the heat. Half-naked natives sat in the shade of huts and in the shadow of vast frilled leaves like green elephants' ears and waited for day to begin.

As we approached the Falls Station I looked out, for I had been told that if the wind is blowing in the right direction spray wets the train windows miles off, but there was no wind that morning, also it was the dry season and the Falls would be low, and so nothing like that happened.

A covered way connects the station to a luxury hotel full of people in white flannels and summer dresses. When you remember it was only yesterday that Livingstone, Baldwin, and Baines spent months in reaching this spot and then had to camp out in considerable peril and discomfort, this great hotel, where the lost arts of cookery and service are preserved intact so far from civilisation, is one of the many wonders of Africa.

My room looked out towards the Falls. As soon as I entered I was drawn to the window by a constant roar of sound and, only a short walk away, a gigantic screen of spray, grey as the smoke of a veld fire, rose several hundreds of feet into the air. It was a surprising and appalling sight, surprising because there is nothing else like it in Africa, appalling because

the height of the spray, the mile-long width of it, and the roar
that accompanied it. spoke of the terrifying power behind it.
I sat down and watched it, unable to leave the window. The
mist was always rising and descending, and constantly in movement as air currents caught it. The roar of the water as it
leapt into space was not like the sea, or like thunder, as I have
heard it described, but like the noise made by an express train
travelling at seventy miles an hour but never getting any
nearer. It forms a constant background to everything, and
listening to its steady roar I could understand why the natives
in Livingstone's day never approached nearer to it than five or
six miles. I listened to it fascinated and then became aware
of a smaller, nearer sound: the lovely sound in a hot land of a
hose spraying a flower bed. There below the window stood a
native boy watering a bed of asters. Every now and then he
would look suspiciously over his shoulder: and I wondered
why.

Upon the parapet of the swimming-pool an old baboon was
hiding. He was a wise old veteran, who from time to time
would peep round a corner at the boy. He had the bright
restless eyes of a Scottish sub-editor in the face of a disillusioned
dog. At last, judging the moment right, he suddenly launched
himself into the air in the direction of a mango tree and
came down to earth with a green mango in his mouth and two
fists full of mangoes en branche: and before the poor boy,
made aware of his adversary by the sound of breaking boughs,
could pick up a stone, the old villain was on the other side of
the hill.

§ 15

I set off after breakfast with Mr Miles, the curator, to see the
Falls, and I must say that I was consumed by uneasiness.
Suppose they were disappointing? Mountains, volcanoes,
valleys, and other natural sights may be described so often, so
enthusiastically, and so well, that to see them for yourself is an
anti-climax. I still remember over the years the feeling of
having been let down when I first observed the Pyramids.

We made for the sound of the Falls and came to a stretch of

land which might be described as the most favoured in Africa ; alone in Africa it possesses what everyone throughout the length and breadth of the southern portion of the Continent prays and longs for : it is land on which rain falls ceaselessly day and night all through the year. It is the land immediately opposite the Falls, which is perpetually drenched in spray; and they call it the Rain Forest.

As we entered this hot, odoriferous jungle, we saw on each side of the path a dense riot of thriving trees, every bright leaf shining and dripping in the wetness. Stray gusts of air came up from the gorge and drove belts of grey spray through the forest as if it were a Highland glen. Those warm little fogs settled in beads upon the leaves and dripped down upon the moss, the bracken, and the great banks of fern. Birds called among the monkey ropes that linked tree to tree ; dragon-flies came darting in and out of the spray, enjoying the thin moisture on their wings. In the warm, perpetual rainfall, moss and lichen climbed the trees and covered every fallen trunk with velvet, while flowers of startling beauty broke into life with the speed of fungi. Those just appearing were clumps of a fuzzy red flower called *Haemanthus multiflores*, which sprang from the earth sudden and leafless like little flames.

All the time, as we walked through this jungle, having to shout ever louder to each other, I was conscious of the thundering monster and impatience to come face to face with it became overwhelming. At last the trees thinned a little and I saw ahead a ledge of glistening wet rock, and about a hundred yards away, on the opposite side of the chasm, the white slide of water falling into the darkness of the gorge.

I was standing on a rock with the mist coming up from the abyss, the dragon-flies in hundreds diving in and out of the falling rain like flying emeralds, and opposite I saw the Zambesi sliding over the mile-long edge of the precipice. It was a sight both frightening and beautiful. Standing there, blinded by the spray and deafened by the roar, I knew that this immense spectacle was unlike anything else in the world.

What makes the view of the Victoria Falls from the edge of the Rain Forest so impressive is that you are not looking up at it, but standing upon the same level as the river. You can see it far away, flowing gently, lapping the shores of the little islands that rise out of it, drawing nearer every moment to the great chasm into which it must fall; then, as it reaches the lip, with sudden acceleration it jumps over and down in long white streamers; and all is confusion, noise, and spray.

If I remember the Niagara Falls correctly, the river before it leaps downward is a tumultuous, violent affair with rapids that are already angry before they fall into space: but the Zambesi is a placid river to within a few yards of its descent. And this contrast between peace and violence, between water flowing calmly over the earth and water falling angrily through the air, makes a first glimpse of these Falls impressive and memorable.

At various points along the edge of the Rain Forest are wooden seats and little thatched huts in which you may sit more or less dryly and watch the tumult. The steady white slide of the mile of falling water, the constant thunder and reverberation of its descent, the ever downward movement of the water, and the ever upward movement of the mist, have an almost mesmeric effect upon the spectator. You sit for a long time concentrating upon some calm eddy, watching it slide nearer to its doom, watching it take the leap and then anxiously following it downward until it loses its individuality, first becoming a thin feather of water and then, as it meets an air current, becoming blown and shredded, mixed with other water and lost, part of it going down and ever down into the darkness and part flung upward in ascending spray. There is a fascination too in watching the very edge of the Falls, where the Zambesi arches itself like a curve of greenish-white glass before it leaps into space.

For a mile you may walk opposite the Falls seeing cascade after cascade and then, if you dare, you may creep to the edge and peer down into the awful cleft where the river, now green, now black, boils onward beneath a grey mist in which a rainbow lies like a tinted hoop.

It is interesting to examine the effect this sight has had upon the minds of those who have described it   Livingstone was impressed by its sublime majesty and thought that " scenes so lovely must have been gazed upon by angels in their flight ";

Chapman was also filled with awe and wonder, but was conscious also of an " invisible spell " tempting the spectator to " fling himself headlong into it "; Major Serpa Pinto, who was there in 1877, was inspired by awe and a kind of horror for " the hell of water and darkness ", which he likened to " the last gasp of age in the arms of death ". A Frenchman, Lionel Declé, agreed with Pinto and compared the Falls to " a dark and terrible hell, from the middle of which you expect every moment to see some repulsive monster rising in anger ". Lord Curzon, who was a connoisseur of waterfalls, was affected by the " beauty and power " of the Falls and thought that they " excel in grandeur any spectacle of the same kind in the world ".

To me the grandeur and the power overwhelmed all other impressions. I did not find it horrible or hellish. It was a stupendous display of natural forces and it created in my mind a feeling of almost fearful admiration. It struck me that of all natural phenomena waterfalls alone have constant sound and movement. Thunderstorms and volcanoes in eruption have these, but only intermittently; the waterfall alone in Nature has them all the time. The great mountains of the world are silent and still, the great gorges and the plains are soundless, and even the great rivers, although they too have movement, have none of the violent catastrophic movement of a waterfall.

In the afternoon we went across the bridge, to a point above the Falls where a canoe was waiting upon the placid river. Far away the opposite bank showed as a line of thick forest from which rose the tufted heads of palm trees. Four ebony boys stabbed their paddles in the water, and we sped out into the stream and made towards the lip of the Falls.

The sun gleamed on the polished bodies of the natives, and I thought that we must have looked very like an illustration in Stanley's *Darkest Africa*. A feature of the Falls is the group of islands near the edge of the precipice; some actually over-hang it in the most terrifying manner. We paddled to one of these, Livingstone Island, in the centre of the river, taking advantage of calm water and paddling against the eddies and swirls which could have swept us on and over the brink. The little island is a shady jungle swept by spray like the Rain Forest opposite. It was a place of tall trees and thick undergrowth. A path has been cut to the lip of the Falls at the point where Livingstone gazed for the first time into the abyss.

We found the tree upon which, surrendering once only to a bad habit, he had carved his initials, but there is no sign of them to-day. Selecting a spot not too near the brink, he planted a little garden of a hundred peach and apricot stones and a quantity of coffee-seeds, but hippopotami soon trampled Rhodesia's first garden into chaos. From the edge of the island the view of the Main Cataract was frightening. As I looked down, it seemed that the little island was trembling with the thunder of the Falls and might at any moment break from its mooring and go whirling down into white foam and darkness.

§ 16

Anything less heroic than my first sight of wild elephants could not be imagined. I had been invited to go up the Zambesi, and this naturally suggested a canoe with ebony bodies swaying back and forth as paddles were dipped into the water. But when I reached the landing stage I saw a motor launch into which were stepping fellow guests from the hotel—elderly visitors, honeymoon couples, and family parties with children—just as if they were going to Hampton Court.

We sat beneath an awning, and as soon as we had exploded into mid-stream every camera was produced and a look-out kept for crocodiles. We saw several, lying upon rocks with their mouths open, exposing gullets the colour of boiled salmon. People became tired of wasting film on hippos.

Turning into a broad reach of the river, Mr Dowell, our skipper, gave a cry and pointed to the distant bank, where several elephants were grouped at the edge of the water. He put on speed, and the animals allowed us to get within two hundred yards before they turned and shambled off into the bush. By the time our boathooks gripped the bank we could hear the sound as they pressed through the bush to the crack of snapping twigs. The place was evidently a regular drinking-pool, for the ground was churned up into yellow mud and impressed with huge, circular footprints, each one filled with a bucketful of blue Zambesi.

Mr Dowell told me that elephants had not been seen in that part for a long time, and indeed he seemed a good deal more excited than his passengers, to whom no doubt the sight of elephants in zoos was an everyday occurrence. Seizing a camera, he leapt ashore and told us he was going to take a photograph of them in the bush. Rashly, I asked if I might accompany him, and together we advanced into a dense thicket.

" The wind's all right," he whispered, " but if they come for us beat it back to the boat as fast as you can."

I readily promised to do this, and we crouched together on an ant-hill, gazing between the leaves into the dappled jungle. The elephants were not far off. We could hear them in the crackling undergrowth, rending branches from the trees. Mr Dowell signed to me in dumb show to stay where I was while he crept forward with the camera.

Left alone on the ant-hill, I began to feel that this modern passion for hunting big game with films is carried to excess in Africa. I felt foolishly helpless, and glancing back I noted that the boat was no longer visible, neither was the cheerful chatter of its passengers audible. I could see Mr Dowell's white shirt some way to the right, and I noticed that he was crouching with the camera at eye level, obviously taking photographs. Following his line of vision, I saw a grey shape swaying among the trees, and realised that if all these were cut down I should have found myself no more than fifty yards from the elephants. Suddenly one of them, with the alarming speed and smoothness of the bulkier wild animals, moved to a frightening sound of snapping boughs, and I was relieved to hear Mr Dowell saying, " Come on, let's go ! "

Back in the boat, I thought that anyone armed with a camera probably stands a better chance with a rhino, whose sight is poor, than with an elephant, whose sight is so keen. And the thought of an elephant, preceded by its sensitive and muscular trunk, is not pleasant as you wait, suddenly and appallingly transported from the security of a large hotel into the reality of the African bush.

The hotel stands like a policeman guarding the visitor from the peril and lawlessness of the wild, and I am sure that few of its visitors realise how lawless the wild still is. The fact that you can book a room and bath from Johannesburg or Cape Town obscures the fact that fundamentally the Zambesi region is still as it was in Livingstone's time. Take away the comfortable buffer of the hotel, and the traveller would be faced by an expedition of the first order with tents, mosquito nets, guns, bearers, quinine, atropin, and all the rest of it. But as far as I could see, my fellow guests were not aware of this. Off they went in the morning to study the Falls; in the afternoon they voyaged upon the Zambesi; and in the evening, while eating an iced soufflé, they would mention that they had taken photographs of crocodile and hippopotami as if it were the most ordinary and normal thing in the world.

When I reached the hotel one evening a young woman told me that she had seen such a sweet little crocodile on a rock, and a man who was sinking an iced whisky and soda informed me that a smell of burning that was steadily rising in the air was caused by a bush fire.

" Dropped cigarettes? " I suggested, thinking of Hindhead in August.

" Oh, no," he replied. " Natives hunting. They fire the bush and then assegai the game as it runs away. Of course they're not supposed to do it, but the police can't always stop them."

So I went up and thoughtfully changed for dinner. There was iced papaw, cream of leek soup, grilled sole with mayonnaise, roast spiced venison with wine sauce, and pêche Melba. But somewhere not far off was a " sweet little crocodile " and a buck with an assegai in its stomach. Which of these two worlds is the real Zambezia I leave you to decide.

§ 17

While I was in Bulawayo, on my way back to Johannesburg, a friend drove me out to the Matopos to see the grave of Cecil Rhodes. Long before his death that extraordinary man chose his burial-place upon a lonely hilltop in the country which bears his name. It was not the first time the Matopos had been selected as a sepulchre. Rhodes, when describing how the Matabele warrior Mzilikazi had been buried in a cave there, seated on a throne, so that even in death he might face the great expanse which he had ruled, exclaimed, " What a poet that man was! "; and maybe it was Mzilikazi who first put the idea in Rhodes' head.

" I admire the grandeur and loneliness of the Matopos in Rhodesia," he wrote in his will, " and therefore I desire to be buried in the Matopos on the hill which I used to visit and which I called the ' View of the World ' in a square to be cut in the rock on the top of the hill covered with a plain brass plate with these words thereon—' Here lie the remains of Cecil John Rhodes '."

After travelling for about fifteen miles we came to a hot, mountainous country which seemed to me singularly eerie. The largest euphorbia trees I had seen lifted their queer surrealist arms against the blueness of the sky, and other trees in some miraculous way managed to find foothold and nourishment between the cracks of granite. The chief features of the scene were the numerous rounded granite boulders, some of them colossal, which in the course of centuries had been left stranded on hill-tops and poised so crazily upon ledges that one puff of wind, it seemed, might send them crashing into the valleys. The boulders and the rocks around them were beautifully tinted by green and saffron lichens. The silence was underlined by insect noises. Between a gap in the hills I caught a glimpse of vast blue distances.

One of the most impressive features in this queer landscape is the place where Rhodes chose to be buried. A natural Stonehenge has been formed by granite boulders which seem to stand guard round a rock platform. A path has been cut to the summit, and when you reach the top you see " the World's View " stretching away for fifty miles, and at your feet is the grave of Cecil Rhodes, covered by a slab of granite bearing his name and the dates of his birth and death, as he directed. He was not fifty.

It could not fail to be an impressive grave, and it occurred to me, as I stood there watching the flame-headed lizards run over it, that it is also the grave of a Trappist monk. I was reminded of a story which W. T. Stead tells in his revealing book about Rhodes' will. A certain Mr G. Wyndham, who was travelling in Rhodesia, happened to go with Rhodes to this place, and when they reached the hill-top the founder of the country, " circling his hands about the horizon ", cried, ' Homes, more homes; that is what I work for '."

The narrator of this story called it " very beautiful ", but surely it is also very pathetic. Homes mean marriage and children, and of these Rhodes himself knew and wished to know nothing. Of all those who have striven in Africa his spirit is surely the least restful and the least home-like. While he could dream of homes for other people, he himself remained a born wanderer on the face of the earth.

This grave in the hills is the one place in Africa where it seems to me you can forget Rhodes the materialist and remember only Rhodes the visionary. Was he not of the same kind as Alexander of Macedon? One dreamed of Hellenising the world, the other of Anglicising it; and both lived to sigh for more worlds to conquer.

As I was going down the hill I met an elderly gentleman dressed in khaki shorts who was painfully climbing up with the aid of a stick. He removed his sombrero and mopped his head.

" Is John Cecil up there? " he asked me.

" You'll find him on the top," I said.

" I just wanted to say good afternoon to him."

" Did you know Rhodes? " I asked.

" Oh, Lor', yes! I knew Rhodes in the old days, but it's fifty years since I was last in Bulawayo. Of course, I was a young lad then."

" Tell me," I asked, " was Rhodes an impressive person to meet? "

" Oh, I don't know," he replied. " He wore an old shirt and an old pair of pants and a wide-awake hat, like the rest of us, but I really couldn't say whether he was impressive or not."

He continued his pilgrimage to the hill top. And there I left him on the Matopos, with the sky and the lizards and the grave of Rhodes.

§ 18

Glancing through the port-hole of the aeroplane at sunrise, I watched a new day dawn over the broad lands that lie north to the Limpopo. In a few hours I should be in another continent, for my travels in South Africa were over. I had been in the country too long to be able to solve its problems and not long enough to be able to express an opinion about them.

I remembered how at that time in the morning Cape Town would be stirring round its blue bay; Port Elizabeth, East London and Durban would be awakening; the smoke would be rising from the kraals of Zululand; the night clouds leaving the peaks of the Drakensberg; the Free State would lie in clarity from horizon to horizon, and the first gold miners would already be at work beneath the rocks of the Transvaal.

All over South Africa at that moment the varied population would be preparing to meet the challenges and responsibilities of a new day: British South Africans, Afrikaners; Cape Coloured, Bantu, Indians; a complex and puzzling passenger list for any country to carry into the future. I could see them in imagination from Table Bay to Durban Bay, and over the mountains upon the northern plateau, preparing to engage in their innumerable activities. And behind them, stretching back in time, I saw also Kruger, Rhodes, and Lobengula; Potgieter and Harry Smith; the Voortrekkers; Piet Retief and Dingaan; Farewell, King and Shaka; the 1820 Settlers; Pringle and Somerset; Lady Anne Barnard and the first British; a century of Dutch Governors; the Huguenots and, last—and first—Jan Anthony van Riebeeck with his South Africans. After unnumbered ages of silence, history, it seems, was determined to crowd as much as possible into three South African centuries, as if to make up for lost time.

The story of South Africa is that of two fine European peoples, as alike as two races can be, who have established their civilisation at great cost and with courage upon the tip of Africa. In spite of their unhappy schism they have managed to exert their sway over, and to accept responsibility for, a greater number of servants than any nation has been blessed or cursed with since the slave empires of antiquity. Most travellers who have moved about among them must go away with the feeling that to them more than to most people in a changed and threatening world the twenty-fourth verse of the third chapter of St Mark applies more than ever it did.

I recollected with affection the many friends, British and Afrikaner, I had made in all the four provinces. The South Africans are a kind, generous, open-hearted people and hospitality is one of their oldest traditions. I remembered also with gratitude the silent ministrations of those servants of another race who had done my bidding and had made my life easier. Then I settled down to face that long journey to the north and the surprising realisation that, vast as South Africa seems to be when you are there, it is merely a small part of a greater whole.

A A

BIBLIOGRAPHY

Baines, Thomas, *The Gold Regions of South Eastern Africa.* 1877.
Baker, Herbert, *Cecil Rhodes by his Architect.* 1934.
—— *Architecture and Personalities.* 1944.
Baldwin, W. C., *African Hunting and Adventure.* 1894.
Barnard, Anne, *South Africa a Century Ago.* n.d.
Barrow, John, *Travels into the Interior of Southern Africa.* 2 vols. 1806.
Beet, George, *The Grand Old Days of the Diamond Fields.* n.d.
Blackwell, L., and May, H. J., *This is South Africa.* 1947.
Botha, C. Graham, *Place Names in the Cape Province.* n.d.
—— *Social Life in the Cape Province in the 18th Century.* n.d.
Bryce, James (Lord), *Impressions of South Africa.* 1899.
Burchell, W. J., *Travels in the Interior of Southern Africa.* 2 vols. 1822–4.
Calpin, G. H., *There are no South Africans.* 1946.
Carter, George, *The Wreck of the Grosvenor* (Van Riebeeck Society). 1927.
Chilvers, Hedley A., *The Seven Wonders of Africa—Out of the Crucible.*
Clements, W. H., *The Glamour and Tragedy of the Zulu War.* 1936.
Cloete, Stuart, *African Portraits.* 1946.
Colvin, Ian D., *South Africa.* n.d.
Cory, Sir G. E., *The Rise of South Africa.* 4 vols. 1910–26.
Coupland, R., *Wilberforce.* 1923.
Cumming, Gordon Roualeyn, *The Lion Hunter of South Africa.* 1863.
Devitt, Napier, *The Spell of South Africa.* 1938.
—— *People and Places.* n.d.
Duggan-Cronin, A. M., *The Bantu Tribes of South Africa.* 1930–39.
—— *The Bushman Tribes of Southern Africa.* 1942.
Du Plessis, J., *Christian Missions in South Africa.* 1911.
Fairbridge, Dorothea, *Historic Farms of South Africa.* 1931.
—— *Lady Anne Barnard at the Cape.* 1924.
Fitzpatrick, Percy, *Jock of the Bushveld.* 1907.
—— *The Transvaal from Within.* 1899.
Fitzsimons, F. W., *The Snakes of South Africa.* n.d.
Gardiner, Allen F., *Narrative of the Journey to the Zoolu Country.* 1836.
Gibson, J. Y., *The Story of the Zulus.* 1911.
Hamilton-Agar, J. A. I., *The Native Policy of the Voortrekkers.* n.d.
—— *The Road to the North.* 1937.
Harris, W. Cornwallis, *The Wild Sports of Southern Africa.* 1839.
Hofmeyr, Jan H., *South Africa* (The Modern World). 1931.
Huizinga, Dirk M., *De Stad der Grachten.* n.d.
Hunter, Monica, *Reaction to Conquest.* 1936.
Hutchinson, John, *A Botanist in Southern Africa.* 1946.

Isaacs, Nathaniel, *Travels and Adventures* (Van Riebeeck Society). 2 vols. 1936.

Joelson, Annette, *South African Yesterdays.* 1940.

Kenyon, J. T., *An Address on the General Council Administrative System of the Transkeian Territories.* 1939.

Krige, E. J., *The Social System of the Zulus.* 1936.

Kruger, S. J. Paul, *The Memoirs of Paul Kruger . . . told by himself.* 2 vols. 1902.

Laidler, P. W., *The Growth and Governance of Cape Town.* 1939.

—— *A Tavern of the Ocean.* n.d.

Le Roux, Servaas D., *Pioneers and Sportsmen of South Africa.* 1939.

Le Vaillant, François, *Travels from the Cape of Good Hope. . . .* etc. 2 vols. 1790.

—— *New Travels into the Interior Parts of Africa.* 3 vols. 1796.

Lewinsohn, Richard, *Barney Barnato.* 1937.

Liebbrandt, H. C. V., *Van Riebeeck's Journal.* 3 vols. 1897.

—— *Letters Despatched from the Cape, 1652–70.* 1901.

—— *Letters and Documents Received, 1695–1708.* 1896.

MacCrone, I. D., *Race Attitudes in South Africa.* 1937.

Macmillan, W. M., *Complex South Africa.* 1930.

—— *The Cape Colour Question.* 1927.

Marais, Eugene N., *The Soul of the White Ant.* 1937.

Marais, J. S., *The Cape Coloured People, 1652–1937.* 1939.

Millin, Gertrude, *Rhodes.* 1933.

—— *South Africans,* 1937.

—— *God's Step-children.* 1924.

Mockford, Julian, *Here are South Africans.* 1944.

Moffat, Robert, *The Matabele Journals.* 2 vols. 1945.

—— *The Matabele Mission.* 1945.

Moodie, J. W. D., *Ten Years in South Africa.* 2 vols. 1835.

Nathan, Manfred, *The Voortrekkers of South Africa.* 1937.

Owen, Francis, *Diary* (Van Riebeeck Society). 1926.

Parr, Henry Hallam, *A Sketch of the Kafir and Zulu Wars.* 1880.

Pettman, Charles, *Africanderisms.* 1913.

Pringle, Thomas, *Narrative of a Residence in South Africa.* 1840.

Reitz, Deneys, *Commando.* 1929.

—— *Trekking On.* 1933.

—— *No Out-span.* 1943.

Roberts, Austin, *The Birds of South Africa.* 1940.

Robertson, T. C., various articles in *Libertas.* 1946–7.

Sauer, Hans, *Ex Africa.* 1937.

Schapera, I. (editor), *The Bantu-speaking Tribes of South Africa.* 1946.

Schreiner, Olive, *Thoughts on South Africa.* 1923.

—— *The Story of a South African Farm.* 2 vols. 1883.

South Africa. (Cambridge History of the British Empire. Vol. VIII.) 1936.

Sowden, Lewis, *The South African Union.* 1945.

Sparrman, A., *A Voyage to the Cape.* 2 vols. 1786.

Stead, W. T., *The Last Will and Testament of Cecil J. Rhodes.* 1902.

Stevenson-Hamilton, J., *Wild Life in South Africa.* 1947.

Stow, G. W., *The Native Races of South Africa.* 1910.

Theal, George MacCall, *History of South Africa.* 5 vols. 1888–93.

Union-Castle Mail Steamship Co. Ltd., *South and East African Year Book and Guide.* 1947.

Voight, J. C., *Fifty Years of the History of the Republic in South Africa.* 2 vols. 1899.

Vulliamy, C. E., *Outlanders.* 1938.

Walker, Eric A., *A History of South Africa.* 1928.

—— *The Great Trek.* 1938.

Waterhouse, G., *Simon van der Stel's Journal.* 1932.

Welch, S. R., *Europe's Discovery of South Africa.* n.d.

Wells, A. W., *South Africa.* 1939.

Young, Francis Brett, *They Seek a Country.* 1937.

—— *The City of Gold.* 1939.

GLOSSARY

OF AFRIKAANS AND OTHER WORDS USED IN THIS BOOK

Aasvoël, vulture.
Afrikaans, the language of the Afrikaner.
Afrikander, the South African breed of red cattle.
Afrikaner, a South African of Dutch–Huguenot–German descent.
agterkis, rear wagon chest.
arak, an eastern spirit of considerable potency.
baas, white master.
bekslaner hek, concertina gate (lit. smack-you-in-the-mouth gate).
blommetjie, little flower.
bobotie, curried mince.
boer, farmer.
bokkeveld, goatveld.
dassie, rock rabbit.
disselboom, wagon-shaft.
donga, a hollow or dip.
dorp, village.
drostdy, magistrate's residence.
erf, building plot.
fontein, spring or fountain.
goed, good.
groot, great.
Groote Schuur, Great Barn.
indaba, native gathering or council.
isiChola, Zulu female headdress.
kabeljou, Cape salmon or salmon-bass.
Kapenaar, Capetownian.
kappie, sunbonnet.
katel, bedstead.
kerkraad, church council, elders.
kiewit, peewit.
kis, chest or trunk.
kombuis, kitchen.
koppie, hill.
korhaan, moor-cock.
kraal, native cattle pen or hut.
laager, defensive formation of ox-wagons.
lammervanger, eagle.

liefling, darling (Dutch).
mebos, salted, crystallised apricots.
meisie, girl.
melk, milk.
meneer, sir, mister.
mooi, pretty.
morg (pl. *morgen*), $2\frac{1}{8}$th acres of land.
mud (*sak*), measure by bag.
onderstel, wagon under-frame.
piccanin, native child.
remskoen, skid, slipper.
riem, leather thong.
rondavel, circular hut.
rust, rus, rest.
sosatie, spiced meat flavoured with curry powder and grilled.
skof, hump.
spruit, rivulet, stream.
steenbras, a fish, Grunter.
stoep, verandah.
stukkie, little pieces.
taal, language.
tarentaal, guinea-fowl.
tert, tart.
tickey, threepenny piece.
tot siens, so long.
uitlander, foreigner, stranger.
vaal, grey.
veld, field, open country.
velskoen, home-made shoe.
vergelegen, far-away.
verskriklik, terrible, frightful.
vlei, valley.
voorhuis, front room or parlour.
voorkis, front wagon chest.
voorloper, forerunner.
vrou (pl. *vrouens*), woman, women.
waaierstertmeerkat, the fan-tailed meercat.
wag 'n bietjie, the wait-a-bit thorn bush.
winkel, shop.
wonderlik, wonderful.

357

(The Plain)

page 285

In peace I rest by the ages caressed,
Unseen, unheard,
And dazed and bewitched by my sun-dreams enriched
Unawakened, unstirred.
    (*Jan Cilliers.   Translation by E. R. Petterson.*)

(Names of a Team of Oxen)

page 291

Storm Mountain.	*Vulture.*
Very Nice.	*Apple.*
Commandant.	*Soldier.*
Pontak (*a sweet wine*).	*Fawn-tail.*
Wagon-road.	*Rocking Man.*
Front Man.	*Carpenter.*
Dirty Beard.	*Sweetveld.*

INDEX

359

PRINTED IN GREAT BRITAIN BY RICHARD CLAY AND COMPANY, LTD.,
BUNGAY, SUFFOLK